SWEET AND LOWDOWN:

America's Popular Song Writers

by
WARREN CRAIG

with a Foreword

by

Milton Ager

The Scarecrow Press, Inc.
Metuchen, N.J. & London
1978

R
784.0922
C 886

Library of Congress Cataloging in Publication Data
Craig, Warren, 1924-
   Sweet and lowdown.

   Bibliography: p.
   Includes indexes.
   1. Music, Popular (Songs, etc.)--United States--
Bio-bibliography. I. Title.
ML106.U3C75   784'.092'2 [B]   77-20223
ISBN 0-8108-1089-1

For

JAMES MARVIN GILLESPIE

who was born too late to hear the
songs--the first time around

CONTENTS

FOREWORD

In the fall of 1976, the postman delivered an unexpected package of recorded tapes to my home. On playing the tape, I heard:

> This is Warren Craig bringing you another chapter from The Broadway Songbook. Each week, The Songbook presents the work of America's top composers and lyricists --songs, famous or obscure, featured in stage and screen attractions from the Turn of the Century to the present.

To my delight, there followed two hours of the melodies I had written in conjunction with Jack Yellen and other lyricists, beginning with my first hit song "Everything Is Peaches Down in Georgia" (published in 1918) and ending with "Sweet Stranger" which was popularized 20 years later.

The program was the most complete anthology of my work that I have heard covering, as it did, the Broadway musicals on which I had worked, the motion pictures to which I had contributed, and the independent songs which had achieved success without the benefit of a theatrical promotion. The first hour of the show was much more than the Milton Ager Songbook. It was, in fact, a musical montage of the Roaring Twenties--when vaudeville was in its glory. Imagine the pleasure of hearing my songs performed again by such legendary entertainers as Harry Richman, Sophie Tucker, Eddie Cantor, Ruth Etting--and 25-year-old Bing Crosby!

I wrote to Mr. Craig to express my appreciation of the thorough job he had done in covering my career. During a later visit with me, he said that he was preparing a book titled Sweet and Lowdown which would be a transferral of The Broadway Songbook oral series to the printed page. And now, the book is a reality. The hundreds of hours of research spent in developing this anthology insure it as one of the most comprehensive references yet com-

piled on the subject of popular songwriters. I am genuinely pleased
to be included in Sweet and Lowdown.

Milton Ager
Los Angeles
March 1977

ACKNOWLEDGMENTS

The author expresses appreciation for their interest, cooperation, and assistance to:

Louis Alter
Rita Belfer
Brad Bennett
Sammy Cahn
Sam Coslow
Nikki Dillon
Ray Evans
Sammy Fain
E. Y. Harburg
Donald Kahn
Burton Lane

Jerry Livingston
David Mann
Buddy Pepper
Don Raye
Mrs. Bob Russell
Carl Sigman
Harry Tobias
Harry Warren
Ned Washington
Mrs. Richard Whiting
Don Wolf

Academy of Motion Picture Arts and Sciences
American Society of Composers, Authors and Publishers
Loyola Marymount University, Los Angeles, California

ATV Music Group
Barton Music Corp.
Belwin Mills Pub. Corp.
Big Seven Music Corp.
Bourne Co. Music Pubs.
Carmichael Music Pub. , Inc.
Edward B. Marks Music Corp.
Edwin H. Morris & Co. , Inc.
Fred Fisher Music Co. , Inc.
GW Famous Music Pub. Co.
Irving & Almo Music Pub.
Irving Caesar
Jimmy McHugh Music

Larry Spier, Inc.
MCA Music
Music Sales Corp.
Octave Music Pub. Corp.
Peer-Southern Organization
Redd Evans Music Co.
Rojon Productions Inc.
Shapiro, Bernstein & Co. , Inc.
Theodore Presser Co.
20th Century Music Corp.
Warner Bros. Music
Warock Corp.
Words & Music, Inc.

PREFACE

Whether you prefer the sweet strains of "After the Ball" and "You'll Never Know," or the lowdown wail of "Love Me or Leave Me" and "Blues in the Night," you're probably able to hum or whistle a few bars from at least one of these famous songs. But if you're an average citizen, you're probably unable to name the men who wrote the music and lyrics to any of them--despite the fact that Charles K. Harris, Harry Warren, Mack Gordon, Walter Donaldson, Gus Kahn, Harold Arlen and Johnny Mercer are all among the most successful popular song writers in American history.

No single group of artists has contributed so much to as many people's daily lives as have popular song writers--yet no single group of artists is more anonymous. The music and lyrics of these writers have been a continuous part of the lives of virtually everyone, but even persons who claim an attachment to a particular song that has played a personal part in their lives are unaware of to whom they are indebted. The anonymity of songwriters is not due to the faulty memories of the millions of people who have adopted their songs as lifetime favorites. People who are able to recall the names of sports figures, politicians, movie stars, novelists, and singers could easily remember the names of songwriters. But with the exception of such giants as Irving Berlin, Jerome Kern, Richard Rodgers, George Gershwin and Cole Porter, the names of America's songwriters have almost never been mentioned!

There was a time when radio announcers were required to identify the name of the motion picture in which a song was introduced before the song was played. The sheet music carried a note in bold print which read: "Please announce title of production when broadcasting this number." Listeners were told that "Love in Bloom" was from the film "She Loves Me Not." No one informed them of the far more important fact that "Love in Bloom" was written by Ralph Rainger and Leo Robin. No wonder these songwriters are little known outside the music industry. Their names have reached the general public only in small print on the covers of sheet music, or in even smaller print on the labels of some phonograph records.

If the music industry has been negligent in spotlighting the men and women who supply its livelihood, the public must share a large part of the blame. Public interest has always been in the performers of the songs without any curiosity as to who wrote the material that skyrocketed the performers to national fame. As far back as the turn of the century, theatregoers talked about Lillian Russell's "Come Down My Evening Star" and ignored its writers John Stromberg and Robert B. Smith. Placards in record stores advertised Bing Crosby's newest hit "Moonlight Becomes You" without mentioning that it was the work of James Van Heusen and Johnny Burke. No one cared that Doris Day's million-selling disc of "It's Magic" would never have existed without the music of Jule Styne and the lyrics of Sammy Cahn. If Barbra Streisand appeared on a New York street today she would be mobbed. The artists who created the song "Happy Days Are Here Again," which helped bring Miss Streisand to America's attention, are Milton Ager and Jack Yellen, who have passed unnoticed on every street they have walked.

While this book is not the first to attempt to uncover the nation's popular song writers from under the rocks that hide them, it is the first to analytically determine their comparative rankings. Appendix A lists the composers and lyricists covered in Sweet and Lowdown in descending order based on the number of hit songs they created. Due to the considerably divergent periods in which the artists worked, the book and Appendix A are divided into three sections: "Before Tin Pan Alley," "Tin Pan Alley," and "After Tin Pan Alley."

The writers of rock and roll and country and western music are excluded from these pages because such forms of popular songs are alien to the author.

INTRODUCTION

About This Work

In 1963, the author undertook the writing of a radio program devoted to the work of Broadway's most celebrated songwriters. The series traced the careers of the acknowledged masters from Victor Herbert to Stephen Sondheim. In performing research to develop the scripts, it was found that available reference books left much to be desired. None of them contained complete chronological listings of every major composer's work. Some listed only Broadway productions for which the composer created the bulk of the score. Dozens of the composer's individual songs which had been interpolated into musicals with basic scores written by others were missing. To locate the interpolations required a review of all musicals ever staged on Broadway. The inclusion of musicals which had closed before reaching Broadway, or were produced elsewhere (London, Paris, St. Louis, Los Angeles, Off Broadway, etc.), required screening over 50 volumes in the annual Best Plays series.

Books on motion picture musicals listed all films in which a composer's songs had been heard regardless of whether or not they were written for the film. For example, the many films in which "Blue Skies" and "I Can't Give You Anything but Love" were used were listed despite neither song having been written for any film. In addition, adaptations of Broadway musicals were included even though no new songs were added to the motion picture version. Since such films represented no new effort on the composer's part, it would be redundant to include them in a summation of the composer's work. It was therefore necessary to edit the lists and delete films which did not present new compositions.

Reconstructing the composer's output was simple compared to

1

researching the careers of lyricists. Most reference books rele-
gate the lyric writers to the back seat as though they were coinci-
dental. Instead of listings of their work, readers are instructed to
"See Rudolf Friml, Jerome Kern and Sigmund Romberg" or "See
music by George Gershwin, Ray Henderson, Victor Herbert and
Jerome Kern." This practice is ludicrous since the words of a song
are unquestionably as important to its success as its music. This is
proven by the extremely small number of instrumental compositions
that have achieved popularity compared to songs having words. What
a disservice to Oscar Hammerstein for History to refer to Jerome
Kern's "The Last Time I Saw Paris" or to praise Victor Herbert's
"A Kiss in the Dark" with no mention of B. G. DeSylva's memorable
words! The task of reconstructing the complete careers of lyricists
required another screening of all the composer listings since most
lyric writers worked with several composers.

The fruit of hundreds of hours of research was a complete
digest of productions on which each of Broadway's most noted songwriters had worked, the songs from each production and the independent songs (not written for stage, screen or television productions)
integrated chronologically from the time of the artist's initial recognition through his latest effort, his retirement, or his death. The
careers of these artists began to come into focus for the first time.
The digests revealed at a glance the total span of the subject's cre-
ativity, his most active years and the volume of his output. But
one ingredient was missing. The subject's creative span and the
volume of his output were not true indications of his success. He
may have written hundreds of songs but he had been successful only
because the public embraced a large per cent of them. The degree
of his success must then be the number of his songs which became
popular in their day or survived the test of time to become popular
music standards.

There is no credible explanation as to why one song becomes
popular while another fails. Thousands of songs pass into oblivion
because of mundane arrangements, lackluster performances by the
artists who introduce them or lack of proper promotion. "Begin

the Beguine" went almost unnoticed until outstanding recordings by
both the Artie Shaw Orchestra and vocalist Tony Martin put the song
over to the extent that it became one of the four most-recorded
songs of all time.   Many noteworthy melodies have failed because
of the lyrics they accompanied.   "Easter Parade," "I Guess I'll
Have to Change My Plan," "Blue Moon" and "Sometimes I'm Happy"
were all failures when they were first heard with different titles and
lyrics.

For purposes of Sweet and Lowdown, popular songs are qualified as those which sold sizable quantities of sheet music or individual (single) phonograph records.   Some songs, particularly those
from Broadway original cast albums, received considerable air play
but did not sell any volume of copies or single records due to their
specialized nature.   Hence, songs such as "Trouble" (from "The Music Man"),   "The Rain in Spain" (from "My Fair Lady") and "If I
Were a Rich Man" (from "Fiddler on the Roof") were not considered
to be popular even though they are well known songs.   In addition,
only songs having lyrics were considered.

The measure of a composer's or lyricist's success was added
to each digest by including a column showing chronologically each of
the subject's songs which were listed in various histories as having
been popular.   Success was in no way equated with quality.   Music
critics may dispute the quality of a song such as "Mairzy Doats"
but the public bought it in large quantities!   The financial gain the
artist may have received from his work was also ignored as a cri-
terion of success.   In the days before the American Society of Composers, Authors and Publishers (ASCAP) was founded, it was rare
for songwriters to amass personal fortunes such as those accumulated by artists working after popular music became as well organized as the steel industry.   Today ASCAP, and Broadcast Music,
Inc. (BMI), take in over one hundred million dollars annually and
distribute the bulk of it among their members.   Most of Broadway's
contemporary songwriters (Harold Rome, Alan Jay Lerner, Stephen
Sondheim, etc.) have derived great wealth from their musical comedy
scores but relatively few of their songs have become popular.   Art-

ists such as these have achieved success from both the standpoint
of quality and dollars earned but not from the standpoint of the number of their hit songs.

The addition of the "Popular Songs" column to each digest
revealed the subject's most successful years and how each ranked
with his contemporaries. When publication of the digests was considered, the question arose as to why they should be limited only to
Broadway's top songwriters. Since there was no purpose in such a
restriction, digests were developed for every songwriter of sufficient
stature to have been recognized by popular music historians. While
the original artists who had been researched had each created dozens of hits, many of the others acknowledged by historians had sur-
prisingly few successes to their credit. For this reason, the digests
of 129 composers and lyricists were eliminated. Their names, however, have been listed in Appendix A.

Setting the Record Straight

If reference books on baseball, locomotives, modern dance
and other subjects contain as much erroneous information as those
written about popular music, future generations will be hard put to
learn the true facts about anything. Myths are perpetuated by authors who parrot stories which are false. Several repeat how Dorothy Fields and Jimmy McHugh wrote their most famous song "I
Can't Give You Anything but Love" when the team had to come up
with a number for the Broadway revue "Blackbirds" in 1928. The
song was actually written for "Harry Delmar's Revels" the previous
year. Another story has Jerome Kern composing "I Won't Dance"
after Fred Astaire tapped out a few rhythm steps during the filming
of "Roberta" in 1935. An earlier version of that song was featured
in Kern's London musical "Three Sisters" the year before. Other-
wise admirable authors have been extremely careless with facts
about popular music and its creators.

Sigmund Spaeth's A History of Popular Music in America
was hailed as so complete that no other book on the subject need
be written. It is truly a fascinating chronicle. However, accord-

ing to Spaeth, "Ragtime Cowboy Joe" was a popular song of 1902.
If that were true, Grant Clarke would have been eleven years old
when he wrote the song's lyrics (actually created ten years later).
Further errors include the omission of credits for Ted Snyder on
"It Was Only a Sun Shower" and Harry Tobias on "Miss You," at-
tributing "If I Were King" to lyricist Al Dubin instead of Leo Robin,
and including DeSylva, Brown and Henderson as collaborators on "Con-
stantinople'"when they were actually the song's publishers. Spaeth in-
vents his own song titles such as "I'll Teach You a Thousand Love
Songs" (for "I'll Sing You a Thousand Love Songs") and "You Go to My
Heart" (for "You Go to My Head"). He lists "Goodnight My Love" as
being from the 1934 film "We're Not Dressing, " and then includes it
later in 1936 without its correct film credit "Stowaway. " He also states
that "The Loveliness of You" is from the film "Love in Bloom" instead
of from "You Can't Have Everything. " His listings of songs by year
are ambiguous in many cases due to lack of specific identification. He
frequently supplies last names only such as "Sterling," "Edwards, " or
"Meyer, " leaving the reader to wonder whether he means "Andrew B.
Sterling" or "Raymond A. Sterling, " "Gus Edwards" or "Leo Edwards, "
"George Meyer" or "Joseph Meyer, " etc.

   Variety Music Cavalcade, by Julius Mattfeld, fails to recog-
nize the hit stage musical "Bells Are Ringing" as anything other
than a film, although the original production ran on Broadway for
924 performances. It also lists "Ten Cents a Dance" as being from
the film of the same name instead of from the Broadway musical
"Simple Simon." It credits the song "She's Such a Comfort to Me"
to Cole Porter instead of Arthur Schwartz, Donovan Parsons, and
Douglas Furber, and gives away Johnny Burke's lyric for "Sunday,
Monday or Always" to Johnny Mercer. Its readers are told that
"Two Blue Eyes, Two Little Baby Shoes" is two songs: "Two Blue
Eyes" and "Two Little Baby Shoes." Lyricist Leo Robin's name ap-
pears as "Leo Dubin," "Leo Rubin," and "Leon Robin," while Rob-
ert Wright is referred to as "Bob White."

   Jack Burton's The Blue Book of Tin Pan Alley (Volume II)
attributes Vincent Youmans' "I Know That You Know" to Jerome

Kern, E. Y. Harburg's "Last Night When We Were Young" to lyricist Ted Koehler, Joseph McCarthy's entire score for "Rio Rita" to
lyricist Fred Thompson, and Cole Porter's words for "In the Still
of the Night" to Gus Kahn.   Burton volunteers the information that
Jimmy McHugh was still a bachelor at 56.   McHugh was survived
by a grown son, several grandchildren, and one great grandchild!
Burton comments on "Stardust" as having been a Hit Parade favorite
in 1939 (It was never on "Your Hit Parade"), and identifies Sammy
Fain as comedian Willie Howard's nephew (they were cousins).   In
addition, he lists the film "Argentine Nights" complete with the correct cast but with all the songs from "Down Argentine Way."

     In Burton's The Blue Book of Broadway Musicals the reader
learns that "I Might Be Your Once-in-Awhile" and "To the Land of
My Own Romance" are both from the operetta "Sweethearts." Neither
song is.   Further wrong credits include listing "Esmeralda" by E.
Ray Goetz and Edgar Smith (instead of Cole Porter), "I Won't Say
I Will" by Arthur Jackson (instead of Arthur Francis), "Get Happy"
by Edward Eliscu (instead of Ted Koehler), and "I'll Take an Option
on You" by Howard Dietz (instead of Leo Robin).

     The Blue Book of Hollywood Musicals is the most erroneous
in Burton's series.   It gives away Jerome Kern's "All the Things
You Are" to Cole Porter, Vernon Duke's "April in Paris" to Kurt
Weill, and Johnny Mercer's "Tangerine" to Frank Loesser.   Confu-
sion runs rampant among the "Harrys" with Harry Revel for Harry
Warren, Harry Warren for Harry Owens, and Harry Tobias for
Charles Tobias.   Ralph Freed is referred to as both Ralph Blane
and Arthur Freed, Harold Arlen is repeatedly called Richard Arlen,
and Marilyn Monroe emerges as Marilyn Moore.   Burton excites the
imagination at the prospect of a musical starring Spencer Tracy,
Lionel Barrymore, James Stewart, Sydney Greenstreet, and John
Hodiak.   The film is called "Malaya" and lists all the songs from
Dorothy Lamour's "Beyond the Blue Horizon."   The numerous in-
correct song titles include the suggestive "Hang Your Clothes on a
Hickory Limb" instead of "Hang Your Heart on a Hickory Limb."
Burton's "Errata" apologizes for not listing the film "Moonlight

Masquerade" under the year 1942 although it does appear in that
year. The book's "Errata" is even in error.

The American Movies Reference Book: The Sound Era, by
Paul Michael, presents facts on memorable films listed in alpha-
betical order.   Before the reader has finished with the "A's," he
has been told that "Moonlight and Shadows" and "I Have Eyes" are
from "Artists and Models" (instead of "The Jungle Princess" and
"Paris Honeymoon") and that the film's score also included "Public
Enemy No. 1" by Burton Lane (the song was "Public Melody No. 1"
by Harold Arlen).   The "F's" include "Jungle Jingle" in the Loretta
Young nonmusical "The Farmer's Daughter" (that number was performed by Martha Raye in the earlier musical of the same title).
The "G's" credit Walter Donaldson and Harold Adamson with "It's
Delightful to Be Married" heard in "The Great Ziegfeld" (it was the
work of Anna Held and Vincent Scotti).   The "H's" list all the songs
from the 1929 musical "Honky Tonk" under the 1941 nonmusical of
the same name, and attribute Ned Washington's "Oscar"-winning "Do
Not Forsake Me" (from "High Noon") to Johnny Mercer.

The Appendix of They All Sang, by Edward B. Marks, is
a list of "Songs Outstanding in My Memory" and includes a column headed "Author/Composer. "   The Appendix omits lyricists
Edward Heymen, Robert Sour, and Frank Eyton on "Body and
Soul, " lyricists Sam Lewis and Joe Young on "Dinah" and lyricists Gus Kahn on "I'll See You in My Dreams. "   According
to Marks, these famous songs were the sole work of composers
Johnny Green, Harry Akst, and Isham Jones.   Marks apparently
remembered "Just a Memory" as a poem since he credits it to
lyricist B. G. DeSylva with no mention of composer Ray Henderson.

The most prolific author on American popular music is David
Ewen, whose more than 50 books have contributed much valuable material on the subject.   They have also contributed their share of mis-
information.   His Complete Book of the American Musical Theatre
repeats the mistake in identifying Sammy Fain as Willie Howard's
nephew.   It also credits George Marion Jr.'s lyrics for the score

of "Toplitsky of Notre Dame" to Jack Barnett, and identifies "I'll
Be Seeing You" as a film song even though it was introduced in the
1938 Broadway musical "Right This Way." In his plot synopsis of
"On the Town," Mr. Ewen reverses the characters played by Betty
Comden and Nancy Walker.

Ewen's Great Men of American Popular Song places "We're
in the Money" in the film "Forty-Second Street" instead of "Gold
Diggers of 1933." It states that the Rogers and Astaire musical
"Flying Down to Rio" followed "The Gay Divorcee" when it actually
preceded it. The book points out that Vincent Youmans wrote songs
for only two motion pictures, yet "What a Widow!," "Song of the
West," "Hit the Deck," and "Flying Down to Rio" add up to four.
Mr. Ewen states that the songs written by Jimmy Van Heusen and
Sammy Cahn were so good that the films in which they were fea-
tured were frequently retitled using the same name as the hit song.
As examples, he cites "Be My Love," "It's Magic," and "All the
Way" yet "Be My Love" was from "The Toast of New Orleans,"
"It's Magic" was from "Romance on the High Seas," and "All the
Way" was from "The Joker Is Wild." More importantly, Van Heu-
sen had nothing to do with either "Be My Love" (music by Nicholas
Brodszky) or "It's Magic" (music by Jule Styne). In his discussion
of Harry Warren, Ewen refers to "Go into Your Dance" as "Get into
Your Dance," "Sun Valley Serenade" as "Sun Valley," and shortens
"There Will Never Be Another You" to "There Will Never Be An-
other."

In American Popular Songs from the Revolutionary War to
the Present, Ewen states that the score for the film "Alexander's
Ragtime Band" consisted of all Irving Berlin standards. He apparently never heard "Now It Can Be Told" which was written for the
picture and was on "Your Hit Parade" nine times the year the film
was released. This book informs the student that "Lovely to Look
At" was the Number One song on the first broadcast of "Your Hit
Parade" and that "Soon," by George and Ira Gershwin, was the
Number Three song. According to "This Was Your Hit Parade,"

by John R. Williams, "Soon" was the first Number One song and
"Lovely to Look At" was Number Three on the initial broadcast.
In any case, it was Rodgers and Hart's "Soon"--not the Gershwins.

David Ewen frequently contradicts himself. In the Complete
Book of the American Musical Theatre, he cites "My Baby Just
Cares for Me" as one of the outstanding show tunes of 1928.   Then,
in American Popular Songs from the Revolutionary War to the Present, he states that it was written for the film version of "Whoopee"
in 1930. He attributes "In the Shadow of the Pyramids" (which he
calls "In the Shade of the Pyramids") to Cecil Mack and Ernest R.
Ball and then lists it as a song by Ren Shields.   In his Life and
Death of Tin Pan Alley, Ewen lists "Mickey" as the work of Neil
Williams. The lyrics for that hit were written by Neil Moret and
the music was by Harry Williams.

The four-volume Complete Encyclopedia of Popular Music
and Jazz, by Roger D. Kinkle, lists "In the Evening by the Moon-
light, Dear Louise" as "In the Evening by the Moonlight" and "Dear
Louise." It omits Jack Yellen from the credits of the song "Big
Boy," Sammy Lerner from "Falling in Love Again," and attributes
Irving Berlin's "There's a Girl in Havana" to E. Ray Goetz and A.
Baldwin Sloane. It gives away Arthur J. Lamb's "When the Bell in
the Lighthouse Rings Ding Dong" to Andrew B. Sterling, Harry Wil-
liams' "It Looks Like a Big Night Tonight" to Gus Kahn, George
White's "Bigger and Better Than Ever" to Irving Caesar, and Her-
bert Stothart and Clifford Grey's "Montana Call" to Nacio Herb
Brown and Arthur Freed. Arthur also collects his brother Ralph's
"No More Tears." "Try to See It My Way" is attributed to Harry
Warren and Al Dubin instead of Allie Wrubel and Mort Dixon. Harry Ruby is listed as composer on "Only When You're in My Arms"
which was written by Herman Ruby. Mr. Kinkle also contradicts
himself. In his list of popular songs of 1930, he includes Nacio
Herb Brown and Arthur Freed's "Pagan Love Song." By the time
he reaches his list of 1950 motion pictures, Harry Warren has re-
placed Brown as the song's composer. "The House Is Haunted" ap-

pears with Edward Heyman as lyricist, but two pages later Billy
Rose becomes the author.

In his biographical section on lyricist Hal David, Kinkle ig-
nores the 1968 stage hit "Promises, Promises" even though it's the
17th longest-running musical in Broadway history.   He identifies the
film "So Dear to My Heart," in which Burl Ives and Luana Patten
appeared, as a cartoon!   The book defeats the basic purpose of an
encyclopedia by listing incorrect song titles.   If a researcher tries
to look up "Too Romantic, " "There's Nothing Too Good for My Baby, "
or "When the Moon Comes Over Madison Square," he won't find
them.   They're listed as "I'm Too Romantic," "Nothing Too Good
for My Baby," and "Moon Over Madison Square."   Kinkle, too, frequently eliminates first names causing the reader to guess whether
he means Wayne King or Robert A. King, Chris Smith or Harry B.
Smith or Robert B. Smith or Edgar Smith, etc.   The book claims
to list songs in the year in which they first became popular yet lists
many numbers in years after they placed on "Your Hit Parade" which
was the national barometer of song popularity for 23 years.   It also
omits many songs that made "Your Hit Parade."

Marian Klamkin is the author of Old Sheet Music.   She credits
the lyrics to "Lovely to Look At" to Otto Harbach (instead of Dorothy
Fields and Jimmy McHugh), the music to "Vict'ry Polka" to Johnny
Mercer (instead of Jule Styne), and refers to Irving Berlin's "Dinah"
which was written by Harry Akst, Sam Lewis, and Joe Young.
Lyricists Lewis and Young get full credit for "How Ya Gonna Keep
'em Down on the Farm" with no mention of composer Walter Donaldson.   Ms. Klamkin points out that "I Found a Million Dollar Baby"
by Billy Rose and Fred Fisher was featured in the revue "Crazy
Quilt."   There were two songs by that title and the one in the revue
was by Harry Warren, Mort Dixon, and Billy Rose.   Her captions
for illustrations of sheet music inform the reader that Ruth Etting
was in the "Ziegfeld Follies" in 1908 (Miss Etting was five years
old that year), identify Dolores Del Rio as Ginger Rogers, and
place the film "Coney Island" ten years ahead of its time.

The frequency with which the same mistakes appear in book

after book causes one to wonder if their authors have verified anything. Two writers repeat Sigmund Spaeth's errors regarding "Goodnight My Love" and "The Loveliness of You." Three others list
"Long Before You Came Along" as being from the 1929 film "Rio
Rita" when it was actually written for the 1942 remake of that picture. Jack Burton and Roger D. Kinkle both credit Harry Warren's
"This Is Always" to Josef Myrow. The discrepancies cited in the
foregoing books which are sold to the public as reference material
are merely examples--hundreds more exist!

Other than locating a sheet music copy of every song ever
published, the most accepted method of insuring accuracy is to veri-
fy song titles, composers, and lyricists by using the ASCAP three
volume Index covering most songs written by its members through
1963. A publication compiled by the organization representing the
majority of the nation's songwriters should be infallible. Regret-
tably, this source also contains errors--but they are minimal, in-
deed, compared to other references.

The prize for the most confused reporting of song credits
goes to the hit "Toot, Toot Tootsie" which was written by from
three to five collaborators--depending on which book is taken from
the shelf: American Popular Songs from the Revolutionary War to
the Present--Ernie Erdman, Gus Kahn, Dan Russo; The Complete
Encyclopedia of Popular Music and Jazz--Ernie Erdman, Ted Fiorito, Gus Kahn, Robert A. King; ASCAP Biographical Dictionary--
Ernie Erdman, Ted Fiorito, Gus Kahn, Robert A. King, Dan Russo.
Not one of the above is correct according to the sheet music which
lists Ernie Erdman, Ted Fiorito, Gus Kahn, and Dan Russo.

In summary, readers are cautioned not to make bets regarding popular music if they expect to settle them by referring to any
"authoritative" reference. While Sweet and Lowdown sets the record straight by correcting hundreds of previous errors, it may still
contain some which were undetected because this author's suspicions
were not aroused.

About the Digests

Lest the reader become confused at finding the same song or

production listed in the digests of several different artists, it should
be remembered that many lyricists worked in teams, the majority
of composers did not write the words to their melodies, and several
writers often contributed to a single production.

The keys to the digests are:

1. Production Titles in all upper case represent stage productions.
   Parenthetical notes identify those which were not produced on
   Broadway or were plays rather than musicals.

2. Production Titles in both upper and lower case represent motion
   picture or television (TV) productions

3. When more than one popular song derived from a single production, the song titles are single-spaced into one group.

4. Song titles within quotation marks represent independent songs
   (not from stage, screen or television productions).

5. The titles of songs recognized by the Academy of Motion Picture
   Arts and Sciences are followed by AN (Academy Nomination) or
   AA (Academy Award).

6. The titles of songs which ranked among the top ten on "Your
   Hit Parade," which was broadcast weekly from April 1935 to
   June 1958, are followed by HP (Hit Parade). HP-1 indicates
   that the song made the Number One spot from coast to coast.
   In some cases, the songs were written years before the program
   began but were successful revivals.

Since one of the purposes of the digests is to indicate each
subject's productivity by year, songs were generally placed in the
year in which their final versions are believed to have been written.
However, some references were based on copyright years while others were based on the years in which songs became popular. Neither year necessarily represents that in which the song was written.
Only the artist could supply the actual year of composition and most
of the artists concerned are no longer living.

Whether or not a song was written with a particular production in mind is also questionable. When an idea for a song occurs,
it is written. If the writer has not been commissioned to create a
specific score or supply work for a specific film, the song may be
published as an independent number or it may wind up in the songwriter's proverbial trunk. In either case, the number may later

find its way into a production. For this reason, the songs have been associated with the first production in which they were heard regardless of when they were written or for what they were originally intended. Hence, songs such as "I've Got a Crush on You" (written for the first version of "Strike Up the Band" but actually introduced on Broadway in "Treasure Girl"), "From This Moment On" (intended for the musical comedy "Out of This World" but not used until the film version of "Kiss Me, Kate"), and "It's De-Lovely" (created for the film "Born to Dance" and later added to the Broadway hit "Red, Hot and Blue") are associated with the production in which they finally achieved popularity. The necessity for this is substantiated by the fact that the music for several popular show tunes ("Hallelujah," "You're Devastating," "The Donkey Serenade") was written earlier than the final lyrics which would have required the song to appear in one year for the composer and in a different year for the lyricist. The narratives preceding the digests attempt to clarify some of these unusual cases.

Songs such as "Deep Purple," "The Donkey Serenade," "Riverboat Shuffle," and "Manhattan Serenade" are credited to the year in which lyrics were added to them instead of the year the instrumental compositions were first heard.

Songs are related to a motion picture only if they had not already achieved popularity as independent numbers, and only the first film in which a song (with lyrics) was heard is listed.

BEFORE TIN PAN ALLEY

Before 1880, the popular songs were published as a sideline by firms throughout the United States whose main product was classical or sacred music. A "popular" song was generally published after its rendition by traveling minstrels and variety artists, such as "The Singing Hutchinson Family," had created a demand for it. Publishers did not solicit songs from composers nor promote the sales of songs. Sheet music was found only in the nation's more affluent homes furnished with pianos. The sale of 75,000 copies of a single song, such as Stephen Foster's "Massa's in de Cold, Cold Groun'," was considered phenomenal. Since popular song writing during this era was not a profession, most composers and lyricists had to support themselves working at other occupations. The following songwriters are included in this section:

James A. Bland

Daniel Decatur Emmett

Stephen Collins Foster

William Shakespeare Hays

George Frederick Root

Henry Russell

Septimus Winner

Henry Clay Work

* * *

JAMES A. BLAND

James Bland was the nation's first successful Negro songwriter and ranks second among the composers before Tin Pan Alley. He was born in 1854 and was raised in Washington, D.C. Bland studied law at Howard University and worked as a page boy in the House of Representatives. He had just come of age when he decided to quit college and become a singer in a minstrel troupe. Three years later, he composed the music and lyrics for the immortal "Carry Me Back to Old Virginny." His income from his songs was minimal but he earned a substantial living as a top minstrel in both the United States and Europe. For 20 years, he was a major attraction in English Music Halls and appeared before Queen Victoria during Command Performances. James Bland died penniless in 1911 at the age of fifty-seven. In 1940, Virginia adopted "Carry Me Back to Old Virginny" as its state song.

Year   Popular Songs

1878   "Carry Me Back to Old Virginny"

1879   "In the Evening by the Moonlight"
        "(Oh, Dem) Golden Slippers"
        "In the Morning by the Bright Light"

1880   "Hand Me Down My Walking Cane"
        "De Golden Wedding"

Unknown: "Close Dem Windows"
            "Come Along, Sister Mary"
            "Dancing on the Kitchen Floor"
            "Dandy Black Brigade"
            "Farmer's Daughter"
            "Gabriel's Band"
            "Listen to the Silver Trumpets"
            "Old-Fashioned Cottage"
            "Old Homestead"
            "Rose Pachoula"
            "Tapioca"
            "Way Up Yonder"
            "You Could Have Been True"

* * *

DANIEL DECATUR EMMETT

Dan Emmett was the son of an Ohio blacksmith. While working as a newspaper printer, Emmett taught himself to play the violin. When he was in his late teens, he joined a circus where he
performed in blackface. By 1843, he was appearing in New York
City variety houses with his own troupe "Virginia Minstrels." Included in their repertoire was Emmett's first hit song "Old Dan
Tucker." In addition to his talent as a violinist, he played the
banjo, sang, wrote plays, and was a popular comedian. While touring with the "Bryant Minstrels" in 1859, he created the classic "I
Wish I Was in Dixie Land" which was the last of his songs to achieve
fame. At the age of fifty-five, Emmett settled in Chicago where he
managed a saloon and gave violin concerts. In 1888, he retired to
his birthplace in Mount Vernon, Ohio. He came out of retirement
to make a farewell tour seven years later. Dan Emmett, known
as "The Father of the Minstrel Show," died in 1904 at the age
of 79.

Year   Popular Songs

1843   "Old Dan Tucker"
        "De Boatman's Dance"
        "My Old Aunt Sally"

1846   "Blue Tail Fly (Jim Crack Corn)"

Year   Popular Songs

1853   "Jordan Is a Hard Road to Travel"

1859   "I Wish I Was in Dixie Land"

* * *

STEPHEN COLLINS FOSTER

Stephen Foster was the most successful of all popular song-writers before Tin Pan Alley. He is also the only songwriter of that period whose name is known to the general public. Foster was born in Lawrenceville, Pennsylvania, in 1826 and was eighteen years old when his first published song "Open Thy Lattice, Love" went on sale. He had no personal contact with his publishers during the early years of his composing career. Foster mailed his song manuscripts to New York and the publisher's checks were posted to him in Cincinnati, Ohio, where he was employed as a bookkeeper. By 1850, he was able to support his family with the money he derived from such successes as "Oh, Susanna," "Nelly Bly," and "De Camptown Races." Before he was thirty years old he had also written both words and music for the classics "Old Folks at Home (Swanee River)," "Jeanie with the Light Brown Hair," and "My Old Kentucky Home" which was later adopted as Kentucky's official song. In the mid-1850's, Foster finally journeyed to New York where he created another of his most famous songs "Old Black Joe." He became an alcoholic and died broke in Bellevue Hospital at the age of only thirty-eight. Foster's "Beautiful Dreamer" was published the year he died and was one of the most popular songs of 1864. The short life of Stephen Foster was dramatized in the films "Harmony Lane" (1935), "Swanee River" (1939), and "I Dream of Jeanie" (1952). He was elected to the Hall of Fame for Great Americans in 1940.

Year   Popular Songs

1844   "Open Thy Lattice, Love"

1847   "Lou'siana Belle"

1848   "Oh, Susanna"
        "Old Uncle Ned"
        "Away Down Souf"

1849   "Nelly Bly"
        "My Brudder Gum"
        "Nelly Was a Lady"

1850   "De Camptown Races"
        "Angelina Baker"
        "I Would Not Die in Springtime"

Year   Popular Songs

1850   "Oh, Lemuel"
        "Dolly Day"
        "Ah, May the Red Rose Live Always"

1851   "Old Folks at Home (Swanee River)"
        "Oh, Boys, Carry Me 'Long"
        "My Hopes Have Departed Forever"
        "Wilt Thou Be Gone, Love?"
        "Sweetly She Sleeps, My Alice Fair"
        "Ring de Banjo"
        "Laura Lee"
        "Willie, My Brave"
        "Once I Love Thee, Mary Dear"

1852   "Massa's in de Cold, Cold Groun'"

1853   "My Old Kentucky Home"
        "Old Dog Tray"

1854   "Jeanie with the Light Brown Hair"
        "Hard Times, Come Again No Mo'"
        "Willie, We Have Missed You"
        "Ellen Bayne"

1855   "Come Where My Love Lies Dreaming"
        "Comrade, Fill No Glass for Me"
        "Village Maiden"
        "Some Folks Like to Sigh"

1856   "Gentle Annie"

1858   "Fairy Belle"

1860   "Old Black Joe"
        "Under the Willow She's Sleeping"
        "The Glendy Burk"
        "Down Among the Cane Breaks"

1861   "Don't Bet Your Money on de Shanghai"
        "Our Bright Summer Days Are Gone"
        "Why Have My Loved Ones Gone?"
        "If You've Only Got a Moustache"
        "Mr. and Mrs. Brown"

1862   "We Are Coming, Father Abraham"
        "We're a Million in the Field"
        "The Merry, Merry Month of May"
        "Little Jenny Dow"
        "That's What's the Matter"
        "Willie Has Gone to War"
        "I Will Be True to Thee"

Year   Popular Songs

1862   "Why?"
        "No One to Love"

1864   "Beautiful Dreamer"

* * *

WILLIAM SHAKESPEARE HAYS

The third most successful popular song writer before Tin Pan
Alley was William Shakespeare Hays who wrote both music and lyrics. His work came into prominence during the Civil War when
he composed "Drummer Boy of Shiloh." Hays was then in his mid-
twenties. After the war, his successes continued with "We Parted
by the River," "Susan Jane" and "Roll Out! Heave Dat Cotton."
His last popular song was the 1880 favorite "Walk in de Middle of
de Road." Will S. Hays was born in Louisville, Kentucky, in 1837
and lived to be seventy years old.

Year   Popular Songs

1862   "Drummer Boy of Shiloh"
        "Evangeline"

1866   "We Parted by the River"
        "Write Me a Letter from Home"

1868   "Driven from Home"

1870   "Nobody's Darling"

1871   "Little Old Log Cabin in the Lane"
        "Mollie Darling"
        "Number Twenty-Nine"
        "Susan Jane"

1872   "Oh! Sam"

1875   "Angels Meet Me at the Crossroads"

1877   "Roll Out! Heave Dat Cotton"
        "Early in de Mornin'"

1880   "Walk in de Middle of de Road"

* * *

GEORGE FREDERICK ROOT

Sheffield, Massachusetts, was the birthplace of George Frederick Root. He moved to New York when he was twenty-four years old and supported himself teaching music and playing the organ. During this period, he composed his first popular song "The Hazel Dell." In 1859, he settled in Chicago where he co-founded a music publishing house and wrote such famous Civil War songs as "Tramp, Tramp, Tramp (The Boys Are Marching)" and "The Battle Cry of Freedom" which sold 350,000 copies. His success as a composer continued for two decades after the war's end. During his retirement, he resumed his work as a music teacher. George Frederick Root was seventy-five when he died in 1895.

Year	Popular Songs
1853	"The Hazel Dell"
1854	"There's Music in the Air"
1855	"Rosalie, the Prairie Flower"
1857	"Departed Days"
1860	"The First Shot Is Fired"
1861	"The Vacant Chair"
1862	"The Battle Cry of Freedom"
1863	"Tramp, Tramp, Tramp (The Boys Are Marching)" "Just Before the Battle, Mother"
1865	"Farewell, Father, Friend and Guardian"
1884	"Blaine for Our President" "The Plumed Knight"

* * *

HENRY RUSSELL

Henry Russell was the first English-born composer to become a successful writer of American popular songs. He was born in Sheerness in 1812 and began his performing career as a boy singer. After studying music in Italy, Russell came to the United States where he settled in Rochester, New York, and worked as a church organist. He was twenty-five years old when he wrote the music for the first of his outstanding songs "Woodman, Spare That Tree." After eight years in America, Russell returned to England in 1841 and continued to write until his death in 1900.

Year   Popular Songs

1837   "Woodman, Spare That Tree"
        "The Indian Hunter"

1838   "A Life on the Ocean Wave"

1840   "The Old Arm Chair"

1841   "My Mother's Bible"
        "Our Native Song"

1850   "Cheer, Boys, Cheer"

1888   "The Ivey Green"

                        * * *

SEPTIMUS WINNER

      Septimus Winner was born in Philadelphia, Pennsylvania,
where he became a successful music publisher. While he is credited with composing "Listen to the Mocking Bird," several historians
believe that it was actually written by a Negro barber who was a
talented whistler. Even without that classic, Winner's reputation as
a composer is assured by his music and lyrics for "Where, Oh
Where, Has My Little Dog Gone?" and "Whispering Hope." Septimus Winner's popular songs were all created over a 16 year period.
He died in 1902 at the age of seventy-six.

Year   Popular Songs

1854   "What Is Home Without a Mother?"
        "I Set My Heart upon a Flower"

1855   "Listen to the Mocking Bird"

1861   "Abraham's Daughter"

1862   "Give Us Back Our Old Commander"

1864   "Where, Oh Where, Has My Little Dog Gone?"

1865   "Ellie Rhee"

1866   "What Care I?"

1868   "Whispering Hope"
        "Ten Little Injuns"

Year   Popular Songs

1870   "Come Where the Woodbine Twineth"
        "Love Once Gone Is Lost Forever"

* * *

HENRY CLAY WORK

        The parents of Henry Clay Work settled in Middletown, Con-
necticut, when he was thirteen years old.   His abolitionist father
served a prison term for helping slaves escape to freedom through
the "underground railway."   In his early twenties, Work moved to
Chicago where he was employed as a music type printer.   He was
a self-taught pianist and composed his first successful song, "Grafted into the Army," in 1862, just after the outbreak of the American
Civil War.   Work was a temperance crusader and his 1864 song
"Come Home, Father" was performed as part of the melodrama
"Ten Nights in a Bar Room."   His last hit, "Grandfather's Clock,"
was published in 1876.   Henry Clay Work died eight years later at
the age of fifty-two.

Year   Popular Songs

1862   "Grafted into the Army"
        "Kingdom Coming"

1863   "Babylon Is Fallen"

1864   "Come Home, Father"
        "Wake, Nicodemus"

1865   "Marching Through Georgia"
        "The Ship That Never Returned"

1876   "Grandfather's Clock"

Unknown: "The Lost Letter"

TIN PAN ALLEY

By 1880, music publishers had begun to realize that large profits could be made from popular songs. New inventions and manufacturing processes were enabling mass production of pianos, guitars, and ukuleles. As retail prices came within reach of the average worker, these instruments found their ways into more and more homes creating a vastly larger market for sheet music. Publishers began soliciting songs and sending out salesmen to vend them on a nationwide basis. Within a dozen years, most firms had located in New York's Union Square and were employing pianists, arrangers, and song pluggers who demonstrated the latest songs to the general public and to entertainers who were looking for new material. Songwriters not only became associated with specific publishers, but frequently opened their own firms. By 1895, the hub of America's popular music business was 28th Street between Fifth Avenue and Broadway--an area nicknamed "Tin Pan Alley."

Before the new century began, the Edison Phonograph was introduced and brought recorded music to persons who were unskilled with instruments. During these formative years, performers-songwriters such as Edward Harrigan and George M. Cohan pioneered livelier forms of theatrical entertainment than had been provided by the operettas of Gilbert and Sullivan and Reginald De Koven. More and more legitimate theatres opened until the name of Broadway became synonymous with American Theatre. Even in this early era, theatre meant sophistication and sheet music which carried a Broadway credit ("As introduced in 'The Ziegfeld Follies'") had a special appeal.

In 1915, organization within Tin Pan Alley reached the point at which the American Society of Composers, Authors and Publishers (ASCAP) was blessed by the Supreme Court. While promotion and merchandising enabled the songs of the nation's writers to reach far greater audiences, and songs sometimes sold three million or more copies, music was still not available at the turn of a switch. The following songwriters are included in this section:

Ernest R. Ball	Will D. Cobb
Henry Blossom	George M. Cohan
David Braham & Edward Harrigan	Bob Cole
Gene Buck	Paul Dresser

Jack Drislane   Edgar Smith

Charles K. Harris   Harry B. Smith

Victor Herbert   Robert B. Smith

Louis A. Hirsch   Andrew B. Sterling

William Jerome   John Stromberg

Arthur J. Lamb   James Thornton

Edward Madden   Egbert Van Alstyne

Kerry Mills   Harry Von Tilzer

Theodore F. Morse   Harry Williams

Monroe Rosenfeld   P. G. Wodehouse

Chris Smith   Rida Johnson Young

* * *

ERNEST R. BALL

     Ernest Ball was born in Cleveland, Ohio, in 1878, and was teaching piano by the time he was thirteen years old. After graduating from the Cleveland Conservatory of Music, he worked as a pianist in New York City vaudeville theatres. In 1904, twenty-six year old Ball set Cecil Mack's lyric "In the Shadow of the Pyramids" to music. The following year, he had a hit with words by New York City's future mayor Jimmy Walker--"Will You Love Me in December as You Do in May?" The lyrics for two of Ball's biggest successes, "When Irish Eyes Are Smiling" and "Mother Machree," were written by Broadway singing star Chauncey Olcott (the latter song in conjunction with Rida Johnson Young). Composer Ernest Ball was touring the country with his vaudeville act in 1927 when he was stricken with a heart attack and died in Santa Ana, California, at the age of forty-nine. Seventeen years later, he was the subject of a screen biography titled "Irish Eyes Are Smiling."

Year	Production Title	Popular Songs
1904		"In the Shadow of the Pyramids"
		"My Honey Moon"
1905	THE ROLLICKING GIRL	
		"Will You Love Me in December as You Do in May?"

Year	Production Title	Popular Songs
1906		"Love Me and the World Is Mine"
1907		"When the Birds in Georgia Sing of Tennessee" "As Long as the World Rolls On" "When Sweet Marie Was Sweet Sixteen" "My Dear"
1908		"To the End of the World with You" "All for Love of You" "In the Garden of My Heart" "When Mary Smiles" "When the Summer Days Have Gone"
1910	BARRY OF BALLYMORE	Mother Machree I Love the Name of Mary "My Heart Has Learned to Love You" "Your Love Means the World to Me" "Allah, Give Me Mine!"
1911		"Till the Sands of the Desert Grow Cold"
1912	THE ISLE OF DREAMS	Isle o' Dreams When Irish Eyes Are Smiling
1913		"To Have, to Hold, to Love" "On the Good Old-Time Straw Ride"
1914	THE HEART OF PADDY WHACK	A Little Bit of Heaven "After the Roses Have Faded Away" "You Planted a Rose in the Garden of Love" "In the Garden of the Gods"

Year	Production Title	Popular Songs
1915	MACUSHLA	That's How the Shannon Flows
		"Ireland Is Ireland to Me"
		"She's the Daughter of Mother Machree"
1916		"For Dixie and Uncle Sam"
		"Turn Back the Universe and Give Me Yesterday"
		"Goodbye, Good Luck, God Bless You"
		"And They Called It Dixieland"
		"The Story of Old Glory, the Flag We Love"
1917		"All the World Will Be Jealous of Me"
		"My Sunshine Jane"
1918		"Dear Little Boy of Mine"
		"One More Day"
		"Who Knows?"
		"With All My Heart and Soul"
1919		"Let the Rest of the World Go by"
1920		"Down the Trail to Home Sweet Home"
1921		"I'll Forget You"
		"Saloon"
1922		"Down the Winding Road of Dreams"
1923		"Out There in the Sunshine with You"
		"Ten Thousand Years from Now"
1924		"West of the Great Divide"
1925		"Hollywood Rose"
1927		"Rose of Killarney"

HENRY BLOSSOM

      Henry Blossom achieved his greatest success writing lyrics
for the melodies of Victor Herbert. Blossom was educated at the
Stoddard School in St. Louis, Missouri, where he was born in 1866.
Before becoming a writer, he worked for an insurance company
Blossom was thirty-six years old when his work was first heard by
a Broadway audience in 1902. His initial collaboration with Herbert, "Mlle Modiste," took place three years later. Its score included Blossom's memorable lyric "Kiss Me Again." The following
year, he and Herbert managed to create no less than seven hit
songs for the operetta "The Red Mill" including the classic "The
Streets of New York." Among Blossom's later successes were
"When You're Away" (1914), and "Thine Alone" (1917). Henry Blossom had two shows running on Broadway when he died in 1919 at
the age of fifty-three. He had contributed lyrics to 16 stage musicals in almost as many years.

Year	Production Title	Popular Songs
1901		"Since I Joined the Buffaloes, I Can't Lay Up a Cent"
1902	FAD AND FOLLY	"Don't Forget You're Talking to a Lady"
1904	THE YANKEE CONSUL	Ain't It Funny What a Difference Just a Few Hours Make?
		My San Domingo Maid
1905	MLLE MODISTE	Kiss Me Again
		I Want What I Want When I Want It
		The Mascot of the Troop
1906	THE RED MILL	The Streets of New York
		Moonbeams
		Every Day Is Ladies Day with Me
		Because You're You
		The Isle of Our Dreams
		When You're Pretty and the World Is Fair
		I Want You to Marry Me
1907	THE HOYDEN	
1908	THE PRIMA DONNA	I'll Be Married to the Music of a Military Band
		If You Were I and I Were You

Year	Production Title	Popular Songs
1911	THE SLIM PRINCESS	
1912	THE MAN FROM COOKS ALL FOR THE LADIES	
1913	A GLIMPSE OF THE GREAT WHITE WAY	
1914	THE ONLY GIRL	When You're Away Tell It All Over Again When You're Wearing the Ball and Chain
1915	THE PRINCESS PAT	Neopolitan Love Song All for You Love Is the Best of All Two Laughing Irish Eyes
1916	THE CENTURY GIRL	
1917	EILEEN	Thine Alone Eileen Alana Asthore When Shall I Again See Ireland? The Irish Have a Great Day Tonight Free Trade and a Misty Moon
1919	THE VELVET LADY AMONG THE GIRLS	Spooky Ookum

* * *

DAVID BRAHAM & EDWARD HARRIGAN

Ned Harrigan was considerably more than a songwriter. He and his partners were responsible for introducing a new type of theatrical entertainment which paved the way for the productions of George M. Cohan and the eventual art form known as musical comedy. Harrigan was born in New York City in 1845. He went to sea in his youth and then became a West Coast dock worker. When he was in his early twenties, he began singing in saloons on San Francisco's Barbary Coast. He made his legitimate stage debut in 1868 and his bookings took him from San Francisco to Chicago where he formed a partnership with female impersonator Tony Hart. Harrigan and Hart appeared in variety theatres in the nation's major cities and eventually became a prime attraction at Tony Pastor's cabaret on New York City's Bowery.

It was at Tony Pastor's that Harrigan met London-born composer David Braham. Braham was an accomplished violinist who had come to the United States in his late teens. After working as violinist-conductor for minstrel shows, Braham was hired as orchestra conductor at Pastor's. Between performances at the cabaret, Ned Harrigan and David Braham began writing songs and had their first hit with "The Mulligan Guard" in 1873. During the next four years, Harrigan and Hart popularized other Braham melodies. It was Ned Harrigan who then conceived the idea of presenting musicals about the daily experiences of the Jewish, Irish and German immigrants who inhabited New York City.

The first of the more than two dozen musicals on which Harrigan and Braham collaborated was produced in 1878. Harrigan was then thirty-three years old and Braham was forty. In addition to providing the lyrics for their musicals, Harrigan wrote the stories and dialogue, produced and directed them, and was Tony Hart's co-star in half of them. Braham conducted the orchestra for the shows. From the start, their offerings attracted large audiences who found welcome relief from the implausible fantasies provided in the operettas of Gilbert and Sullivan. For eight years, Harrigan, Hart and Braham were Broadway's most successful team. In 1885, Tony Hart dissolved his association with Harrigan. The remaining partners continued their efforts for ten more years. After 1896, the vogue they had enjoyed had passed. David Braham died in 1905 at the age of sixty-seven. Ned Harrigan lived for only six more years and was sixty-six at the time of his passing.

Year	Production Title	Popular Songs
1873		"The Mulligan Guard"
1874		"The Skidmore Guard" "Patrick's Day Parade"
1875		"Malone at the Back of the Bar"
1878	THE MULLIGAN GUARD'S BALL MALONE'S NIGHT OFF	The Skidmore Fancy Ball The Babies on Our Block Sweet Mary Ann
1879	THE MULLIGAN GUARD'S CHOWDER THE MULLIGAN GUARD'S CHRISTMAS	The Little Widow Dunn The Casey Social Club "The Plain Gold Ring"
1880	THE MULLIGAN GUARD'S SURPRISE THE MULLIGAN GUARD'S PICNIC	The Full Moon Union Never Take the Horse- shoe from the Door Locked Out After Nine Mary Kelly's Beau

Year	Production Title	Popular Songs
1880	THE MULLIGAN GUARD'S NOMINEE	The Skidmore Masquerade The Mulligan Braves
1881	THE MAJOR THE MULLIGAN'S SILVER WEDDING	Major Gilfeather John Reilly's Always Dry
1882	SQUATTER SOVEREIGNTY THE McSORLEYS MORDECAI LYONS	Paddy Duffy's Cart The Widow Nolan's Goat I Never Drink Behind the Bar The Market on Saturday Night McNally's Row of Flats When the Clock in the Tower Strikes Twelve
1883	CORDELIA'S ASPIRATIONS THE MUDDY DAY	My Dad's Dinner Pail Just Across from Jersey Sam Johnson's Colored Cakewalk Two More to Come
1884	DAN'S TRIBULATIONS	Coming Home from Meeting "Plum Pudding"
1885	OLD LAVENDER McALISTER'S LEGACY INVESTIGATIONS THE GRIP	Poverty's Tears Ebb and Flow
1886	THE LEATHER PATCH THE O'REAGANS	Danny Grady's Hack
1887	PETE McNOONEY'S VISIT	Slavery's Passed Away
1888	WADDY GOOGAN	Old Boss Barry The Midnight Squad Isabelle St. Clair Where the Sparrows and the Chippies Parade
1889	THE LORGAIRE	
1890	REILLY AND THE 400	Maggie Murphy's Home I've Come Home to Stay

Year	Production Title	Popular Songs
1890	REILLY AND THE 400	Jolly Commodore Taking in the Town
1891	THE LAST OF THE HOGANS	Danny by My Side The Last of the Hogans Hats Off to Me Knights of the Mystic Star De Rainbow Road Take a Day Off, Mary Ann
1893	THE WOOLEN STOCKING	They Never Tell All What They Know Little Daughter Nell
1896	MARTY MALONE	

* * *

GENE BUCK

Almost all of Gene Buck's popular songs were introduced in "The Ziegfeld Follies." Buck was born in Detroit, Michigan, in 1885 and attended the Detroit Art Academy. He became a commercial artist and succeeded in changing the covers of sheet music from their previous simple black and white designs into colorful posters. He designed thousands of covers before he turned to lyric writing at the age of twenty-six. Buck's association with producer Florenz Ziegfeld began with the sixth edition of "The Follies" and he became the showman's chief assistant. His songs were heard in 15 of the famous revues plus half a dozen other Ziegfeld productions. Among his hit songs were "Hello, Frisco," "Tulip Time," "My Rambler Rose" and "Florida, the Moon and You" which became Florida's official state song. The composers with whom he worked included Dave Stamper, Louis Hirsch and Rudolf Friml. He also wrote sketches for "The Follies." In 1927, he produced and directed a show of his own. Edward Eugene Buck served as the president of ASCAP from 1924 until 1941. He died in 1957 at the age of seventy-two.

Year	Production Title	Popular Songs
1911		"Some Boy"
1912	THE ZIEGFELD FOLLIES	Daddy Has a Sweetheart and Mother Is Her Name

Year	Production Title	Popular Songs
1913	THE ZIEGFELD FOLLIES	
1914	THE ZIEGFELD FOLLIES	Underneath the Japanese Moon
		"Everything Is Different Nowadays"
1915	THE ZIEGFELD FOLLIES	Hello, Frisco Hold Me in Your Loving Arms In the Cool of Evening
1916	THE ZIEGFELD FOLLIES	Have a Heart Beautiful Island of Girls Bachelor Days
1917	THE ZIEGFELD FOLLIES	Hello, My Dearie
		"Tiger Rose"
1918	THE ZIEGFELD FOLLIES ZIEGFELD 9 O'CLOCK FROLIC	Garden of My Dreams
1919	THE ZIEGFELD FOLLIES	Tulip Time Sweet Sixteen
	ZIEGFELD'S MIDNIGHT FROLIC	
1920	THE ZIEGFELD FOLLIES	The Love Boat Sunshine and Shadows
	ZIEGFELD'S MIDNIGHT FROLIC ZIEGFELD GIRLS OF 1920	
1921	THE ZIEGFELD FOLLIES	Bring Back My Blushing Rosie Sally, Won't You Come Back?
	ZIEGFELD'S MIDNIGHT FROLIC	
1922	THE ZIEGFELD FOLLIES	My Rambler Rose Throw Me a Kiss Some Sweet Day 'Neath the South Sea Moon It's Getting Dark on Old Broadway
1923	THE ZIEGFELD FOLLIES	
1924	THE ZIEGFELD FOLLIES	Lovely Little Melody

Year	Production Title	Popular Songs
1925	THE ZIEGFELD FOLLIES	
1926	NO FOOLIN'	Florida, the Moon and You Poor Little Marie No Foolin'
1927	TAKE THE AIR	We'll Have a New Home in the Mornin' Lullaby
1931	THE ZIEGFELD FOLLIES	

* * *

WILL D. COBB

Will Cobb was born in Philadelphia, Pennsylvania, in 1876. He attended Girard College in New York, and began earning his living as a department store clerk. He was twenty-three years old when he began his collaboration with composer/performer Gus Edwards in 1899. During the next decade, the hit songs with lyrics by Cobb and music by Edwards included "I'll Be with You When the Roses Bloom Again," "Sunbonnet Sue" and the immortal "School Days." Cobb wrote one of his biggest successes, "Waltz Me Around Again, Willie," with composer Ren Shields in 1906. After World War I, few of his songs found favor with the public. Will D. Cobb died in 1930 at the age of fifty-four.

Year	Production Title	Popular Songs
1899		"The Singer and the Song" "I Couldn't Stand to See My Baby Lose" "You Are the Only Girl I'll Ever Care About"
1900		"Goodbye, Dolly Gray" "I Can't Tell Why I Love You, but I Do" "All for a Man Whose God Was Gold" "A Face Behind a Mask"
1901		"I'm Dreaming of a Bygone Day" "Mamie"

Year	Production Title	Popular Songs
1901		"I'll Be with You When the Roses Bloom Again" "I Don't Want Money" "It's Awfully Nice to Be a Regular Soldier" "Way Down Yonder in the Corn Field"
1902		"Could You Be True to Eyes of Blue?" "Fare Thee Well, Molly Darling" "Over the Ocean" "Have You Seen My Sweetheart in His Uniform of Blue?" "On the Proper Side of Broadway on a Saturday P.M."
1903	MR. BLUEBEARD THE WIZARD OF OZ	
1904	THE MEDAL AND THE MAID	In Zanzibar "The Girl Who Cares for Me" "Goodbye, Little Girl, Goodbye"
1905		"If a Girl Like You Loved a Boy Like Me" "Somebody's Sweetheart I Want to Be" "Goodbye, Sweet Marie"
1906	HIS HONOR THE MAYOR	Waltz Me Around Again, Willie
	THE PARISIAN MODEL	I'd Like to See a Little More of You I Just Can't Make My Eyes Behave
	ABOUT TOWN	"Sunbonnet Sue" "Rose Bud" "Two Little Dirty Hands" "I'll Do Anything, Dear, in the World for You"

Year	Production Title	Popular Songs
1907	THE ZIEGFELD FOLLIES	On the Grand Old Sand Good-bye Dear Old Broadway
	THE GAY WHITE WAY	"Laddie Boy" "There's a Girl in This World for Every Boy" "The Welcome on the Mat Ain't Meant for Me"
1908	SCHOOL DAYS	School Days "Yip-I-Addy-I-Ay" "Sunburnt Salome"
1910		"If I Was a Millionaire" "Go 'Way from Me, I Hate You" "Hoop-La!"
1911		"Dusky Sandy from Sandusky"
1912		"Honest True"
1913		"I'll Get You"
1916		"I Lost My Heart in Honolulu"
1917		"For You a Rose" "Just a Simple Country Maiden"
1921		"I Want You Morning, Noon and Night"
1922	THE FRENCH DOLL	

Posthumous:

| 1950 | | "The Beer That I Left on the Bar" |

* * *

GEORGE M. COHAN

The man chiefly responsible for integrating vaudeville tech-

nique into Broadway musicals to produce a bright, fast-moving show
was George Michael Cohan whose talents were limitless. He was
equally successful as an actor, singer, dancer, composer, lyricist,
playwright, producer, and director. He also made phonograph records and appeared in motion pictures!

        Cohan was born in Rhode Island in 1878 and began his pro-
fessional career as a child appearing in the act "The Four Cohans"
with his father Jerry, his mother Helen, and his sister Josie. His
first song, "Why Did Nellie Leave Home?," was published when he
was barely in his teens. Cohan's chief ambition was to raise the
status of his family from vaudeville troupers to stars of the legitimate stage. His ambition began to reach fulfillment in 1901 when
"The Four Cohans" opened on Broadway in "The Governor's Son"--
a production with book, music and lyrics by twenty-three year old
George. Two years later, the foursome appeared in his "Running
for Office," and Cohan had songs featured in the extravaganza
"Mother Goose."

        Cohan was one of America's first image makers--more than
50 years before Madison Avenue learned to make a business out of
promoting images. Cohan's name became synonymous with the
word "Broadway." The mere mention of his name conjured up vi-
sions of bright lights and the smell of greasepaint in the imagina-
tions of most Americans. Cohan worked continuously to establish
and perpetuate this image, writing and singing songs such as "Too
Many Miles from Broadway," "Busy Little Broadway," "Hello,
Broadway," "It's a Long Way from Broadway to Edinboro Town"
and "I Wanted to Come to Broadway." The second facet of the image he created for himself was his role as a super patriot. His
musical catalog abounds with such titles as "I Want to Hear a Yankee Doodle Tune," "Yankee Doodle's Come to Town," "Any Old
Place the Flag Flies" and "My Flag."

        In 1904, Cohan formed a partnership with Sam H. Harris to
produce "Little Johnny Jones" with book, music and lyrics by Cohan. In the cast were Jerry, Helen, and George. The production
was Cohan's most successful to date and introduced both "Give My
Regards to Broadway" and "Yankee Doodle Boy." 1906 was ushered
in with the opening of "Forty-Five Minutes from Broadway." It was
the first Cohan musical in which none of the family appeared. The
show's title song aroused considerable displeasure among the citi-
zens of the New York suburb of New Rochelle when it described
them as "hicks" with "whiskers like hay." In addition to "Forty-
Five Minutes from Broadway," Cohan's play "Popularity" was produced in 1906, and he starred in another Cohan musical "George
Washington, Jr." together with his parents and his wife Ethel Levey. "You're a Grand Old Rag" was part of the score for "George
Washington, Jr." Protests from several patriotic societies forced
him to change "rag" to "flag." The following year, he and Ethel
Levey were divorced and he married dancer Agnes Nolan.

        Plays and musicals continued to flow with profusion from Cohan's pen. "Get-Rich-Quick Wallingford" was one of Broadway's hit plays of 1910. By 1911, his personal wealth was estimated at over one million dollars and he was an owner of the Cohan Theatre. His offering that year was aptly titled "The Little Millionaire." He made his film debut in the 1916 silent movie adaptation of his play "Broadway Jones."

With his reputation as a "Yankee Doodle Boy," it would have been ironic if Cohan had failed in his attempt to write a rousing war song when the United States entered World War I. The song he created was not only successful--it was sensationally successful! Even today, his song "Over There" immediately recalls what was then known as "The Great War."

In 1919, performers belonging to Actor's Equity went on strike against Broadway's major producers. Although he had begun his career as a performer, producer Cohan took sides against the actors. When stagehands and musicians walked out in sympathy with the actors, 23 productions were forced to close. Actor's Equity won the strike but for the rest of his life Cohan continued his feud with the union. The end of the strike coincided with the end of his sixteen year partnership with Sam Harris. Three years later, he presented his twenty-two year old daughter Georgette in "Madelaine and the Movies" but the Cohan heiress failed to generate much excitement. In 1925, he wrote his autobiography Twenty Years on Broadway and the Years It Took to Get There.

Cohan's swan song as a Broadway composer was the 1928 musical "Billie" but it was by no means the end of his career. During the next twelve years he made his first talking motion picture and starred in six plays on Broadway including the Rodgers and Hart musical "I'd Rather Be Right" in which he impersonated President Franklin Roosevelt. He made his final stage appearance in "The Return of the Vagabond" in 1940. That same year, he was awarded the Congressional Medal of Honor for his songs "Over There" and "You're a Grand Old Flag." During World War II he attempted to repeat the success of "Over There" but his songs "This Is Our Side of the Ocean" and "We Must Be Ready" failed to catch the public's fancy.

The last tribute George M. Cohan lived to receive was his 1942 motion picture biography "Yankee Doodle Dandy." The picture was highly fictionized since he refused to allow a true presentation of his private life. The sixty-four year old theatrical "Jack of All Trades" died of cancer in November of 1942 in New York City, leaving a legacy of some 200 songs and 40 musicals and plays. Twenty-six years after his death, the 1968 production "George M!" had its New York premiere. The show was a musical biography featuring his most famous songs--with lyric and musical revisions by his daughter Mary.

Today, visitors to Manhattan may notice a statue which was erected in Times Square in 1959. On close inspection, they'll dis-

cover George M. Cohan overlooking the theatrical district in which
he was once "The Man Who Owns Broadway."

Year	Production Title	Popular Songs
1893		"When the Girl You Love Is Many Miles Away"
1894		"Venus, My Shining Love"
1895		"Hot Tamale Alley"
1896		"The Songs That Maggie Sings" "The Warmest Baby in the Bunch"
1898		"I Guess I'll Have to Telegraph My Baby"
1899		"My Little Lady" "Telephone Me, Baby"
1900		"I Won't Be an Actor No More"
1901	THE GOVERNOR'S SON	
1902		"Then I'd Be Satisfied with Life" "You Won't Do Any Business If You Haven't Got a Band"
1903	MOTHER GOOSE	I Want to Hear a Yankee Doodle Tune Always Leave Them Laughing
	RUNNING FOR OFFICE	
1904	LITTLE JOHNNY JONES	Give My Regards to Broadway The Yankee Doodle Boy Good-Bye, Flo Life's a Funny Proposition After All
1906	FORTY-FIVE MINUTES FROM BROADWAY	Mary's a Grand Old Name Forty-Five Minutes from Broadway

Year	Production Title	Popular Songs
1906	FORTY-FIVE MINUTES FROM BROADWAY	So Long, Mary Stand Up and Fight Like Hell
	GEORGE WASHINGTON JR.	You're a Grand Old Flag You Can Have Broadway I Was Born in Virginia If Washington Should Come to Life
1907	THE HONEYMOONERS	My Musical Comedy Maid Nothing New Beneath the Sun I'm a Popular Man If I'm Going to Die, I'm Going to Have Some Fun
	THE TALK OF NEW YORK	Under Any Old Flag at All I Want the World to Know I Love You I Want You When a Fellow's on the Level with a Girl That's on the Square When We Are M-A Double R-I-E-D
1908	FIFTY MILES FROM BOSTON	Harrigan
	THE YANKEE PRINCE	Come on Down Town
	THE AMERICAN IDEA	That's Some Love "Take Your Girl to the Ball Game"
1909	THE MAN WHO OWNS BROADWAY	There's Something About a Uniform The Man Who Owns Broadway
1911	THE LITTLE MILLIONAIRE	Barnum Had the Right Idea Any Old Place the Flag Flies
	VERA VIOLETTA	That Haunting Melody

Year	Production Title	Popular Songs
1914	HELLO, BROADWAY!	Hello, Broadway!
1916	THE COHAN REVUE	
1917	THE COHAN REVUE OF 1918	
		"Over There"
1918	THE VOICE OF McCONNELL	
		"When You Come Back"
1919	THE ROYAL VAGABOND	In a Kingdom of Our Own
1922	LITTLE NELLIE KELLY	You Remind Me of My Mother Nellie Kelly, I Love You
1923	THE RISE OF ROSIE O'REILLY	When June Comes Along with a Song
1927	MERRY MALONES	Molly Malone
		"When Lindy Comes Home"
1928	BILLIE	Where Were You, Where Was I? Billie
1933	The Phantom President	

* * *

BOB COLE

Lyricist Bob Cole was born in Athens, Georgia, in 1863 and was thirty-four years old when his first hit song was published. At the turn of the century, he formed a partnership with composer J. Rosamond Johnson and the team soon became a leading attraction in both vaudeville and Broadway musicals. Cole supplied the words for a dozen of Johnson's melodies including their biggest hit "Under the Bamboo Tree" which Marie Cahill introduced in the 1902 production "Sally in Our Alley." Cole worked constantly to change the stereotyped image of his race as it was portrayed on the stage to a truer representation of Negro life. His last success, "I've Just Lost My Teddy Bear," was heard in the 1909 production "The Red Moon." Bob Cole died two years later at the age of only forty-eight.

Year	Production Title	Popular Songs
1897		"La Hoola Boola"
		"I Hope These Few Lines Will Find You Well"
1899		"Louisiana Liza"
		"Chicken"
1900	THE BELLE OF BRIDGEPORT	Magdaline, My Southern Queen
		"I Must Been a-Dreamin'"
1901	THE LITTLE DUCHESS	Maiden with the Dreamy Eyes
	SLEEPING BEAUTY AND THE BEAST	Tell Me, Dusky Maiden
		Come Out, Dinah, on the Green
		The Owl and the Moon
		"Ain't That Scand'lous?"
		"My Castle on the Nile"
1902	SALLY IN OUR ALLEY	Under the Bamboo Tree
		"Oh, Didn't He Ramble?"
		"The Old Flag Never Touched the Ground"
1903	NANCY BROWN	Congo Love Song
	WHOOP-DEE-DO	Maid of Timbuctoo
	THE GIRL FROM DIXIE	
	MR. BLUEBEARD	
		"Lazy Moon"
		"Mandy, Won't You Let Me Be Your Beau?"
		"The Katydid, the Cricket and the Frog"
		"My Mississippi Belle"
1904	AN ENGLISH DAISY	Big Indian Chief
	HUMPTY DUMPTY IN NEWPORT	
		"Moonlight on the Mississippi"
		"Countess of Alagazam"
1905		"My Lulu San"

Year	Production Title	Popular Songs
1906	MARRYING MARY	Hottentot Love Song
1909	THE RED MOON	I've Just Lost My Teddy Bear

* * *

PAUL DRESSER*

Paul Dresser was noted as the composer of sentimental ballads guaranteed to bring tears to the eyes of listeners. He was the younger brother of Theodore Dreiser who wrote the best-selling novels Sister Carrie and An American Tragedy. Dresser was born in Terra Haute, Indiana in 1857. When he was sixteen, he left home to join the company of a traveling medicine show, and later became the lead comic in a minstrel troupe. While still struggling for a foothold in the acting profession, Dresser wrote newspaper columns and supplied special material for his fellow comedians. He made his debut as a songwriter when he was twenty-eight. The title of his early hit "The Letter That Never Came" was typical of the many sad songs he created during his 20 year career. Dresser wrote the music and lyrics for the plaintive "The Pardon Came Too Late," "I Was Looking for My Boy, She Said," "The Curse of the Dreamer," and "Where Are the Friends of Other Days?" With his continued success as a songwriter, Dresser became a partner in a New York music publishing company. He also achieved his ambition to become a legitimate actor and played prominent roles in several Broadway productions. His 1897 song "On the Banks of the Wabash" was adopted by Indiana as its official state song. Paul Dresser was approaching fifty when he wrote his last hit "My Gal Sal" in 1905. He died the next year. In 1942, Twentieth Century-Fox released "My Gal Sal" based on Dresser's life.

Year	Popular Songs
1885	"Wide Wings"
1886	"The Letter That Never Came"
1887	"The Outcast Unknown"
1888	"The Convict and the Bird"
1890	"Her Tears Drifted Out with the Tide" "The Lone Grave" "Little Jim"
1891	"The Pardon Came Too Late"

*Dresser Americanized spelling from Dreiser.

Year	Popular Songs

1893   "Rosie, Sweet Rosabel"

1894   "Take a Seat, Old Lady"
       "Once Ev'ry Year"

1895   "We Were Sweethearts for Many Years"
       "Jean"
       "Just Tell Them That You Saw Me"
       "I Was Looking for My Boy, She Said"

1896   "Show Me the Way"
       "A Dream of My Boyhood Days"
       "He Brought Home Another"
       "I'se Your Nigger If You Wants Me, Liza Jane"
       "Don't Tell Her That You Love Her"
       "He Fought for a Cause He Thought Was Right"
       "I Wish That You Were Here Tonight"
       "I Wonder If She'll Ever Come Back to Me?"

1897   "On the Banks of the Wabash"
       "You're Going Far Away, Lad"
       "If You See My Sweetheart"

1898   "The Path That Leads the Other Way"
       "You're Just a Little Nigger Still You're Mine, All Mine"
       "Your God Comes First, Your Country Next, Then
           Mother Dear"
       "We Fight Tomorrow, Mother"
       "Every Night There's a Light"
       "The Old Flame Flickers and I Wonder Why"
       "Sweet Savannah"
       "Come Tell Me What's Your Answer, Yes or No?"
       "Our Country, May She Always Be Right"

1899   "Come Home, Dewey, We Won't Do a Thing to You"
       "We Came from the Same Old State"
       "There's Where My Heart Is Tonight"
       "The Curse of the Dreamer"
       "In Good Old New York Town"
       "I Wonder Where She Is Tonight?"

1900   "The Blue and the Gray"
       "Calling to Her Boy Just Once Again"
       "I'd Still Believe You True"
       "My Heart Still Clings to the Old First Love"
       "When de Moon Comes Up Behind de Hill"

1901   "I Just Want to Go Back and Start the Whole Thing Over"
       "When the Birds Have Sung Themselves to Sleep"
       "There's No North or South Today"
       "Way Down in Old Indiana"

Year   Popular Songs

1901   "In the Great Somewhere"
        "Mr. Volunteer"

1902   "When You Come Back They'll Wonder Who the ____
            You Are"
        "In Dear Old Illinois"

1903   "Where Are the Friends of Other Days?"
        "The Boys Are Coming Home Today"
        "Lincoln, Grant or Lee"
        "The Voice of the Hudson"

1904   "Your Mother Wants You Home, Boy"
        "When I'm Away from You, Dear"
        "She Went to the City"

1905   "The Town Where I Was Born"
        "The Day That You Grew Colder"
        "Bethlehem"
        "Jim Judson--from the Town of Hackensack"
        "My Gal Sal"

                          * * *

JACK DRISLANE

        Lyricist Jack Drislane is the forgotten man among America's
popular song writers. Although he wrote the words for over two
dozen of the nation's favorite melodies from 1904 through 1912, the
only mention he receives from historians is in their lists of song
titles.   Drislane's hits included "Keep a Little Cozy Corner in Your
Heart," "Arrah Wanna" and "Honey-Love." His most frequent collaborator was composer Theodore F. Morse.

Year   Popular Songs

1904   "What the Brass Band Played"

1905   "Keep a Little Cozy Corner in Your Heart"
        "Just a Little Rocking Chair and You"
        "Longing for You"
        "My Yankee Irish Girl"

1906   "Arrah Wanna"
        "The Good Old U.S.A."
        "Keep on the Sunny Side"
        "Crocodile Isle"
        "You Never Can Tell by the Label"

Year   Popular Songs

1907   "It's Great to Be a Soldier Man"
        "Nobody's Little Girl"
        "Won't You Be My Honey?"
        "In Monkey Land"
        "The Old Street Band"
        "Since Arrah Wanna Married Barney Carney"

1909   "I'm Awfully Glad I Met You"
        "Monkey Doodle Dandy"
        "You Taught Me How to Love You, Now Teach Me to Forget"

1910   "You Remind Me of the Girl That Used to Go to School
            with Me"
        "Somebody Else, It's Always Somebody Else"
        "Cupid's I.O.U."

1911   "Honey-Love"

1912   "Dear Old Rose"
        "After All That I've Been to You"
        "In Dixie Land with Dixie Lou"

* * *

CHARLES K. HARRIS

        Charles K. Harris wrote the words and music for one of
the most famous songs in popular music history--"After the Ball"
(1892). It sold over 5,000,000 copies of sheet music! Harris
taught himself to play the banjo when he was ten years old, and
began composing melodies six years later. He settled in Milwau-
kee, Wisconsin, and worked as a bellhop, pawnbroker's assistant,
and music teacher. The success of "After the Ball" enabled him
to open his own music publishing firm in Chicago. Harris was
then twenty-five. Although a score of his songs were popular over
the next two decades, none came even close to the fame of his biggest hit. He also wrote plays and scripts for silent motion pictures. When syncopation became the order of the day, he was unable to adjust his musical style to the new vogue. One of Harris'
last songs to attract public favor was "Songs of Yesterday" published in 1916. Charles K. Harris died 14 years later at the age
of sixty-three. He was born in Poughkeepsie, New York.

Year   Popular Songs

1891   "When the Sun Has Set"

1892   "After the Ball"

Year	Popular Songs

1892   "Fallen by the Wayside"
       "Can Hearts So Soon Forget?"

1893   "After Nine"
       "Since Katie Rides a Wheel"

1894   "I Heard Her Voice Again"

1895   "There'll Come a Time"
       "Better Than Gold"

1896   "Just Behind the Times"

1897   "I've Just Come Back to Say Goodbye"
       "Break the News to Mother"

1898   "'Mid the Green Fields of Virginia"
       "I've Been Faithful to You"

1899   "One Night in June"
       "Is Life Worth Living?"
       "A Rabbi's Daughter"

1900   "For Old Times' Sake"
       "I've a Longing in My Heart for You, Louise"
       "Just One Kiss"

1901   "Hello, Central, Give Me Heaven"

1902   "I'm Wearing My Heart Away for You"

1903   "Always in the Way"
       "For Sale, a Baby"

1904   "Why Don't They Play with Me?"
       "I'm Trying So Hard to Forget You"

1905   "Would You Care?"

1907   "The Best Things in Life"

1909   "Nobody Knows, Nobody Cares"

1910   "It's Always June When You're in Love"

1916   "Songs of Yesterday"

* * *

VICTOR HERBERT

Musical comedy is one of the few art forms originated in the United States. It was developed partly from the European art form of operetta--a development that took nearly three decades to produce its first major milestone with the 1927 production "Show Boat."

The word "operetta" is a synonym for "light opera." In light opera, the musical compositions are bridged with spoken dialogue as opposed to true opera in which communication is accomplished only through singing. The foremost exponent of operetta composition in America was Victor Herbert.

Herbert was born in Dublin, Ireland, in 1859 and came to the United States at the age of twenty-seven as cellist in an opera company orchestra. His first operetta, produced in 1894, failed to generate much excitement but his second--"The Wizard of the Nile"--entertained audiences for three months.

For many years after Herbert began writing for the theatre, the plots of operettas were constructed as pure escapist entertainment. They generally dealt with romances between exotic persons and commoners with the true identity of the "Prince" or "Princess" unknown to the heroine or hero until just before the curtain fell. The settings for the productions were invariably European or Oriental. There was virtually no attempt at relevance and no relationship to reality as known to the audience.

After creating the scores for "The Gold Bug," "The Serenade," "The Idol's Eye," and "The Fortune Teller," Victor Herbert accepted the post of Director of the Pittsburgh Symphony--a position he held for three years. He returned to Broadway for the 1903 production "Babes in Toyland." The biggest success of his career was "The Red Mill" (1906) which ran for eight months. Three dozen productions followed including "Naughty Marietta," "Sweethearts" and "The Princess Pat."

In the days when Herbert was writing his operettas, composers generally sold their songs to a publisher for a flat sum and perhaps a penny or so for each sheet music copy sold. That was all the artist ever earned from his songs no matter how popular they became. Likewise, the publisher's only income was from the copies of sheet music purchased. Regardless of how many times the song was played, neither the composer nor the publisher received another dime. This practice was a great concern to Victor Herbert and his contemporaries. Each time he attended a vaudeville performance or dined at a restaurant which employed musicians, he was disturbed by the fact that everyone was making more money out of popular songs than the artists who had brought them into being. Herbert discussed the situation with other songwriters and publishers and they decided to form an organization which would prohibit the public performance of their music for profit unless royalties were paid. The royalties were to be prorated among the various members. In order to test the legality of the organization,

a New York restaurant owner whose orchestra had played the title
song from "Sweethearts" without Herbert's permission was sued.
The suit ended up in the United States Supreme Court and the historic 1915 decision was in favor of the newly-formed American
Society of Composers, Authors and Publishers.   The court ruled
that all establishments in which songs were performed for the public and for profit were required to pay annual dues to the organization which soon became known as "ASCAP."   From that time on,
the more often a particular song was performed, the more money
the composer, lyricist and publisher were paid.   When radio became a source of entertainment, the dues requirements were levied
on broadcasters.   The same enforcement greeted the birth of commercial television.   Today ASCAP pays over 80 million dollars annually to its 25,000 members based on the popularity of the members' compositions.

Even before "The Jazz Age" of the 1920's began, the climate in the musical theatre started to change.   Rhythms became
faster, romantic fantasies gave way to more realistic stories, and
the public's craving for light opera diminished.   Victor Herbert
was well aware of the changes but, although he contributed songs
to several editions of the lively "Ziegfeld Follies," he continued to
write mainly in the style which was his tradition.

Herbert died of a heart attack in May of 1924 at the age of
sixty-five--just three months before the opening of his operetta
"The Dream Girl."   A few years after his death, sound came to
motion pictures and his music was soon enjoyed by vaster audiences than ever before.   During the 1930's, screen adaptations of
"Babes in Toyland," "Naughty Marietta" and "Sweethearts" were
released.   In 1939, Paramount Studios paid tribute to the famous
composer with the motion picture biography "The Great Victor Herbert."   That same year, Al Dubin added lyrics to Herbert's instrumental number "Indian Summer" (1919) and it became the Number
One song on "Your Hit Parade."   Another resurrection occurred
in 1940 when Stanley Adams wrote words for "Yesterthoughts" (1900)
and it proved to be a best-selling Glenn Miller recording.   In addition to frequent revivals of his operettas, a new musical titled
"Gypsy Lady" opened on Broadway in 1946.   The score consisted
of a dozen Herbert melodies written before the turn of the century.

Victor Herbert occupies the Number Three position in Tin
Pan Alley's "Winner's Circle."

Year	Production Title	Popular Songs
1894	PRINCE ANANIAS	
1895	THE WIZARD OF THE NILE	My Angeline Star Light, Star Bright
1896	THE GOLD BUG	

Year	Production Title	Popular Songs
1897	THE SERENADE	The Cupid and I I Love Thee, I Adore Thee
	THE IDOL'S EYE	
1898	THE FORTUNE TELLER	Gypsy Love Song Romany Life
1899	THE SINGING GIRL	If Only You Were Mine Love Is a Tyrant
	CYRANO DE BERGERAC THE AMEER	
1900	THE VICEROY	
1903	BABES IN TOYLAND	Toyland Never Mind, Bo Peep I Can't Do That Sum Go to Sleep, Slumber Deep
	BABETTE	There Once Was an Owl
1904	IT HAPPENED IN NORDLAND	A Knot of Blue Absinthe Frappe Bandanna Land
1905	MISS DOLLY DOLLARS	A Woman Is Only a Woman (But a Good Cigar Is a Smoke)
	MLLE MODISTE	Kiss Me Again I Want What I Want When I Want It The Mascot of the Troop
	WONDERLAND	
1906	THE RED MILL	Moonbeams Every Day Is Ladies' Day with Me The Streets of New York Because You're You The Isle of Our Dreams When You're Pretty and the World Is Fair I Want You to Marry Me
	ABOUT TOWN DREAM CITY and THE MAGIC KNIGHT	
1907	THE TATTOOED MAN	
1908	ALGERIA	Ask Her While the Band Is Playing Rose of the World Love Is Like a Cigarette

Year	Production Title	Popular Songs
1908	THE PRIMA DONNA	If You Were I and I Were You I'll Be Married to the Music of a Military Band
	LITTLE NEMO	
1909	THE ROSE OF ALGERIA OLD DUTCH	
1910	NAUGHTY MARIETTA	Ah! Sweet Mystery of Life I'm Falling in Love with Someone Italian Street Song Tramp! Tramp! Tramp! 'Neath the Southern Moon Live for Today
1911	WHEN SWEET SIXTEEN THE ENCHANTRESS THE DUCHESS	The Wild Rose To the Land of My Own Romance
1912	THE LADY OF THE SLIPPER	Bagdad
1913	SWEETHEARTS THE MADCAP DUCHESS	Sweethearts For Every Lover Must Meet His Fate The Angelus Pretty as a Picture The Cricket on the Hearth Jeanette and Her Little Wooden Shoes
1914	THE ONLY GIRL THE DEBUTANTE	When You're Away Tell It All Over Again When You're Wearing the Ball and Chain The Springtime of Life
1915	THE PRINCESS PAT	Neopolitan Love Song Love Is the Best of All Two Laughing Irish Eyes All for You
1916	THE CENTURY GIRL	You Belong to Me
1917	EILEEN	Thine Alone Eileen Alanna Asthore When Shall I Again See Ireland?

Year	Production Title	Popular Songs
1917	EILEEN	The Irish Have a Great Day Tonight Free Trade and a Misty Moon
	THE ZIEGFELD FOLLIES MISS 1917 HER REGIMENT	
1919	THE VELVET LADY ANGEL FACE	Spooky Ookum I Might Be Your Once-in-awhile Someone Like You
1920	THE ZIEGFELD FOLLIES OUI, MADAME MY GOLDEN GIRL GIRL IN THE SPOTLIGHT	The Love Boat The Wooing of the Violin
1921	THE ZIEGFELD FOLLIES	
1922	ORANGE BLOSSOMS THE ZIEGFELD FOLLIES	A Kiss in the Dark
1923	THE ZIEGFELD FOLLIES	
1924	THE DREAM GIRL THE ZIEGFELD FOLLIES	My Dream Girl

Posthumous:

1925	SKY HIGH	Give Me a Heart in June Time
1939		"Indian Summer" (HP-1)
1940		"Yesterthoughts"

* * *

LOUIS A. HIRSCH

Louis Achille Hirsch taught himself to play the piano as a child, and attended high school and college in his home town of New York City. He completed his last year of musical studies at the Stern Conservatory in Berlin. Hirsch was nineteen years old when he went to work as a staff pianist for a New York music publishing firm. One year later he was engaged by the Shubert Brothers as a staff composer. His melodies were featured in half a dozen Shubert productions, one of which ("Vera Violetta") introduced Hirsch's hit song "The Gaby Glide." He left the Shubert organization in 1912 and became one of Broadway's most respected free lance composers.

Among his outstanding successes were "Hello, Frisco" (lyrics by
Gene Buck) in 1915, and "The Love Nest" (lyrics by Otto Harbach)
in 1920. "The Love Nest" eventually became the theme song of
comics George Burns and Gracie Allen. The career of Louis
Hirsch was cut short by his untimely death. He was only thirty-
seven years old when he died in 1924--just a few months before
the curtain went up on his musical comedy "Betty Lee."

Year	Production Title	Popular Songs
1907	THE GAY WHITE WAY	
		"My Twilight Queen"
1908	THE SOUL KISS THE MIMIC WORLD MISS INNOCENCE	
1909	THE GIRL AND THE WIZARD	
1910	HE CAME FROM MILWAUKEE	Love Is Like a Red, Red Rose
1911	VERA VIOLETTA	The Gaby Glide Come and Dance with Me When You Hear Love's Hello
	REVUE OF REVUES	
1912	THE WHIRL OF SOCIETY THE PASSING SHOW	My Sumurum Girl Always Together
1914		"Sweet Kentucky Lady"
1915	THE ZIEGFELD FOLLIES	Hello, Frisco Hold Me in Your Loving Arms
	AROUND THE MAP	
1916	THE ZIEGFELD FOLLIES	Beautiful Island of Girls Bachelor Days
	MY HOME TOWN GIRL	When I Found You
1917	GOING UP	Going Up If You Look in Her Eyes Everybody Ought to Know How to Do the Tickle Toe
	THE GRASS WIDOW	
1918	THE RAINBOW GIRL THE ZIEGFELD FOLLIES OH, MY DEAR!	I Am Thinking of You Garden of My Dreams
1919	SEE-SAW	

LOUIS A. HIRSCH   53

Year	Production Title	Popular Songs
1920	MARY	The Love Nest Mary Waiting
1921	THE O'BRIEN GIRL	Learn to Smile
1922	THE GREENWICH VILLAGE FOLLIES	Sixty Seconds Every Minute, I Think of You Nightingale, Bring Me a Rose
	THE ZIEGFELD FOLLIES	My Rambler Rose Some Sweet Day Throw Me a Kiss 'Neath the South Sea Moon It's Getting Dark on Old Broadway
1923	THE GREENWICH VILLAGE FOLLIES	Annabel Lee
1924	BETTY LEE	

* * *

WILLIAM JEROME

The second most successful songwriter during the heyday of Tin Pan Alley was lyricist William Jerome who was born in Cornwall-on-the-Hudson, New York, in 1865. He ran away from home when he was 18 and trod the path of many future songwriters by joining a troupe of minstrels. Almost a dozen years passed before his first hit song, "My Pearl's a Bowery Girl" (music by Andrew Mack) was published in 1894. Shortly after the turn of the century, he met composer Jean Schwartz with whom he wrote most of his popular songs including "Don't Put Me Off at Buffalo Anymore" (1901), "Bedelia" (1903), and "Chinatown, My Chinatown" (1910). The lyrics of William Jerome were heard in three dozen Broadway musicals from 1900 through 1918. In addition to his work with Schwartz, he collaborated with composer Jimmy Monaco on "Row, Row, Row" (introduced in "The Ziegfeld Follies" of 1912) and with Harry Von Tilzer on "And the Green Grass Grew All Around" that same year. Jerome's last song to become popular was the 1928 publication "Get Out and Get Under the Moon." He died four years later at the age of sixty-seven.

Year	Production Title	Popular Songs
1894		"My Pearl's a Bowery Girl"
1900	STAR AND GARTER	

Year	Production Title	Popular Songs
1900		"I Took the Heavy Part"
1901	THE STROLLERS HOITY TOITY	I'm Tired When Mr. Shakespeare Comes to Town
	THE SLEEPING BEAUTY AND THE BEAST	Rip Van Winkle Was a Lucky Man Nursery Rhymes
		"Don't Put Me Off at Buffalo Anymore" "Any Old Place I Can Hang My Hat Is Home Sweet Home to Me" "My Lady Hottentot" "It's All Right, Mayme"
1902	THE WILD ROSE A CHINESE HONEYMOON	I'm Unlucky Mr. Dooley
		"Just Kiss Yourself Goodbye" "Back to the Woods" "Since Sister Nell Heard Paderewski Play" "The Gambling Man" "I Wonder Why Bill Bailey Won't Come Home?"
1903	MR. BLUEBEARD THE JERSEY LILY MOTHER GOOSE	Hamlet Was a Melancholy Dane Bedelia
		"My Hula Lula Girl" "Why Don't You Go, Go, Go?"
1904	PIFF! PAFF!! POUF!!!	The Ghost That Never Walked Love, Love, Love Goodbye, My Own True Love
		"When You're Broke"
1905	SERGEANT BRUE LIFTING THE LID THE WHITE CAT THE HAM TREE FRITZ IN TAMMANY HALL	My Irish Molly O Oh, Marie Goodbye, Maggie Doyle
1906	THE LITTLE CHERUB THE RICH MR. HOGGENHEIMER	My Irish Rosie Any Old Time at All

Year	Production Title	Popular Songs
1907	THE ZIEGFELD FOLLIES LOLA FROM BERLIN	Handle Me with Care
		"Miss Killarney"
1908	THE ZIEGFELD FOLLIES	When the Girl You Love Is Loving
		"White Wash Man" "Over the Hills and Far Away" "Goodbye, Mr. Ragtime" "Love Days" "Kiss Your Minstrel Boy Goodbye" "Take Your Girl to the Ball Game"
1909	SILVER STAR	Franco-American Ragtime The Cooney Spooney Dance
	IN HAYTI	"Meet Me in Rose Time, Rosie" "The Hat My Father Wore on St. Patrick's Day" "Honey on Our Honeymoon" "I'm a Member of the Mid- night Crew"
1910	UP AND DOWN BROADWAY	Chinatown, My Chinatown
		"I'll Make a Ring Around Rosie" "Isn't It Exasperating, Sadie?"
1911		"Come, Love, and Play Peek-a-boo" "I'm Going Back to Reno" "Just Think of All the Money You Could Save" "Sarah's Hat"
1912	THE ZIEGFELD FOLLIES OVER THE RIVER HOKEY-POKEY A WINSOME WIDOW THE WALL STREET GIRL MY BEST GIRL	Row, Row, Row
		"And the Green Grass Grew All Around"

Year	Production Title	Popular Songs
1913	THE PLEASURE SEEKERS THE HONEYMOON EXPRESS	Sit Down, You're Rocking the Boat Goodbye Boys (I'm Going to Be Married in the Morning) "Where the Red, Red Roses Grow" "A Little Bunch of Shamrocks" "On the Old Fall River Line" "You Can't Get Away from It"
1914		"Sweet Kentucky Lady"
1915	HANDS UP	I'm Simply Crazy Over You "Just Try to Picture Me Down Home in Tennessee" "In Winky, Blinky Chinatown"
1916	BETTY	"I'm Going Back Home and Have a Wonderful Time"
1917	CHEER UP	"If I Catch the Guy Who Wrote 'Poor Butterfly'"
1918	EVERYTHING	"Every Day Will Be Sunday When the Town Goes Dry"
1920		"That Old Irish Mother of Mine" "If I Meet the Guy Who Made This Country Dry"
1923		"Ev'ry Day Is Mother's Day" "Old King Tut"
1928		"Get Out and Get Under the Moon"

* * *

ARTHUR J. LAMB

Lyricist Arthur J. Lamb emigrated to America from Somerset, England while still in his youth. He became an actor in minstrel shows and was employed on the staff of a music publishing firm. The first of his songs to achieve popularity was published in 1894 when he was twenty-four years old. His successes spanned almost two decades and included "Asleep in the Deep" (music by H. W. Petrie), "A Bird in a Gilded Cage" (music by Harry Von Tilzer), and "The Bird on Nellie's Hat" (music by Alfred Solman). Arthur J. Lamb died in 1928 at the age of fifty-eight.

Year	Production Title	Popular Songs
1894		"I'm Mamma's Little Girl"
1895		"Will You Love Me Sweetheart, When I'm Old?"
1897		"Asleep in the Deep"
1898		"Dreaming of Mother and Home"
1899		"At the Bottom of the Deep Blue Sea"
1900		"A Bird in a Gilded Cage" "The Spider and the Fly"
1902		"The Mansion of Aching Hearts" "Jennie Lee" "I Know She Waits for Me"
1903	THE FISHER MAIDEN	
		"In the Garden of Faded Flowers"
1904		"Tell Me with Your Eyes" "You Mustn't Pick Plums from My Plum Tree"
1905		"When the Bell in the Lighthouse Rings Ding Dong" "When the Mocking Birds Are Singing in the Wildwood" "Goodbye, Sweetheart, Goodbye" "A Picnic for Two"
1906		"The Bird on Nellie's Hat" "The Linger Longer Girl" "I'm in Love with a Slide Trombone"
1907		"When the Birds in Georgia Sing of Tennessee"

Year	Production Title	Popular Songs
1907		"You Splash Me and I'll Splash You"
1908		"Any Old Port in a Storm" "The Story the Picture Blocks Told"
1912		"When You've Had a Little Love, You Want a Little More"

* * *

EDWARD MADDEN

Lyricist Edward Madden was born in New York City where he attended Fordham and Columbia universities. He was twenty-five years old when two of his songs, with music by Theodore Morse, became popular in 1903. For the next five years, Madden continued turning out hits in collaboration with Morse, and created special material for comedienne Fanny Brice. In 1907, his lyrics were introduced to theatre audiences in "The Rogers Brothers in Panama." He contributed songs to seven more Broadway productions before his career went into a decline in 1915. His two most famous lyrics were written for "By the Light of the Silvery Moon" (1909) and "Moonlight Bay" (1912). Edward Madden died in 1952.

Year	Production Title	Popular Songs
1903		"A Wise Old Owl" "Up in the Cocoanut Tree"
1904		"Blue Bell" "I've Got a Feeling for You" "A Little Boy Called 'Taps'" "Nan! Nan! Nan!" "Please Come and Play in My Yard" "My Sweet Egyptian Maid" "Come Down from the Big Fig Tree" "Louisiana Anna" "Make a Fuss Over Me"
1905		"Daddy's Little Girl" "Starlight" "The Leader of the German Band" "She Waits by the Deep Blue Sea"

Year	Production Title	Popular Songs
1906		"Just for Auld Lang Syne" "Farewell Killarney" "Colleen Bawn"
1907	THE ROGERS BROTHERS IN PANAMA	
		"Two Blue Eyes, Two Little Baby Shoes" "I'd Rather Be a Lobster Than a Wise Guy" "I Want to Be a Merry, Merry Widow" "I Want a Gibson Man"
1908	LONESOME TOWN MISS INNOCENCE MR. HAMLET OF BROADWAY THE MIMIC WORLD	The Lanky Yankee Boys in Blue My Cousin Carus'
		"Consolation" "Down in Jungle Town" "I've Taken Quite a Fancy to You" "When You Wore a Pinafore" "Santiago Flynn"
1909	THE ZIEGFELD FOLLIES	By the Light of the Silvery Moon Up, Up in My Aeroplane Come on and Play Ball with Me
	THE GIRL AND THE WIZARD	
1910	HE CAME FROM MILWAUKEE	Love Is Like a Red, Red Rose
		"Silver Bell" "The Chanticleer Rag"
1911	VERA VIOLETTA LA BELLE PAREE LITTLE BOY BLUE	Rum Tum Tiddle
		"Look Out for Jimmy Valentine" "Skeleton Rag" "Red Rose Rag"
1912		"Moonlight Bay" "The Hold Up Rag"

Year	Production Title	Popular Songs
1913		"That Devil Rag" "Goodbye Summer, So Long Fall, Hello Wintertime"
1915	COUSIN LUCY	
1920	BUZZIN' AROUND	

* * *

KERRY MILLS

When Frederick Allen (Kerry) Mills was unable to realize his ambition to become a concert violinist, he turned to teaching at the University of Michigan School of Music and opened his own studio in Ann Arbor. He began writing songs when he was in his mid-twenties and published them himself. His music is credited with having popularized the dance "The Cakewalk." Mills' two best-known melodies were the 1904 hit "Meet Me in St. Louis, Louis" (lyrics by Andrew B. Sterling) and "Red Wing" (lyrics by Thurland Chattaway) which was written three years later. Kerry Mills was born in Philadelphia, Pennsylvania in 1869 and lived to be seventy-nine years old.

Year	Production Title	Popular Songs
1895		"Rastus on Parade"
1897		"Let Bygones Be Bygones"
1899		"Whistling Rufus" "At a Georgia Camp Meeting"
1902		"Fare Thee Well, Molly Darling" "In the City of Sighs and Tears" "I Know She Waits for Me"
1903	THE GIRL FROM DIXIE	
1904		"Meet Me in St. Louis, Louis" "When the Bees Are in the Hive" "Don't Cry, Katie Dear" "Just for the Sake of Society" "Let's All Go Up to Maud's"
1905		"Goodbye, Sweet Marie"
1907		"Red Wing" "Take Me Around Again"

Year	Production Title	Popular Songs
1908		"Any Old Port in a Storm" "The Longest Way 'Round Is the Sweetest Way Home"
1909		"Lonesome" "Take Me Out for a Joy Ride"
1910		"My Friend Jim-a-da-Jeff"
1911		"Love Is the Theme of My Dreams"

* * *

THEODORE F. MORSE

Theodore Morse dropped out of the Maryland Military Academy when he was fourteen years old. He went to New York City where he progressed from clerking in music stores to clerking in music publishing houses. Morse played the violin and formed a trio which entertained at private parties. He was in his early thirties when he began collaborating with lyricist Edward Madden and the team provided Tin Pan Alley with two dozen hit songs in six years. He also worked with lyricist Jack Drislane during that period. In 1915, Morse supplied the music for Howard Johnson's sentimental ballad "M-O-T-H-E-R." Two years later, he created the most famous of his songs "Hail, Hail the Gang's All Here." Morse wrote the words and adapted the music from Sir Arthur Sullivan's "The Pirates of Penzance" score. After his success as a composer, he toured the vaudeville circuit as the star of his own act. His wife, Dorothy Terris, was an accomplished lyricist but her best-known song "Three O'Clock in the Morning" was written with composer Julian Robledo. Theodore Morse was born in Washington, D.C. and died in 1924 at the age of fifty-one.

Year	Production Title	Popular Songs
1901		"Sweet Morning Glory" "When They Play 'God Save the King'"
1902	THE TOREADOR	In the Moonlight
		"Love's Own Sweet Way" "The Proper Way to Kiss"
1903	THE WIZARD OF OZ MR. BLUEBEARD	Hurray for Baffin's Bay

Year	Production Title	Popular Songs
		"Up in the Cocoanut Tree"
		"A Wise Old Owl"
		"In the Valley of Broken Hearts"
		"Dear Old Girl"
1904		"Can't You See My Heart Beats All for You?"
		"My Faithful Rose"
		"Where the Southern Roses Grow"
		"Blue Bell"
		"I've Got a Feeling for You"
		"A Little Boy Called 'Taps'"
		"Nan! Nan! Nan!"
		"Please Come and Play in My Yard"
		"What the Brass Band Played"
		"Come Down from the Big Fig Tree"
		"Make a Fuss Over Me"
		"My Sweet Egyptian Maid"
1905		"Just a Little Rocking Chair and You"
		"She Waits by the Deep Blue Sea"
		"Daddy's Little Girl"
		"Starlight"
		"The Leader of the German Band"
		"Keep a Little Cozy Corner in Your Heart"
		"One Called 'Mother' and the Other 'Home Sweet Home'"
		"Longing for You"
		"My Yankee Irish Girl"
1906		"Arrah Wanna"
		"The Good Old U.S.A."
		"Keep on the Sunny Side"
		"Crocodile Isle"
		"You Never Can Tell by the Label"
1907		"It's Great to Be a Soldier Man"
		"She's the Fairest Little Flower Dear Old Dixie Ever Grew"
		"Nobody's Little Girl"
		"Won't You Be My Honey?"
		"Two Blue Eyes, Two Little Baby Shoes"

Year	Production Title	Popular Songs
1907		"I'd Rather Be a Lobster Than a Wise Guy" "In Monkey Land" "I Want to Be a Merry, Merry Widow" "The Old Street Band" "Since Arrah Wanna Married Barney Carney"
1908	LONESOME TOWN	The Lanky Yankee Boys in Blue "The Land of the Heart's Desire" "Consolation" "Down in Jungle Town" "I've Taken Quite a Fancy to You" "When You Wore a Pinafore" "Santiago Flynn"
1909		"He's a College Boy"
1910		"Good-Bye, Betsy Brown" "To Arms! To Arms!"
1911		"Another Rag"
1912		"When Uncle Joe Plays a Rag on His Old Banjo" "Whistling Jim"
1913		"Bobbin' Up and Down" "Down in Monkeyville" "Salvation Nell"
1915		"M-O-T-H-E-R" "Auntie Skinner's Chicken Dinners"
1917		"Sing Me Love's Lullaby" "We'll Knock the Heligo-Into-Heligo Out of Heligoland" "Hail, Hail, the Gang's All Here"

* * *

MONROE ROSENFELD

Monroe Rosenfeld is another popular song writer who is sometimes overlooked by historians despite the more than 30 hits he created, and the fact that he is generally credited with having given "Tin Pan Alley" its name. He was born in Richmond, Virginia, in 1861, and migrated to New York City in the early 1880's. He worked as a newspaper reporter, press agent, and short story writer. He was twenty-three years old when four of his numbers became favorites in 1884. Although he wrote both words and music, he frequently collaborated with other lyricists and composers. His best known songs were "Johnny, Get Your Gun," "Those Wedding Bells Shall Not Ring Out" and "Take Back Your Gold." Monroe Rosenfeld was a compulsive gambler and died penniless in 1918. He was fifty-seven years old.

Year	Popular Songs
1884	"Climbing Up the Golden Stairs" "Hush, Little Baby, Don't You Cry" "Her Golden Hair Was Hanging Down Her Back" "Good-bye, My Boy, Good-bye"
1886	"Johnny, Get Your Gun"
1888	"Our Champion" "I'm Gone" "Kutchy, Kutchy, Coo!" "Good-bye, My Honey" "With All Her Faults I Love Her Still"
1890	"Finnegan, the Umpire" "Song of the Steeple" "They're After Me"
1891	"The Old Tin Dipper on the Nail" "Speak Easy"
1893	"Columbus Was an Irishman"
1894	"There's Nothing Too Good for the Irish"
1896	"Those Wedding Bells Shall Not Ring Out" "The Cross of Gold" "She Was Just as Good as You"
1897	"Take Back Your Gold" "I Don't Care If You Nebber Come Back" "Just for the Sake of Our Daughter"
1898	"Gold Will Buy 'Most Anything"
1899	"She Was Happy Till She Met You" "Her Word Is Just as Good as Yours" "The Home of the Girl I Love"

Year   Popular Songs

1902   "Hitch on de Golden Trolley"
        "The Lily or the Rose?"
        "The Lion and the Mouse"
        "Nothing Can Come Between Us Now"
        "Only to Meet Once More"

1904   "Upon a Sunday Morning When the Church Bells Chime"

1905   "Down Where the Silv'ry Mohawk Flows"

* * *

CHRIS SMITH

        Negro composer Chris Smith was just twenty-one when his
song "Never Let the Same Bee Sting You Twice" became a hit in
1900. Smith was a piano player and performed on the vaudeville
stage and in night clubs. His most famous melody, "Ballin' the
Jack" (lyrics by James Henry Burris), was written in 1913. His
success as a composer ended in 1925 although he lived for another
24 years. Chris Smith was born in Charleston, South Carolina, in
1879.

Year	Production Title	Popular Songs
1900		"Never Let the Same Bee Sting You Twice"
1901		"Good Morning Carrie"
1904		"Jasper Johnson, Shame on You"
1906	MARRYING MARY	He's a Cousin of Mine
		"All in Down and Out"
1907		"The Sounds of Chicken Frying in a Pan, Dat's Music to Me"
1908	LONESOME TOWN	There's a Big Cry-Baby in the Moon
		"Down Among the Sugar Cane"
		"You're in the Right Church but the Wrong Pew"

Year	Production Title	Popular Songs
1909		"Come After Breakfast, Bring 'Long Your Lunch and Leave 'Fore Supper Time" "Trans-mag-hi-fi-can-bam-u-al-ity"
1910		"If He Comes In, I'm Going Out" "Constantly"
1912	THE OPERA BALL	I Want a Little Lovin' Sometime "Beans! Beans! Beans!" "After All That I've Been to You" "Love, Honor and Obey"
1913		"Ballin' the Jack" "Fifteen Cents"
1916		"Down in Honky Tonky Town" "It's a Pretty Thing"
1920		"The Irish Were Egyptians Long Ago"
1921	ZIEGFELD'S MIDNIGHT FROLIC	
1923		"Cruel Daddy Blues" "Darktown Reveille"
1924		"Cake Walking Babies from Home" "Of All the Wrongs You've Done to Me, They're Bound to Come Back to You"
1925		"The Camel Walk" "Fly Roun' Young Ladies"
1927	BOTTOMLAND	

* * *

EDGAR SMITH

Edgar Smith was forty years old before he became known as a lyricist. He was born in Brooklyn, New York, in 1857, and was

educated at a military academy in Pennsylvania. Smith began his
career as an actor and playwright. In 1897, he formed a partnership with composer John Stromberg which ended prematurely with
Stromberg's suicide five years later. The team supplied the
scores for a series of musicals starring famed comedians Joe Weber and Lew Fields. The most lasting of their songs was "Ma
Blushin' Rosie" from "Fiddle-Dee-Dee" (1900). Smith's most famous lyric, the melodramatic "Heaven Will Protect the Working
Girl" (music by A. Baldwin Sloane), was introduced by Marie Dres-
sler in "Tillie's Nightmare" in 1910. He also worked with composers Sigmund Romberg, Victor Herbert, and Gus Edwards. In addition to the 23 Broadway musicals which featured his songs, Edgar Smith wrote the books for a score of others and produced several of his shows. He was eighty-one years old at the time of
his death in 1938.

Year	Production Title	Popular Songs
1897	THE GLAD HAND	How I Love My Lou
1898	HURLY BURLY	Keep Away from Emmaline Kiss Me, Honey, Do (Dinah)
1899	HELTER SKELTER IN GAY PAREE	What, Marry Dat Girl?
1900	FIDDLE-DEE-DEE	Come Back, My Honey Boy, to Me I'm a Respectable Working Girl Ma Blushin' Rosie Tell Us Pretty Ladies
	SWEET ANNE PAGE	"When in Flanders" "Nothing Doing"
1901	HOITY TOITY	De Pullman Porter's Ball When Two Hearts Are One
1902	TWIRLY-WHIRLY	
1903	WHOOP-DEE-DO	
1904	HIGGLEDY-PIGGLEDY AN ENGLISH DAISY	A Great Big Girl
1906	TWIDDLE-TWADDLE DREAM CITY and THE MAGIC KNIGHT	
1907	HIP! HIP! HOORAY!	What's the Good?
1910	TILLIE'S NIGHTMARE	Heaven Will Protect the Work- ing Girl

Year	Production Title	Popular Songs
1910	TILLIE'S NIGHTMARE	Life Is Only What You Make It, After All
1911	A CERTAIN PARTY	
1912	HOKEY-POKEY	
1913	LIEBER AUGUSTIN	
1915	HANDS UP THE BLUE PARADISE	
1916	ROBINSON CRUSOE JR. THE GIRL FROM BRAZIL	
1921	THE WHIRL OF THE WORLD	

Posthumous:

1939   "Creole Love Song"

* * *

HARRY B. SMITH

Harry Bache Smith was born in Buffalo, New York, in 1860. He was educated in Chicago and gained his experience as a professional writer while serving as the drama and music critic for Chicago newspapers. His career as a lyricist and librettist began when he was twenty-seven years old and collaborated with composer Reginald DeKoven on the score for the unsuccessful 1887 Broadway operetta "The Begum." Three years later, their operetta "Robin Hood" was one of New York's biggest attractions. Smith continued his association with DeKoven while also working with newcomer Victor Herbert. The most popular of the songs he created with Herbert was "Gypsy Love Song" from the 1898 production "The Fortune Teller." Smith was the most prolific lyricist and librettist in the history of the American theatre. He contributed songs to more than 100 musical comedies and revues and wrote the books for over 300 of them. Smith was one of Jerome Kern's first lyricists working with him as early as 1906. He was also a frequent collaborator of composer Sigmund Romberg. While most of Smith's popular songs were ballads written for operettas, one of his biggest hits was the fox trot "The Sheik of Araby" (music by Ted Snyder) which he wrote with co-lyricist Francis Wheeler in 1922. Harry B. Smith's last success was his English adaptation of Franz Lehar's Hungarian operetta "The Land of Smiles" in which the memorable "Yours Is My Heart Alone" was introduced in 1931. Smith died five years later at the age of seventy-five.

Year	Production Title	Popular Songs
1887	THE BEGUM	
1889	DON QUIXOTE	
1890	ROBIN HOOD	Brown October Ale The Armorer's Song
1892	THE KNICKERBOCKERS JUPITER	
1893	THE ALGERIAN THE FENCING MASTER	
1894	ROB ROY	
1895	THE WIZARD OF THE NILE	Star Light, Star Bright My Angeline
1896	THE MANDARIN	
1897	THE SERENADE	The Cupid and I I Love Thee, I Adore Thee
	THE HIGHWAYMAN	Do You Remember Love? Moonlight Song
	THE IDOL'S EYE	
1898	THE FORTUNE TELLER	Gypsy Love Song (Slumber on, My Little Gypsy Sweetheart) Romany Life
1899	THE SINGING GIRL	If You Were Only Mine Love Is a Tyrant
	WHIRL-I-GIG	The Queen of Bohemia Say You Love Me, Sue When Chloe Sings a Song
	LITTLE ROBINSON CRUSOE THE ROUNDERS THE THREE DRAGOONS PAPA'S WIFE CYRANO DE BERGERAC	
		"I'm Making a Bid for Popu- larity". "Only a Hundred Girls" "The Kissing Bug" "My Josephine"
1900	FOXY QUILLER THE CASINO GIRL THE CADET GIRL THE BELLE OF BOHEMIA THE VICEROY	Quiller Has the Brains

Year	Production Title	Popular Songs
1900		"De Cake Walk Queen"
1901	THE STROLLERS THE PRIMA DONNA THE ROGERS BROTHERS IN WASHINGTON THE LIBERTY BELLES LITTLE DUCHESS	Strollers We
1902	MAID MARIAN THE BILLIONAIRE	
		"The Gipsy Wedding" "The Little Gypsy Maid"
1903	BABETTE THE JEWEL OF ASIA THE BLONDE IN BLACK THE OFFICE BOY THE GIRL FROM DIXIE	There Once Was an Owl
1904	A MADCAP PRINCESS A CHINA DOLL	
1905	MISS DOLLY DOLLARS THE WHITE CAT	A Woman Is Only a Woman (But a Good Cigar Is a Smoke)
1906	THE FREE LANCE THE RICH MR. HOGGENHEIMER MAM'SELLE SALLIE THE PARISIAN MODEL	
1907	THE TATTOOED MAN	
1908	THE SOUL KISS THE ZIEGFELD FOLLIES THE GOLDEN BUTTERFLY LITTLE NEMO MISS INNOCENCE	
1909	THE ZIEGFELD FOLLIES THE SILVER STAR THE AIR KING	
1910	THE ZIEGFELD FOLLIES THE GIRL IN THE TRAIN THE BACHELOR BELLES THE SPRING MAID	

Year	Production Title	Popular Songs
1911	THE ENCHANTRESS	To the Land of My Own Romance
	THE PARADISE OF MAHOMMET	
	LITTLE MISS FIX-IT	
	THE RED ROSE	
	THE SIREN	
	THE DUCHESS	
	GYPSY LOVE	
	THE WEDDING TRIP	
1912	MODEST SUZANNE	
	THE ROSE MAID	
	THE GIRL FROM MONTMARTRE	
	THE ZIEGFELD FOLLIES	
1913	OH, I SAY!	I Can't Forget Your Eyes
	MY LITTLE FRIEND	
	THE DOLL GIRL	
1914	THE LAUGHING HUSBAND	You're Here and I'm Here
	THE GIRL FROM UTAH	The Land of Let's Pretend
		Same Sort of Girl
	PAPA'S DARLING	
1915	A MODERN EVE	
	NED WAYBURN'S TOWN TOPICS	
	ALL OVER TOWN	
1916	THE CENTURY GIRL	You Belong to Me
	MOLLY O'	
	SYBIL	
1917	LOVE O' MIKE	I Wonder Why
		Drift with Me
	RAMBLER ROSE	
1918	LADIES FIRST	
	THE CANARY	
	FOLLOW THE GIRL	
1919	THE LADY IN RED	
1920	BETTY BE GOOD	
		"Bright Eyes"
		"I Wonder If You Still Care for Me?"
1922	MAKE IT SNAPPY	The Sheik of Araby

Year	Production Title	Popular Songs
1922		"Dancing Fool"
1923	CAROLINE FASHIONS OF 1924	Argentina
1925	THE LOVE SONG NATJA PRINCESS FLAVIA	
1926	COUNTESS MARITZA NAUGHTY RIQUETTE	Play, Gypsies, Dance, Gypsies The One I'm Looking For
1927	THE CIRCUS PRINCESS CHERRY BLOSSOMS HALF A WIDOW THE LOVE CALL	You Are Mine Evermore Dear Eyes That Haunt Me We Two Shall Meet Again
1928	THE RED ROBE	
1930	THREE LITTLE GIRLS	
1931	THE LAND OF SMILES	Yours Is My Heart Alone

* * *

ROBERT B. SMITH

Chicago-born Robert B. Smith was the younger brother of Broadway's most prolific lyricist and librettist Harry B. Smith. Robert was educated in Brooklyn, New York and worked as a reporter and theatrical press agent while writing acts for vaudeville and burlesque performers. By the time he was twenty-seven, he was following in his brother's footsteps. His first hit "Come Down, My Evening Star" was the last song written by composer John Stromberg before Stromberg's death. It was introduced by Lillian Russell in the 1902 Weber and Fields' production "Twirly Whirly." More than two dozen musicals followed during Smith's 21 year Broadway career. He also wrote the librettos for many of them. The most successful of his shows was "Sweethearts" (1913) with music by Victor Herbert. Six songs from its score became national favorites. Anna Held sang two of his best lyrics in "Follow Me" (1916): "It's a Cute Little Way of My Own" (music by Harry Tierney) and "I Want to Be Good but My Eyes Won't Let Me" (music by Sigmund Romberg). When sound was added to motion pictures, he worked in Hollywood adapting stage musicals for films. Robert B. Smith was seventy-six years old when he died in 1951.

Year	Production Title	Popular Songs
1902	TWIRLY WHIRLY	Come Down, My Evening Star
1904	A CHINA DOLL	
1905	FANTANA	Just My Style The Farewell Waltz My Word
	WHEN WE WERE FORTY-ONE THE BABES AND THE BARON	Meet Me Under the Wisteria
1906	MEXICANA THE GIRL AT THE HELM	
1907	A KNIGHT FOR A DAY	The Little Girl in Blue "Does Anybody Want a Blonde?"
1909	THE GIRL AND THE WIZARD BREAKING INTO SOCIETY	
1910	THE SPRING MAID	Daydreams Fountain Fay Two Little Love Bees
1911	GYPSY LOVE THE RED ROSE THE PARADISE OF MOHAMMET	Melody of Love
1912	MODEST SUZANNE THE ROSE MAID THE GIRL FROM MONTMARTRE	All the World Loves a Lover Roses Bloom for Lovers
1913	SWEETHEARTS	Sweethearts For Every Lover Must Meet His Fate Pretty as a Picture The Cricket on the Hearth Jeanette and Her Little Wooden Shoes The Angelus
	MY LITTLE FRIEND	
1914	THE LILAC DOMINO THE DEBUTANTE	Tell Me, Lilac Domino The Springtime of Life
1915	NED WAYBURN'S TOWN TOPICS	

Year	Production Title	Popular Songs
1916	FOLLOW ME	It's a Cute Little Way of My Own I Want to Be Good but My Eyes Won't Let Me
	MOLLY O' THE AMBER EXPRESS	
1919	ANGEL FACE	I Might Be Your Once-in-Awhile Someone Like You
	A LONELY ROMEO	
1920	OUI, MADAME	Wooing of the Violin
1923	SUNBONNET SUE	

* * *

ANDREW B. STERLING

Lyricist Andrew B. Sterling was born and educated in New York City and began his career in show business writing special material for vaudeville performers. He was twenty-four years old when he wrote the lyrics for his first hit "My Old New Hampshire Home." In 1900, he collaborated with composer Charles B. Ward on "Strike Up the Band, Here Comes a Sailor." His 1904 favorite "Meet Me in St. Louis, Louis" (music by Kerry Mills) was followed by "Wait Till the Sun Shines, Nellie" (music by Harry Von Tilzer). The next decade he worked with Von Tilzer and co-lyricist Billy Munro to create "When My Baby Smiles at Me" which was introduced in the 1919 edition of "The Greenwich Village Follies." Andrew B. Sterling was eighty-one at the time of his death in 1955.

Year	Production Title	Popular Songs
1898		"My Old New Hampshire Home" "That's No Dream"
1899		"Where the Sweet Magnolias Grow" "You'll Get All That's Coming to You" "I Wonder If She's Waiting for You" "I Wouldn't Leave My Home If I Were You" "I've Lost Ma Baby" "Rosey, Rosey, Just Supposey" "The Lady with the Auburn Hair" "The Coldest Coon in Town"

Year	Production Title	Popular Songs
1899		"Don't Forget Your Mother" "The Girl I Loved in Old Virginia"
1900		"Strike Up the Band, Here Comes a Sailor" "Hey There!"
1901		"Down Where the Cotton Blossoms Grow" "When the Orange Blossoms Bloom" "Eyes of Blue, Eyes of Brown" "The Only Pair of Eyes"
1902		"On a Sunday Afternoon" "When Kate and I Were Comin' Through the Rye" "Hearts Win, You Lose" "Here's to the Old Folks at Home" "In the City of Sighs and Tears" "Louisiana Louise" "I Just Can't Help from Loving That Man" "On a Saturday Night"
1903		"Goodbye, Eliza Jane" "My Little Coney Isle" "Under the Anheuser Bush"
1904		"Meet Me in St. Louis, Louis" "All Aboard for Dreamland" "Alexander, Don't You Love Your Baby No More?" "Coax Me" "Hannah, Won't You Open That Door?"
1905		"Wait Till the Sun Shines, Nellie" "What You Goin' to Do When the Rent Comes 'Round? (Rufus Rastus Johnson Brown)" "Where the Morning Glories Twine Around the Door" "In Vacation Time" "In a Hammock Built for Two"
1906		"Ida, My Idaho"
1907		"Take Me Back to New York Town"

Year	Production Title	Popular Songs
1907		"Darling Sue" "Bye, Bye Dearie" "Mariutch"
1909		"I Wonder If She's Waiting"
1910		"Under the Yum Yum Tree" "All Aboard for Blanket Bay" "My Friend Jim-a-da-Jeff" "I Want Somebody to Flirt With" "Mr. Johnson, Good Night"
1911		"Knock Wood"
1912		"In the Evening by the Moon- light, Dear Louise" "Last Night Was the End of the World" "Just a Little Lovin'"
1913	THE HONEYMOON EXPRESS THE PASSING SHOW	Goodbye, Boys (I'm Going to Be Married in the Morning) Do You Take This Woman for Your Lawful Wife? "On the Old Fall River Line" "A Little Bunch of Shamrocks"
1915		"You'll Always Be the Same Sweet Girl" "Close to My Heart" "Under the American Flag"
1917		"We're Going Over"
1918		"Can You Tame Wild Wimmen?"
1919	THE GREENWICH VILLAGE FOLLIES ZIEGFELD'S MIDNIGHT FROLIC	When My Baby Smiles at Me All the Boys Love Mary "They're All Sweeties"
1920		"Why Did You Do It to Me, Babe?"
1922		"Mammy Lou"
1925		"Keep Your Skirts Down, Mary Ann"

Year	Production Title	Popular Songs
1929	Rainbow Man	Sleepy Valley

* * *

JOHN STROMBERG

Composer John Stromberg worked as an arranger for the Witmark Music Corporation. After his first hit song, "My Best Girl's a New Yorker," was published in 1895, he wrote almost exclusively for Broadway musicals which the comedy team of Joe Weber and Lew Fields produced and starred in. Stromberg was also the musical conductor for the shows. He invested most of the money he made from the dozen popular songs he created in a New York real estate venture which failed. He committed suicide in 1902 at the age of forty-nine. John Stromberg's best-known melody, "Come Down, My Evening Star" (lyrics by Robert B. Smith), was popularized by Lillian Russell after the composer's death.

Year	Production Title	Popular Songs
1895		"My Best Girl's a New Yorker (Corker)"
1896	ART OF MARYLAND THE GEEZER	
		"My Young Man"
1897	THE GLAD HAND POUSSE CAFE	How I Love My Lou
1898	HURLY BURLY	Keep Away from Emmaline Kiss Me, Honey, Do (Dinah)
1899	WHIRL-I-GIG	When Chloe Sings a Song Say You Love Me, Sue Queen of Bohemia
	HELTER SKELTER	What, Marry Dat Girl?
		"My Josephine" "I'm Making a Bid for Popularity" "The Kissing Bug"
1900	FIDDLE-DEE-DEE	Ma Blushin' Rosie Come Back, My Honey Boy, to Me I'm a Respectable Working Girl Tell Us Pretty Ladies

Year	Production Title	Popular Songs
1900		"Nothing Doing" "De Cake Walk Queen"
1901	HOITY TOITY	De Pullman Porter's Ball When Two Hearts Are One
1902	TWIRLY WHIRLY	Come Down, My Evening Star

* * *

JAMES THORNTON

Liverpool, England, was the birthplace of James Thornton whose parents settled in Boston, Massachusetts when he was nine years old. After working as a singing waiter, he became part of a vaudeville team in which he played the piano, sang, and exhibited considerable flair as a comedian. Thornton generally wrote both words and music and was in his late twenties when his first hit "Upper Ten, Lower Five" was published. His most outstanding song "The Benches in the Park" is better known as "Strolling Through the Park One Day." In 1903, he abandoned his songwriting career and returned to vaudeville where he was a headliner through the 1920's. James Thornton was seventy-seven when he died in 1938.

Year	Production Title	Popular Songs
1889		"Upper Ten, Lower Five"
1890	THE IRISH JUBILEE	The Irish Jubilee
1892		"My Sweetheart's the Man in the Moon" "When the Days Grow Longer" "I'm the Man Who Wrote 'Ta-Ra-Ra-Boom-De Aay'"
1894		"She May Have Seen Better Days" "Maggie Mooney"
1895		"Don't Give Up the Old Love for the New" "The Streets of Cairo"
1896		"The Benches in the Park" "It Don't Seem Like the Same Old Smile" "Going for a Pardon"

Year	Production Title	Popular Songs
1897		"There's a Little Star Shining for You" "The Concert Hall Singer"
1898		"When You Were Sweet Sixteen" (HP)
1900		"The Bridge of Sighs"

* * *

EGBERT VAN ALSTYNE

   Composer Egbert Van Alstyne learned to play the organ when he was seven years old and became so proficient that he was awarded a scholarship at the Chicago Musical College. After completing his studies, he formed an act with Harry Williams and toured the country in circuses and in vaudeville. He and Williams became song pluggers at the Remick Music Corporation, and Van Alstyne had barely come of age when the team's "Navajo" became a favorite in 1903. Their songs were featured in five Broadway musicals during the next seven years. Van Alstyne's hit melodies included "In the Shade of the Old Apple Tree," "Good Night, Ladies," and "That Old Girl of Mine." He also worked with lyricist Gus Kahn with whom he created "Memories," "Pretty Baby" and "Your Eyes Have Told Me So." Van Alstyne spent the last 20 years of his life in retirement. He was born in Illinois in 1882 and was sixty-nine years old at the time of his death in 1951.

Year	Production Title	Popular Songs
1903		"Navajo"
1904		"Seminole" "Back, Back, Back to Baltimore" "Mr. Wilson, That's All"
1905		"In the Shade of the Old Apple Tree" "In Dear Old Georgia" "Why Don't You Try?"
1906	THE RED MILL	Good-a-bye, John "Cheyenne" "Won't You Come Over to My House?" "Camp Meetin' Time" "My Dreamy China Lady"

Year	Production Title	Popular Songs
1906		"Ashy Africa" "Just Because I'm from Missouri"
1907	THE HOYDEN	"The Tale the Church Bells Tolled" "I'm Afraid to Come Home in the Dark" "San Antonio" "There Never Was a Girl Like You"
1908	NEARLY A HERO	"It Looks Like a Big Night Tonight" "Rebecca" "I Used to Be Afraid to Go Home in the Dark, Now I'm Afraid to Go Home at All"
1909	A BROKEN IDOL	"We'll All Go Home"
1910	GIRLIES	Who Are You with Tonight? "I'm Just Pinin' for You" "What's the Matter with Father?"
1911		"Good Night, Ladies" "When I Was Twenty-One and You Were Sweet Sixteen" "Naughty, Naughty, Naughty" "Down in the Old Meadow Lane" "Oh, That Navajo Rag"
1912		"That Old Girl of Mine" "The Hold Up Rag"
1913		"That Devil Rag" "Sunshine and Roses"
1914		"Way Down on Tampa Bay" "When I Was a Dreamer and You Were My Dream"
1915		"Memories" "Ypsilanti"

Year	Production Title	Popular Songs
1916	THE PASSING SHOW	Pretty Baby
		"I'm Going Right Back to Chicago"
		"Just a Word of Sympathy"
1917	GOOD NIGHT, PAUL	Sailin' Away on the Henry Clay
1918		"My Chocolate Soldier Sammy Boy"
1919	ZIEGFELD'S MIDNIGHT FROLIC	Baby
		"Your Eyes Have Told Me So"
1924		"Old Pal"
1925		"Drifting and Dreaming"
		"Kentucky's Way of Sayin' Good Mornin'"
1928		"You're in Style When You're Wearing a Smile"
1931		"Beautiful Love"
		"The Little Old Church in the Valley"

* * *

HARRY VON TILZER

Harry Von Tilzer was the most successful of all the songwriters who functioned exclusively during the period in which Tin Pan Alley controlled American popular music. From 1897 through 1925, he composed 89 hit songs! He was born in Detroit, Michigan, in 1872, and left home at the age of fourteen to join a circus. After less than a year under the Big Top, Von Tilzer graduated to burlesque and stock companies. He was twenty-five when he enjoyed his first success as a composer with his hits "De Swellest Gal in Town" and "Jack, How I Envy You." One of the top favorites of 1900 was Von Tilzer's ballad "A Bird in a Gilded Cage" (lyrics by Arthur J. Lamb). In 1902, he became his own publisher and the classics that followed included "In the Sweet Bye and Bye," "On a Sunday Afternoon," "Wait Till the Sun Shines, Nellie," "Under the Yum Yum Tree" and "I Want a Girl Just Like the Girl That Married Dear Old Dad." After achieving stature as a leading songwriter, he returned to the stage where he performed his hit songs on the vaudeville circuit.   Harry Von Tilzer's days as a songwriter ended when radio became the nation's chief purveyor of popular music.   He died in 1946 at the age of seventy-four.

Year	Production Title	Popular Songs
1897		"De Swellest Gal in Town" "Jack, How I Envy You"
1898		"My Old New Hampshire Home" "That's No Dream"
1899		"You'll Get All That's Coming to You" "Where the Sweet Magnolias Grow" "I'd Leave My Happy Home for You" "I Wonder If She's Waiting for You" "When Susan Thompson Tries to Reach High C" "I Wouldn't Leave My Home If I Were You" "I've Just Received a Telegram from Baby" "Mammy's Kinky-Headed Coon" "I've Lost Ma Baby" "The Coldest Coon in Town" "Her Name Is Rose" "I Guess That Will Be About All"
1900		"Rauss Mit Ihm" "A Bird in a Gilded Cage" "When the Harvest Days Are Over, Jessie Dear" "The Spider and the Fly" "My Jersey Lily"
1901	THE LIBERTY BELLES	"Down Where the Cotton Blossoms Grow" "My Lady Hottentot"
1902	THE WILD ROSE	"In the Sweet Bye and Bye" "On a Sunday Afternoon" "When Kate and I Were Comin' Through the Rye" "The Train Rolled On"

Year	Production Title	Popular Songs
1902		"Pardon Me, My Dear Alphonse, After You, My Dear Gaston" "Jennie Lee" "The Mansion of Aching Hearts" "Down on the Farm" "Down Where the Wurzburger Flows" "Please Go 'Way and Let Me Sleep" "I Just Can't Help from Loving That Man"
1903	THE FISHER MAIDEN	"Goodbye, Eliza Jane" "My Little Coney Isle" "Under the Anheuser Bush"
1904		"All Aboard for Dreamland" "Alexander, Don't You Love Your Baby No More?" "Coax Me" "Hannah, Won't You Open That Door?"
1905	LIFTING THE LID	Making Eyes "Wait Till the Sun Shines, Nellie" "Where the Morning Glories Twine Around the Door" "What You Goin' to Do When the Rent Comes 'Round? (Rufus Rastus Johnson Brown)" "Goodbye, Sweetheart, Goodbye" "In Vacation Time" "In a Hammock Built for Two"
1906		"Ida, My Idaho"
1907	THE DAIRYMAIDS	"Take Me Back to New York Town" "Darling Sue" "Bye, Bye Dearie" "Mariutch"
1908	NEARLY A HERO	"Don't Take Me Home"

Year	Production Title	Popular Songs
1909		"I Love, I Love, I Love My Wife, but Oh, You Kid" "The Cubanola Glide"
1910	THE KISSING GIRL	"Under the Yum Yum Tree" "All Aboard for Blanket Bay" "I Love It"
1911		"I Want a Girl Just Like the Girl That Married Dear Old Dad" "All Alone" "They Always Pick on Me" "Knock Wood"
1912		"And the Green Grass Grew All Around" "Last Night Was the End of the World" "In the Evening by the Moonlight, Dear Louise" "Just a Little Lovin'"
1913	THE HONEYMOON EXPRESS THE PASSING SHOW	Goodbye, Boys (I'm Going to Be Married in the Morning) Do You Take This Woman for Your Lawful Wife? "On the Old Fall River Line" "A Little Bunch of Shamrocks" "What's the Good of Being Good--When No One's Good to Me?"
1915		"You'll Always Be the Same Sweet Girl" "Close to My Heart" "Under the American Flag"
1916		"On the South Sea Isle" "On the Hoko Moko Isle"
1917		"Constantinople"
1918		"Can You Tame Wild Wimmen?" "I Remember You" "I Want a Doll"
1919	THE GREENWICH VILLAGE FOLLIES	When My Baby Smiles at Me

HARRY VON TILZER

Year	Production Title	Popular Songs
1919		"They're All Sweeties"
1920		"That Old Irish Mother of Mine" "Why Did You Do It to Me Babe?" "If I Meet the Guy Who Made This Country Dry"
1922		"Mammy Lou"
1923		"Old King Tut"
1925		"Just Around the Corner"

* * *

HARRY WILLIAMS

Harry Williams was born in Faribault, Minnesota, in 1879. After his primary education at both public and military schools, he joined the circus as a performer in an act with Egbert Van Alstyne. The team progressed to the vaudeville stage and finally landed in New York City where they both took jobs at the Remick music publishing house. The year 1903 saw the publication of their first hit song "Navajo." Williams was then twenty-four years old. During the next thirteen years of their partnership, their successes included "In the Shade of the Old Apple Tree" and "Good Night, Ladies." In 1914, Williams wrote the words for one of the most famous of all World War I songs "It's a Long Way to Tipperary" (music by Joe Judge). He also became a silent film director and one of his last popular songs, "Mickey" (1918), was written to promote one of Mabel Normand's starring vehicles. Harry Williams died four years later at the age of forty-three.

Year	Production Title	Popular Songs
1903		"Navajo"
1904		"Seminole" "Back, Back, Back to Baltimore" "Mr. Wilson, That's All"
1905	A YANKEE CIRCUS ON MARS	"In the Shade of the Old Apple Tree" "In Dear Old Georgia" "Why Don't You Try?"

Year	Production Title	Popular Songs
1906	THE RED MILL	Good-a-bye, John
		"Cheyenne"
		"Won't You Come Over to My House?"
		"Camp Meetin' Time"
1907	THE HOYDEN	"The Tale the Church Bells Tolled"
		"I'm Afraid to Come Home in the Dark"
		"There Never Was a Girl Like You"
		"San Antonio"
1908	NEARLY A HERO	"It Looks Like a Big Night Tonight"
		"Rebecca"
		"I Used to Be Afraid to Go Home in the Dark, Now I'm Afraid to Go Home at All"
1909	A BROKEN IDOL	"We'll All Go Home"
1910	THE YOUNG TURK GIRLIES	Who Are You with Tonight?
		"What's the Matter with Father?"
		"I'm Just Pinin' for You"
		"That Ragtime Suffragette"
1911		"Good Night, Ladies"
		"When I Was Twenty-One and You Were Sweet Sixteen"
		"Naughty, Naughty, Naughty"
		"Down in the Old Meadow Lane"
		"Oh, That Navajo Rag"
1912		"Oh, You Cutie--You Ever, Ever Loving Child"
1913	THE PLEASURE SEEKERS	Don't Blame It All on Broadway
1914	DANCING AROUND	It's a Long Way to Tipperary
1916		"I'm Going Right Back to Chicago"

Year	Production Title	Popular Songs
1918		"Mickey"
1919		"Rose Room" "Peggy"
1921		"Mello Cello"

* * *

P. G. WODEHOUSE

Pelham Grenville Wodehouse is better known as a novelist than as a songwriter. He was born in Guildford Surrey, England, in 1881, and wrote his first story at the age of seven. He studied finance at Dulwich College and began his career as a banker. After two years, during which he began writing about sports and had his first book (The Pothunters) published, he left the banking world to become a columnist for the London Globe. The success of his novel Psmith in the City in 1910 enabled him to become a full-time novelist, and he perpetuated his characters "Psmith" and a comical butler named "Jeeves" in a series of best-sellers.

Wodehouse made his third trip to the United States in 1915. He renewed his acquaintance with composer Jerome Kern whom he had met in London in 1902. Kern's work with lyricist-librettist Guy Bolton on musicals staged at the Princess Theatre had received widespread praise and Wodehouse agreed to supply lyrics for the third and fourth productions ("Oh, Boy!" and "Oh, Lady! Lady!") in the successful series. He was also Kern's lyricist on the 1917 Broadway hit "Leave It to Jane." In addition to Kern, Wodehouse collaborated with composers Ivan Caryll and Rudolf Friml. During his career as a lyricist, he was the drama critic for Frank Crowninshield's chic periodical Vanity Fair, and wrote humorous pieces for the Saturday Evening Post. Among the popular songs for which Wodehouse provided the words were "Till the Clouds Roll By," "The Siren's Song," "Bill," and "March of the Musketeers." "Bill" was written for "Oh, Lady! Lady!" (1918) and became a hit when it was added to the score of "Show Boat" nine years later.

P. G. Wodehouse wrote popular songs for only twelve years after which he concentrated on novels and musical comedy librettos. During World War II, he and his wife were captured by the Nazis in France. He was accused of collaborating with the Germans but was cleared of the charge after the armistice. In 1955, he became a United States citizen. Wodehouse was ninety-two years old when his last novel was published in 1973. He was knighted by Queen Elizabeth II in 1975 and died that same year at the age of ninety-four.

Year	Production Title	Popular Songs
1903	THE BEAUTY AND THE BATH (London)	Mr. Chamberlain
1916	MISS SPRINGTIME	Throw Me a Rose
1917	HAVE A HEART	You Said Something
		Honeymoon Inn
		And I'm All Alone
	OH, BOY!	Till the Clouds Roll By
		An Old-Fashioned Wife
		Rolled into One
		You Never Knew About Me
		Nesting Time in Flatbush
		Ain't It a Grand and Glorious Feeling?
	LEAVE IT TO JANE	The Siren's Song
		The Crickets Are Calling
		Leave It to Jane
		Just You Watch My Step
		Cleopatterer
		The Sun Shines Brighter
	RIVIERA GIRL	A Bungalow in Quogue
	MISS 1917	The Land Where Good Songs Go
		Go, Little Boat
	KITTY DARLIN'	
1918	OH, LADY! LADY!	Moon Song
		Before I Met You
		Our Little Love Nest
		Oh, Lady! Lady!
	THE GIRL BEHIND THE GUN	There's a Light in Your Eyes
		There's Life in the Old Dog Yet
	THE CANARY	
	OH, MY DEAR!	
1919	THE ROSE OF CHINA	
1920	SALLY	The Church 'Round the Corner
1924	SITTING PRETTY	
1927	SHOW BOAT	Bill
	THE NIGHTENGALE	
1928	ROSALIE	Oh Gee! Oh Joy!
		Say So
	THE THREE MUSKETEERS	Ma Belle
		March of the Musketeers

Year	Production Title	Popular Songs
1928	THE THREE MUSKETEERS	Your Eyes With Red Wine

* * *

RIDA JOHNSON YOUNG

Lyricist-librettist Rida Johnson Young began her professional career as an actress in a stock company and appeared opposite
famed actor E. H. Sothern. She worked with three of Broadway's
top composers during her fourteen years in the musical theatre.
She was forty-one years old when she collaborated with the then
Dean of Popular Music Victor Herbert on the score for the 1910
operetta "Naughty Marietta." Five of the songs it introduced became standards. In 1917, the highlight of the production "Maytime"
was "Will You Remember? (Sweetheart, Sweetheart, Sweetheart)"
with words by Miss Young and music by Sigmund Romberg. The
following year, her partner on "Sometime" was composer Rudolf
Friml. She was reunited with Victor Herbert on his last score for
"The Dream Girl" in 1924. It also proved to be her farewell to
Broadway. Rida Johnson Young died two years later at the age of
fifty-seven. She was a native of Baltimore, Maryland.

Year	Production Title	Popular Songs
1904		"I Can't Take My Eyes Off You"
1906		"When Love Is Young in the Springtime"
1910	BARRY OF BALLYMORE NAUGHTY MARIETTA	Mother Machree Ah, Sweet Mystery of Life I'm Falling in Love with Some- one Tramp, Tramp, Tramp Italian Street Song 'Neath the Southern Moon Live for Today
1912	ISLE OF DREAMS	
1914	LADY LUXURY	
1915	MACHUSHLA	
1916	HER SOLDIER BOY	Mother
1917	MAYTIME	Will You Remember?

Year	Production Title	Popular Songs
1917	MAYTIME	The Road to Paradise
		Jump Jim Crow
1918	SOMETIME	Sometime
		Any Kind of Man
	LITTLE SIMPLICITY	
1924	THE DREAM GIRL	My Dream Girl

AFTER TIN PAN ALLEY

While the first commercial broadcasts emanated from Pittsburgh, Pennsylvania (KDKA) and Detroit, Michigan (WWJ) in 1920, several years passed before the nation could count any appreciable number of transmitters and receivers. The first network broadcast in 1926 reached only from New York (WEAF) to Kansas City, but it was the turning point for radio. The small electrical boxes soon outnumbered pianos in parlors, and the music of the Vincent Lopez and Ben Bernie orchestras reached hundreds of millions.

The concern of the publishers who ruled Tin Pan Alley--that free music would mean their ruin--proved false. The slogan "The Music You Want When You Want It" reflected the public's attitude and it continued to buy sheet music. The slogan backfired when the quality of phonograph records improved and the money previously passed across the sheet music counters began moving across the record counters instead.

The final blow to Tin Pan Alley came when sound in motion pictures became practical. Realizing that music would be a staple of the film industry, and not wishing to be at the mercy of music publishers, the major studios began acquiring publishing houses. Within a short time, Metro-Goldwyn-Mayer, Paramount, Warner Bros., etc., were in the music business--and the Tin Pan Alley moguls were reduced to taking orders from the West Coast.

Popular music was now available to the masses through radio and motion pictures. The advantage to songwriters was that songs became favorites in days instead of months, and the span of their popularity was sharply reduced by incessant repetition. The new media consumed material at such a rapid rate that more and more songwriters were required to meet the public demand for new numbers. The following songwriters are included in this section:

Harold Adamson
Milton Ager
Fred Ahlert
Harry Akst
Louis Alter
Harold Arlen
Burt Bacharach
Irving Berlin
Lew Brown
Nacio Herb Brown
Alfred Bryan

Johnny Burke
Joseph A. Burke
Irving Caesar
Sammy Cahn
Hoagy Carmichael
Grant Clarke
Con Conrad
J. Fred Coots
Sam Coslow
Hal David
Mack David

Benny Davis
Peter DeRose
B. G. DeSylva
Howard Dietz
Mort Dixon
Walter Donaldson
Al Dubin
Gus Edwards
Duke Ellington
Ray Evans & Jay Livingston
Sammy Fain
Dorothy Fields
Ted Fiorito
Fred Fisher
Arthur Freed
Cliff Friend
Rudolf Friml
George Gershwin
Ira Gershwin
L. Wolfe Gilbert
Mack Gordon
Oscar Hammerstein
Otto Harbach
E. Y. Harburg
Lorenz Hart
Ray Henderson
Edward Heyman
Bob Hilliard
Al Hoffman
Gus Kahn
Bert Kalmar
Jerome Kern
Ted Koehler
Burton Lane
Edgar Leslie
Samuel M. Lewis
Jerry Livingston
Frank Loesser
Herbert Magidson
Joseph McCarthy
Jimmy McHugh
Johnny Mercer

Bob Merrill
George W. Meyer
Joseph Meyer
Irving Mills
Sidney D. Mitchell
James V. Monaco
Mitchell Parish
Cole Porter
Ralph Rainger
Don Raye
Andy Razaf
Harry Revel
Leo Robin
Richard Rodgers
Sigmund Romberg
Billy Rose
Harry Ruby
Bob Russell
Arthur Schwartz
Jean Schwartz
Carl Sigman
Abner Silver
Sam H. Stept
Al Stillman
Jule Styne
Charles Tobias
Harry Tobias
Roy Turk
James Van Heusen
Albert Von Tilzer
Thomas (Fats) Waller
Harry Warren
Ned Washington
Paul Francis Webster
Richard A. Whiting
Harry M. Woods
Allie Wrubel
Jack Yellen
Vincent Youmans
Joseph Young
Victor Young

* * *

HAROLD ADAMSON

Although Harold Adamson began writing verse while still in prep school, he planned to become an actor. While attending the University of Kansas, he performed in summer stock. He later appeared in the Hasty Pudding Club shows when he was a student at

Harvard. Adamson was barely out of college when he collaborated
with lyricist Mack Gordon in 1930 on the song "Time on My Hands"
(music by Vincent Youmans). Its success convinced him that his
future was in popular music. The year after his first hit, Adamson teamed with composer Burton Lane with whom he wrote songs
for Broadway revues before they left for Hollywood. Their initial
film assignment produced the classic "Everything I Have Is Yours."
In 1936, Adamson worked with composer Walter Donaldson to create "Did I Remember?" and "You," and formed his long-lasting
partnership with composer Jimmy McHugh. During the next decade,
Adamson and McHugh wrote such popular motion picture songs as
"You're a Sweetheart," "Where Are You?," "I Couldn't Sleep a
Wink Last Night" and "Here Comes Heaven Again."

Louis Alter's instrumental composition "Manhattan Serenade"
became a 1942 favorite with words added by Adamson, and his lyric
for "Comin' in on a Wing and a Prayer" made it one of the biggest
successes of World War II. Adamson's work was also heard on
Broadway in the productions "Banjo Eyes" (1941) and "As the Girls
Go" (1948). After his partnership with McHugh ended, he worked
with composers Victor Young and Harry Warren on songs for the
films "Around the World in 80 Days," "An Affair to Remember"
and "Separate Tables." He also collaborated with composer Sammy
Fain on the score for a stage adaptation of "Around the World in
80 Days" which became a popular attraction at New York's Jones
Beach Amphitheatre. Harold Adamson has received five Academy
Award nominations. He was born in Greenville, New Jersey in
1906.

Year	Production Title	Popular Songs
1930	SMILES	Time on My Hands
		I'm Glad I Waited
	EARL CARROLL'S VANITIES	
1931	EARL CARROLL'S VANITIES	Heigh Ho, the Gang's All Here
		Have a Heart
		Love Came into My Heart
	THE THIRD LITTLE SHOW	
1932		"Here's Hoping"
1933	Dancing Lady	Everything I Have Is Yours
	Turn Back the Clock	Tony's Wife
		"Look Who's Here"
		"Sittin' in the Dark"
1934	Bottoms Up	Little Did I Dream
	Palooka	Like Me a Little Bit Less
		(Love Me a Little Bit More)

94

AFTER TIN PAN ALLEY

Year	Production Title	Popular Songs
1934	Kid Millions	Your Head on My Shoulder
	Coming Out Party	
	Strictly Dynamite	
	Long Lost Father	
	The Band Plays On	
1935	Shadow of Doubt	Beyond the Shadow of a Doubt
	Folies Bergere	You Took the Words Right Out of My Mouth
	Reckless	Ev'rything's Been Done Before (HP)
	Here Comes the Band	Tender Is the Night
	The Perfect Gentleman	
1936	Suzy	Did I Remember? (AN) (HP-1)
	The Great Ziegfeld	You (HP-1)
		You Never Looked So Beautiful
	Banjo on My Knee	There's Something in the Air (HP)
		Where the Lazy River Goes By
	The Voice of Bugle Ann	
	Piccadilly Jim	
	His Brother's Wife	"It's Been So Long" (HP)
1937	Hitting a New High	I Hit a New High
		Let's Give Love Another Chance
		This Never Happened Before
	You're a Sweetheart	You're a Sweetheart (HP-1)
		My Fine Feathered Friend
		Broadway Jamboree
	Top of the Town	Where Are You? (HP)
		That Foolish Feeling
		Top of the Town
		Blame It on the Rhumba
		Jamboree
	Merry-Go-Round	You're My Dish
	of 1938	More Power to You
	When Love Is Young	When Love Is Young
	Breezing Home	
1938	Mad About Music	I Love to Whistle (HP)
		Chapel Bells
		A Serenade to the Stars
	That Certain Age	My Own (AN) (HP)
		You're as Pretty as a Picture
	Youth Takes a Fling	For the First Time
	Road to Reno	
	Devil's Party	
	Reckless Living	

HAROLD ADAMSON

Year	Production Title	Popular Songs
1939	The Family Next Door	"The Little Man Who Wasn't There"
1940	Ride, Tenderfoot, Ride	The Woodpecker Song (HP-1)
		"Ferry Boat Serenade" (HP-1)
		"It's a Wonderful World" (HP)
		"This Changing World" (HP)
		"720 in the Books"
1941	BANJO EYES	We're Having a Baby (My Baby and Me)
	Hold That Ghost	Aurora
1942		"Manhattan Serenade" (HP)
		"Moonlight Mood" (HP)
		"Sentimental Rhapsody"
		"Five O'Clock Drag"
1943	Higher and Higher	I Couldn't Sleep a Wink Last Night (AN) (HP-1)
		A Lovely Way to Spend an Evening (HP)
		The Music Stopped
	Hit Parade of 1943	Change of Heart (AN)
	Thousands Cheer	Daybreak (HP)
	Around the World	Don't Believe Everything You Dream
		Candlelight and Wine
	Follow the Band	
1944	Something for the Boys	Wouldn't It Be Nice?
		I Wish We Didn't Have to Say Goodbye
		In the Middle of Nowhere
	Four Jills in a Jeep	How Blue the Night (HP)
		You Send Me
		How Many Times Do I Have to Tell You?
	Two Girls and a Sailor	Thrill of a New Romance
	The Princess and the Pirate	
	Bathing Beauty	"Comin' in on a Wing and a Prayer" (HP-1)
1945	Doll Face	Here Comes Heaven Again
		Dig You Later--a Hubba, Hubba, Hubba
		Somebody's Walkin' in My Dreams

Year	Production Title	Popular Songs
1945	Nob Hill	I Don't Care Who Knows It (HP)
		I Walked in with My Eyes Wide Open
	Bring on the Girls	
1946	Do You Love Me?	
1947	Smash-Up	Life Can Be Beautiful (HP)
		I Miss That Feeling
	Calendar Girl	
	Big Town	
	Hit Parade of 1947	
1948	AS THE GIRLS GO	You Say the Nicest Things, Baby
		I Got Lucky in the Rain
		There's No Getting Away from You
	A Date with Judy	It's a Most Unusual Day
	If You Knew Susie	
		"Just a Shade on the Blue Side"
1950		"A Woman Likes to Be Told"
1951	His Kind of Woman	
1952	The Las Vegas Story	My Resistance Is Low
1953	Gentlemen Prefer Blondes	When Love Goes Wrong
		"Gigi"
1955	The Legend of Wyatt Earp (TV)	
1956	STRIP FOR ACTION (closed in tryout)	Too Young to Go Steady
		Love Me as Though There Were No Tomorrow
		I Just Found Out About Love
	Around the World in 80 Days	Around the World (HP-1)
1957	An Affair to Remember	An Affair to Remember (AN)
	China Gate	
1958	Separate Tables	Separate Tables

HAROLD ADAMSON

Year	Production Title	Popular Songs
1958	The Seven Hills of Rome	
1962	AROUND THE WORLD IN 80 DAYS (St. Louis) Satan Never Sleeps	Satan Never Sleeps
1963	A Ticklish Affair	
1964	The Incredible Mr. Limpet	I Wish I Were a Fish

* * *

MILTON AGER

Composer Milton Ager was born in Chicago in 1893. After graduating from McKinley High School, he was employed as a song plugger in the Chicago branch of a New York music publishing firm. He also worked as a pianist in motion picture and vaudeville theatres, and accompanied vaudeville performers. After serving in an Army morale corps in Georgia during World War I, he wrote his first success "Everything Is Peaches Down in Georgia." He was then twenty-five years old. His biggest hits during the first decade of his career were those with words by Jack Yellen and included "A Young Man's Fancy," "I Wonder What's Become of Sally" and "Ain't She Sweet?" The team's "I'm the Last of the Red Hot Mamas" was one of Sophie Tucker's standards, and their "Happy Days Are Here Again" has been played at every Democratic political convention held since it was written in 1930. Ager frequently shared his credits with other composers such as George Meyer, Cliff Hess, Jean Schwartz and Jimmie Grier.

Year	Production Title	Popular Songs
1918		"Everything Is Peaches Down in Georgia"
1919		"Freckles" "Anything Is Nice If It Comes from Dixie Land"
1920	WHAT'S IN A NAME THE ZIEGFELD FOLLIES	A Young Man's Fancy Smart Little Feller, Stock Up Your Cellar "I'm in Heaven When I'm in My Mother's Arms"

Year	Production Title	Popular Songs
1921		"I'm Nobody's Baby" (HP)
		"East Is East, West Is West"
		"High Brown Blues"
		"Tom Boy Girl"
		"Two Sweet Lips"
1922	BOMBO	Who Cares?
	THE BUNCH AND JUDY	Lovin' Sam, the Sheik of Alabam'
	ZIG ZAG	
1923	TED LEWIS FROLIC	
		"Mamma Goes Where Papa Goes"
		"Louisville Lou, the Vampin' Lady"
1924		"I Wonder What's Become of Sally?"
		"Big Boy"
		"Big Bad Bill Is Sweet William Now"
		"Bagdad"
		"Hardhearted Hannah"
1925		"Are You Sorry?"
		"Away from You"
		"No One"
1926		"I Wish I Had My Old Gal Back Again"
		"Lay Me Down to Sleep in Carolina"
		"In Your Green Hat"
1927		"Forgive Me" (HP)
		"Ain't She Sweet?"
		"Crazy Words, Crazy Tune"
		"Ain't That a Grand and Glorious Feeling?"
		"Is She My Girl Friend?"
		"Vo-Do-Do-De-O Blues"
		"Could I? I Certainly Could"
1928	RAIN OR SHINE	Falling Star
		Forever and Ever
		Rain or Shine
	WHOOPEE	Hungry Women
		"I Still Love You"
		"My Pet"
		"If You Don't Love Me"

Year	Production Title	Popular Songs
1929	MURRAY ANDERSON'S ALMANAC	Wait for the Happy Ending
	Honky Tonk	I'm the Last of the Red Hot Mamas
		He's a Good Man to Have Around
	Glad Rag Doll	Glad Rag Doll
1930	Chasing Rainbows	Happy Days Are Here Again
		Lucky Me, Lovable You
	King of Jazz	I Like to Do Things for You
		Song of the Dawn
		A Bench in the Park
		Happy Feet
	They Learned About Women	
		"Blame It on the Moonlight"
1931		"If I Didn't Have You"
		"What Good Am I Without You?"
1932		"Sweet Muchacha"
		"Auf Wiedersehn, My Dear"
		"Sing a New Song"
1933		"Trouble in Paradise"
		"Little You Know"
		"Roll Out of Bed with a Smile"
1934		"If I Didn't Care"
		"In a Little Red Barn (on a Farm Down in Indiana"
		"I Hate Myself (for Being So Mean to You)"
		"Dream Man, Make Me Dream Some More"
1935		"Seein' Is Believin'" (HP)
		"I Threw a Bean Bag at the Moon"
		"Loafin' Time"
1936		"You Can't Pull the Wool Over My Eyes" (HP)
		"West Wind" (HP)
		"It's No Fun"
		"You're Giving Me a Song and a Dance"
1937		"Trust in Me" (HP)
		"The Shag"
		"You Can Tell She Comes from Dixie"

Year	Production Title	Popular Songs
1938	Listen, Darling	Ten Pins in the Sky
		"There's Rain in My Eyes"
		"Sweet Stranger"
1939		"Sweet Dreams, Sweetheart"
		"Old Mill Wheel"
		"You're Letting the Grass Grow Under Your Feet"
		"There's a New Day Coming"
1942		"Only a Moment Ago"

* * *

FRED AHLERT

Fred Ahlert was among several successful songwriters who started out to become attorneys. A native of New York City, Ahlert was educated at Townsend Harris High School and New York City College. He studied law at Fordham University but dropped the profession to become an arranger for a music publishing company. Among his clients was glee club director Fred Waring. Ahlert's first hit, the novelty song "Who Played Poker with Pocahontas When John Smith Went Away?" (lyrics by Sam Lewis and Joe Young), was published in 1919 when Ahlert was twenty-seven years old. Before the Twenties ended, he had collaborated with lyricist Roy Turk to create his two most famous songs: "I'll Get By" and "Mean to Me." His 1931 melody "Where the Blue of the Night Meets the Gold of the Day" was Bing Crosby's theme on his weekly broadcasts. Ahlert's success continued throughout the Depression with the favorites "I Don't Know Why (I Just Do)" and "I'm Gonna Sit Right Down and Write Myself a Letter." He was an infrequent contributor to films and his only Broadway offering was "It Happens on Ice" in 1940. Composer Fred Ahlert died at sixty-one in 1953.

Year	Production Title	Popular Songs
1919		"Who Played Poker with Pocahontas When John Smith Went Away?"
1920		"I'd Love to Fall Asleep and Wake Up in My Mammy's Arms"
		"You Oughta See My Baby"
1922		"I Gave You Up Just Before You Threw Me Down"

Year	Production Title	Popular Songs
1924		"Put Away a Little Ray of Golden Sunshine for a Rainy Day" "In Shadowland" "Maybe She'll Write Me"
1927		"There's a Cradle in Caroline"
1928	Stepping High	"I'll Get By" (HP) "Evening Star"
1929	Port of Dreams Marianne Girl on the Barge	"Mean to Me" "I'll Never Ask for More" "The One That I Love Loves Me" "To Be in Love"
1930	Free and Easy In Gay Madrid Children of Pleasure Navy Blues	It Must Be You The "Free and Easy" Into My Heart The Whole Darned Thing's for You "Walkin' My Baby Back Home" (HP-1) "We're Friends Again"
1931	Blonde Crazy	"I Don't Know Why (I Just Do)" (HP) "Why Dance?" "Can't You See?"
1932	The Big Broadcast	Where the Blue of the Night Meets the Gold of the Day "How Can You Say You Love Me?" "I'll Follow You" "Love, You Funny Thing" "Just a Little Home for the Old Folks" "I'm Still Without a Sweetheart with Summer Coming On"
1933		"The Moon Was Yellow" "I Wake Up Smiling"
1934		"Lovely"

Year	Production Title	Popular Songs
1934		"Were You Foolin'?" "And I Still Do"
1935		"I'm Gonna Sit Right Down and Write Myself a Letter" (HP) "Sing an Old-Fashioned Song" "Life Is a Song (Let's Sing It Together)" (HP-1) "I'm Keeping Those Keepsakes You Gave Me"
1936		"Take My Heart" (HP-1) "You Dropped Me Like a Red Hot Penny" "There's Two Sides to Ev'ry Story"
1937		"Sweet Thing" "The Goona Goo" "I'm Happy, Darling, Dancing with You" "The Image of You" "I've Got a New Lease on Love" "There's Frost on the Moon"
1939		"Many Dreams Ago"
1940	IT HAPPENS ON ICE	"Where Do You Keep Your Heart?"
1945		"In the Middle of May"

* * *

HARRY AKST

Composer Harry Akst's father played the violin in symphony orchestras and with the Metropolitan Opera. His son made his debut as a concert pianist when he was ten years old. After high school, the young man entered the popular music business as a song plugger in a music store and later became the accompanist of fabled Broadway star Nora Bayes. While serving in the medical corps at Camp Upton during World War I, Akst met Irving Berlin. Berlin had become a music publisher and hired Akst as a staff pianist. Akst had just turned thirty when he wrote the music for what became his best-known song "Dinah." He proved to be one of the most prolific of all film composers contributing music to almost 60 motion pictures including "On with the Show" in which Ethel Wa-

ters introduced the classic "Am I Blue?" During World War II,
Akst toured overseas bases as Al Jolson's accompanist. Towards
the end of his career, he composed "May I Sing to You?" which
Eddie Fisher used as his theme. The New York-born composer
was sixty-nine when he died in 1963.

Year	Production Title	Popular Songs
1918		"Laddie Boy"
1919		"You Don't Need the Wine to Have a Wonderful Time"
1920		"Home Again Blues"
1921	ZIEGFELD 9 O'CLOCK FROLIC	
1922		"Dearest, You're the Nearest to My Heart" "Hello, Hello, Hello"
1923	NIFTIES OF 1923	"A Smile Will Go a Long, Long Way" "First, Last and Always" "Stella" "South Sea Eyes"
1924		"Dinah"
1926		"Baby Face" (HP) "Everything's Gonna Be All Right" "There's a Little White House"
1927	ARTISTS AND MODELS	"It's a Million to One You're in Love" "Gorgeous" "No Wonder I'm Happy"
1928		"Revenge" "In My Bouquet of Memories" "Right or Wrong, I Love You"
1929	On with the Show Is Everybody Happy? This Is Heaven Broadway Babies	Am I Blue? Birmingham Bertha I'm the Medicine Man for the Blues Wouldn't It Be Wonderful? This Is Heaven Wishing and Waiting for Love

Year	Production Title	Popular Songs
1929	Bulldog Drummond The Squall Saturday's Children Mississippi Gambler Sacred Flame	
1930	So Long Letty Dancing Sweeties Golden Dawn No, No Nanette Song of the Flame Song of the West Leathernecking	My Strongest Weakness Is You
1931	Palmy Days Bright Lights	There's Nothing Too Good for My Baby Nobody Cares If I'm Blue "Guilty" (HP)
1932	The Kid from Spain High Pressure Husband's Holiday	What a Perfect Combination I Can't Get Mississippi Off My Mind "If Love Were All"
1933	Broadway Bad Professional Sweetheart Diplomaniacs	 "Was My Face Red?"
1934	CALLING ALL STARS Stand Up and Cheer Loud Speaker Change of Heart Let's Talk It Over Marie Galante Pursued Now I'll Tell Cat's Paw	Stand Up and Cheer
1935	Coronado After the Dance Paddy O'Day	
1936	The Music Goes 'Round Star for a Night Crack-Up Can This Be Dixie? Big Town Girl	Taking Care of You

Year	Production Title	Popular Songs
1937	Sing and Be Happy Holy Terror Wild and Woolly Fight for Your Lady Think Fast, Mr. Moto	What a Beautiful Beginning
1938	Rascals Battle of Broadway International Settlement Up the River Walking Down Broadway	
1939	Boy Friend	
1940	Shooting High	
1943	Is Everybody Happy? Harvest Melody Lady of Burlesque	
1944	The Impatient Years She's a Sweetheart	
1947	This Time for Keeps	"The Egg and I" "All My Love"
1953	JOHN MURRAY ANDER- SON'S ALMANAC	Anema e Core (With All My Heart and Soul)
1954		"May I Sing to You?"

* * *

LOUIS ALTER

Composer Louis Alter is a concert pianist who has appeared as guest soloist at the Hollywood Bowl. At the age of thirteen,
the accompaniment he played for silent films was frequently of his
own invention instead of that provided with the picture. A native
of Haverhill, Massachusetts, he received his formal training at the
New England Conservatory of Music. Alter toured America and
Europe with singer Nora Bayes, and also accompanied such celebrated performers as Helen Morgan and Irene Bordoni. Broadway
first heard his melodies in the 1925 edition of "Earl Carroll's
Vanities" when he was twenty-three years old. Paul Whiteman's
instrumental recording of Alter's "Manhattan Serenade" was pressed
five years later. The composer began writing for motion pictures

in 1929 and his outstanding film songs include "A Melody from the
Sky" and "Dolores" which won "Oscar" nominations in 1936 and
1941.   During World War II, Alter worked for the Armed Services
organizing entertainments in which he appeared at Air Force bases
on the West Coast.   Among the successful lyricists with whom
Louis Alter has collaborated have been Oscar Hammerstein, Ira
Gershwin, Lew Brown, Paul Francis Webster, Frank Loesser and
Harold Adamson who added words to "Manhattan Serenade" in 1942.

Year	Production Title	Popular Songs
1925	EARL CARROLL'S VANITIES	Hugs and Kisses
		"To Be Loved"
1926		"I'm in Love with You"
1927	A LA CARTE	"Au Revoir but Not Goodbye"
1928	EARL CARROLL'S VANITIES	Blue Shadows
	PARIS	Paris
	AMERICANA	My Kinda Love
1929	Hollywood Revue of 1929	Gotta Feelin' for You
	Untamed	That Wonderful Something Is Love
	Iron Mask	
1930	SWEET AND LOW	Overnight
	BALLYHOO	I'm One of God's Children Who Hasn't Got Wings
		No Wonder I'm Blue
	Lord Byron of Broadway	Love Ain't Nothin' but the Blues
1931	THE SOCIAL REGISTER (play)	The Key to My Heart
	BILLY ROSE'S CRAZY QUILT	
1932		"What a Life"
1933	TATTLE TALES	
	HOLD YOUR HORSES	
	Take a Chance	Come Up and See Me Sometime
		"Morning, Noon and Night"
		"What Have We Got to Lose?"
		"Hi Ho Lack a Day"

Year	Production Title	Popular Songs
1934	CASINO VARIETIES	"(If Love Makes You Give Up) Steak and Potatoes" "Last Year's Girl"
1935	The Rain Makers Convention Girl Going Highbrow The Old Homestead	Isn't Love the Grandest Thing? I've Got Sand in My Shoes
1936	Trail of the Lonesome Pine Sing, Baby, Sing Rainbow on the River Dizzy Dames	A Melody from the Sky (AN) (HP-1) Twilight on the Trail You Turned the Tables on Me (HP) A Thousand Dreams of You Rainbow on the River I Was Taken by Storm "I Had a Dream Last Night"
1937	Make a Wish Vogues of 1938	
1940	Youth Will Be Served	
1941	Las Vegas Nights Caught in the Draft	Dolores (AN) "The Sky Fell Down"
1942		"Manhattan Serenade" (HP) "Fun to Be Free" "The Things I Should Have Said" "We All Together"
1944		"A Yankee Christmas"
1946	Breakfast in Hollywood	If I Had a Wishing Ring
1947	New Orleans Living in a Big Way	Do You Know What It Means to Miss New Orleans? Endie "Without Music"
1948	Moonrise	"Strange What a Song Can Do"
1949		"Circus" "Arizona Sundown"

Year	Production Title	Popular Songs
1952		"Nina Never Knew"
1961		"My Ecstasy"

* * *

HAROLD ARLEN

Harold Arlen, nee Hyman Arluck, was born in Buffalo, New York, in 1905. He dropped out of high school to work as a pianist in silent movie houses. He then formed a jazz group for which he did the arranging, piano playing, and singing. His first composition was published in 1926. Arlen's vocal efforts landed him in vaudeville engagements and he was hired to appear in the Broadway musical "Great Day" (1929). The twenty-four year old performer's part was cut from the show before it opened. The following year, he hit his stride as a songwriter and his early hits included "Get Happy," "I Gotta Right to Sing the Blues," and "It's Only a Paper Moon." He also became a successful recording artist.

One of New York City's most popular cabarets during the Thirties was The Cotton Club located at 142nd St. and Lennox Avenue in Harlem. The extravagant productions staged there featured Cab Calloway, Ethel Waters, Adelaide Hall, and sixteen year old Lena Horne. Arlen and his chief lyricist Ted Koehler supplied most of the numbers for the club's revues. Among them were "I Love a Parade," "Between the Devil and the Deep Blue Sea," "I've Got the World on a String," and the phenomenally successful "Stormy Weather." In 1934, Arlen and Koehler wrote their first complete film score for "Let's Fall in Love" starring Ann Sothern. That same year, Broadway audiences were entertained by "Life Begins at 8:40" (lyrics by E. Y. Harburg and Ira Gershwin). Harburg was also Arlen's lyricist on the stage musical "Hooray for What" (1937), and the "Oscar" winning song "Over the Rainbow" which was sung by fourteen year old Judy Garland in the 1939 release "The Wizard of Oz." The award marked the beginning of four years in which his music was heard almost exclusively in films. Arlen's work earned him Academy nominations for "Blues in the Night" (1941), "That Old Black Magic" (1942), "Happiness Is a Thing Called Joe," and "My Shining Hour" (both 1943), and "Ac-cent-tchu-ate the Positive" and "Now I Know" (both 1944).

Arlen left Hollywood in 1944 to create the music for the long-run hit "Bloomer Girl." It was followed by the less successful "St. Louis Woman" (1946) in which Pearl Bailey made her Broadway debut. Arlen composed two more outstanding motion picture scores: "Casbah" (1948), and "A Star Is Born" (1954). The latter marked Judy Garland's return to the screen after a five year absence, and won Arlen an "Oscar" nomination for "The Man That

Got Away" (lyrics by Ira Gershwin). He also supplied the title song
for Miss Garland's last film "I Could Go on Singing" (1963).   Of
Arlen's three stage musicals in the Fifties, only "Jamaica" was an
unqualified hit.   His most serious work has been a blues opera
titled "Free and Easy" which was presented in Amsterdam in 1959.
Its content included songs from "St. Louis Woman" and several of
his film scores.   During the Sixties, Arlen's autobiography Happy
with the Blues was published, and he recorded an album of his
songs.   His sixty-eighth birthday was celebrated nationwide in a
television tribute in which he appeared.   Composer George Gershwin once referred to Harold Arlen as "the most original of us all."

Year	Production Title	Popular Songs
1929		"The Album of My Dreams" "Gladly"
1930	9:15 REVUE EARL CARROLL'S VANITIES	Get Happy The March of Time Hittin' the Bottle "Linda"
1931	YOU SAID IT	Sweet and Hot You Said It "Between the Devil and the Deep Blue Sea" "Kickin' the Gong Around" "I Love a Parade" "Tell Me with a Love Song"
1932	EARL CARROLL'S VANITIES AMERICANA THE GREAT MAGOO (play) GEORGE WHITE'S MU- SIC HALL VARIE- TIES	I Gotta Right to Sing the Blues Satan's Li'l Lamb It's Only a Paper Moon (HP) "I've Got the World on a String" "Minnie the Moocher's Wedding Day" "Music, Music, Everywhere"
1933		"Stormy Weather" "Happy as the Day Is Long" "Calico Days" "Shame on You" "Raisin' the Rent"
1934	LIFE BEGINS AT 8:40	Let's Take a Walk Around the Block

Year	Production Title	Popular Songs
1934	LIFE BEGINS AT 8:40	You're a Builder-Upper
		Fun to Be Fooled
		What Can You Say in a Love Song?
		Shoein' the Mare
	Let's Fall in Love	Let's Fall in Love
		Love Is Love Anywhere
		This Is Only the Beginning
		"Ill Wind"
		"As Long as I Live"
		"Here Goes (a Fool)"
		"Breakfast Ball"
1936	THE SHOW IS ON	Song of the Woodman
	Gold Diggers of 1937	Speaking of the Weather
		Let's Put Our Heads Together
	The Singing Kid	You're the Cure for What Ails Me
		I Love to Sing-a
	Stage Struck	Fancy Meeting You
		In Your Own Quiet Way
	Strike Me Pink	The Lady Dances
		First You Have Me High
		"Last Night When We Were Young"
1937	HOORAY FOR WHAT	God's Country
		Down with Love
		In the Shade of the New Apple Tree
		Moanin' in the Mornin'
		I've Gone Romantic on You
	Artists and Models	
1939	The Wizard of Oz	Over the Rainbow (AA) (HP-1)
		Ding, Dong, the Witch Is Dead
		We're Off to See the Wizard
	At the Circus	Lydia, the Tattooed Lady
		Two Blind Loves
	Love Affair	Sing, My Heart
1941	Blues in the Night	Blues in the Night (AN) (HP-1)
		This Time the Dream's on Me
		Says Who? Says You, Says I!
		"When the Sun Comes Out"
1942	Star Spangled Rhythm	That Old Black Magic (AN) (HP)
		Hit the Road to Dreamland
	Cairo	Buds Won't Bud
	Rio Rita	
	Captains of the Clouds	

Year	Production Title	Popular Songs
1942		"The Moment I Laid Eyes on You"
1943	Cabin in the Sky	Happiness Is a Thing Called Joe (AN)
		Life's Full o' Consequence
	The Sky's the Limit	My Shining Hour (AN) (HP)
		One for My Baby
	They Got Me Covered	
	Riding High	
1944	BLOOMER GIRL	Evelina (HP)
		The Eagle and Me
		Right as the Rain
		I Got a Song
	Here Come the Waves	Ac-cent-tchu-ate the Positive (AN) (HP-1)
		Let's Take the Long Way Home (HP)
		I Promise You (HP)
	Up in Arms	Now I Know (AN)
	Kismet	Tess's Torch Song
1945	Out of This World	Out of This World (HP)
		June Comes Around Every Year
1946	ST. LOUIS WOMAN	Come Rain or Come Shine (HP)
		Anyplace I Hang My Hat Is Home
		Legalize My Name
		It's a Woman's Prerogative
1948	Casbah	For Every Man There's a Woman (AN)
		It Was Written in the Stars
		Hooray for Love
		What's Good About Goodbye?
1950	The Petty Girl	Fancy Free
	My Blue Heaven	
1951	Mr. Imperium	Andiamo
1953	The Farmer Takes a Wife	Today I Love Everybody
	Down Among the Sheltering Palms	
1954	HOUSE OF FLOWERS	A Sleepin' Bee
	A Star Is Born	The Man That Got Away (AN)
		It's a New World
		Here's What I'm Here For

Year	Production Title	Popular Songs
1954	The Country Girl	The Search Is Through
1957	JAMAICA	Take It Slow, Joe Cocoanut Sweet
1959	SARATOGA FREE AND EASY (Amsterdam)	
1962	Gay Purr-ee	Little Drops of Rain "The Morning After"
1963	I Could Go on Singing	I Could Go on Singing "So Long, Big Time" "Silent Spring"

* * *

BURT BACHARACH

Burt Bacharach is the only living composer under the age of fifty who qualified for inclusion in this book. He was born in Kansas City, Missouri in 1928, and was educated in public schools in Forest Hills, New York. He received his formal training as a musician at the David Mannes School of Music in New York, the Berkshire Music Center, and McGill University in Montreal. Bacharach is an accomplished instrumentalist and plays the cello, drums, and piano. After two years of service in the Armed Forces, he performed with dance bands and jazz combos, and worked as an arranger and accompanist in Los Angeles.

Bacharach's music first attracted nationwide attention when he collaborated with lyricist Hal David on the songs "The Story of My Life" and "Magic Moments" in 1957. Among their subsequent hits are "Wives and Lovers," "Do You Know the Way to San Jose?," and "One Less Bell to Answer." Bacharach's contributions to motion pictures have earned him four Academy Award nominations including his "Raindrops Keep Fallin' on My Head" which won the 1969 "Oscar." He and David also won the Antoinette Perry "Tony" award for their score for the 1968 Broadway hit "Promises, Promises." Another of his collaborators has been lyricist Bob Hilliard with whom he wrote "Tower of Strength." Burt Bacharach has made many appearances throughout the world as accompanist-conductor for Marlene Dietrich's one-woman show. He is also seen frequently on television and in concert performances.

Year	Production Title	Popular Songs
1955		"Keep Me in Mind"
1957	The Sad Sack Lizzie	
		"The Story of My Life" "Magic Moments"
1958	The Blob	The Blob
1960		"I Cry Alone"
1961		"Tower of Strength" "Baby, It's You" "(Don't Go) Please Stay" "Don't Envy Me" "You're Following Me"
1962	Forever My Love The Man Who Shot Liberty Valance Wonderful to Be Young!	Forever My Love The Man Who Shot Liberty Valance Wonderful to Be Young
		"Any Day Now" "Don't Make Me Over" "Don't You Believe It" "I Just Don't Know What to Do with Myself" "Make It Easy on Yourself" "Only Love Can Break a Heart" "True Love Never Runs Smooth"
1963		"Wives and Lovers" "Close to You" "Anonymous Phone Call" "Anyone Who Had a Heart" "Blue on Blue" "Message to Michael" "Please Make Him Love Me" "Twenty-Four Hours from Tulsa" "Walk on By" "Wishin' and Hopin'" "Who's Been Sleeping in My Bed?" "This Empty Place" "To Wait for Love"
1964	A House Is Not a Home Send Me No Flowers	A House Is Not a Home "Always Something There to Re- mind Me" "Trains and Boats and Planes"

Year	Production Title	Popular Songs
1964		"Any Old Time of Day" "A Lifetime of Loneliness" "Reach Out for Me" "You'll Never Get to Heaven"
1965	What's New Pussycat?	What's New Pussycat? (AN) Here I Am My Little Red Book "What the World Needs Now Is Love" "Are You There (with Another Girl?)" "Don't Go Breakin' My Heart"
1966	Alfie Promise Her Anything After the Fox	Alfie (AN) "Another Night"
1967	Casino Royale	The Look of Love (AN) Casino Royale "One Less Bell to Answer" "Do You Know the Way to San Jose?" "I Say a Little Prayer" "Who Is Gonna Love Me?" "Windows of the World"
1968	PROMISES, PROMISES	I'll Never Fall in Love Again Promises, Promises "This Guy's in Love with You"
1969	Butch Cassidy and the Sundance Kid	Raindrops Keep Fallin' on My Head (AA) "April Fools" "I'm a Better Man (for Having Loved You)" "Odds and Ends (of a Beautiful Love Affair)"
1973	Lost Horizon	

* * *

IRVING BERLIN

Irving Berlin is both the most successful and best known popular song writer the United States has produced. Sixty-one percent of his hits were published during the reign of Tin Pan Alley but he continued to create songs which became popular for 32 years after the Alley's decline.

Berlin's family emigrated to America from Russia in the 1890's when he was a small child. He ran away from his home on New York's East Side when he was fourteen. While working as a singing waiter in 1907, he wrote the words for "Marie, from Sunny Italy." The following year, he succeeded in placing a song in the Broadway musical "The Boys and Betty." In 1910, Berlin appeared in vaudeville at the Palace Theatre, and made his legitimate stage debut in the revue "Up and Down Broadway" in which two more of his song lyrics were featured.

The year 1911 was a milestone in Berlin's career. Singer Emma Carus, appearing in vaudeville in Chicago, included a Berlin number in her act and within a few months it swept the country. "Alexander's Ragtime Band" is listed among the 16 songs on the ASCAP list of all-time popular hits. The year after its success, tragedy touched Berlin when his bride contracted typhoid fever on their Cuban honeymoon and died after only five months of marriage. The death of Dorothy Goetz inspired the twenty-four year old songwriter to write his first successful ballad--"When I Lost You." The song sold over two million copies.

Although his songs were featured in a dozen Broadway productions, it wasn't until 1914 that Berlin was engaged to write his first complete score. The show "Watch Your Step" starred Vernon and Irene Castle, and the score included the perennial "Play a Simple Melody." The next important steps in his Broadway career were his collaborations with the two top theatrical composers of the time. Working with Victor Herbert, he created the score for the 1916 musical "The Century Girl" and then joined George M. Cohan writing songs for the second edition of "The Cohan Revue" which opened in 1917. In April of that year, the United States entered the war which had been raging in Europe for three years, and Irving Berlin enlisted in the Army. While stationed at Camp Upton, he composed the songs for an all-soldier revue in which he also appeared singing "Oh, How I Hate to Get Up in the Morning."

Berlin was a frequent contributor to Florenz Ziegfeld's annual "Follies." His score for the thirteenth edition of "The Ziegfeld Follies" was hailed as the finest ever heard in the revue and "A Pretty Girl Is Like a Melody" became the theme song for subsequent editions. "The Follies" was a widely-imitated production and the musical stage of the 1920's was crowded with such annual revues as "The Greenwich Village Follies," "The Passing Show" and "Kitchy-Koo." In 1921, still another yearly revue was inaugurated. The new production had the distinction of opening in the only theatre

ever constructed especially to present the work of a single compos-
er--The Music Box Theatre financed by Irving Berlin and producer
Sam H. Harris.   The first "Music Box Revue" opened the million
dollar showcase and a new edition was presented every fall for
four years.   Berlin's "Say It with Music" was the theme of all editions.   The revues ran for a total of 2,227 performances.

One of the reasons why Berlin's songs have been so popular
is because people are usually able to identify themselves personal-
ly with his lyrics.   Some of his most successful songs have been
those concerned with common emotions experienced by everyone.
Such Berlin classics as "Lazy," "All by Myself," "Always" and
"Remember" illustrate the simplicity of his lyric approach.   He
helped perpetuate his notoriety by having his photograph on the
cover of several of the songs published by his own company.

Berlin celebrated two decades of songwriting by returning to
the Ziegfeld fold to compose the score for "The Follies" of 1927.
Two months after its premiere, an event occurred that launched
Berlin into a new phase of his career.   The use of sound in motion
pictures had been in the experimental stage for several years when
Hollywood's Warner Brothers decided to gamble their future on the
first talking picture.   "The Jazz Singer" opened in Manhattan in
October and one of its highlights was Al Jolson's rendition of Berlin's "Blue Skies."   Berlin was in on the ground floor of the talking
picture industry!   During the next three years, a stream of musical films brought his songs to larger audiences than ever.

Berlin returned to New York in 1932 after four years in
Hollywood.   The following year, his revue "As Thousands Cheer"
became the longest-running musical of 1933.   The show's theme
was a daily tabloid.   Each song in the production depicted a particular section or column of a newspaper: "Heat Wave" was a
weather report; "Easter Parade" represented the fashion column;
and "Supper Time" recounted a news item about a lynching in the
South.   "Easter Parade" is one of the ten most popular and financially profitable songs of all time.   It was written in 1917 and the
original title was "Smile and Show Your Dimple."   After "As
Thousands Cheer," Berlin composed the scores for six of the most
popular film musicals of the 1930's including "Top Hat," "Follow
the Fleet" and "On the Avenue."   Almost every song from each of
these three motion pictures became standards.   Berlin celebrated
his fiftieth birthday in 1938 and was as apprehensive as most Americans about the European conquests of Adolph Hitler and Benito
Mussolini.   One of radio's top personalities, Kate Smith, introduced
a patriotic song by Berlin on her nationwide broadcast in November
of that year.   It was so well received that she repeated it weekly
and in a few months, more Americans knew the words to "God
Bless America" than to the National Anthem.   The first version of
the song had been written twenty years earlier.

The year 1940 saw the Broadway premiere of Berlin's
"Louisiana Purchase" which ran until the summer of 1941.   Six

months after it closed, the United States declared war on Japan and World War II was underway. Just as he had done during World War I, Berlin helped raise funds for the Army by organizing a revue with an all-soldier cast. The New York opening of "This Is the Army" was on the Fourth of July in 1942. After a three month run in Manhattan, the revue toured the United States, Europe and the Pacific, and was adapted as a motion picture. It ultimately raised ten million dollars for Army Emergency Relief. Berlin also wrote "Any Bonds Today?" to promote the sale of U. S. Savings Bonds, and donated his royalties from "I Threw a Kiss in the Ocean" to the Navy Relief Fund.

One of the most successful of the film musicals which helped Americans escape from war news during the early years of the global conflict was Irving Berlin's "Holiday Inn." The plot of the picture concerned two song and dance men who operated a hotel and restaurant which was open only on holidays. The floor show included a special song celebrating the particular holiday. The film proved to be another milestone in Berlin's career when a simple melody he composed to celebrate Christmas turned out to be one of the most financially profitable songs of all time! "White Christmas" has sold over 92,000,000 records and more than five and a half million printed editions. Berlin has said that he wouldn't accept a million dollars for his copyright to this one song. "White Christmas" was awarded the "Oscar" as the Best Film Song of 1942, and was on "Your Hit Parade" a total of 32 times--the highest number ever attained by any song.

Berlin's first Academy Award-nominated song was the 1935 hit "Cheek to Cheek." Despite six more nominations, "White Christmas" was his only winner. Berlin has been greatly out-distanced in the "Oscar" Derby by four-time winners Sammy Cahn, Jimmy Van Heusen and Johnny Mercer.

Irving Berlin's contemporary, composer Jerome Kern, once wrote "Irving Berlin has no place in American music--he is American music." Ironically, the death of Kern resulted in Berlin's musical comedy masterpiece. Kern had been engaged to create the score for a musical about the legendary sharpshooter Annie Oakley when he suffered a fatal stroke in 1945, and Berlin was selected to replace him. A year later, the curtain went up on "Annie Get Your Gun" and six of the songs from its score became standards. The original production ran for nearly three years to become the twenty-third longest-running musical in Broadway history. It was also successful in England, France, Austria, Australia, Southern Rhodesia and Venezuela.

"Annie Get Your Gun" was followed by the film musicals "Easter Parade" and "Blue Skies." Berlin's next Broadway effort, "Miss Liberty," opened in 1949 and fell considerably short of the bullseye scored by "Annie." The disappointment over it was quickly forgotten the following year when "Call Me Madam" had its premiere and was an immediate success. One of the highlights of Berlin's career occurred in 1954 when President Eisenhower signed a bill authorizing Congress to strike a gold medal to honor the composer for "God Bless America." Berlin's last new Broadway musical has been the 1962 offering "Mr. President" which was a financial loss. In the spring of 1966, "Annie Get Your Gun" was revived on Broadway. Berlin added "Old-Fashioned Wedding" to his original score and it stopped every performance.

In 1977, the eighty-seven year old songwriter was awarded a Medal of Freedom by President Gerald Ford. Berlin's career has spanned well over half a century. He is second only to Oscar Hammerstein as Broadway's most successful lyricist and ranks third after Richard Rodgers and Jerome Kern as its top composer. He's the only songwriter to have three of his numbers on ASCAP's list of 16 All-time favorites: "Alexander's Ragtime Band," "God Bless America," and "White Christmas."

Irving Berlin's success is best summed-up in his own composition "There's No Business Like Show Business."

Year	Production Title	Popular Songs
1908	THE BOYS AND BETTY	
1909	THE GIRL AND THE WIZARD	
		"My Wife's Gone to the Country (Hurrah! Hurrah!)"
		"That Mesmerizing Mendelssohn Tune"
		"Next to Your Mother, Who Do You Love?"
		"Sadie Salome (Go Home)"
		"Wild Cherries"
		"I Didn't Go Home at All"
		"If I Thought You Wouldn't Tell"
		"Do Your Duty, Doctor"
		"Just Like a Rose"
		"Dorando"
1910	THE JOLLY BACHELORS	Stop That Rag (Keep on Playing, Honey)
	UP AND DOWN BROADWAY	That Beautiful Rag
	THE ZIEGFELD FOLLIES	Sweet Italian Love
	GETTING A POLISH	The Dance of the Grizzly Bear
	HE CAME FROM MILWAUKEE	That Opera Rag
	JUMPING JUPITER	

Year	Production Title	Popular Songs
1910		"Yiddle on Your Fiddle (Play Some Ragtime)"
		"Piano Man"
		"Call Me Up Some Rainy Afternoon"
		"Stop! Stop! Stop! (Love Me Some More)"
1911	TEMPTATIONS	Keep a Taxi Waiting, Dear
		Answer Me
		Spanish Love
		I Beg Your Pardon, Dear Old Broadway
	THE ZIEGFELD FOLLIES	Woodman, Woodman, Spare That Tree
		Ephraham Played Upon the Piano
	THE NEVER HOMES	There's a Girl in Havana
	FASCINATING WIDOW	
		"The Ragtime Violin"
		"Take a Little Tip from Father"
		"Kiss Me, My Honey, Kiss Me"
		"Run Home and Tell Your Mother"
		"When I'm Alone, I'm Lonesome"
		"Bring Back My Lovin' Man"
		"When You Kiss an Italian Girl"
		"Virginia Lou"
		"Whistling Rag"
		"Everybody's Doing It Now"
		"Alexander's Ragtime Band" (HP)
1912	THE PASSING SHOW	Ragtime Jockey Man
	THE WHIRL OF SOCIETY	That Society Bear
		I Want to Be in Dixie
	HOKEY POKEY	
	HANKY PANKY	
	MY BEST GIRL	
	THE ZIEGFELD FOLLIES	
		"That Mysterious Rag"
		"At the Devil's Ball"
		"When the Midnight Choo-Choo Leaves for Alabam'"
		"Do It Again"
		"Wait Until Your Daddy Comes Home"
		"When I Lost You"
		"Ragtime Soldier Man"

Year	Production Title	Popular Songs
1912		"Keep Away from the Fellow Who Owns an Automobile" "Snookey Ookums" "Welcome Home" "Fiddle Dee Dee" "Goody Goody Goody Goody Goody Good" "Pick, Pick, Pick, Pick on the Mandolin, Antonio" "That's How I Love You" "Lead Me to That Beautiful Band"
1913	ALL ABOARD	Somebody's Coming to My House "The International Rag" "Happy Little Country Girl" "We Have Much to Be Thankful For" "Monkey Doodle Doo" "In My Harem" "You've Got Your Mother's Big Blue Eyes" "Pullman Porters' Parade" "If You Don't Want Me, Why Do You Hang Around?" "San Francisco Bound" "Take Me Back" "The Old Maid's Ball"
1914	WATCH YOUR STEP	Play a Simple Melody (HP) Watch Your Step Minstrel Parade Syncopated Walk When I Discovered You
	THE QUEEN OF THE MOVIES	"I Want to Go Back to Michigan (Down on the Farm)" "He's a Devil in His Own Home Town" "Along Came Ruth" "He's a Rag Picker" "This Is the Life"

Year	Production Title	Popular Songs
1914		"When It's Night-Time in Dixieland" "If That's Your Idea of a Wonderful Time (Take Me Home)" "Stay Down Here Where You Belong"
1915	STOP! LOOK! LISTEN!	I Love a Piano The Girl on the Magazine Cover "My Bird of Paradise" "Araby" "When I Leave the World Behind" "Cohen Owes Me Ninety-Seven Dollars" "Si's Been Drinking Cider" "When You're Down in Louisville (Call on Me)"
1916	STEP THIS WAY THE CENTURY GIRL	I've Got a Sweet Tooth Bothering Me "Someone Else May Be There While I'm Gone" "In Florida Among the Palms" "When the Black Sheep Returns to the Fold" "He's Getting Too Darn Big for a One-Horse Town"
1917	JACK O'LANTERN RAMBLER ROSE THE COHAN REVUE OF 1918 DANCE AND GROW THIN	I'll Take You Back to Italy "Whose Little Heart Are You Breaking Now?" "Let's All Be Americans Now" "How Can I Forget? (When There's So Much to Remember?)" "For Your Country and My Country" "My Sweetie" "From Here to Shanghai"

Year	Production Title	Popular Songs
1918	THE ZIEGFELD FOLLIES	Blue Devils of France I'm Gonna Pin My Medal on the Girl I Left Behind Me
	YIP, YIP YAPHANK	Oh! How I Hate to Get Up in the Morning Mandy
	EVERYTHING	The Circus Is Coming to Town Come Along to Toy Town
	THE CANARY	"They Were All Out of Step but Jim"
1919	THE ZIEGFELD FOLLIES	A Pretty Girl Is Like a Melody You'd Be Surprised You Cannot Make Your Shimmy Shake on Tea
	THE ROYAL VAGABOND	That Revolutionary Rag "Nobody Knows (and Nobody Seems to Care)" "I've Got My Captain Working for Me Now" "Sweeter Than Sugar (Is My Sweetie)" "Eyes of Youth" "Was There Ever a Pal Like You?"
1920	ZIEGFELD MIDNIGHT FROLIC THE ZIEGFELD FOLLIES	I'll See You in C-U-B-A The Girls of My Dreams Bells Tell Me, Little Gypsy The Syncopated Vamp I'm a Vamp from East Broadway
	BROADWAY BREVITIES	Beautiful Faces (Need Beautiful Clothes)
	ZIEGFELD GIRLS OF 1920	"After You Get What You Want You Don't Want It" "Home Again Blues"
1921	MUSIC BOX REVUE	Say It with Music Everybody Step I Like It
	ZIEGFELD 9 O'CLOCK FROLIC	"All by Myself"

Year	Production Title	Popular Songs
1922	MUSIC BOX REVUE	Lady of the Evening Pack Up Your Sins (and Go to the Devil) Crinoline Days Will She Come from the East? (North, West or South?) "Some Sunny Day" "Homesick"
1923	MUSIC BOX REVUE	Tell Me a Bedtime Story Learn to Do the Strut When You Walked Out Someone Else Walked Right In Little Butterfly An Orange Grove in California Waltz of Long Ago "Tell All the Folks in Kentucky (I'm Comin' Home)"
1924	MUSIC BOX REVUE	Tell Her in the Springtime The Call of the South "Lazy" "What'll I Do?" "All Alone"
1925	THE COCOANUTS	Lucky Boy Ting-a-ling (the Bells'll Ring) A Little Bungalow "Always" (HP) "You Forgot to Remember"
1926	BETSY	Blue Skies "How Many Times?" "I'm on My Way Home" "At Peace with the World" "Because I Love You" "That's a Good Girl "Just a Little Longer"

Year	Production Title	Popular Songs
1927	THE ZIEGFELD FOLLIES	Shaking the Blues Away It All Belongs to Me Ooh! Maybe It's You "The Song Is Ended (But the Melody Lingers On)" "Russian Lullaby" "What Does It Matter?" "Together, We Two"
1928	The Awakening	Marie "Roses of Yesterday" "Sunshine" "How About Me?" "To Be Forgotten" "I Can't Do Without You"
1929	Lady of the Pavements	Where Is the Song of Songs for Me?
	Hallelujah	Waiting at the End of the Road Swanee Shuffle
	Coquette	Coquette
	The Cocoanuts	When My Dreams Come True
1930	Mammy	Let Me Sing--and I'm Happy To My Mammy (Across the Breakfast Table) Looking at You
	Puttin' on the Ritz	With You Puttin' on the Ritz "The Little Things in Life" "Just a Little While"
1931	SHOOT THE WORKS	(Just) Begging for Love
	Reaching for the Moon	Reaching for the Moon "Me!" "I Want You for Myself" "I'll Miss You in the Evening"
1932	FACE THE MUSIC	Let's Have Another Cup o' Coffee Soft Lights and Sweet Music

Year	Production Title	Popular Songs
1932	FACE THE MUSIC	On a Roof in Manhattan
		"How Deep Is the Ocean? (How High Is the Sky?)" (HP)
		"Say It Isn't So"
		"I'm Playing with Fire"
1933	AS THOUSANDS CHEER	Easter Parade (HP)
		Heat Wave
		Not for All the Rice in China
		Supper Time
		How's Chances?
		Lonely Heart
		Harlem on My Mind
		"I Can't Remember"
		"Maybe I Love You Too Much"
1934		"I Never Had a Chance"
		"So Help Me"
		"Butterfingers"
1935	Top Hat	Cheek to Cheek (AN) (HP-1)
		Isn't This a Lovely Day? (To Be Caught in the Rain) (HP)
		The Piccolino
		No Strings (I'm Fancy Free) (HP)
		Top Hat, White Tie, and Tails (HP)
1936	Follow the Fleet	Let Yourself Go (HP)
		Let's Face the Music and Dance (HP)
		We Saw the Sea
		I'm Putting All My Eggs in One Basket (HP)
		Get Thee Behind Me, Satan
		But Where Are You?
		I'd Rather Lead a Band
1937	On the Avenue	I've Got My Love to Keep Me Warm (HP)
		This Year's Kisses (HP-1)

Year	Production Title	Popular Songs
1937	On the Avenue	Slumming on Park Avenue (HP) He Ain't Got Rhythm You're Laughing at Me (HP) The Girl on the Police Gazette
1938	Alexander's Ragtime Band Carefree	Now It Can Be Told (AN) (HP) My Walking Stick Change Partners (AN) (HP-1) I Used to Be Color Blind "God Bless America"
1939	Second Fiddle	I Poured My Heart into a Song (AN) (HP) I'm Sorry for Myself Back to Back When Winter Comes An Old Fashioned Tune Always Is New
1940	LOUISIANA PURCHASE	It's a Lovely Day Tomorrow You're Lonely and I'm Lonely (HP) You Can't Brush Me Off It'll Come to You Latins Know How Fools Fall in Love "Everybody Knew but Me"
1941		"Any Bonds Today?" "A Little Old Church in England"
1942	THIS IS THE ARMY Holiday Inn	I Left My Heart at the Stage Door Canteen (HP) I'm Getting Tired So I Can Sleep (HP) This Is the Army, Mister Jones This Time (Is the Last Time) White Christmas (AA) (HP-1)

Year	Production Title	Popular Songs
1942	Holiday Inn	Be Careful, It's My Heart (HP) Happy Holiday I've Got Plenty to Be Thankful For Let's Start the New Year Right You're Easy to Dance With "Me and My Melinda" (HP) "I Threw a Kiss in the Ocean" "When This Crazy World Is Sane Again" "Arms for the Love of America" "Angels of Mercy" "When That Man Is Dead and Gone"
1943	THIS IS THE ARMY (overseas tour)	
1944		"All of My Life" (HP)
1945		"Just a Blue Serge Suit"
1946	ANNIE GET YOUR GUN	They Say It's Wonderful (HP-1) Doin' What Comes Natur'lly (HP) I Got the Sun in the Morning (HP) (There's No Business Like) Show Business The Girl That I Marry I Got Lost in His Arms Anything You Can Do
	Blue Skies	You Keep Coming Back Like a Song (AN) (HP) A Couple of Song and Dance Men "Let's Go West Again"
1947		"Love and the Weather" "Kate (Have I Come Early, Too Late?)"

Year	Production Title	Popular Songs
1948	Easter Parade	It Only Happens When I Dance with You (HP) Steppin' Out with My Baby A Fella with an Umbrella A Couple of Swells Better Luck Next Time
		"The Freedom Train"
1949	MISS LIBERTY	Let's Take an Old-Fashioned Walk (HP) Just One Way to Say I Love You (HP) Homework
		"I'm Beginning to Miss You"
1950	CALL ME MADAM	(I Wonder Why) You're Just in Love (HP) It's a Lovely Day Today The Best Thing for You Marrying for Love
1954	White Christmas	Count Your Blessings Instead of Sheep (AN) (HP)
	There's No Business Like Show Business	
1957	Sayonara	Sayonara
1962	MR. PRESIDENT	This Is a Great Country
1966	ANNIE GET YOUR GUN (revival)	

* * *

LEW BROWN

     Lyricist Lew Brown was born in Russia in 1893. His family came to the United States when he was a child, and he received his schooling in Connecticut and New York. When he was only nineteen years old, he began working with composer Albert Von Tilzer to create such hits as "I'm the Lonesomest Gal in Town" and "Oh, By Jingo." Broadway audiences heard their first Lew Brown lyric in the 1917 edition of the revue "Hitchy-Koo." In 1925, Brown became a partner in one of the best-known songwriting teams of the decade--DeSylva, Brown & Henderson. As such, he co-founded the music publishing firm that carried their names. Together with lyricist B. G. DeSylva, Brown wrote some of his most popular songs for the annual "George White's Scandals" including "The Birth of the Blues" which ASCAP lists as one of the 16 most famous songs of all time. Other hit Broadway musicals on which he worked were "Good News," "Follow Thru," "Flying High" and "Strike Me Pink."

Brown's first year in Hollywood produced the Al Jolson classic "Sonny Boy." DeSylva, Brown & Henderson ended their collaboration in 1930, and Brown went on to receive a 1937 "Oscar" nomination for his lyrics to "That Old Feeling" (music by Sammy Fain). One of the biggest hits of his career, "Beer Barrel Polka," swept the country in 1939 making "Your Hit Parade" for 16 weeks! Brown augmented his film work with Broadway musicals until 1940. He died in 1958 at the age of sixty-five. Brown's 142 hit songs make him the most successful member of DeSylva, Brown & Henderson.

Year	Production Title	Popular Songs
1912		"I'm the Lonesomest Gal in Town" "Kentucky Sue" "Please Don't Take My Lovin' Man Away" "Parisienne" "Here Comes the Bride That Took My Lovin' Man Away"
1913		"Kiss Me Good Night"
1916		"If You Were the Only Girl"
1917	HITCHY-KOO	I May Be Gone for a Long, Long Time "Au Revoir, but Not Goodbye, Soldier Boy" "Give Me the Moonlight, Give Me the Girl"
1919	LINGER LONGER LITTY	Oh, By Jingo "Wait Till You Get Them Up in the Air, Boys"

Year	Production Title	Popular Songs
1920		"Chili Bean" "I Used to Love You but It's All Over Now" "(Oh Gee! Say Gee! You Ought to See) My Gee Gee from the Fiji Isles"
1921		"Dapper Dan" "I've Got the Travelling Choo Choo Blues" "Big Chief Walley Ho Wo (He'd Wiggle His Way to Her Wigwam)"
1922	MAKE IT SNAPPY	Seven or Eleven--My Dixie Pair O'Dice
	THE GREENWICH VILLAGE FOLLIES	Georgette "I Got It, You'll Get It, Just the Same as Me" "Oh, How I Hate That Fellow Nathan"
1923	GEORGE WHITE'S SCANDALS	"Last Night on the Back Porch" "Ain't You Ashamed?" "Annabelle" "Why Did I Kiss That Girl?" "When It's Night Time in Italy, It's Wednesday Over Here" "Counterfeit Bill from Louisville" "I've Got the 'Yes, We Have No Bananas' Blues"
1924		"Shine"
1925	BIG BOY	It All Depends on You How I Love You (I'm Tellin' the Birds, I'm Tellin' the Bees)
	GEORGE WHITE'S SCANDALS GAY PAREE	I Want a Lovable Baby "Don't Bring Lulu"

Year	Production Title	Popular Songs
1925		"Then I'll Be Happy" "Dummy Song (I'll Take the Legs from Some Old Table)"
1926	GEORGE WHITE'S SCANDALS	The Birth of the Blues Black Bottom Lucky Day The Girl Is You and the Boy Is Me "I'd Climb the Highest Mountain"
1927	GOOD NEWS	The Best Things in Life Are Free (HP) Lucky in Love Just Imagine Good News The Varsity Drag The Girls of Pi Beta Phi
	MANHATTAN MARY	Manhattan Mary Broadway The Five Step It Won't Be Long Now
	ARTISTS AND MODELS	Here Am I--Broken Hearted
	PIGGY	"Just a Memory" "Without You, Sweetheart" "So Blue" "South Wind" "One Sweet Letter from You" "Magnolia" "I Wonder How I Look When I'm Asleep?" "The Church Bells Are Ringing for Mary"
1928	GEORGE WHITE'S SCANDALS	I'm on the Crest of a Wave What D'ya Say? Pickin' Cotton American Tune
	HOLD EVERYTHING	You're the Cream in My Coffee Don't Hold Everything
	THREE CHEERS	Maybe This Is Love Pompanola

Year	Production Title	Popular Songs
1928	The Singing Fool	Sonny Boy
		"Together" (HP) "For Old Times Sake" "The Song I Love" "Sorry for Me" "That's Just My Way of Forgetting You"
1929	FOLLOW THRU	Button Up Your Overcoat My Lucky Star You Wouldn't Fool Me, Would You? I Want to Be Bad Follow Thru
	GEORGE WHITE'S SCANDALS Sunny Side Up	Sunny Side Up (I'm a Dreamer) Aren't We All? If I Had a Talking Picture of You Turn on the Heat
	Say It with Songs	Why Can't You? I'm in Seventh Heaven Little Pal Used to You
	In Old Arizona	My Tonia
		"My Sin"
1930	FLYING HIGH	Without Love Wasn't It Beautiful While It Lasted? Thank Your Father Good for You, Bad for Me Red Hot Chicago
	Just Imagine	(There's Something About an) Old-Fashioned Girl (I Am the Words) You Are the Melody
	Happy Days	
		"Don't Tell Her What Happened to Me" "(I Am the Words) You Are the Melody"
1931	GEORGE WHITE'S SCANDALS	Life Is Just a Bowl of Cherries My Song This Is the Missus The Thrill Is Gone That's Why Darkies Were Born

Year	Production Title	Popular Songs
1931	Indiscreet	Come to Me If You Haven't Got Love "You Try Somebody Else" "One More Time"
1932	HOT-CHA!	You Can Make My Life a Bed of Roses There I Go Dreaming Again
1933	STRIKE ME PINK	Let's Call It a Day Strike Me Pink "I May Be Dancing with Somebody Else" "I've Got to Pass Your House"
1934	CALLING ALL STARS CASINO VARIETIES Stand Up and Cheer Loud Speaker Carolina	Baby, Take a Bow She's Way Up Thar Stand Up and Cheer "This Is Our Last Night Together" "(If Love Makes You Give Up) Steak and Potatoes"
1936	The Music Goes 'Round Strike Me Pink	Taking Care of You Life Begins When You're in Love The Lady Dances First You Have Me High
1937	Vogues of 1938 New Faces of 1937	That Old Feeling (AN) (HP-1) Love Is Never Out of Season Our Penthouse on Third Avenue
1938	Straight, Place and Show Hold That Co-ed Tarnished Angel	With You on My Mind "Oh, Ma, Ma (The But- cher Boy)" (HP)
1939	YOKEL BOY	Beer Barrel Polka (HP)

Year	Production Title	Popular Songs
1939	YOKEL BOY	Comes Love (HP) I Can't Afford to Dream Let's Make Memories Tonight
	Barricade Girl from Brooklyn	"Down Home Rag"
1940	Sing, Dance, Plenty Hot	"Wait Till I Catch You in My Dreams"
1941		"I Came Here to Talk for Joe" (HP) "Don't Cry, Cherie"
1942	Private Buckaroo	Don't Sit Under the Apple Tree (HP-1)
1943	DuBarry Was a Lady	Madame, I Love Your Crepe Suzette
	Thousands Cheer Swing Fever	I Dug a Ditch in Wichita "I Have Faith, So Have You"
1944		"Let Us All Sing Auld Lang Syne"
1948		"An Old Sombrero (and an Old Spanish Shawl)"
1950		"On the Outgoing Tide" "The Beer That I Left on the Bar"

* * *

NACIO HERB BROWN

Composer Nacio Herb Brown was the son of a New Mexico law enforcement officer who moved his family to Los Angeles in 1904. Brown studied both piano and violin and graduated from Manual Arts High School. He worked as a vaudeville accompanist for a short time, and then opened a retail shop which supplied custom-tailored clothes to some of Hollywood's best-known silent screen stars. He soon branched out into selling Southern California real estate. While writing music was only a hobby during the first fifteen years of his career, he had three popular songs to his cre-

dit when he celebrated his thirty-second birthday in 1928.   One of
them ("When Buddha Smiles") was written in collaboration with lyricist Arthur Freed.   In 1929, Brown and Freed were hired by
MGM Studios to provide songs for one of the first all-talking musicals "Broadway Melody."   In addition to its hit title song, their
score included the memorable "You Were Meant for Me."   That
same year, the film "Hollywood Revue" introduced Brown and
Freed's "Singin' in the Rain."   Brown's career at MGM spanned
more than two decades during which his music was heard in such
box office successes as "Going Hollywood," "Broadway Melody of
1936," "San Francisco," "Babes in Arms" and "Ziegfeld Girl."
His only Broadway musical was the 1932 hit "Take a Chance" on
which he shared credits with composers Richard Whiting and Vincent Youmans.   Nacio Herb Brown was sixty-eight when he died
in 1964.

Year	Production Title	Popular Songs
1920		"Coral Sea"
1921		"When Buddha Smiles"
1924		"The Hoodoo Man"
1927	HOLLYWOOD MUSIC BOX REVUE (Los Angeles)	
1928		"Avalon Town"
1929	Broadway Melody	Broadway Melody You Were Meant for Me The Wedding of the Paint- ed Doll The Love Boat
	Hollywood Revue of 1929 The Pagan Untamed Marianne	Singin' in the Rain Pagan Love Song The Chant of the Jungle Blondy
1930	Lord Byron of Broadway	Should I? The Woman in the Shoe A Bundle of Old Love Letters The Moon Is Low I'll Still Belong to You
	Montana Moon Whoopee One Heavenly Night Good News	
1932	TAKE A CHANCE	Eadie Was a Lady You're an Old Smoothie Turn Out the Light Paradise
	A Woman Commands	

Year	Production Title	Popular Songs
1933	The Barbarian	Love Songs of the Nile
	Going Hollywood	Temptation
		After Sundown
		We'll Make Hay While the Sun Shines
		Our Big Love Scene
	Hold Your Man	Hold Your Man
	Stage Mother	Beautiful Girl
	Peg O' My Heart	
1934	Sadie McKee	All I Do Is Dream of You
	Student Tour	A New Moon Is Over My Shoulder
		From Now On
	Hollywood Party	
	Hide-Out	
	Riptide	
1935	Broadway Melody of 1936	You Are My Lucky Star (HP-1)
		Broadway Rhythm (HP)
		I've Got a Feelin' You're Foolin' (HP)
		On a Sunday Afternoon
		Sing Before Breakfast
	A Night at the Opera	Alone (HP-1)
	China Seas	
1936	San Francisco	Would You? (HP)
	After the Thin Man	Smoke Dreams
	The Devil Is a Sissy	
1937	Broadway Melody of 1938	Yours and Mine (HP)
		I'm Feelin' Like a Million
		Everybody Sing
		Sun Showers
1939	Babes in Arms	Good Morning (HP)
	The Ice Follies of 1939	
1940	Two Girls on Broadway	My Wonderful One, Let's Dance
1941	Ziegfeld Girl	You Stepped Out of a Dream
1943	Wintertime	Later Tonight
	Swing Fever	
1944	Greenwich Village	

Year	Production Title	Popular Songs
1946	Holiday in Mexico	
1948	The Kissing Bandit	Love Is Where You Find It If I Steal a Kiss
	On an Island with You	
1949	The Bribe	
1952	Singin' in the Rain	Make 'em Laugh

* * *

ALFRED BRYAN

Alfred Bryan was a staff writer for a music publishing firm and realized his first success as a popular song writer in 1901. Two years later, the Ontario-born lyricist's work was introduced to Broadway audiences in "Mr. Bluebeard." In 1910, he collaborated with composer Fred Fisher on "Come, Josephine, in My Flying Machine," and their "Peg O' My Heart" was featured in "The Ziegfeld Follies" in 1913. Bryan was among the first lyricists to collaborate with newcomers George Gershwin ("I Was So Young"--1919) and Vincent Youmans ("The Country Cousin"--1920). He and composer George Meyer, with whom he had worked frequently for 20 years, supplied songs for more than a dozen films during the early days of talking pictures. Alfred Bryan was eighty-seven at the time of his death in 1958.

Year	Production Title	Popular Songs
1901		"Casey's Wedding Night" "When They Play 'God Save the King'"
1902		"The Train Rolled On"
1903	MR. BLUEBEARD	
1904		"When the Bees Are in the Hive"
1906		"Bonnie Jean"
1907		"And a Little Bit More"
1908		"Are You Sincere?" "Rainbow"

Year	Production Title	Popular Songs
1909		"You Taught Me How to Love You, Now Teach Me to Forget"
1910		"Come, Josephine, in My Flying Machine" "I've Got Your Number" "Winter" "Think It Over, Mary" "Cupid's I.O.U." "Dill Pickles" "I'd Rather Say Hello Than Say Good-Bye"
1911		"After That I Want a Little More" "If Every Hour Were a Day" "Make Me Love You Like I Never Loved Before" "Bring Back My Golden Dream" "That Was Before I Met You" "First You Get the Money, Then You Get the Flat, Then It's Time Enough to Get the Girl" "Yiddisha Luck and Irisha Love"
1912		"Big Blond Baby" "When I Waltz with You" "Roll Me Around Like a Hoop, My Dear" "When I Get You Alone Tonight"
1913	THE ZIEGFELD FOLLIES	Peg O' My Heart (HP) "I'm on My Way to Mandalay" "Tango Town" "That Tango Tokio"
1914	THE BELLE OF BOND STREET	Who Paid the Rent for Mrs. Rip Van Winkle? "When It's Moonlight on the Alamo"

Year	Production Title	Popular Songs
1914		"When It's Night Time Down in Burgundy" "Smother Me with Kisses and Kill Me with Love"
1915		"I Didn't Raise My Boy to Be a Soldier" "Ypsilanti" "She Went Over the Hills to Moonshine Valley"
1916	FOLLOW ME	It's a Cute Little Way of My Own I Want to Be Good but My Eyes Won't Let Me "Ireland Must Be Heaven for My Mother Came from There" "Come Back to Arizona" "She's Dixie All the Time"
1917		"Sweet Little Buttercup" "Lorraine, My Beautiful Alsace Lorraine" "Joan of Arc, They Are Calling You" "My Yokohama Girl" "Cleopatra" "My Mother's Eyes"
1918		"Madelon" "When Alexander Takes His Ragtime Band to France" "Eyes of Youth" "Sahara"
1919	GOOD MORNING, JUDGE MONTE CRISTO JR. SHUBERT GAIETIES HELLO, ALEXANDER	I Was So Young "Goodbye, Teddy Roosevelt (You Were a Real American)" "I'm Gonna Break That Mason-Dixon Line"
1920	KISSING TIME ED WYNN CARNIVAL	Oui, Oui, Marie

Year	Production Title	Popular Songs
1920	CENTURY REVUE THE MIDNIGHT ROUNDERS	"Beautiful Anna Bell Lee" "Hiawatha's Melody of Love" "The Country Cousin" "Who Ate Napoleons with Josephine When Bona- parte Was Away?" "Daddy, You've Been a Mother to Me" "The Irish Were Egyp- tians Long Ago" "The Hen and the Cow" "They'll Never Miss the Wine in Dixieland"
1921	THE MIDNIGHT ROUNDERS	
1922	THE HOTEL MOUSE	"(O-hi-O) Round on the End and High in the Middle"
1925		"Brown Eyes, Why Are You Blue?" "Row! Row! Rosie" "I Want You to Want Me to Want You"
1926		"Her Beaus Are Only Rainbows"
1927		"Blue River" "Red Lips, Kiss My Blues Away" "There's Something Nice About Everyone but There's Everything Nice About You"
1928		"Don't Keep Me in the Dark, Bright Eyes" "Japansy" "Wear a Hat with a Silver Lining"
1929	Drag Wolf Song	My Song of the Nile Yo Te Amo Means I Love You

Year	Production Title	Popular Songs
1929	Footlights and Fools	If I Can't Have You
	Show of Shows	Just an Hour of Love
	Careers	
	Broadway Babies	
	Girl from Woolworth's	
	Her Private Life	
	Hard to Get	
	A Man's Man	
	Two Weeks Off	
1930	Paris	Miss Wonderful
	Dancing Sweeties	
	Bride of the Regiment	
	No, No Nanette	
	Isle of Escape	
	Wedding Rings	
		"Looking in the Window, Thinking of You"
1931	Holy Terror	Lonesome Lover
	Bright Lights	
		"Give Me Your Affection, Honey"
		"Pagan Moon"
1932		"Dream Serenade"
1933		"Puddin' Head Jones"
		"Baby"
1934		"Down in the Old Cherry Orchard"
1936		"Wintertime Dreams"
1937		"It's Raining Sunshine"
		"In a Little Dutch Kindergarten"
1938		"Hearts Are Never Blue in Blue Kalua"

Posthumous:

| 1966 | | "When the Harbor Lights Are Burning" |

* * *

JOHNNY BURKE

     Johnny Burke's family moved from Antioch, California, to Chicago where his father was a building contractor. Burke attended the University of Wisconsin and played the piano in the college orchestra. After graduation in 1926, he was employed as a staff pianist at Irving Berlin's music publishing firm. He was twenty-five years old when he collaborated with composer Harold Spina and lyricist Joe Young on the 1933 hit "Annie Doesn't Live Here Anymore." The following year, Burke joined Paramount Studios where he worked almost exclusively for 18 years. His first film collaborator was composer Arthur Johnston with whom he received his first "Oscar" nomination for "Pennies from Heaven" (1936). The next composer to set Burke's words to music was Jimmy Monaco, and their partnership produced the hits "On the Sentimental Side," "I've Got a Pocketful of Dreams," and "Too Romantic" which was heard in the first of the Bing Crosby/Bob Hope "Road" films.

     In 1939, Burke formed his third major alliance with composer James Van Heusen, and five years later they received the Academy Award for "Swinging on a Star." The more than two dozen popular motion picture songs written by Burke and Van Heusen included "Moonlight Becomes You," "Sunday, Monday or Always," and "But Beautiful." The team created the scores for two Broadway musicals--"Nellie Bly" (1946) and "Carnival in Flanders" (1953)--but neither was successful. Johnny Burke is the lyricist most closely associated with Bing Crosby who starred in over half of the 40 films in which Burke's songs were heard. He made another attempt on Broadway in 1961 when he wrote both music and lyrics for "Donnybrook!" but it also suffered an early closing. Johnny Burke died three years later at the age of fifty-five. He ranks fourth among Hollywood's top lyricists.

Year	Production Title	Popular Songs
1930		"Yours and Mine"
1933		"Annie Doesn't Live Here Anymore"
1934		"Irresistible" "Beat of My Heart" "It's Dark on Observatory Hill" "I've Got a Warm Spot in My Heart for You" "You're Not the Only Oyster in the Stew"
1935		"My Very Good Friend, the Milkman" "Love Dropped in for Tea"

Year	Production Title	Popular Songs
1935		"Now You've Got Me Doing It"
		"Once Upon a Midnight"
		"You're So Darn Charming"
1936	Pennies from Heaven	Pennies from Heaven (AN) (HP-1)
		One, Two, Button Your Shoe
		So Do I
		Let's Call a Heart a Heart
	Go West, Young Man	I Was Saying to the Moon
		"So This Is Heaven?"
		"Too Much Imagination"
1937	Double or Nothing	The Moon Got in My Eyes (HP)
		It's the Natural Thing to Do
		All You Want to Do Is Dance
	Midnight Madonna	
1938	Sing You Sinners	I've Got a Pocketful of Dreams (HP-1)
		Don't Let That Moon Get Away
		Laugh and Call It Love
	Doctor Rhythm	On the Sentimental Side (HP)
		My Heart Is Taking Lessons
		This Is My Night to Dream
		"Between a Kiss and a Sigh"
1939	That's Right--You're Wrong	Scatterbrain (HP-1)
	The Star Maker	An Apple for the Teacher (HP)
		Go Fly a Kite (HP)
		A Man and His Dream (HP)
		Still the Bluebird Sings
	East Side of Heaven	East Side of Heaven
		That Sly Old Gentleman from Featherbed Lane
		Hang Your Heart on a Hickory Limb
		Sing a Song of Sunbeams
		"Imagination" (HP-1)
		"What's New?" (HP)
		"Oh, You Crazy Moon" (HP)
1940	Rhythm on the River	Only Forever (AN) (HP-1)

Year	Production Title	Popular Songs
1940	Rhythm on the River	That's for Me When the Moon Comes Over Madison Square Ain't It a Shame About Mame?
	Road to Singapore	Too Romantic (HP) The Moon and the Willow Tree Sweet Potato Piper
	If I Had My Way	I Haven't Time to Be a Millionaire April Played the Fiddle Meet the Sun Half-way
	Love Thy Neighbor	Do You Know Why? Isn't That Just Like Love? Dearest, Darest I? "Devil May Care" (HP) "Polka Dots and Moonbeams" "Charming Little Faker" "Let's All Meet at My House"
1941	Playmates	Humpty Dumpty Heart (HP) How Long Did I Dream?
	Road to Zanzibar	It's Always You (HP) Birds of a Feather
1942	Road to Morocco	Moonlight Becomes You (HP-1) Road to Morocco Ain't Got a Dime to My Name Constantly
	My Favorite Spy	Got the Moon in My Pocket Just Plain Lonesome "Absent-Minded Moon"
1943	Dixie	Sunday, Monday or Always (HP-1) If You Please (HP)
1944	Going My Way	Swinging on a Star (AA) (HP) Going My Way The Day After Forever
	Lady in the Dark	Suddenly It's Spring
	And the Angels Sing	It Could Happen to You (HP)
	Belle of the Yukon	Like Someone in Love Sleigh Ride in July (HP)
1945	The Bells of St. Mary's	Aren't You Glad You're You? (AN) (HP)

Year	Production Title	Popular Songs
1945	Road to Utopia	Personality (HP) Put It There, Pal Welcome to My Dream It's Anybody's Spring A Friend of Yours (HP)
	The Great John L Duffy's Tavern	"Yah-Ta-Ta, Yah-Ta-Ta"
1946	NELLIE BLY Cross My Heart	Just My Luck That Little Dream Got No- where So Would I My Heart Goes Crazy
	My Heart Goes Crazy	
1947	Welcome Stranger	As Long as I'm Dreaming My Heart Is a Hobo Country Style Smile Right Back at the Sun
	Road to Rio	But Beautiful (HP) You Don't Have to Know the Language Apalachicola, Florida
	Variety Girl Magic Town	
1948	The Emperor Waltz Mystery in Mexico	
1949	Top O' the Morning A Connecticut Yankee in King Arthur's Court	You're in Love with Someone Once and for Always When Is Sometime? If You Stub Your Toe on the Moon
1950	Riding High	Sunshine Cake Someplace on Anywhere Road
	Mr. Music	And You'll Be Home Life Is So Peculiar High on the List
		"Early American"
1952	Road to Bali	To See You Moonflowers
1953	CARNIVAL IN FLANDERS Little Boy Lost	Here's That Rainy Day The Magic Window
		"Wild Horses" "Now That I'm in Love"

Year	Production Title	Popular Songs
1955		"Misty"
1956	The Vagabond King	
		"From the First Hello to the Last Goodbye"
1961	DONNYBROOK!	He Makes Me Feel I'm Lovely
1963		"If Love Ain't There, It Ain't There"

* * *

JOSEPH A. BURKE

Joseph Burke was already thirty-two years old when he composed the music for his first hit "Down Honolulu Way" in 1916. He was born in Philadelphia, Pennsylvania and was educated at Philadelphia Catholic High School and the University of Pennsylvania. Before becoming a songwriter, he earned his livelihood as an arranger in a music publishing firm. Burke's first year creating for films produced "Painting the Clouds with Sunshine" and the most famous song he was ever to write--"Tip-Toe Through the Tulips." His lyric writer for these 1929 hits was Al Dubin but their partnership was cut short when Dubin began working with composer Harry Warren. In the mid-Thirties, Burke teamed with lyricist Edgar Leslie and their string of hits included "In a Little Gypsy Tea Room," "Robins and Roses," and "It Looks Like Rain in Cherry Blossom Lane." The magnitude of their success was evidenced by the January 4, 1936, broadcast of "Your Hit Parade" when the Number 1, Number 2, and Number 4 spots were occupied by Burke and Leslie's "A Little Bit Independent," "On Treasure Island," and "Moon Over Miami." Joe Burke came out of retirement to write the music for "Rambling Rose" in 1948. He died two years later at the age of sixty-six. In 1968, a bizarre entertainer named "Tiny Tim" rose to fame with a falsetto rendition of Burke's "Tip-Toe Through the Tulips."

Year	Production Title	Popular Songs
1916		"Down Honolulu Way"
1924		"Oh, How I Miss You To-night" "Dear One"
1925		"Yearning Just for You" "Who Wouldn't Love You?"

Year	Production Title	Popular Songs
1925		"No Other, No One but You" "She Was Just a Sailor's Sweetheart"
1926		"Roses Remind Me of You"
1927		"Heaven Help a Sailor on a Night Like This" "Oh, What a Pal Was 'Whoozis'" "Baby Your Mother"
1928	EARL CARROLL'S VANITIES	"Who Wouldn't Be Blue?" "Carolina Moon"
1929	Gold Diggers of Broadway	Tip-Toe Through the Tulips with Me Painting the Clouds with Sunshine
	In the Headlines Sally	Love Will Find a Way If I'm Dreaming, Don't Wake Me Up Too Soon Sally
	Show of Shows Applause	
1930	Dancing Sweeties She Couldn't Say No Oh, Sailor Beware Hold Everything The Cuckoos Top Speed Let's Go Places	The Kiss Waltz Watching My Dreams Go By
		"Dancing with Tears in My Eyes" "For You"
1931		"Crosby, Columbo and Vallee" "Many Happy Returns of the Day" "When the Rest of the Crowd Goes Home" "If You Should Ever Need Me" "Pagan Moon" "To Have and Hold You in My Arms"

Year	Production Title	Popular Songs
1932	Blessed Event The Crooner	
		"The Whisper Waltz" "Little Locket of Long Ago" "You'll Always Be the Same Sweetheart"
1933		"Shadows on the Swanee" "In the Valley of the Moon" "Good Night, Little Girl of My Dreams"
1934	Girl from Missouri Palooka	
		"I'm Lonesome for You, Caroline"
1935		"Moon Over Miami" (HP-1) "On Treasure Island" (HP-1) "A Little Bit Independent" (HP-1) "In a Little Gypsy Tea Room" (HP-1)
1936	THE ZIEGFELD FOLLIES	Midnight Blue "Cling to Me" (HP) "Robins and Roses" (HP) "A Little Rendezvous in Honolulu"
1937		"It Looks Like Rain in Cherry Blossom Lane" (HP-1) "Getting Some Fun Out of Life" "Moonlight on the Highway"
1938		"At a Perfume Counter" (HP) "Sailing at Midnight"
1939		"Rainbow Valley"
1940		"Dream Valley" (HP) "Harbor of Dreams"
1941		"A Tale of Two Cities"
1942	When Johnny Comes Marching Home	We Must Be Vigilant

Year	Production Title	Popular Songs
1943		"By the River of the Roses"
1944		"Diana"
1947	Trail to San Antone	
1948		"Rambling Rose"

* * *

IRVING CAESAR

Irving Caesar was born in New York City in 1895, and attended the Chappaqua Mountain Institute and the City College of New York. He was twenty-three years old when he became one of George Gershwin's first collaborators in 1918. Their "Swanee" is one of the two most famous songs in the Caesar catalog. The other, "Tea for Two" is one of the four most-recorded songs of all time. Caesar's lyrics have been featured in over three dozen Broadway musicals and he supplied the books for several of them. In addition to his show tunes, his hits include "Just a Gigolo," "If I Forget You" and "Is It True What They Say about Dixie?" Irving Caesar has worked with such widely disparate composers as Sigmund Romberg and Jimmy Durante. He has recorded an album of his best-known songs and was approaching eighty when he appeared on Broadway in a series featuring America's great lyric writers.

Year	Production Title	Popular Songs
1918	HITCHY-KOO THE RAINBOW GIRL SINBAD	You--oo, Just You I Am Thinking of You
1919	GOOD MORNING, JUDGE THE LADY IN RED MORRIS GEST'S MIDNIGHT WHIRL	I Was So Young "Swanee"
1920	BROADWAY BREVITIES THE SWEETHEART SHOP KISSING TIME DERE MABLE (closed in tryout)	 "The Hen and the Cow"
1921	BLUE EYES THE PERFECT FOOL	

Year	Production Title	Popular Songs
1921		"Swanee Rose" "Yan-kee" "No One Else but That Girl of Mine"
1922	MAKE IT SNAPPY SPICE OF 1922 THE GREENWICH VILLAGE FOLLIES PINS AND NEEDLES RAYMOND HITCHCOCK'S PINWHEEL	I Love Her, She Loves Me The Yankee Doodle Blues Sixty Seconds Every Minute, I Think of You Nightingale, Bring Me a Rose
1923	POPPY NIFTIES OF 1923 THE GREENWICH VILLAGE FOLLIES THE DANCING GIRL JACK AND JILL	Someone Will Make You Smile What Do You Do Sunday, Mary? Nashville Nightingale Annabel Lee
1924	BETTY LEE	
1925	NO, NO NANETTE CHARLOT'S REVUE THE GREENWICH VILLAGE FOLLIES A NIGHT OUT (closed in tryout)	Tea for Two I Want to Be Happy You Can Dance with Any Girl at All Too Many Rings Around Rosie Gigolette
1926	SWEETHEART TIME NO FOOLIN' BETSY	
1927	HIT THE DECK YES, YES YVETTE TALK ABOUT GIRLS	Sometimes I'm Happy I'm a Little Bit Fonder of You
1928	HERE'S HOWE	Crazy Rhythm Imagination

Year	Production Title	Popular Songs
1928	WHOOPEE	My Blackbirds Are Bluebirds Now
	AMERICANA	
		"Dear, on a Night Like This"
		"It Goes Like This"
		"You're a Real Sweetheart"
1929	POLLY	
		"Buy, Buy for Baby"
		"Satisfied"
		"Blue Hawaii"
1930	NINA ROSA	Serenade of Love
		Nina Rosa
		Your Smiles, Your Tears
	RIPPLES	There's Nothing Wrong in a Kiss
		"Just a Gigolo"
		"Lady, Play Your Mandolin"
1931	THE WONDER BAR	Elizabeth
		Good Evening Friends
		Oh, Donna Clara
		"Under a Roof in Paree"
1932	The Crooner	Sweethearts Forever
	The Kid from Spain	What a Perfect Combination
		"What! No Mickey Mouse? What Kind of a Party Is This?"
1933	MELODY	Give Me a Roll on the Drum
		You Are the Song
		"If I Forget You"
1934	George White's Scandals	(Oh, You) Nasty Man
		Hold My Hand
		My Dog Loves Your Dog
	Palooka	Count Your Blessings
		"South American Joe"
1935	Curly Top	Animal Crackers in My Soup
		"Dust Off That Old Pianna"

Year	Production Title	Popular Songs
1936	WHITE HORSE INN	Blue Eyes I Cannot Live Without Your Love
	Stowaway	That's What I Want for Christmas
		"Is It True What They Say About Dixie?" (HP-1) "Saskatchewan"
1937		"Vienna Dreams"
1939		"Love Is Such a Cheat"
1943	MY DEAR PUBLIC	
1944	Music for Millions	Umbriago

* * *

SAMMY CAHN

Lyricist Sammy Cahn has received more Academy Award nominations than any song writer in history. Over a period of thirty-three years, he's received 26 nominations--and has won four "Oscars"! In four separate years he competed against himself having two songs nominated for the same award. Cahn ranks third, in a tie with lyricist Mack Gordon, in the number (11) of his songs that made the Number One spot on Your Hit Parade.

Samuel "Cohen" was born in New York City in 1913. During the early years of his career, he made his living working at odd jobs and writing special material for night club performers and dance bands. He also played the violin in vaudeville orchestras, and formed his own band with Saul Chaplin. In 1937, an adaptation he and Chaplin made of a Yiddish popular song was recorded by a new trio named The Andrews Sisters. The song "Bei Mir Bist Du Schön" swept the country and was a juke box favorite for months.

Cahn's success in Tin Pan Alley attracted the attention of filmmakers and he and composer Chaplin were hired to write for the screen. A milestone in Cahn's movie career occurred when he began a partnership with composer Jule Styne in the early 1940's. Their hits "I've Heard That Song Before" and "I'll Walk Alone" earned Academy Award considerations in 1942 and 1944. They also created the score for the 1944 stage musical "Glad to See You." Although the show closed during its tryouts, their song "Guess I'll Hang My Tears Out to Dry" survived. Styne and Cahn went on to another "Oscar" nomination for "I Fall in Love Too Easily" in 1945. Two years later they made their second try at invading Broadway. Their success was in sharp contrast to the failure of their first attempt. "High Button Shoes" not only made it to New York but became the longest-running musical of its season.

After the success of "High Button Shoes," Cahn returned to Hollywood where he worked on half a dozen films at Warner Bros. The most important was "Romance on the High Seas" in which band singer Doris Day was introduced to movie audiences. The film included "It's Magic" which earned Cahn his fifth Academy Award nomination. In 1950, MGM released "The Toast of New Orleans" in which its new discovery, tenor Mario Lanza, sang the memorable "Be My Love." The song was one of Cahn's earliest collaborations with composer Nicholas Brodszky. Cahn and Brodszky accumulated four nominations during their partnership. After nine chances at the "Oscar," Cahn finally collected his first for "Three Coins in the Fountain" with music by Styne.

Another name heard frequently at the Academy ceremonies is that of composer James Van Heusen. In 1955, Cahn and Van Heusen began one of the most profitable collaborations in popular music history. Their initial efforts earned them an Academy nomination for the title song from "The Tender Trap," and won them television's "Emmy" for "Love and Marriage" written for a musical adaptation of Thornton Wilder's "Our Town." The golden statuette won for "Three Coins in the Fountain" became twins in 1957, triplets in 1959, and quadruplets in 1963!

The performer most closely associated with Cahn is Frank Sinatra. Their association began when Sinatra was first singing with the Tommy Dorsey Orchestra. He's sung Cahn's lyrics in a dozen films and his numerous record albums abound with Cahn numbers. On the brink of his first retirement in 1965, Sinatra recorded an album of middle-age-oriented numbers and Cahn wrote the lyrics for the album's title song "September of My Years."

Sammy Cahn's 1965 Broadway musical "Skyscraper" ran for a disappointing 241 performances despite such songs as "Everybody Has the Right to Be Wrong" and "I'll Only Miss Her When I Think of Her." The following year, he supplied the lyrics for "Walking Happy" which had an even shorter New York run but managed to tour the United States. While theatre audiences were enjoying live performances of "Walking Happy," moviegoers were flocking to see Julie Andrews in the 1967 release "Thoroughly Modern Millie." The next year, Miss Andrews appeared in a film biography of Gertrude Lawrence. It almost goes without saying that Sammy Cahn and Jimmy Van Heusen's title songs for both films were nominated as the Best Film Song of the Year.

Cahn's most recent Broadway musical has been "Look to the Lilies." The production, with music by Jule Styne, opened in 1970

and ran for less than a month. The year 1974 found sixty-one
year old Cahn appearing in person on Broadway in "Words and Music"--a presentation of his own songs. The show ran for four
months after which it was staged in London and Los Angeles. Cahn
has published an autobiography titled "I Should Care" (a hit song
from the 1945 film "Thrill of a Romance"), and has been approached
regarding a motion picture based on a segment of his career.

    Sammy Cahn has contributed songs to more than 100 motion
pictures, and seven stage productions. Which composer writes the
music for his lyrics appears to be incidental. In 1973, composer
George Barrie collaborated with Cahn on a song for the film "A
Touch of Class." "All That Love Went to Waste" won newcomer
Barrie his first "Oscar" nomination--and Sammy Cahn his twenty-
fifth! Cahn's latest nomination has been for "Now That We're in
Love" from the 1975 release "Whiffs." He was featured in a segment of the 1976 film "That's Entertainment--Part II."

Year	Production Title	Popular Songs
1935		"Rhythm in My Nursery Rhymes" (HP) "Rhythm Is Our Business"
1936		"Until the Real Thing Comes Along" (HP) "Shoe-Shine Boy" "I'm One Step Ahead of My Shadow" "Rhythm Saved the World"
1937		"Bei Mir Bist Du Schön" (HP-1) "If It's the Last Thing I Do" (HP) "Posin'" "If You Ever Should Leave" "Dedicated to You"
1938		"Please Be Kind" (HP-1) "Saving Myself for You" "Joseph, Joseph" "Wait Till My Heart Finds Out"
1939		"I Want My Share of Love" (HP) "It's Easy to Blame the Weather" "It's My Turn Now" "You're a Lucky Guy"
1940	Ladies Must Live	I Could Make You Care

SAMMY CAHN

Year	Production Title	Popular Songs
1940	Argentine Nights	
1941	Time Out for Rhythm	As If You Didn't Know Twiddlin' My Thumbs
	Go West, Young Lady Sing for Your Supper Rookies on Parade Two Latins from Manhattan Honolulu Lu	
		"The End of the Rainbow"
1942	Youth on Parade	I've Heard That Song Before (AN) (HP-1)
	Two Yanks in Trinidad Johnny Doughboy Blondie Goes to College Blondie's Blessed Event	
		"We All Together"
1943	Crazy House Let's Face It Thumbs Up Lady of Burlesque The Heat's On	
1944	GLAD TO SEE YOU (closed in tryout) Follow the Boys Jam Session Carolina Blues	Guess I'll Hang My Tears Out to Dry I'll Walk Alone (AN) (HP-1) The Vict'ry Polka There Goes That Song Again (HP) Poor Little Rhode Island
	Step Lively	Come Out, Come Out Wher- ever You Are And Then You Kissed Me (HP)
	Knickerbocker Holiday Janie	
		"It's Been a Long, Long Time" (HP-1) "Saturday Night (Is the Lone- liest Night in the Week)" (HP)
1945	Anchors Aweigh	I Fall in Love Too Easily (AN) The Charm of You I Begged Her What Makes the Sunset?
	Tonight and Every Night	Anywhere (AN)

Year	Production Title	Popular Songs
1945	Thrill of a Romance	I Should Care (HP)
	The Stork Club	
	A Song to Remember	"Day by Day" (HP)
		"Let It Snow, Let It Snow, Let It Snow" (HP-1)
		"Can't You Read Between the Lines?" (HP)
1946	Cinderella Jones	When the One You Love Simply Won't Love Back
	Earl Carroll's Sketch Book	I've Never Forgotten
	Tars and Spars	I'm Glad I Waited for You
	Sweetheart of Sigma Chi	Five Minutes More (HP-1)
	The Kid from Brooklyn	I Love an Old-Fashioned Song
		You're the Cause of It All
		"The Things We Did Last Summer" (HP)
1947	HIGH BUTTON SHOES	You're My Girl
		Papa, Won't You Dance with Me?
		On a Sunday by the Sea
		I Still Get Jealous
	It Happened in Brooklyn	Time After Time (HP)
		It's the Same Old Dream
		I Believe
	Ladies' Man	What Am I Gonna Do About You?
		I Gotta Gal I Love
1948	Romance on the High Seas	It's Magic (AN) (HP-1)
		It's You or No One
	Two Guys from Texas	Every Day I Love You
		I Don't Care If It Rains All Night
	Sons of Adventure	
	Miracle of the Bells	
1949	It's a Great Feeling	It's a Great Feeling (AN) (HP)
		Fiddle Dee Dee (HP)
		Blame My Absent-Minded Heart
		At the Cafe Rendezvous
	Always Leave Them Laughing	
1950	The Toast of New Orleans	Be My Love (AN) (HP)
		I'll Never Love You
	Young Man with a Horn	Melancholy Rhapsody

Year	Production Title	Popular Songs
1950	The West Point Story	"Go to Sleep, Go to Sleep, Go to Sleep"
1951	Rich, Young and Pretty Two Tickets to Broadway Double Dynamite	Wonder Why (AN)
1952	Because You're Mine April in Paris She's Working Her Way Through College	Because You're Mine (AN) (HP)
1953	Three Sailors and a Girl Peter Pan	Face to Face
1954	Three Coins in the Fountain Indiscretion of an American Wife A Woman's World Vera Cruz	Three Coins in the Fountain (AA) (HP-1) Autumn in Rome Indiscretion "Teach Me Tonight" (HP-1)
1955	Love Me or Leave Me The Tender Trap Pete Kelly's Blues You're Never Too Young How to Be Very, Very Popular Our Town (TV)	I'll Never Stop Loving You (AN) (Love Is) The Tender Trap (AN) Pete Kelly's Blues Love and Marriage (HP) The Impatient Years Look to Your Heart
1956	THE LITTLEST REVUE Written on the Wind Somebody Up There Likes Me Forever Darling Meet Me in Las Vegas The Opposite Sex Anything Goes Serenade The Court Jester Pardners	Written on the Wind (AN) Somebody Up There Likes Me Forever Darling "Hey, Jealous Lover" (HP) "It's Better in the Dark"

Year	Production Title	Popular Songs
1957	The Joker Is Wild Until They Sail Don't Go Near the Water Ten Thousand Bedrooms	All the Way (AA) (HP-1)
1958	Some Came Running The Long Hot Summer Indiscreet Rock-A-Bye Baby Party Girl Paris Holiday Kings Go Forth	To Love and Be Loved (AN) The Long Hot Summer Indiscreet Dormi, Dormi, Dormi "Only the Lonely" "Come Fly with Me"
1959	A Hole in the Head Best of Everything They Came to Cordura This Earth Is Mine Say One for Me Journey to the Center of the Earth Night of the Quarter Moon	High Hopes (AA) All My Tomorrows The Best of Everything (AN) They Came to Cordura
1960	High Time Wake Me When It's Over Let's Make Love Ocean's Eleven The World of Suzie Wong Who Was That Lady?	The Second Time Around (AN) Wake Me When It's Over
1961	Pocketful of Miracles By Love Possessed The Pleasure of His Company	Pocketful of Miracles (AN)
1962	COME ON STRONG (play) How the West Was Won Boys' Night Out Road to Hong Kong	Home in the Meadow The Boys' Night Out Warmer Than a Whisper "If and When"
1963	Papa's Delicate Condition My Six Loves Come Blow Your Horn Under the Yum Yum Tree Johnny Cool	Call Me Irresponsible (AA)

SAMMY CAHN

Year	Production Title	Popular Songs
1964	Robin and the 7 Hoods	My Kind of Town (AN) Style I Like to Lead When I Dance
	Where Love Has Gone The Pleasure Seekers	Where Love Has Gone (AN) Everything Makes Music When You're in Love
		"Love Is a Bore"
1965	SKYSCRAPER	I Only Miss Her When I Think of Her Everybody Has the Right to Be Wrong
		"September of My Years"
1966	WALKING HAPPY	What Makes It Happen? Walking Happy
1967	Thoroughly Modern Millie	Thoroughly Modern Millie (AN)
1968	Star! A Flea in Her Ear	Star! (AN)
1969	The Great Bank Robbery	
1970	LOOK TO THE LILIES	
1971	Journey Back to Oz (TV)	
1973	A Touch of Class	
1975	Whiffs Paper Tiger	
1976	I Will, I Will...for Now The Duchess and the Dirtwater Fox	
1977	Once Upon a Brothers Grimm (TV)	

* * *

HOAGY CARMICHAEL

The name of Hoagy Carmichael is familiar to the public

mainly because of his motion picture roles and his recordings.
Carmichael was born in Bloomington, Indiana in 1899, and dropped
out of high school in his freshman year to work as a laborer.
When he returned to school after World War I, he organized a
small band which played at local dances.   His original vocation was
law, and he worked his way through Indiana University arranging
bookings for orchestras he organized and playing the piano in summer resorts.   His interest in jazz music crystallized during his
school years, and he composed "Washboard Blues" a year before
he obtained his degree.   He cut a record of the song with the Paul
Whiteman Orchestra and its success caused him to abandon law in
favor of a career in music.

        Carmichael's most famous melody "Stardust" was published
when he was thirty years old.   It became one of the four most-recorded songs in popular music history.   The composer continued as
a recording artist while writing such hits as "Rockin' Chair," "Lazybones" and "Little Old Lady."   He began supplying music for motion
pictures in 1936 and his film scores produced "Small Fry," "Heart
and Soul" and "Two Sleepy People"--all with lyrics by Frank Loesser.   The climax of his career in Hollywood was winning the "Oscar" for his music to "In the Cool, Cool, Cool of the Evening" in
1951.   Although he generally works with a lyricist, Hoagy Carmichael wrote both words and music for the 1939 success "Blue Or-
chids."   Among his best-remembered screen performances are
those in "To Have and Have Not," "Night Song," "Canyon Passage,"
"The Best Years of Our Lives" and "Belles on Their Toes."

Year	Production Title	Popular Songs
1925		"Washboard Blues"
1929		"Stardust" "One Night in Havana"
1930		"Rockin' Chair" "Georgia on My Mind" (HP)
1931		"Lazy River" "After Twelve O'Clock" "Come Easy, Go Easy Love"
1932		"Daybreak" "Thanksgivin'" "New Orleans" "In the Still of the Night"
1933		"Lazybones" "One Morning in May" "Ole Faithful" "Snowball" "Old Man Harlem"

Year	Production Title	Popular Songs
1934		"Judy" "Moon Country (Is Home to Me)"
1935		"Ballad in Blue" "Down 't Uncle Bill's" "Mister Bluebird"
1936	THE SHOW IS ON Anything Goes	Little Old Lady (HP-1) Moonburn "Sing Me a Swing Song"
1937	Topper Every Day's a Holiday I Met Him in Paris	Old Man Moon Jubilee
1938	Romance in the Dark Sing You Sinners Say It in French Thanks for the Memory A Song Is Born (short subject) College Swing Men with Wings	The Nearness of You (HP) Small Fry (HP) April in My Heart Two Sleepy People (HP) Heart and Soul (HP)
1939	St. Louis Blues	Kinda Lonesome "Blue Orchids" (HP-1) "I Get Along without You Very Well" (HP) "Hong Kong Blues" "Riverboat Shuffle" "Vagabond Dreams"
1940	WALK WITH MUSIC	The Rhumba Jumps I Walk with Music Way Back in 1939 A. D. Ooh, What You Said "Can't Get Indiana Off My Mind"
1941	Road Show Mr. Bug Goes to Town	I Should Have Known You Years Ago We're the Couple in the Castle (HP)
1942		"Skylark" (HP) "Lamplighter's Serenade"

Year	Production Title	Popular Songs
1942		"Don't Forget to Say 'No,' Baby"
1943	True to Life Hands Across the Border	The Old Music Master Hands Across the Border "Drip Drop"
1944	To Have and Have Not	How Little We Know "When Love Walks By"
1945	The Stork Club Johnny Angel	Doctor, Lawyer, Indian Chief (HP) Memphis in June "Baltimore Oriole" "No More Toujours L'Amour"
1946	Canyon Passage	Ole Buttermilk Sky (AN) (HP-1) Rogue River Valley "Things Have Changed"
1947	Ivy Night Song	Ivy (HP) Who Killed 'er (Who Killed the Black Widder?) "Casanova Cricket" "Put Yourself in My Place, Baby"
1948		"Bubble-Loo" "Sad Cowboy" "Just a Shade on the Blue Side"
1949		"The Three Rivers" "Follow the Swallow to Hide-a-way Hollow" "Grandma Teeter-Totter"
1950	ALIVE AND KICKING	If You Don't Love Me "A Woman Likes to Be Told"
1951	Here Comes the Groom	In the Cool, Cool, Cool of the Evening" (AA) (HP-1)

Year	Production Title	Popular Songs
1952	The Las Vegas Story	My Resistance Is Low
		"Watermelon Weather"
1953	Gentlemen Prefer Blondes Those Redheads from Seattle	When Love Goes Wrong
1955	Timberjack	
1957		"Music, Always Music"
1958		"Mediterranean Love"
1962	Hatari	Just for Tonight
1963		"There Goes Another Pal of Mine"

* * *

GRANT CLARKE

Lyricist Grant Clarke was a product of Akron, Ohio, where he was born in 1891. After high school, he became an actor in a stock company and then joined a music publisher's staff. He celebrated his eighteenth birthday and the success of his first hit in 1909. Three years later, his "Ragtime Cowboy Joe" (music by Maurice Abrahams and Lewis Muir) swept the country. Songs with words by Clarke were heard in 13 Broadway productions before he became associated with motion pictures. One of his best show tunes was "Second Hand Rose" (music by James Hanley) which Fanny Brice introduced in "The Ziegfeld Follies" in 1921. He also wrote material for Bert Williams, Eva Tanguay, and Al Jolson, and provided the words for Harry Akst's melody "Am I Blue" which Ethel Waters sang in the 1929 film "On with the Show." Grant Clarke had just completed work on his 13th motion picture in two years when he died in 1931. He was only forty years old.

Year	Production Title	Popular Songs
1909		"When You're in Love with Someone"
1911	THE ZIEGFELD FOLLIES	Dat's Harmony
1912	MODEST SUZANNE BROADWAY TO PARIS	
		"Ragtime Cowboy Joe"

Year	Production Title	Popular Songs
1913	THE PLEASURE SEEKERS	He'd Have to Get Under (Get Out and Get Under)
		Sit Down, You're Rocking the Boat
		"Oh, You Million Dollar Doll"
		"Down in Monkeyville"
		"Salvation Nell"
		"You Can't Get Away from It"
1914	OUR AMERICAN BOY	I Love the Ladies
		"He's a Devil in His Own Home Town"
		"On the Steps of the Great White Capitol"
		"The 20th Century Rag"
		"Back to the Carolina You Love"
1915		"Beatrice Fairfax"
		"Goodbye, Virginia"
1916	ROBINSON CRUSOE JR.	You're a Dog Gone Dangerous Girl
		"The Honolulu Blues"
		"Honolulu, America Loves You"
		"You Can't Get Along with 'em or without 'em"
		"I Know I Got More Than My Share"
		"There's a Little Bit of Bad in Every Good Little Girl"
1917	THE COHAN REVUE OF 1918	
1918		"In the Land of Beginning Again"
		"I Hate to Lose You"
		"If He Can Fight Like He Can Love, Good Night, Germany"
		"Everything Is Peaches Down in Georgia"
		"You'll Find Old Dixieland in France"

Year	Production Title	Popular Songs
1919		"Anything Is Nice If It Comes from Dixie Land"
1920	THE ZIEGFELD FOLLIES	Smart Little Feller, Stock Up Your Cellar
	SILKS AND SATINS	My Little Bimbo Down on the Bamboo Isle
	ED WYNN CARNIVAL	I Love the Land of Old Black Joe
		"Tired of Me"
1921	THE ZIEGFELD FOLLIES	Second Hand Rose
	SNAPSHOTS OF 1921	Now I Know
1922		"Blue (and Broken-Hearted)"
		"Don't Feel Sorry for Me"
		"Oogie Oogie Wa Wa (Means 'I Wanna Mama' to an Eskimo)"
1923		"Dirty Hands, Dirty Face"
		"Home in Pasadena"
1924	DIXIE TO BROADWAY	Mandy, Make Up Your Mind
		Dixie Dreams
		I'm a Little Blackbird Looking for a Bluebird
1928		"Avalon Town"
1929	On with the Show	Am I Blue?
		Birmingham Bertha
	Weary River	Weary River
	Broadway Babies	Wishing and Waiting for Love
	Is Everybody Happy?	I'm the Medicine Man for the Blues
		Wouldn't It Be Wonderful?
	Saturday's Children	
	The Squall	
	Sacred Flame	
1930	So Long Letty	My Strongest Weakness Is You
	Dancing Sweeties	
	Golden Dawn	
	No, No Nanette	
	Song of the Flame	
	Song of the West	

Year	Production Title	Popular Songs
1931	Bright Lights	Nobody Cares If I'm Blue
		"Thanks to You"

* * *

CON CONRAD

The Academy of Motion Picture Arts and Sciences established its Best Song category in 1934. The first composer to win the Award was forty-three year old Con Conrad for "The Continental." He was born in New York City in 1891 where he was christened Conrad K. Dober. After military academy schooling, he played the piano in movie houses and toured the United States and Europe as a vaudeville performer. During the 1920's, Conrad had songs featured in 13 Broadway productions. When sound revolutionized the film industry, Conrad transferred his talents permanently to Hollywood where he worked primarily with lyricists Sidney Mitchell and Herb Magidson. His music was heard in over two dozen motion pictures before he died in 1938-- four years after receiving popular music's first Academy Award.

Year	Production Title	Popular Songs
1912		"Down in Dear Old New Orleans"
1918		"Oh, Frenchy"
1920	ED WYNN CARNIVAL	"Margie" "Palesteena" "Singin' the Blues (Till My Daddy Comes Home)"
1921	THE MIDNIGHT ROUNDERS SNAPSHOTS OF 1921 BOMBO	Ma, He's Making Eyes at Me "That Barber in Seville" "Mimi" "Moonlight" "Mandy 'n' Me"
1922		"Barney Google" "You Gotta See Mama Every Night" "California"
1923	THE GREENWICH VILLAGE FOLLIES	

Year	Production Title	Popular Songs
1923		"Come On, Spark Plug" "Steppin' Out" "Somebody Else Took You Out of My Arms"
1924	MOONLIGHT BETTY LEE	"She's Everybody's Sweet- heart" "Mah Jong" "Memory Lane"
1925	BIG BOY MERCENARY MARY THE COMIC SUPPLEMENT	Miami Mercenary Mary
1926	KITTY'S KISSES AMERICANA LIDO LADY (London)	"Lonesome and Sorry"
1927	TAKE THE AIR	
1928		"Dear, on a Night Like This" "The Song I Love"
1929	Fox Movietone Follies of 1929 Broadway Words and Music Christiana Skin Deep Song of Kentucky They Had to See Paris Cock-Eyed World	Look What You've Done to Me That's You, Baby The Breakaway Walking with Susie Big City Blues Hittin' the Ceiling Sing a Little Love Song "Why Can't I Be Like You?"
1930	Happy Days New Movietone Follies of 1930 Let's Go Places	Crazy Feet Mona Here Comes Emily Brown "Football Freddie, My Colle- giate Man" "Skippy" "Don't Send My Boy to Prison"

Year	Production Title	Popular Songs
1930		"Nine Little Miles from Ten-Ten Tennessee"
1931	Palmy Days	Bend Down, Sister My Baby Said Yes, Yes
	Age for Love	
		"At Last I'm Happy" "You Call It Madness but I Call It Love"
1932		"Lonesome Me"
1933	Wine, Women and Song	
		"I May Be Dancing with Somebody Else"
1934	The Gay Divorcee	The Continental (AA) A Needle in a Haystack
	Gift of Gab	Talking to Myself Blue Sky Avenue
	Goodbye Love Social Register	
		"Champagne Waltz"
1935	Here's to Romance	Midnight in Paris Here's to Romance (HP)
	Reckless King Solomon of Broadway	
1936	I'd Give My Life	

Posthumous:

1939	The Story of Vernon and Irene Castle	Only When You're in My Arms
1940	Nobody's Children	

* * *

J. FRED COOTS

One of the most successful Broadway composers of the 1920's was Brooklyn-born J. Fred Coots. After completing high school, he worked for a bank, as a stock clerk, and playing the piano in vaudeville, night clubs, and music publishing houses. He soon began writing special material for vaudeville artists and then became a performer himself. He was twenty-five years old when the producer of "Sally, Irene

and Mary" engaged him to supply the music for the show. It proved to
be one of the longest running Broadway productions of 1922. One of
the last of his stage musicals was the long-run 1929 hit "Sons O' Guns."
Coots' work for Broadway was largely eclipsed by his music for the
standards "For All We Know," "You Go to My Head" and "Santa Claus
Is Coming to Town." He was one of the few songwriters of the Thirties
who remained successful without the benefit of motion pictures to promote his music. Coots' "Goodbye, Mama, I'm Off to Yokohama" was
one of the earliest hits of World War II. J. Fred Coots was born in
1897 and retired from popular music activities in 1970.

Year	Production Title	Popular Songs
1922	SPICE OF 1922 SALLY, IRENE AND MARY	In My Little Red Book Time Will Tell I Wonder Why
1923	DEW DROP INN	"Home Town Blues" "Not Yet, Suzette"
1924	INNOCENT EYES ARTISTS AND MODELS	Innocent Eyes Tomorrow's Another Day
1925	ARTISTS AND MODELS JUNE DAYS MAYFLOWERS GAY PAREE	The Promenade Walk Remembering You Put Your Troubles in a Candy Box
1926	THE MERRY WORLD A NIGHT IN PARIS	Sunday
1927	WHITE LIGHTS	
1928		"Doin' the Racoon" "It Was the Dawn of Love" "Moonlight Madness" "A Love Tale of Alsace Lor- raine"
1929	SONS O' GUNS Shopworn Angel Why Be Good?	Cross Your Fingers Why? It's You I Love A Precious Little Thing Called Love "Pal of My Sweetheart Days" "Here Comes My Ball and Chain"
1930	RIPPLES	

Year	Production Title	Popular Songs
1930		"I Miss a Little Miss" "I Still Get a Thrill (Thinking of You)"
1931		"Love Letters in the Sand" (HP-1)
1932		"Here's Hoping" "You'll Get By" "Strangers" "I Wouldn't Trade the Silver in My Mother's Hair" "There's Oceans of Love by the Beautiful Sea"
1933		"Two Tickets to Georgia" "I Want to Ring Bells" "One Minute to One" "This Time It's Love"
1934		"Santa Claus Is Comin' to Town" (HP) "For All We Know" "I Knew You When"
1935		"A Beautiful Lady in Blue" (HP) "Things Might Have Been So Diff'rent" "Louisiana Fairy Tale" "Whose Honey Are You?" "It Never Dawned on Me" "It's Mating Time"
1936		"You Started Me Dreaming" (HP) "Who Loves You?" (HP) "Yours Truly Is Truly Yours" "Copper-Colored Gal" "Until Today" "I'll Stand By" "I'm Grateful to You" "Doin' the Suzi-Q" "In My Estimation of You" "A Little Robin Told Me So" "Isn't Love the Strangest Thing?" "The More I Know You" "Why Do I Lie to Myself About You?" "Friendly Moon"

Year	Production Title	Popular Songs
1936		"Frisco Flo" "Alabama Barbecue"
1937		"In Your Own Little Way"
1938		"You Go to My Head" (HP) "There's Honey on the Moon Tonight" (HP) "Summer Souvenirs" (HP) "I'm Madly in Love with You" "Miss Hallelujah Brown" "Blue and Disillusioned"
1939		"Let's Stop the Clock"
1940		"I'll Wait for You Forever" "Wait Till I Catch You in My Dreams" "Wrap Your Dreams in the Red, White and Blue"
1941		"Goodbye, Mama, I'm Off to Yokohama"
1947		"Encore, Cherie" "I Can't Believe It Was All Make Believe Last Night"
1949		"It's Too Late Now"
1952		"When the Teddy Bears Go Marching on Parade"
1953		"Me and My Teddy Bear"
1958		"Let's Make Memories To-night"
1961		"What's Gonna Be with You and Me?"

* * *

SAM COSLOW

New York-born Sam Coslow writes both music and lyrics but generally works with another composer and frequently with a co-lyricist. His first popular song was published in 1919 when he was

only seventeen.   Ten years later, he migrated to Hollywood where
he was one of the busiest writers on the Paramount lot.   His songs
"Sing, You Sinners," "Learn to Croon," "Moon Song" and "My Old
Flame" were introduced by such box office favorites as Lillian
Roth, Bing Crosby, Kate Smith and Mae West.   Coslow made recordings as a vocalist during the Thirties.   In 1940, he and Col.
James Roosevelt founded "Soundies"--a firm that manufactured
coin-operated machines which showed film short subjects.   He won
his only "Oscar" for the short subject "Heavenly Music" which he
produced in 1943.   He soon branched out into producing full-length
motion pictures.   After writing for English stage and screen attractions in 1954 and 1955, he devoted himself full-time to publishing
trade periodicals serving the investment business.   Seventy-six
year old Sam Coslow now lives in retirement in New York.

Year	Production Title	Popular Songs
1919		"Alleesamee"
1920		"Grieving for You" "It Might Have Been You"
1921		"Dixie"
1922		"Kitten on the Keys"
1923		"Bebe, Be Mine" "Not Yet, Suzette"
1924	ARTISTS AND MODELS	Tomorrow's Another Day
1926		"I'm Just Wild About Animal Crackers" "Hello! Swanee--Hello!" "Don't Take That Black Bot- tom Away"
1927		"Lonely Melody" "One Summer Night"
1928		"Was It a Dream?"
1929	Dance of Life Fast Company Why Bring That Up? The Time, the Place and the Girl Thunderbolt River of Romance	True Blue Lou You Want Lovin' (but I Want Love) "Can You Read in My Eyes?"

Year	Production Title	Popular Songs
1930	Vagabond King	If I Were King
	Honey	Sing, You Sinners
		In My Little Hope Chest
	Paramount on Parade	Sweepin' the Clouds Away
	Reno	
	Silent Enemy	
1931	Monkey Business	Just One More Chance
		"You Didn't Know the Music"
		"Tabu"
		"Is This the Music of Love?"
1932	This Is the Night	This Is the Night
	Blonde Venus	
	Lady and Gent	
1933	College Humor	Learn to Croon
		Down the Old Ox Road
		Moonstruck
	Too Much Harmony	Thanks
		The Day You Came Along
		Black Moonlight
		I Guess It Had to Be That Way
	Hello, Everybody!	Moon Song
	Her Bodyguard	
	Way to Love	
	Disgraced!	
	From Hell to Heaven	
1934	Murder at the Vanities	Cocktails for Two
		Live and Love Tonight
		Ebony Rhapsody
	Eight Girls in a Boat	This Little Piggie Went to Market
	Belle of the Nineties	My Old Flame
		Troubled Waters
	You Belong to Me	When He Comes Home to Me
	Search for Beauty	
	Many Happy Returns	
	Limehouse Blues	
	You're Telling Me	
1935	College Scandal	In the Middle of a Kiss (HP-1)
	The Big Broadcast of 1936	Crooner's Lullaby
	All the King's Horses	A Little White Gardenia

Year	Production Title	Popular Songs
1935	Coronado	How Do I Rate with You?
		You Took My Breath Away
	Goin' to Town	Now I'm a Lady
	Remember Last Night	
	The Gilded Lily	
	Ruggles of Red Gap	
	Oh! Daddy	
	One Hour Late	
1936	Rhythm on the Range	(If You Can't Sing It) You'll Have to Swing It
	It's Love Again	It's Love Again
	The Texas Rangers	The Texas Ranger Song
	Klondike Annie	
	Poppy	
	Fatal Lady	
	Heart of the West	
1937	True Confession	True Confession (HP)
	100 Men and a Girl	It's Raining Sunbeams
	This Way Please	Is It Love or Infatuation?
	Turn Off the Moon	Turn Off the Moon
	Every Day's a Holiday	Every Day's a Holiday
	Mountain Music	Good Mornin'
	Thrill of a Lifetime	Thrill of a Lifetime
	Double or Nothing	After You
	Swing High, Swing Low	
	Champagne Waltz	
	Hideaway Girl	
	Make Way for Tomorrow	
		"Tea on the Terrace"
1938	Love on Toast	I'd Love to Play a Love Scene Opposite You
		I Want a New Romance
	Booloo	Beside a Moonlit Stream
	Romance in the Dark	
	You and Me	
		"Have You Forgotten So Soon?" (HP)
1939	Society Lawyer	I'm in Love with the Honorable Mr. So and So
		Kinda Lonesome
	St. Louis Blues	
		"At a Little Hot Dog Stand"
		"Tomorrow Night"
		"A New Moon and an Old Serenade" (HP)
		"An Old Curiousity Shop"

Year	Production Title	Popular Songs
1939		"A Table in a Corner"
1940	Dreaming Out Loud Brigham Young	Dreaming Out Loud "Make-Believe Island" (HP-1)
1943	Heavenly Music (short subject) Hangmen Also Die	Heavenly Music
1944	Practically Yours	
1945	Out of This World	I'd Rather Be Me
1946	Song of the South	
1947	Carnegie Hall Copacabana	Beware, My Heart Je Vous Aime "Everybody Loves Somebody"
1948	Sleep, My Love	
1951	His Kind of Woman	
1953	Affair with a Stranger	
1955		"Blue Mirage"
1956		"One Kiss Away from Heaven"

* * *

HAL DAVID

Hal David graduated from high school in his home town of
Brooklyn, New York, and studied journalism at New York University. He began writing lyrics while serving with an entertainment
unit in Hawaii during World War II. After the armistice, he supplied special material for orchestra leader Sammy Kaye. David
was twenty-seven years old when his first hit "Schoene Mädel"
(Music by Don Rodney) was published in 1948. Nine years later,
he began working with composer Burt Bacharach and their "The
Story of My Life" and "Magic Moments" were national favorites in
1957. David's lyrics for the film songs "What's New Pussycat?,"
"Alfie," and "The Look of Love" earned him Academy Award nominations, and he won the 1969 "Oscar" for "Raindrops Keep Fallin' on

My Head." He and Bacharach wrote the score for the 1968 stage
hit "Promises, Promises" which is the 17th longest-running musical in Broadway history. Their partnership was dissolved after
completing the score for the 1973 film "Lost Horizon." Many of
David's lyrics are included in his book "What the World Needs Now
and Other Lyrics." He's the younger brother of popular song writer Mack David.

Year	Production Title	Popular Songs
1948		"Schoene Mädel (Pretty Girl)"
1949		"Four Winds and the Seven Seas" (HP)
1950		"American Beauty Rose"
1951		"A House Is a Home"
1953		"Bell Bottom Blues"
1954		"The Heart of a Fool"
1955		"What Do You See in Her?"
1957	The Sad Sack Lizzie	"The Story of My Life" "Magic Moments"
1958		"My Heart Is an Open Book"
1959		"Broken-Hearted Melody"
1960		"I Cry Alone" "Sea of Heartbreak" "Our Concerto"
1961		"No Regrets" "You'll Answer to Me" "Don't Envy Me" "La Charanga"
1962	The Man Who Shot Liberty Valance Hatari! Forever My Love Wonderful to Be Young!	The Man Who Shot Liberty Valance Baby Elephant Walk Forever My Love Wonderful to Be Young! "True Love Never Runs Smooth"

Year	Production Title	Popular Songs
1962		"Only Love Can Break a Heart" "Don't Make Me Over" "I Just Don't Know What to Do with Myself" "Johnny Get Angry" "Make It Easy on Yourself"
1963		"Wives and Lovers" "Close to You" "Anonymous Phone Call" "Twenty-Four Hours from Tulsa" "Walk on By" "Wishin' and Hopin'" "Please Make Him Love Me" "Anyone Who Had a Heart" "Blue on Blue" "Message to Michael" "Who's Been Sleeping in My Bed?" "This Empty Place" "To Wait for Love"
1964	A House Is Not a Home Send Me No Flowers	A House Is Not a Home "Sole, Sole, Sole" "Any Old Time of Day" "Trains and Boats and Planes" "Always Something There to Remind Me" "A Lifetime of Loneliness" "You'll Never Get to Heaven" "First Night of the Full Moon" "Reach Out for Me"
1965	What's New Pussycat?	What's New Pussycat? (AN) Here I Am My Little Red Book "Don't Go Breakin' My Heart" "Are You There (with Another Girl?)" "What the World Needs Now Is Love"
1966	Alfie Promise Her Anything	Alfie (AN)

Year	Production Title	Popular Songs
1966	After the Fox	
		"Another Night"
1967	Casino Royale	The Look of Love (AN)
		Casino Royale
		"One Less Bell to Answer"
		"Do You Know the Way to San Jose?"
		"I Say a Little Prayer"
		"Who Is Gonna Love Me?"
		"Windows of the World"
1968	PROMISES, PROMISES	I'll Never Fall in Love Again
		Promises, Promises
		"This Guy's in Love with You"
1969	Butch Cassidy and the Sundance Kid	Raindrops Keep Fallin' on My Head (AA)
		"Paper Mache"
		"April Fools"
		"I'm a Better Man (for Having Loved You)"
		"Odds and Ends (of a Beautiful Love Affair)"
1973	Lost Horizon	
	Oklahoma Crude	
	Emperor of the North	
1975	Return of the Pink Panther	

* * *

MACK DAVID

Mack David is a native of New York City where he was born in 1912. After attending Cornell and St. John universities, his interest in music surmounted his interest in law. He was twenty years old when his song "Rain, Rain, Go Away" became popular. While David writes both music and lyrics, he usually works with another composer or lyricist. His hit "Sixty Seconds Got Together" was written with Jerry Livingston and he collaborated with Duke Ellington on the songs "Don't You Know I Care?" and "I'm Just a Lucky So-and So." An even dozen of his numbers placed on "Your

Hit Parade" in the 1940's. During the 1950's, he added English
lyrics to Edith Piaf's French favorite "La Vie en Rose," and transformed Max Steiner's main theme from "Gone with the Wind" into
"My Own True Love." Mack David received his first "Oscar" nomination in 1950 and, although he now has seven more, he has yet
to win an Academy Award. Since 1959, his most notable output
has been motion picture title songs. He received considerable publicity in the late 1960's when he sued Broadway composer Jerry
Herman for plagiarism claiming that Herman's title song from "Hello, Dolly!" was partially lifted from "Sunflower" which David had
written in 1948. Herman settled out of court for a quarter of a
million dollars. In 1973, Mack David supplied the lyrics for the
Broadway musical comedy "Molly" which closed after only 68 performances.

Year	Production Title	Popular Songs
1932		"Rain, Rain, Go Away"
1935		"Quicker Than You Can Say Jack Robinson"
1936		"Bermuda Buggyride"
1937		"Oh, Oh, What Do You Know About Love?" "I Wouldn't Change You for the World" "It's Raining Sunshine"
1938		"Sixty Seconds Got Together" (HP) "Just a Kid Named Joe"
1939		"Moon Love" (HP-1) "That's All, Brother" "Blue and Sentimental"
1940		"The Singing Hills" (HP) "On the Isle of May" (HP) "Falling Leaves"
1941	Pot o' Gold	
1942		"A Sinner Kissed an Angel" (HP) "Take Me" (HP) "Sweet Eloise"
1943	BRIGHT LIGHTS OF 1944	"It's Love, Love, Love" (HP-1)

Year	Production Title	Popular Songs
1943		"Johnny Zero" (HP) "My First Love"
1944	Meet Miss Bobby Socks Westward Bound	
		"Candy" (HP-1) "Don't You Know I Care?" (HP)
1945		
1945		"I'm Just a Lucky So-and-So" "I've Got a Locket in My Pocket" "Spellbound"
1946		"You're Too Dangerous, Cherie"
1947		"Chi-Baba, Chi-Baba" (HP) "Give Me Something to Dream About"
1948	My Girl Tisa To the Victor Whiplash	At the Candlelight Cafe "Sunflower" (HP) "There's a Barber in the Harbor of Palermo" "Don't You Love Me Anymore?" "Come with Me, My Honey"
1949	Cinderella	Bibbidi-Bobbidi-Boo (AN) (HP) A Dream Is a Wish Your Heart Makes So This Is Love "I Don't Care If the Sun Don't Shine"
1950	Montana At War with the Army	"La Vie en Rose" (HP-1) "My Destiny" "I've Got a Sunday Feeling in My Heart" "Dreaming Is My Business"
1951	Sailor Beware Alice in Wonderland Teresa	I Like It, I Like It The Unbirthday Song

Year	Production Title	Popular Songs
1952	Jumping Jacks The Stooge Glory Alley Room for One More	
1953	Shane Those Redheads from Seattle	The Call of the Far Away Hills "My Jealous Eyes (That Turned from Blue to Green)"
1954		"My Own True Love"
1955	The Trouble with Harry	"Cherry Pink and Apple Blossom White" (HP-1)
1956	The Birds and the Bees	"It Only Hurts for a Little While" "My Dream Sonata"
1958	The Blob	The Blob
1959	The Hanging Tree 77 Sunset Strip (TV) Verboten! Lawman (TV) Bronco (TV) Bourbon Street Beat (TV) Hawaiian Eye (TV) Alaskans (TV) Room for One More (TV)	The Hanging Tree (AN) Kookie's Love Song "Bimbombey"
1960	Sergeant Rutledge Guns of the Timberland Roaring Twenties (TV) Surfside 6 (TV)	Captain Buffalo
1961	Bachelor in Paradise Ada	Bachelor in Paradise (AN) "Baby, It's You"
1962	Walk on the Wild Side Bird Man of Alcatraz A Girl Named Tamiko Taras Bulba	Walk on the Wild Side (AN)

Year	Production Title	Popular Songs
1962	Follow That Dream	"Young Emotions"
1963	It's a Mad, Mad, Mad Mad World Tom Jones For Those Who Think Young	It's a Mad, Mad, Mad, Mad World (AN) "The Willow"
1964	The Chalk Garden Hush, Hush Sweet Charlotte	Madrigal Hush, Hush Sweet Charlotte (AN)
1965	Cat Ballou Love Has Many Faces The Love Goddesses	The Ballad of Cat Ballou (AN) Love Has Many Faces
1966	Hawaii	My Wishing Doll (AN) Them "It Must Be Him"
1967	The Dirty Dozen Enter Laughing	 "The Lesson"
1968	How to Save a Marriage and Ruin Your Life The Wrecking Crew	
1969	Pendulum Krakatoa, East of Java	
1971	Bunny O'Hare	
1973	MOLLY	

* * *

BENNY DAVIS

     Benny Davis left his New York City home at the age of four-
teen and traveled to San Francisco where he supported himself as a
cafe performer. He advanced to vaudeville and his success as a
song and dance man won him a place in the act of singing favorites
Blossom Seeley and Benny Fields. Davis was twenty-two when he
wrote the lyrics for one of the first hit songs of World War I:
"Goodbye, Broadway--Hello, France." The next decade added "Ma

gie, " "I'm Nobody's Baby, " "Oh, How I Miss You Tonight" and "Baby Face" to his list of successes.   While contributing songs to half a dozen Broadway revues, he produced his own shows spotlighting such new talents as Eleanor Powell, Martha Raye and The Andrews Sisters.   He also wrote lyrics for floor shows staged at Harlem's Cotton Club, and operated his own restaurant.   Few of the motion pictures on which Davis worked produced any memorable songs.   He was a frequent collaborator of composers Milton Ager, Harry Akst, and J. Fred Coots.   The team of Davis and Coots wrote the astounding number of 16 hits in the single year of 1936!

Year	Production Title	Popular Songs
1917	THE PASSING SHOW	Goodbye, Broadway--Hello, France
1920		"Margie"
1921		"I'm Nobody's Baby" (HP) "Make Believe"
1922	SPICE OF 1922	Angel Child
		"Say It While Dancing" "Dearest, You're the Nearest to My Heart" "Lost a Wonderful Girl"
1923	NIFTIES OF 1923	"Stella" "First, Last and Always" "A Smile Will Go a Long, Long Way" "Indiana Moon" "When Will the Sun Shine for Me?"
1924		"Oh, How I Miss You Tonight" "Show Me the Way"
1925		"Are You Sorry?" "Yearning, Just for You" "Who Wouldn't Love You?" "Oh, How She Can Love" "No Other, No One but You" "Away from You"
1926		"Baby Face" (HP) "Somebody's Lonely" "Lonesome and Sorry" "Everything's Gonna Be All Right"

Year	Production Title	Popular Songs
1926		"Sleepy Head" "Reaching for the Moon" "Roses Remind Me of You" "Falling in Love (with You)"
1927	ARTISTS AND MODELS	"I'm Gonna Meet My Sweetie Now" "Gorgeous" "It's a Million to One You're in Love" "No Wonder I'm Happy"
1928		"Carolina Moon" "Mary Ann" "Who Wouldn't Be Blue?" "Right or Wrong, I Love You"
1929	SONS O' GUNS	Cross Your Fingers Why? It's You I Love
	EARL CARROLL'S SKETCH BOOK Why Be Good? Saturday's Children	"All That I'm Asking Is Sympathy" "Pal of My Sweetheart Days"
1930	RIPPLES Dixiana Leathernecking	"I Still Get a Thrill (Thinking of You)" "Skippy"
1931	Palmy Days	There's Nothing Too Good for My Baby "There's No Other Girl" "If You Haven't Got a Girl" "Little Mary Brown"
1932	Husband's Holiday	
1934		"There Goes My Heart" "I Hate Myself (for Being So Mean to You)"

BENNY DAVIS

Year	Production Title	Popular Songs
1935		"Chasing Shadows" (HP-1)
1936		"You Started Me Dreaming" (HP)
		"In My Estimation of You"
		"Doin' the Suzy-Q"
		"I'll Stand By"
		"I'm Grateful to You"
		"Until Today"
		"Yours Truly Is Truly Yours"
		"Copper-Colored Gal"
		"Who Loves You?" (HP)
		"Isn't Love the Strangest Thing?"
		"A Little Robin Told Me So"
		"The More I Know You"
		"Why Do I Lie to Myself About You?"
		"Alabama Barbecue"
		"Friendly Moon"
		"Frisco Flo"
1938		"I'm Madly in Love with You"
		"Blue and Disillusioned"
		"Miss Hallelujah Brown"
		"There's Rain in My Eyes"
1939		"To You" (HP)
		"Let This Be a Warning to You, Baby"
		"This Is No Dream" (HP)
		"Sweet Dreams, Sweetheart"
		"Old Mill Wheel"
1942		"All I Need Is You"
		"Please Think of Me"
1943	Harvest Melody	
1944	The Impatient Years	
	She's a Sweetheart	
1947	This Time for Keeps	
1949		"How Green Was My Valley"
1950		"With These Hands"
		"Patricia"
		"Make Believe Land"

Year	Production Title	Popular Songs
1952		"I Laughed at Love"
1955	Bring Your Smile Along	
1961		"Baby's First Christmas"
1962		"Don't Break the Heart That Loves You"
1963	Follow the Boys	Follow the Boys
1964		"This Is My Happiest Moment"

* * *

PETER DE ROSE

Composer Peter DeRose was born in New York City in 1900. He taught himself to play the piano by ear when he was a freshman at Dewitt Clinton High School. He began his career as a stock clerk for the G. Schirmer music publishing firm, and wrote his first successful song when he was eighteen. In 1923, DeRose began 16 years as a radio entertainer in partnership with his wife May Singhi Breen who sang and played the ukulele. During that time he wrote such hits as "Have You Ever Been Lonely?" and "Wagon Wheels" in collaboration with composer-lyricist Billy Hill. DeRose enjoyed his greatest success in 1939 when Mitchell Parish added lyrics to two movements of an instrumental composition DeRose had written five years earlier. The result was "Deep Purple," which held the Number One spot on "Your Hit Parade" seven times, and "Lilacs in the Rain" which rose to third place. Peter DeRose was still an active contributor to motion pictures when he died in 1953.

Year	Production Title	Popular Songs
1918		"Now All the World's at Peace"
1919		"Alleesamee"
1920		"When You're Gone I Won't Forget" "Gretchen"
1922		"Suez"
1926		"Muddy Water"

Year	Production Title	Popular Songs
1927		"I Just Roll Along, Havin' My Ups and Downs" "Lazy Weather" "I Got Worry (Love Is on My Mind)"
1928	EARL CARROLL'S VANITIES Gang War	"Dixie Dawn"
1929		"Walking with My Sweetness Down Among the Sugar Cane"
1930		"Somewhere in Old Wyoming"
1931		"When Your Hair Has Turned to Silver" "I'm Just a Dancing Sweetheart" "You'll Be Mine in Apple Blossom Time" "One More Kiss Then Good Night"
1932		"You'll Always Be the Same Sweetheart" "Nightfall" "Somebody Loves You"
1933		"Have You Ever Been Lonely?" "There's a Home in Wyomin'" "Louisville Lady"
1934	THE ZIEGFELD FOLLIES	Wagon Wheels "Rain" "Song of the Blacksmith"
1935		"Moonlight and Magnolias" "The Oregon Trail" "When Love Knocks at Your Heart"
1936		"Close to Me" "Now or Never" "Just Say Aloha"

Year	Production Title	Popular Songs
1936		"Half of Me Wants to Be Good" "That's Life, I Guess"
1937		"Blue September" "In a Mission by the Sea"
1938		"So Little Time" "When Twilight Comes"
1939		"Deep Purple" (HP-1) "Lilacs in the Rain" (HP) "The Lamp Is Low" (HP)
1940	EARL CARROLL'S VANITIES IT HAPPENS ON ICE	The Starlit Hour (HP) Angel The Moon Fell in the River "Orchids for Remembrance" "On a Little Street in Singapore"
1941	ICE-CAPADES	I Hear America Singing "Orange Blossom Lane" (HP)
1942		"All I Need Is You" "Moonlight Mood" (HP) "Evening Star"
1943		"Never a Day Goes By"
1944	The Fighting Seabees	
1945		"Autumn Serenade" (HP) "White Orchids" "American Waltz"
1946		"Put That Kiss Back Where You Found It"
1947	Song of Love	As Years Go By "That's Where I Came In" "Did the Moon Tap on Your Window Last Night?"
1948		"On the Little Village Green" "In the Market Place in Old Monterey"

Year	Production Title	Popular Songs
1949		"Twenty-Four Hours of Sunshine" (HP)
		"Who Do You Know in Heaven?"
		"There's a Mile Between Esses in Smiles"
		"The Manuelo Tarantel"
1950	Harvey	
		"A Marshmallow World" (HP)
		"Buona Sera"
		"The Breeze Is My Sweetheart"
		"No Range to Ride No More"
1951	On Moonlight Bay	Love Ya
	Callaway Went Thataway	
		"If You Turn Me Down"
1952	About Face	
	Bird of Paradise	

* * *

B. G. DESYLVA

New York-born George Gard DeSylva prefixed his family name with the initials "B. G." and became known as "Buddy." Educated in California, he was persuaded by Al Jolson to try a songwriting career in New York. Jolson plugged two DeSylva lyrics into hits during the 1918 Broadway run of "Sinbad," and made "April Showers" into an even greater success three years later. DeSylva worked with both veteran composers Victor Herbert and Jerome Kern and newcomer George Gershwin. His hits already included the lyrics for "A Kiss in the Dark," "Look for the Silver Lining" and "Somebody Loves Me" at the time he became a member of the celebrated team of DeSylva, Brown and Henderson. The first year of their collaboration DeSylva and Lew Brown supplied the words for "It All Depends on You" which Jolson introduced in the 1925 stage musical "Big Boy." Fourteen more Broadway productions featured such successes as "Black Bottom," "The Best Things in Life Are Free" and "You're the Cream in My Coffee" before the trio followed Jolson to Hollywood for the 1928 film "The Singing Fool."

The partnership of DeSylva, Brown and Henderson terminated with the 1930 Broadway hit "Flying Colors." While DeSylva soon relegated songwriting to second place in favor of film producing, he

managed to write both music and lyrics for the 1939 Academy
Award contender "Wishing." He also co-authored the books and
produced Cole Porter's "DuBarry Was a Lady" and Irving Berlin's
"Louisiana Purchase" on Broadway, and was the head of Paramount
Studios for several years. "Buddy" DeSylva died at the age of
fifty-five in 1950. DeSylva's "April Showers" and "The Birth of
the Blues" are both on ASCAP's list of 16 All-Time Favorites.

Year	Production Title	Popular Songs
1917		"'n Everything"
1918	SINBAD	I'll Say She Does You Ain't Heard Nothin' Yet
1919	LA, LA LUCILLE GOOD MORNING, JUDGE MORRIS GEST'S MIDNIGHT WHIRL ZIP! GOES A MILLION	Nobody but You

1920	THE GREENWICH VILLAGE
	   FOLLIES
	SALLY
		Just Snap Your Fingers at
		   Care
		Look for the Silver Lining
		Whip-poor-will
		
		"Avalon"

1921	BOMBO THE BROADWAY WHIRL THE ZIEGFELD FOLLIES THE PERFECT FOOL	April Showers (HP) Yoo-Hoo "Swanee Rose" "Tallahasee" "Don't Send Your Wife to the Country" "Give Me My Mammy"

1922	THE FRENCH DOLL
	SPICE OF 1922
	GEORGE WHITE'S
	   SCANDALS
	
	ORANGE BLOSSOMS
	THE YANKEE PRINCESS
		Do It Again
		Yankee Doodle Blues
		I'll Build a Stairway to
		   Paradise
		I Found a Four Leaf Clover
		A Kiss in the Dark
		My Bajadere

1923	GEORGE WHITE'S SCANDALS LITTLE MISS BLUEBEARD NIFTIES OF 1923	Let's Be Lonesome Together Life of a Rose I Won't Say I Will "Annabelle"

Year	Production Title	Popular Songs
1924	SWEET LITTLE DEVIL	Someone Who Believes in You
		Virginia, Don't Go Too Far
	GEORGE WHITE'S SCANDALS	Somebody Loves Me
	PRIMROSE (London)	Rose of Madrid
		"California, Here I Come"
		"Memory Lane"
		"May Time"
		"Oh, Baby! Don't Say No, Say Maybe"
		"As Long as I've Got My Mammy"
		"Born and Bred in Old Kentucky"
1925	BIG BOY	It All Depends on You
		If You Knew Susie
		Keep Smiling at Trouble
		Miami
		Hello, 'Tucky
	TELL ME MORE	Kickin' the Clouds Away
		Why Do I Love You?
		Tell Me More
	GEORGE WHITE'S SCANDALS	I Want a Lovable Baby
	GAY PAREE	Sugar Plum
	CAPTAIN JINKS	
		"Alabamy Bound"
		"Headin' for Louisville"
		"Just a Cottage Small--by a Waterfall"
		"Save Your Sorrow for To-morrow"
1926	GEORGE WHITE'S SCANDALS	The Birth of the Blues
		Black Bottom
		Lucky Day
		The Girl Is You and the Boy Is Me
	QUEEN HIGH	Cross Your Heart
		Gentlemen Prefer Blondes
		Everything Will Happen for the Best
	AMERICANA	"When Day Is Done"
1927	GOOD NEWS	The Best Things in Life Are Free (HP)
		The Varsity Drag

Year	Production Title	Popular Songs
1927	GOOD NEWS	Just Imagine
		Lucky in Love
		Good News
		The Girls of Pi Beta Phi
	MANHATTAN MARY	The Five Step
		Broadway
		It Won't Be Long Now
		Manhattan Mary
	ARTISTS AND MODELS	Here Am I--Broken Hearted
		"South Wind"
		"So Blue"
		"Without You, Sweetheart"
		"I Wonder How I Look When I'm Asleep?"
		"The Church Bells Are Ringing for Mary"
		"Magnolia"
		"Just a Memory"
1928	GEORGE WHITE'S SCANDALS	I'm on the Crest of a Wave
		What D'ya Say?
		Pickin' Cotton
		American Tune
	HOLD EVERYTHING	You're the Cream in My Coffee
		Don't Hold Everything
	THREE CHEERS	Maybe This Is Love
		Pompanola
	The Singing Fool	Sonny Boy
		"Together" (HP)
		"For Old Time's Sake"
		"Sorry for Me"
		"That's Just My Way of Forgetting You"
		"The Song I Love"
1929	FOLLOW THRU	Button Up Your Overcoat
		My Lucky Star
		You Wouldn't Fool Me, Would You?
		I Want to Be Bad
		Follow Thru
	GEORGE WHITE'S SCANDALS Sunny Side Up	
		(I'm a Dreamer) Aren't We All?
		If I Had a Talking Picture of You
		Sunny Side Up
		Turn on the Heat

B. G. DESYLVA

Year	Production Title	Popular Songs
1929	Say It with Songs	Why Can't You? Used to You I'm in Seventh Heaven Little Pal
	In Old Arizona Sally	My Tonia "My Sin"
1930	FLYING HIGH	Without Love Wasn't It Beautiful While It Lasted? Thank Your Father Good for You, Bad for Me Red Hot Chicago
	NINA ROSA Just Imagine	(There's Something About an) Old-Fashioned Girl (I Am the Words) You Are the Melody
	Happy Days Queen High	"Minnie, the Mermaid" "Don't Tell Her What Happened to Me" "(I Am the Words) You Are the Melody"
1931	Indiscreet	Come to Me If You Haven't Got Love "One More Time" "You Try Somebody Else"
1932	TAKE A CHANCE	Eadie Was a Lady You're an Old Smoothie Rise 'n' Shine So Do I Turn Out the Light Should I Be Sweet? Oh, How I Long to Belong to You
1933	My Weakness	Gather Lip Rouge While You May
1935	Under the Pampas Moon	
1939	Love Affair	Wishing (AN) (HP-1)

* * *

HOWARD DIETZ

Howard Dietz divided his professional activities between pro-

moting motion pictures and writing lyrics and librettos. His first
successful song, "Alibi Baby," was featured in the 1923 Broadway
musical "Poppy." The number brought him little notice since the
theatre program and sheet music both credited his lyrics to Dorothy Donnelly!

Dietz was born in New York City in 1896 and served in the
Navy during World War I. He edited college publications while enrolled briefly at Columbia University, and contributed to newspaper
columns before becoming an advertising copywriter. He began his
film career on the advertising staff of producer Samuel Goldwyn.
When he was twenty-five, Dietz joined the MGM publicity department where he worked for over 20 years and eventually became an
executive in Loew's Inc.

During the Thirties, Dietz worked with composer Arthur
Schwartz on a series of Broadway revues including the innovative
1931 hit "The Band Wagon." Among the most popular of Dietz's
lyrics were "I Guess I'll Have to Change My Plan," "Moanin' Low,"
"Dancing in the Dark," "A Shine on Your Shoes" and "You and the
Night and the Music." He was one of the creators of the World
War II Coast Guard production "Tars and Spars." After the war,
his Broadway revue "Inside U. S. A." ran for a year and then
toured the United States. Dietz's "That's Entertainment" (music
by Schwartz) was introduced in the 1953 film "The Band Wagon"
and became an anthem of show business. Dietz and Schwartz supplied the scores for two Broadway musicals in the Sixties but
neither was successful. Howard Dietz was seventy-eight years old
when his autobiography "Dancing in the Dark" was published in
1974.

Year	Production Title	Popular Songs
1923	POPPY	Alibi Baby
1924	DEAR SIR	
1926	OH, KAY!	
1927	MERRY-GO-ROUND	
1929	THE LITTLE SHOW	I Guess I'll Have to Change My Plan Moanin' Low I've Made a Habit of You
	GRAND STREET FOLLIES Battle of Paris	
1930	THREE'S A CROWD	Something to Remember You By The Moment I Saw You All the King's Horses Right at the Start of It Practicing Up on You

Year	Production Title	Popular Songs
1930	SECOND LITTLE SHOW Lottery Bride	Lucky Seven "Got a Man on My Mind"
1931	THE BAND WAGON	Dancing in the Dark High and Low New Sun in the Sky I Love Louisa Hoops Confession
1932	FLYING COLORS	A Shine on Your Shoes Louisiana Hayride Alone Together A Rainy Day Fatal Fascination
1933		"Love Lost"
1934	REVENGE WITH MUSIC	You and the Night and the Music If There Is Someone Lovelier Than You When You Love Only One Wand'rin' Heart
	Girl from Missouri Hollywood Party	Born to Be Kissed Feelin' High "How High Can a Little Bird Fly?" "How Can We Be Wrong?"
1935	AT HOME ABROAD	Farewell, My Lovely What a Wonderful World Loadin' Time Love Is a Dancing Thing Got a Bran' New Suit
1936	Under Your Spell	Under Your Spell
1937	BETWEEN THE DEVIL	I See Your Face Before Me (HP) By Myself You Have Everything
1940	KEEP OFF THE GRASS	On the Old Park Bench
1942	Crossroads	
1943	DANCING IN THE STREET (closed in tryout)	

Year	Production Title	Popular Songs
1944	SADIE THOMPSON JACKPOT	The Love I Long For
1948	INSIDE U. S. A.	Haunted Heart (HP) Rhode Island Is Famous for You My Gal Is Mine Once More Blue Grass
	Three Daring Daughters	The Dickey Bird Song (HP)
1953	The Band Wagon	That's Entertainment
1956	A Bell for Adano (TV)	
1957	THE ZIEGFELD FOLLIES	
1961	THE GAY LIFE	Magic Moment
1963	JENNIE	Before I Kiss the World Goodbye Waitin' for the Evening Train

* * *

MORT DIXON

Lyricist Mort Dixon attended DeWitt Clinton High School in New York City and drove a streetcar in the Bronx. He served three years in the Army and then reenlisted during World War I. After the armistice, he remained in France as director of an American Expeditionary Forces revue. When he returned to the United States, he worked as a bank clerk, waiter, bartender, and actor before the success of his song "That Old Gang of Mine" (music by Ray Henderson) enabled him to become a full-time lyricist. He was then in his early thirties. Dixon's success continued in partnership with composer Harry Warren. The team contributed songs to three Broadway hits in a row: "Sweet and Low," "Billy Rose's Crazy Quilt" and "The Laugh Parade." The productions introduced the songs "Would You Like to Take a Walk?" and "I Found a Million Dollar Baby" (both written with co-lyricist Billy Rose) and "You're My Everything" (written with co-lyricist Joe Young). Another of Dixon's collaborators was composer Harry Woods with whom he wrote the alcoholic's lament "Pink Elephants." The 1930's found Dixon employed at Warner Bros. where his most outstanding film lyric proved to be "The Lady in Red" from the 1935 release "In Caliente." His "I'm Looking Over a Four Leaf Clover" became

the Number One song on "Your Hit Parade" in 1948--more than two
decades after it was written.   Mort Dixon died eight years later
at the age of sixty four.

Year	Production Title	Popular Songs
1923		"That Old Gang of Mine"
1924		"Follow the Swallow" "I Wonder Who's Dancing with You Tonight?" "You're in Love with Everyone but the One Who's in Love with You"
1925		"'Bam, 'Bam, 'Bamy Shore" "If I Had a Girl Like You" "Where Is My Old Girl Tonight?"
1926		"Bye, Bye Blackbird" "I'm in Love with You, That's Why" "Who'd Be Blue?" "Too Many Parties and Too Many Pals"
1927		"I'm Looking Over a Four Leaf Clover" (HP-1) "Just Like a Butterfly That's Caught in the Rain" "Where the Wild Wild Flowers Grow" "Cover Me Up with Sunshine" "I'll Take Care of Your Cares" "Is It Possible?" "Moonbeam, Kiss Her for Me" "You're So Easy to Remember"
1928	My Man	If You Want the Rainbow "Nagasaki" "Old Man Sunshine--Little Boy Bluebird" "Hello, Montreal" "In a Sing Song Sycamore Tree"

Year	Production Title	Popular Songs
1929		"Where the Sweet Forget-Me-Nots Remember" "My Old Man"
1930	SWEET AND LOW	Would You Like to Take a Walk? He's Not Worth Your Tears "The River and Me" "Cover a Clover with Kisses" "Wasting My Love on You"
1931	BILLY ROSE'S CRAZY QUILT THE LAUGH PARADE	I Found a Million Dollar Baby Sing a Little Jingle You're My Everything Ooh! That Kiss The Torch Song "River Stay 'Way from My Door"
1932		"Pink Elephants"
1933		"Marching Along Together"
1934	Happiness Ahead Flirtation Walk Dames The Key Housewife	Pop Goes Your Heart Happiness Ahead Mr. and Mrs. Is the Name Flirtation Walk I See Two Lovers Try to See It My Way "I Raised My Hat"
1935	In Caliente Sweet Music I Live for Love We're in the Money Bright Lights Broadway Hostess Little Big Shot	The Lady in Red (HP) Fare-Thee-Well, Annabelle Mine Alone I Live for Love So Nice Seeing You Again Toddlin' Along with You
1936		"Did You Mean It?" (HP) "Every Once in Awhile"
1937		"I Can't Lose That Longing for You"

Year	Production Title	Popular Songs
1939		"Tears from My Inkwell" (HP)
1944		"On the Corner of Dream Street and Main"

* * *

WALTER DONALDSON

Walter Donaldson began his career writing melodies for shows staged at his high school. After graduation, he joined a Wall Street brokerage firm which he left when offered a position with a music publisher. Tin Pan Alley first took notice of the twenty-two year old composer/lyricist in 1915 when three of his melodies became best-sellers. During World War I, Donaldson entertained soldiers at home camps. One of his first post-war hits, "How Ya Gonna Keep 'em Down on the Farm?" was popularized by Eddie Cantor, and his 1921 success "My Mammy" became the almost personal property of Al Jolson. In the late 1920's, Donaldson co-founded a music publishing company and began writing some of his own lyrics. After his 1928 Broadway hit "Whoopee," in which "Love Me or Leave Me" was introduced, he worked primarily on motion pictures produced by MGM. He received his only "Oscar" nomination for "Did I Remember?" which Jean Harlow sang in "Suzy" (1936). The 1947 film "Big Town" was the last in which a new Walter Donaldson song was heard. The fifty-four year old Brooklyn-born songwriter died that same year. Georgia's official state song is Donaldson's "Georgia."

Year	Production Title	Popular Songs
1915		"Just Try to Picture Me Down Home in Tennessee" "You'd Never Know the Old Home-Town of Mine" "We'll Have a Jubilee in My Old Kentucky Home"
1916		"When Verdi Plays the Hurdy Gurdy"
1917		"Suki-San"
1918		"The Daughter of Rosie O'Grady"
1919	THE LADY IN RED	

Year	Production Title	Popular Songs
1919		"How Ya Gonna Keep 'em Down on the Farm?"
		"You're a Million Miles from Nowhere (When You're One Little Mile from Home)"
		"Don't Cry, Frenchy, Don't Cry"
		"I'll Be Happy When the Preacher Makes You Mine"
		"Upstairs and Down"
1920	ED WYNN CARNIVAL	I Love the Land of Old Black Joe
	SILKS AND SATINS	My Little Bimbo Down on the Bamboo Isle
		"I'm Telling You"
		"Tired of Me"
1921		"My Mammy"
		"Down South"
		"Give Me My Mammy"
1922	MAKE IT SNAPPY	Seven or Eleven--My Dixie Pair o' Dice
	THE PASSING SHOW	Carolina in the Morning
		"Georgia"
		"My Buddy"
		"On the 'Gin, 'Gin, 'Ginny Shore"
		"Dixie Highway"
		"Sweet Indiana Home"
1923		"Beside a Babbling Brook"
		"Mindin' My Business"
		"Chili Bom Bom"
1924	ROUND THE TOWN	
		"My Best Girl"
		"In the Evening"
		"Back Where the Daffodils Grow"
		"Oh, Baby! Don't Say No, Say Maybe"
		"Sioux City Sue"
1925		"Yes Sir, That's My Baby"

WALTER DONALDSON

Year	Production Title	Popular Songs
1925		"That Certain Party" "Isn't She the Sweetest Thing?" "Let It Rain! Let It Pour!" "In the Middle of the Night" "My Sweetie Turned Me Down" "I Wonder Where My Baby Is Tonight?" "The Midnight Waltz" "Swanee Butterfly" "Down by the Winegar Woiks"
1926	SWEETHEART TIME	"(What Can I Say, Dear) After I Say I'm Sorry?" "For My Sweetheart" "Where'd You Get Those Eyes?" "Don't Be Angry with Me" "That's Why I Love You" "There Ain't No Maybe in My Baby's Eyes" "Thinking of You" "But I Do--You Know I Do" "It Made You Happy When You Made Me Cry" "I've Got the Girl" "Just a Birds-Eye View of My Old Kentucky Home" "Let's Talk About My Sweetie"
1927		"My Blue Heaven" "At Sundown" "Sam, the Old Accordian Man" "My Ohio Home" "Dixie Vagabond" "A Shady Tree" "Changes" "Sing Me a Baby Song" "Mary" "He's the Last Word" "If You See Sally" "Just Once Again"
1928	WHOOPEE	Makin' Whoopee Love Me or Leave Me I'm Bringing a Red, Red Rose

Year	Production Title	Popular Songs
1928	Warming Up Hit of the Show	Out of the Dawn "Because My Baby Don't Mean Maybe Now" "Anything You Say" "Out of Town Gal" "Say 'Yes' Today" "Just Like a Melody Out of the Sky" "She's Wonderful" "If I Can't Have You"
1929	Hot for Paris	"Kansas City Kitty" "Junior" "Reaching for Someone"
1930	SMILES Cameo Kirby Whoopee	You're Driving Me Crazy Romance My Baby Just Cares for Me "Little White Lies" (HP) "'Tain't No Sin" "There's a Wah-Wah Girl in Agua Caliente" "Sweet Jennie Lee" "Lazy Lou'siana Moon"
1931	THE ZIEGFELD FOLLIES	I'm with You "Nobody Loves No Baby Like My Baby Loves Me" "Goodnight Moon" "Without That Gal" "Hello, Beautiful" "Blue Kentucky Moon" "You Didn't Have to Tell Me" "An Evening in Caroline"
1932		"I'm So in Love" "My Mom" "You're Telling Me"
1933	The Prizefighter and the Lady	You've Got Everything
1934	Operator 13	Sleepy Head Once in a Lifetime

Year	Production Title	Popular Songs
1934	Hollywood Party	I've Had My Moments
		Feelin' High
	Riptide	Riptide
	Kid Millions	An Earful of Music
		Okay, Toots
		When My Ship Comes In
	Let's Talk It Over	
	Forsaking All Others	
	Million Dollar Ransom	
	Gay Bride	
		"Dancing in the Moonlight"
		"A Thousand Goodnights"
1935	Here Comes the Band	Tender Is the Night
	Reckless	
		"Clouds"
1936	Suzy	Did I Remember? (AN) (HP-1)
	The Great Ziegfeld	You (HP-1)
		You Never Looked So Beautiful
	Sinner Take All	I'd Be Lost Without You
	The Old Soak	
	Piccadilly Jim	
	After the Thin Man	
	His Brother's Wife	
		"It's Been So Long" (HP)
1937	Madame X	
	Saratoga	
	Man of the People	
1938		"Could Be" (HP)
		"Why'd Ya Make Me Fall in Love?"
1939	That's Right-You're Wrong	I'm Fit to Be Tied
	Broadway Serenade	
		"(Gotta Get Some) Shut Eye" (HP)
		"Cuckoo in the Clock"
1940	Two Girls on Broadway	
		"Mister Meadowlark"
		"On Behalf of the Visiting Firemen"
1942	Panama Hattie	
	Give Out, Sisters	

Year	Production Title	Popular Songs
1943	What's Buzzin' Cousin?	Nevada
		"Never a Day Goes By"
1944	Beautiful but Broke Follow the Boys	
1947	Big Town	

* * *

AL DUBIN

Al Dubin was born in Zurich, Switzerland. His family emigrated to the United States where his father began practicing medicine in Philadelphia in 1893. Dubin started writing lyrics while a teenaged student at the Perkiomen Seminary in Pennsylvania and eventually became one of the five most successful lyricists in the history of motion pictures. He served overseas in an entertainment unit during World War I, and then worked as a singing waiter until he was able to support himself with his lyrics. After four Broadway productions and a dozen popular music hits, Dubin moved to Hollywood. From 1929 through 1938, he wrote the words to over 70 hit film songs introduced in Warner Bros. musicals such as the legendary "Forty-Second Street," and the "Gold Diggers" series. Thirteen of the films boasted at least three hits from each score. His initial collaborator was composer Joseph Burke but the majority of his successes had music by Harry Warren. Three of his songs were nominated for "Oscars" and he won the 1935 statuette for "Lullaby of Broadway." Al Dubin lived to be fifty-four.

Year	Production Title	Popular Songs
1916		"'Twas Only an Irishman's Dream"
1917		"All the World Will Be Jealous of Me"
1920		"Tripoli--on the Shores of Tripoli"
1921	THE GREENWICH VILLAGE FOLLIES	
		"Crooning"
1923		"Just a Girl That Men Forget"

Year	Production Title	Popular Songs
1924		"What Has Become of Hinky Dinky Parlez Voo?" "I Don't Care What You Used to Be, I Know What You Are Today"
1925	CHARLOT'S REVUE	A Cup of Coffee, a Sandwich and You "The Lonesomest Girl in Town" "Nobody Knows What a Red-headed Mama Can Do" "Cross Words, Why Were They Spoken?" "Waters of Perkiomen"
1926		"My Dream of the Big Parade"
1927	WHITE LIGHTS TAKE THE AIR	"Heaven Help a Sailor on a Night Like This" "All by My Ownsome"
1928		"I Must Be Dreaming" "Half-way to Heaven" "Memories of France"
1929	Gold Diggers of Broadway In the Headlines Show of Shows Sally Evidence	Tip-Toe Through the Tulips with Me Painting the Clouds with Sunshine Love Will Find a Way Your Love Is All That I Crave If I'm Dreaming, Don't Wake Me Up Too Soon Sally "Ev'rybody Loves You"
1930	Dancing Sweeties She Couldn't Say No Hold Everything Oh, Sailor Beware Top Speed The Cuckoos	The Kiss Waltz Watching My Dreams Go By

Year	Production Title	Popular Songs
1930		"Dancing with Tears in My Eyes" "For You" (HP)
1931		"Crosby, Columbo and Vallee" "Many Happy Returns of the Day" "When the Rest of the Crowd Goes Home" "Pagan Moon" "To Have and Hold You in My Arms" "If You Should Ever Need Me"
1932	The Crooner Blessed Event	Three's a Crowd "Too Many Tears" "Deep in Your Eyes"
1933	Forty-Second Street	Forty-Second Street Shuffle Off to Buffalo You're Getting to Be a Habit with Me Young and Healthy
	Footlight Parade	Shanghai Lil Honeymoon Hotel
	Gold Diggers of 1933	We're in the Money (Gold Digger's Song) I've Got to Sing a Torch Song Pettin' in the Park The Shadow Waltz Remember My Forgotten Man
	Roman Scandals	No More Love Build a Little Home Keep Young and Beautiful "My Temptation"
1934	Moulin Rouge	The Boulevard of Broken Dreams Coffee in the Morning, Kisses at Night Song of Surrender
	Twenty Million Sweethearts	I'll String Along with You Fair and Warmer
	Dames	I Only Have Eyes for You

AL DUBIN   207

Year	Production Title	Popular Songs
1934	Wonder Bar	Goin' to Heaven on a Mule
		Don't Say Good Night
		Wonder Bar
		Why Do I Dream Those Dreams?
1935	Gold Diggers of 1935	Lullaby of Broadway (AA) (HP-1)
		The Words Are in My Heart
		I'm Goin' Shoppin' with You
	Go into Your Dance	She's a Latin from Manhattan (HP)
		About a Quarter to Nine (HP)
		The Little Things You Used to Do
		Go into Your Dance
	Page Miss Glory	Page Miss Glory (HP)
	Broadway Gondolier	The Rose in Her Hair (HP)
		Lulu's Back in Town (HP)
		Outside of You
		Sweet and Slow
	Shipmates Forever	Don't Give Up the Ship (HP)
		I'd Rather Listen to Your Eyes
		I'd Love to Take Orders from You
	Stars Over Broadway	Where Am I? (HP)
		You Let Me Down
	Sweet Music	Sweet Music
	Living on Velvet	Living on Velvet
	In Caliente	Muchacha
1936	Cain and Mabel	I'll Sing You a Thousand Love Songs (HP-1)
	Gold Diggers of 1937	With Plenty of Money and You (HP-1)
		All's Fair in Love and War
	Sing Me a Love Song	Summer Night
		The Little House That Love Built
	Hearts Divided	My Kingdom for a Kiss
	Colleen	
	Sons O' Guns	
	Stolen Holiday	
1937	Mr. Dodd Takes the Air	Remember Me? (AN) (HP-1)
	The Singing Marine	Am I in Love?
		The Song of the Marines (We're Shoving Right Off)

Year	Production Title	Popular Songs
1937		I Know Now (HP)
		'Cause My Baby Says It's So (HP)
		The Lady Who Couldn't Be Kissed
		You Can't Run Away from Love Tonight
	Melody for Two	September in the Rain (HP-1)
		Melody for Two
	San Quentin	How Could You? (HP)
	Marked Woman	
1938	Gold Diggers in Paris	The Latin Quarter
		A Stranger in Paree
		Put That Down in Writing
		I Wanna Go Back to Bali
	Garden of the Moon	Garden of the Moon
		Confidentially
		The Girl Friend of the Whirling Dervish
		Love Is Where You Find It
		"You're an Education"
1939	STREETS OF PARIS	South American Way
		Is It Possible?
		Rendezvous Time in Paree
		"Indian Summer" (HP-1)
1940	KEEP OFF THE GRASS	Clear Out of This World
		A Latin Tune, a Manhattan Moon and You
	The Santa Fe Trail	Along the Santa Fe Trail
		"I Never Felt This Way Before"
		"Where Was I?" (HP)
1941		"The Anniversary Waltz"
		"The Angels Came Thru"
		"It Happened in Hawaii"
1943	Stage Door Canteen	We Mustn't Say Goodbye (AN)
1944	LAFFING ROOM ONLY	Feudin' and Fightin' (HP-1)
		"Diana"

GUS EDWARDS

   Hohensalza, Germany, was the birthplace of Gus Edwards
whose family came to the United States when he was eight years
old. He was a self-taught pianist and earned pocket money working in a cigar store and singing on ferry boats and in New York
City saloons. His talent as a performer led to a spot in the vaudeville act "The Newsboy Quartet." Edwards was nearing his twentieth year when he wrote the music for the 1898 hit "All I Wants Is
My Black Baby Back." The next year, he began collaborating with
lyricist Will D. Cobb with whom he created the favorites "I Just
Can't Make My Eyes Behave" (which Anna Held introduced in the
1906 Broadway musical "A Parisian Model"), "Sunbonnet Sue," and
the classic "School Days." In addition to his work with Cobb, Edwards teamed with lyricist Vincent Bryan on "In the Sweet Bye and
Bye" (co-composer Harry Von Tilzer) in 1902, and "In My Merry
Oldsmobile" in 1905. Before the first decade of the twentieth century ended, Edwards had founded his own publishing firm and added "By the Light of the Silvery Moon" (lyrics by Edward Madden)
to his list of successes. By 1914, he was one of the biggest head-
liners in vaudeville and generally appeared with his own troupes
such as "Gus Edwards' Minstrels." He's credited with helping
George Jessel, Eddie Cantor, Sally Rand, Eleanor Powell and
numerous other performers on their ways to fame. In 1939, Paramount released a film biography of Edwards' career titled "The
Star Maker." That same year, the composer retired due to a serious illness. Gus Edwards died six years later at the age of sixty-six.

Year	Production Title	Popular Songs
1898		"All I Wants Is My Black Baby Back"
1899		"I Couldn't Stand to See My Baby Lose" "The Singer and the Song" "You Are the Only Girl I'll Ever Care About"
1900	HODGE, PODGE & CO.	"All for a Man Whose God Was Gold" "I Can't Tell Why I Love You, but I Do"
1901		"I'm Dreaming of a Bygone Day" "Mamie" "I'll Be with You When the Roses Bloom Again" "I Don't Want Money" "Way Down Yonder in the Corn Field"

Year	Production Title	Popular Songs
1901		"Casey's Wedding Night" "It's Awfully Nice to Be a Regular Soldier"
1902		"In the Sweet Bye and Bye" "Could You Be True to Eyes of Blue?" "Louisiana Louise" "Have You Seen My Sweetheart in His Uniform of Blue?" "On the Proper Side of Broadway on a Saturday P. M. "
1903	MR. BLUEBEARD THE WIZARD OF OZ	
1904	THE MEDAL AND THE MAID	In Zanzibar "The Girl Who Cares for Me" "Goodbye, Little Girl, Goodbye" "Louisiana Anna"
1905	WHEN WE WERE FORTY-ONE FANTANA	Meet Me Under the Wistaria Tammany "Somebody's Sweetheart I Want to Be" "In My Merry Oldsmobile" "He's My Pal" "If a Girl Like You Loved a Boy Like Me"
1906	A PARISIAN MODEL	I Just Can't Make My Eyes Behave I'd Like to See a Little More of You
	HIS HONOR THE MAYOR ABOUT TOWN THE BLUE MOON	"Sunbonnet Sue" "Farewell Killarney" "I'll Do Anything, Dear, in the World for You" "Two Dirty Little Hands"

Year	Production Title	Popular Songs
1907	THE ZIEGFELD FOLLIES	On the Grand Old Sand Bye, Bye Dear Old Broadway
	HIP! HIP! HOORAY!	What's the Good?
		"Does Anybody Want a Blonde?"
1908	MISS INNOCENCE SCHOOL DAYS THE MERRY-GO-ROUND	My Cousin Carus' School Days "Sunburnt Salome" "On the Old Seesaw"
1909	THE ZIEGFELD FOLLIES	By the Light of the Silvery Moon Up, Up, in My Aeroplane Come On and Play Ball with Me
	BREAKING INTO SOCIETY	
1910	THE ZIEGFELD FOLLIES	"If I Was a Millionaire"
1911		"Look Out for Jimmy Valentine"
1913		"I'll Get You" "Little Miss Killarney"
1916		"I Lost My Heart in Honolulu"
1917		"For You a Rose" "Just a Simple Country Maiden"
1918		"Laddie Boy"
1921		"I Want You Morning, Noon and Night"
1922	THE FRENCH DOLL	
1923	SUNBONNET SUE	
1928		"Little Boy Blue Jeans"
1929	Hollywood Revue of 1929	Your Mother and Mine Nobody but You Orange Blossom Time

Year	Production Title	Popular Songs
1930	Chasing Rainbows	
1933	Broadway to Hollywood	
1936	BROADWAY SHO-WINDOW	

* * *

DUKE ELLINGTON

In addition to being one of the greatest jazz musicians the United States has produced, Duke Ellington was a popular song writer of considerable stature.   Instead of studying commercial art on a scholarship he had won while attending high school, nineteen year old Ellington formed a five piece combo which played jazz for the customers of Manhattan's Kentucky Club.   After the success of his first song of 1922, the band was expanded and went on tour. Ellington fan Jimmy McHugh had composed the score for the opening show at Harlem's Cotton Club and convinced its management to engage the Ellington orchestra.   The organization stayed at the Cotton Club for five years during which Ellington composed the music for such popular numbers as "Mood Indigo" and "It Don't Mean a Thing If It Ain't Got That Swing."   The "Duke" and his orchestra were featured in the 1929 Broadway musical "Show Girl" and the 1930 film "Check and Double Check."

By 1933, the composer and his jazz aggregation were so well known that they entertained British royalty at a command performance.   Concerts in France, the Netherlands and Scandanavia culminated in their first appearance at Carnegie Hall in 1943. While neither of Ellington's two stage musicals that reached Broadway succeeded, his list of hit songs includes "Sophisticated Lady," "Solitude," "I Got It Bad and That Ain't Good," "I'm Beginning to See the Light" and "Satin Doll."   The words for many of his successes were written by Irving Mills and Bob Russell.   Conductor-arranger-pianist-composer Edward Kennedy Ellington was born in Washington, D.C. in 1899, and was still a stellar attraction at the time of his death in 1974.   The previous year his autobiography "Music Is My Mistress" was published.

Year	Production Title	Popular Songs
1922		"Blind Man's Buff"
1924		"Pretty Soft for You"
1925		"Jig Walk" "Jim Dandy" "With You"

Year	Production Title	Popular Songs
1930	Check and Double Check	Ring Dem Bells
1931		"Mood Indigo"
1932		"It Don't Mean a Thing If It Ain't Got That Swing" "My Best Wishes"
1933		"Sophisticated Lady" "Drop Me Off at Harlem" "Skrontch"
1934		"Solitude"
1935		"In a Sentimental Mood" "Delta Serenade"
1937		"Caravan" "Clouds in My Heart" "Scattin' at the Kit Cat" "I've Got to Be a Rug Cutter" "Alabamy Home" "Black Butterfly" "Azure"
1938		"I Let a Song Go Out of My Heart" (HP-1) "Prelude to a Kiss" "Dusk on the Desert" "Lost in Meditation" "Please Forgive Me" "Pyramid" "Steppin' into Swing Society" "Gypsy without a Song" "Harmony in Harlem" "If You Were in My Place (What Would You Do?)"
1939		"I'm Checking out, Goombye" "You Gave Me the Gate and I'm Swingin'" "Grievin'" "Gal from Joe's" "Something to Live For" "Boy Meets Horn"
1940		"All Too Soon" "I Never Felt This Way Before"

Year	Production Title	Popular Songs
1941	JUMP FOR JOY (closed in tryout)	I Got It Bad and That Ain't Good (HP) Jump for Joy "Rocks in My Bed" "Just a-Sittin' and a-Rockin'" "Day-Dream" "Warm Valley" "Baby, When You Ain't There" "I'm Satisfied"
1942		"Don't Get Around Much Anymore" (HP-1) "Things Ain't What They Used to Be" "Oh, Miss Jaxson" "Five O'Clock Drag"
1943		"Do Nothin' Til You Hear from Me" (HP) "Tonight I Shall Sleep with a Smile on My Face" "Baby, Please Stop and Think About Me"
1944		"I'm Beginning to See the Light" (HP-1) "I Didn't Know About You" (HP) "Don't You Know I Care?" (HP) "I Ain't Got Nothin' but the Blues"
1945		"I'm Just a Lucky So-and-So" "The Wonder of You" "Ev'ry Hour on the Hour"
1946	BEGGAR'S HOLIDAY People Are Funny	Take Love Easy "Just Squeeze Me" "It Shouldn't Happen to a Dream" "Tell Me, Tell Me, Dream Face (Tulip or Turnip?)"
1947		"Indigo Echoes" "T. T. on Toast" "I Don't Know Why I Love You So"

Year	Production Title	Popular Songs
1947		"It's Kind of Lonesome Out Tonight" "He Makes Me Believe He's Mine"
1958		"Satin Doll"
1959		"I Wish I Was Back in My Baby's Arms" "I'm Gonna Go Fishin'"
1961	Paris Blues	
1962		"Lazy Rhapsody"
1965		"Christmas Surprise"
1966	POUSSE CAFE	

* * *

RAY EVANS & JAY LIVINGSTON

Jay Livingston is the composer in the team of Livingston and Evans and both men write lyrics. They were both born in 1915-- Ray Evans in Salamanca, New York, and Livingston in McDonald, Pennsylvania. The two men met while students at the University of Pennsylvania where pianist Livingston formed a dance band in which Evans played the saxophone and clarinet. They also worked together in orchestras in night clubs and on steamships. They were in their mid-twenties when comedian Ole Olsen provided them with the idea for their first hit song "G'bye Now" which was featured in Olsen and Johnson's Broadway revue "Hellzapoppin'" in the early 1940's.

During World War II, Livingston served in the Armed Forces while Evans worked for an airplane manufacturer. After the war, they became the busiest songwriters on the Paramount lot where they contributed numbers to as many as eight feature films a year starring such favorites as Bob Hope, Marlene Dietrich, Alan Ladd and Paulette Goddard. Livingston and Evans won their first "Oscar" for "Buttons and Bows" (1948). They were also winners in 1950 and 1956. The team appeared playing the piano and singing in a crowded New Year's Eve party scene in "Sunset Boulevard." In the early 1950's, they supplied the score for television's first color presentation of an original musical "Satins and Spurs" starring Betty Hutton. They also created the television theme song for "Bonanza." By the year 1958, they were ready for Broadway and enjoyed a modest success with their score for "Oh Captain!" Three years

later, their second stage attempt, "Let It Ride!," failed.   Since
leaving Paramount, Evans and Livingston have free-lanced frequently writing lyrics only for the melodies of such composers as Victor
Young, Jimmy McHugh and Henry Mancini.   They have also provided special material for TV and night club star Mitzi Gaynor.

Year	Production Title	Popular Songs
1941	HELLZAPOPPIN' SONS O' FUN	G'bye Now (HP)
1944	I Accuse My Parents Swing Hostess	
1945	On Stage Everybody The Stork Club Why Girls Leave Home Crime, Inc.	Stuff Like That There A Square in a Social Circle The Cat and the Canary (AN) "What a Deal"
1946	Monsieur Beaucaire	"To Each His Own" (HP-1)
1947	Golden Earrings The Imperfect Lady My Favorite Brunette	Golden Earrings (HP-1)
1948	The Paleface Isn't It Romantic? Whispering Smith Dream Girl The Sainted Sisters My Own True Love	Buttons and Bows (AA) (HP-1)
1949	Sorrowful Jones My Friend Irma The Great Lover Song of Surrender Streets of Laredo Bride of Vengeance	Havin' a Wonderful Wish Here's to Love Just for Fun A Thousand Violins Song of Surrender The Streets of Laredo "My Love Loves Me"

1950	I LOVE LYDIA (Los
	  Angeles)
	Captain Carey, U.S.A.
	Copper Canyon
	My Friend Irma
	  Goes West
	Fancy Pants
	The Furies
		Mona Lisa (AA) (HP-1)
		Copper Canyon
		I'll Always Love You
		
		Home Cookin'

Year	Production Title	Popular Songs
1950	Paid in Full The Redhead and the Cowboy Sunset Boulevard	
1951	Here Comes the Groom The Lemon Drop Kid Aaron Slick from Punkin Crick My Favorite Spy Rhubarb The Big Carnival Crosswinds That's My Boy	Bonne Nuit Misto Cristofo Columbo Silver Bells Marshmallow Moon My Beloved
1952	Somebody Loves Me What Price Glory? Son of Paleface Anything Can Happen	Love Him
1953	Thunder in the East The Stars Are Singing Off Limits Here Come the Girls Those Redheads from Seattle Casanova's Big Night	The Ruby and the Pearl Haven't Got a Worry
1954	THAT'S LIFE (Los Angeles) Red Garters Satins and Spurs (TV)	
1955	Three Ring Circus The Second Greatest Sex Lucy Gallant	
1956	The Man Who Knew Too Much The Scarlet Hour Istanbul	Whatever Will Be, Will Be (Que Sera, Sera) (AA) (HP-1) Never Let Me Go
1957	Tammy and the Bachelor The James Dean Story The Big Beat Loves of Omar Khayyam	Tammy (AN) (HP-1) Let Me Be Loved As I Love You
1958	OH CAPTAIN!	All the Time You're So Right for Me

Year	Production Title	Popular Songs
1958	Houseboat Another Time, Another Place Saddle the Wind This Happy Feeling Once Upon a Horse Bonanza (TV)	Almost in Your Arms (AN) Another Time, Another Place
1959	A Private's Affair Take a Giant Step	Warm and Willing "Angeltown"
1960	Mr. Lucky (TV)	Dreamsville
1961	LET IT RIDE! All Hands on Deck	Love Let Me Know
1964	Dear Heart	Dear Heart (AN) "Angel" "On My Way"
1965	Harlow Never Too Late The Third Day	Lonely Girl Never Too Late
1966	This Property Is Condemned What Did You Do in the War, Daddy? Torn Curtain The Night of the Grizzly	Wish Me a Rainbow In the Arms of Love
1967	Wait Until Dark	
1976	Foxtrot	

* * *

SAMMY FAIN

Sammy Fain was born in New York City in 1902. He came by his interest in the theatre naturally--being a cousin of the famed comedy team of Willie and Eugene Howard. After finishing high school, Fain left his home on a farm in New York State. He was twenty-three years old when his first published song, "Nobody Knows What a Redheaded Mama Can Do," went on sale in 1925.

SAMMY FAIN 219

That same year, his songs were heard by Broadway audiences in
"Chauve Souris" and "Sky High." In 1927, he collaborated with
lyricists Irving Kahal and Francis Wheeler on "Let a Smile Be
Your Umbrella" which became a national favorite.

Fain joined the cadre of Hollywood songwriters in 1929.
For the next decade, he contributed songs to two dozen motion
pictures and received his first Academy Award nomination for
"That Old Feeling." During that period he made several successful recordings as a vocalist. Fain returned to Broadway for the
1938 production "Right This Way." Although the show closed in
only two weeks, his songs "I'll Be Seeing You" and "I Can Dream,
Can't I?" have remained timeless. The biggest Broadway hit ever
enjoyed by Fain--the revue "Hellzapoppin'" starring zany comics
Olsen and Johnson--opened that same year. It ran for more than
three years and held the record as Broadway's longest-running
musical until the record passed to "Oklahoma!" Ironically, none
of Fain's music from this famous production achieved any popularity. Four more revues featuring his songs followed including the
last edition of "George White's Scandals" (in which his cousins appeared) and Olsen and Johnson's "Sons O' Fun."

In 1943, Sammy Fain resumed his Hollywood career and
worked on films starring such well known personalities as Red
Skelton, Judy Garland, Abbott and Costello, Frank Sinatra and Es-
ther Williams. His book musical, "Toplitsky of Notre Dame,"
opened on Broadway in 1946 and was not a success. Three years
later, his "Dear Hearts and Gentle People" was published as an
independent song and was one of the most-recorded numbers of the
year. During the decade of the 1950's, Fain alternated between
stage and screen work. He was represented on Broadway by four
revues and the book musicals "Flahooley" (1951) and "Ankles A-
weigh" (1955). He received his second Academy Award nomination
for "Secret Love" in 1953. After 24 years of writing for the
screen, he won his first "Oscar." His second win came two years
later for the title song from "Love Is a Many-Splendored Thing."
He also received nominations in 1957, 1958 (two that year), 1961,
1972 ("Strange Are the Ways of Love" from "The Stepmother"), and
1977 ("A World That Never Was" from "Half a House").

Sammy Fain has continued to compose for Broadway even
though he hasn't had a stage hit since 1941. His book musicals
"Christine" (1960) and "Something More" (1964) each ran for less
than a month. His musical version of Jules Verne's "Around the
World in 80 Days" was presented by the St. Louis Municipal Opera
in 1962 after which it opened at Guy Lombardo's Jones Beach Mar-
ine Theatre in New York where it became a seasonal favorite.

Year   Production Title   Popular Songs

1925   CHAUVE SOURIS
       SKY HIGH

Year	Production Title	Popular Songs
1925		"Nobody Knows What a Red-headed Mama Can Do"
1927		"Let a Smile Be Your Umbrella" "I Left My Sugar Standing in the Rain" "I Ain't That Kind of Baby"
1928		"There's Something About a Rose That Reminds Me of You"
1929	Romance of the Underworld	"Wedding Bells Are Breaking Up That Old Gang of Mine"
1930	The Big Pond	You Brought a New Kind of Love to Me Mia Cara (My Dear)
	Dangerous Nan McGrew Follow the Leader Laughter Young Man of Manhattan	
1931	EVERYBODY'S WELCOME	"When I Take My Sugar to Tea" "Was That the Human Thing to Do?"
1932	The Crooner	"Hummin' to Myself"
1933	Footlight Parade	By a Waterfall Ah, the Moon Is Here Sittin' on a Backyard Fence
	College Coach Moonlight and Pretzels	Lonely Lane There's a Little Bit of You in Every Love Song
1934	Harold Teen	How Do I Know It's Sunday? Simple and Sweet
	Fashions of 1934 Easy to Love Mandalay Dames Happiness Ahead Strictly Dynamite	Spin a Little Web of Dreams Easy to Love When Tomorrow Comes

SAMMY FAIN

Year	Production Title	Popular Songs
1934	Desirable Here Comes the Navy	
1935	Sweet Music Goin' to Town G-Men	Ev'ry Day (HP) Now I'm a Lady "I Went Merrily, Merrily on My Way"
1936		"Am I Gonna Have Trouble with You?" "That Never-to-Be-Forgotten Night"
1937	Vogues of 1938 New Faces of 1937	That Old Feeling (AN) (HP-1) Our Penthouse on Third Avenue Love Is Never Out of Season "Don't You Know or Don't You Care?"
1938	RIGHT THIS WAY HELLZAPOPPIN'	I'll Be Seeing You (HP-1) I Can Dream, Can't I? (HP-1) "Who Blew Out the Flame?"
1939	GEORGE WHITE'S SCANDALS BLACKBIRDS	Are You Havin' Any Fun? (HP) Something I Dreamed Last Night Goodnight, My Beautiful "The Moon Is a Silver Dollar" (HP)
1940	BOYS AND GIRLS TOGETHER	Such Stuff as Dreams Are Made Of I Want to Live
1941	SONS O' FUN	Happy in Love (HP)
1943	I Dood It Presenting Lily Mars Swing Fever	
1944	Two Girls and a Sailor Lost in a Harem Meet the People Maisie Goes to Reno	You Dear

Year	Production Title	Popular Songs
1945	Thrill of a Romance Weekend at the Waldorf Anchors Aweigh George White's Scandals	Please Don't Say No And There You Are (HP)
1946	TOPLITSKY OF NOTRE DAME No Leave, No Love Holiday in Mexico Two Sisters from Boston Little Mr. Jim	Love Is a Random Thing All the Time "The Secretary Song"
1947	This Time for Keeps	"The Wildest Gal in Town"
1948	Three Daring Daughters	The Dickey Bird Song (HP)
1949		"Dear Hearts and Gentle People" (HP-1) "Cheap Cigars" "Church Bells on Sunday Morning"
1950	MICHAEL TODD'S PEEP SHOW ALIVE AND KICKING The Milkman	Violins from Nowhere "Lock, Stock and Barrel"
1951	FLAHOOLEY MY L.A. (Los Angeles) Call Me Mister Alice in Wonderland	The World Is Your Balloon Here's to Your Illusions I Just Can't Do Enough for You I'm Late Alice in Wonderland
1953	Calamity Jane The Jazz Singer Three Sailors and a Girl Peter Pan	Secret Love (AA) (HP-1) I Hear the Music Now Face to Face
1954	Lucky Me Young at Heart	I Speak to the Stars There's a Rising Moon
1955	ANKLES AWEIGH CATCH A STAR Love Is a Many- Splendored Thing Ain't Misbehavin'	Love Is a Many-Splendored Thing (AA) (HP-1) A Little Love Can Go a Long, Long Way

SAMMY FAIN

Year	Production Title	Popular Songs
1956	Hollywood or Bust	
	The Revolt of Mamie Stover	
1957	THE ZIEGFELD FOLLIES	
	April Love	April Love (AN) (HP-1)
	Man on Fire	
1958	Marjorie Morningstar	A Very Precious Love (AN)
	A Certain Smile	A Certain Smile (AN)
	Gift of Love	The Gift of Love
	Mardi Gras	I'll Remember Tonight
	Wagon Train (TV)	
1959	The Big Circus	
	Imitation of Life	
1960	CHRISTINE	
1962	AROUND THE WORLD IN 80 DAYS (St. Louis)	
	Tender Is the Night	Tender Is the Night (AN)
1964	SOMETHING MORE	
	The Incredible Mr. Limpet	I Wish I Were a Fish
		"Why Is My Heart Such a Fool?"
1965	Joy in the Morning	
1968	If He Hollers, Let Him Go!	
1972	The Stepmother	
1976	Half a House	
1977	The Rescuers	

* * *

DOROTHY FIELDS

Dorothy Fields is the most successful woman lyricist in the history of American popular music. Miss Fields was born in Allenhurst, New Jersey in 1905. She was the daughter of famed vaudeville comedian Lew Fields. She began her theatrical career in 1926 writing material for floor shows staged at Harlem's Cotton

Club. The following year, she collaborated with composer Jimmy
McHugh on a song for the Broadway revue "Harry Delmar's Revels." Fields and McHugh were then engaged to create the entire
score for an all-Negro revue called "Blackbirds." They inserted
"I Can't Give You Anything but Love," written for "Revels," into
their score for "Blackbirds" and it swept the country. "Blackbirds" ran for 15 months! Her next effort, again with McHugh,
was a family affair. "Hello, Daddy" starred Lew Fields, the
book was written by his son Herbert, and the lyrics were by daughter Dorothy. In 1930, Miss Fields was represented by two Broadway musicals: "The International Revue" and "The Vanderbilt Revue." The former introduced both "On the Sunny Side of the
Street" and "Exactly Like You."

Beginning in 1929, Dorothy Fields' songs were heard in dozens of films starring such personalities as Lawrence Tibbett, Joan
Crawford, Jean Harlow, Ginger Rogers, Ann Sothern and Alice
Faye. While writing lyrics for motion pictures, she also had songs
included in the 1931 Broadway revue "Shoot the Works," and the
opening stage presentation at the Radio City Music Hall in which
she appeared as a singer in 1933.

For the first nine years of her career, Dorothy Fields
worked primarily with McHugh. In the mid-Thirties she began a
long association with veteran composer Jerome Kern. Their first
collaboration was the screen adaptation of his stage musical "Ro-
berta." Fields and McHugh worked with Kern to create the song
"Lovely to Look At," and with lyricists Oscar Hammerstein and
Otto Harbach to rewrite an old Kern melody called "I Won't Dance."
When the first broadcast of "Your Hit Parade" was aired in 1935,
"Lovely to Look At" was the Number Three song across the nation.
It was also nominated for an Academy Award. The same year "Ro-
berta" was released, Fields and Kern wrote the score for "I Dream
Too Much" starring Lily Pons. Opera singers were then a vogue
in Hollywood; RKO had Lily Pons, Paramount had Gladys Swarthout,
MGM had Miliza Korjus, and Columbia had Grace Moore. Miss
Moore's first two films had introduced the hit title songs "One
Night of Love" and "Love Me Forever" and Columbia was eager to
provide its diva with another standout for her third effort. Dorothy
Fields proved equal to the task when she wrote a new lyric for a
Fritz Kreisler melody which had first been heard in the 1919 operet-
ta "Apple Blossoms." The result was the classic "Stars in My
Eyes." In 1936, Dorothy Fields was again nominated for the "Os-
car" for her lyrics to "The Way You Look Tonight." This time,
she won.

Miss Fields returned to Broadway in 1939 after almost ten
years of writing for films. Her assignment was a natural--a musical about a Hollywood screen star titled "Stars in Your Eyes." In
the early 1940's, she expanded her activities to writing the books
for Broadway musicals in conjunction with her brother Herbert. The
team supplied the librettos for three Cole Porter hits in a row:

"Let's Face It," "Something for the Boys" and "Mexican Hayride."
They then joined with composer Sigmund Romberg for "Up in Central Park" for which Miss Fields also supplied the lyrics. Their
score included the hit "Close as Pages in a Book." "Up in Central Park" was followed by the books for "Annie Get Your Gun" and
"Arms and the Girl." Miss Fields was also the lyricist on the
latter production. Her next two Broadway assignments were lyrics
for the Shirley Booth vehicles "A Tree Grows in Brooklyn" and
"By the Beautiful Sea." By 1957, television had gained its hold as
the most popular source of entertainment in the country and Miss
Fields joined with composer Burton Lane to create the score for
a DuPont Show of the Month--a musical adaptation of the novel
"Junior Miss."

Dorothy Fields' last three Broadway efforts were "Redhead,"
"Sweet Charity" and "Seesaw." She was in her late sixties when
"Seesaw" had its premiere in 1973 yet her lyrics were as relevant
and contemporary as any ever written for the musical stage. In
March 1974, the fabled lyricist suffered a fatal heart attack in New
York City at the age of sixty-eight. Dorothy Fields was at the top
of her profession for 46 years! Her songs "I Can't Give You Any-
thing but Love," "On the Sunny Side of the Street," "Exactly Like
You" and "I'm in the Mood for Love" are all included on Variety's
list of the 100 Most Popular Songs of All Time.

Year	Production Title	Popular Songs
1928	BLACKBIRDS	I Can't Give You Anything but Love Diga-Diga-Doo I Must Have that Man Doin' the New Lowdown Porgy Baby!
	HELLO, DADDY	Futuristic Rhythm Out Where the Blues Begin In a Great Big Way Let's Sit and Talk About You
1929	The Time, the Place and the Girl	Collegiana
1930	THE INTERNATIONAL REVUE	On the Sunny Side of the Street Exactly Like You I'm Feeling Blue
	THE VANDERBILT REVUE	Blue Again Button Up Your Heart
	Love in the Rough	Go Home and Tell Your Mother One More Waltz

Year	Production Title	Popular Songs
1931	SHOOT THE WORKS SINGIN' THE BLUES	How's Your Uncle? It's the Darndest Thing Singin' the Blues
	Cuban Love Song Flying High	Cuban Love Song
1932	Meet the Baron	
		"Goodbye Blues"
1933	RADIO CITY MUSIC HALL (opening presentation)	Hey! Young Fella Happy Times With a Feather in My Cap
	Dancing Lady The Prizefighter and the Lady	My Dancing Lady Lucky Fella
		"Don't Blame Me" "Dinner at Eight"
1934	Fugitive Lovers	
		"Thank You for a Lovely Evening" "Lost in a Fog" "Serenade for a Wealthy Widow"
1935	Roberta	Lovely to Look At (AN) (HP-1) I Won't Dance (HP)
	I Dream Too Much	I Dream Too Much Jockey on the Carousel I'm the Echo I Got Love
	Every Night at Eight	I'm in the Mood for Love (HP-1) I Feel a Song Comin' On Speaking Confidentially You're an Angel
	Hooray for Love	I'm in Love All Over Again Hooray for Love I'm Livin' in a Great Big Way
	In Person	Don't Mention Love to Me Out of Sight, Out of Mind
	The Nitwits Alice Adams	Music in My Heart
		"Every Little Moment" (HP)
1936	Swing Time	The Way You Look Tonight (AA) (HP-1) A Fine Romance (HP)

DOROTHY FIELDS   227

Year	Production Title	Popular Songs
1936	Swing Time	Pick Yourself Up Never Gonna Dance Bojangles of Harlem
	The King Steps Out	Stars in My Eyes
1937	When You're in Love	Our Song
1938	Joy of Living	You Couldn't Be Cuter (HP) Just Let Me Look at You
1939	STARS IN YOUR EYES	This Is It (HP) It's All Yours I'll Pay the Check Just a Little Bit More
1940	One Night in the Tropics	Remind Me
1945	UP IN CENTRAL PARK	Close as Pages in a Book It Doesn't Cost You Anything to Dream April Snow When You Walk in the Room
1950	ARMS AND THE GIRL	There Must Be Something Better than Love Nothin' for Nothin'
1951	A TREE GROWS IN BROOKLYN Mr. Imperium Excuse My Dust Texas Carnival	Make the Man Love Me Love Is the Reason Andiamo Spring Has Sprung
1952	Lovely to Look At	
1953	The Farmer Takes a Wife	Today I Love Everybody
1954	BY THE BEAUTIFUL SEA	More Love than Your Love
1957	Junior Miss (TV)	
1959	REDHEAD	Just for Once Two Faces in the Dark Look What's in Love
1966	SWEET CHARITY	Where Am I Going? Big Spender If My Friends Could See Me Now

Year	Production Title	Popular Songs
1968	The Hell with Heroes	
1969	Sweet Charity	
1973	SEESAW	

* * *

TED FIORITO

The name of composer Ted Fiorito is better known than that of most songwriters since he achieved national recognition as an orchestra leader. He wrote almost exclusively for the popular music market having no Broadway credits and only four film credits. Fiorito was born in Newark, New Jersey in 1900, and worked as an accompanist in dancing academies while attending high school. After graduation, he played the piano in cafes and movie houses, and demonstrated songs for music publishing firms. In the early 1920's, he formed a four piece band whose repertoire included his hit songs "No, No Nora," "Charley My Boy" and "Toot, Toot, Tootsie." His primary lyricists were Gus Kahn, Sam Lewis, and Joe Young. The size of the Fiorito musical aggregation soon increased and his Oriole Terrace Orchestra became a favorite in large hotels from coast to coast. One of his featured singers in the 1930's was Betty Grable. Many of his recordings were best sellers, and he was frequently a regular on such popular radio programs as "Hollywood Hotel." By the 1960's, Fiorito had settled in Scottsdale, Arizona, where he had still another dance orchestra. His last engagement was with a combo in Las Vegas in 1970. Ted Fiorito died the next year at the age of seventy.

Year	Production Title	Popular Songs
1921		"By the Pyramids" "Love Bird" "Just Like a Rainbow"
1922		"Toot, Toot Tootsie" "Doo Dah Blues" "Lips"
1923		"No, No Nora" "When Lights Are Low"
1924		"Charley My Boy" "The Little Old Clock on the Mantel" "I Need Some Petting"

TED FIORITO

Year	Production Title	Popular Songs
1925		"I Never Knew" "Sometime" "Alone at Last" "Dreamer of Dreams" "When I Dream of the Last Waltz with You"
1926		"Drifting Apart"
1928		"Laugh, Clown, Laugh" "King for a Day" "I'm Sorry, Sally"
1929		"Then You've Never Been Blue" "Joe College" "I Used to Love Her in the Moonlight"
1930		"Hangin' on the Garden Gate"
1931	Holy Terror	"Now That You're Gone"
1932	Blondie of the Follies	Three on a Match
1933		"Kalua Lullaby"
1934		"King Kamehameha" "How Can It Be a Beautiful Day?" "Soft Green Seas"
1935	Here Comes the Band	Roll Along, Prairie Moon (HP)
1936	Song of the Saddle	"When the Moon Hangs High" "Alone at a Table for Two" "Yours Truly Is Truly Yours" "Knick Knacks on the Mantel"
1937		"Along a Texas Trail"
1940		"Now I Lay Me Down to Dream" (HP)
1942		"Lily of Laguna"
1944		"My Mama Says 'No, No'"

Year	Production Title	Popular Songs
1945		"Boogie Woogie Lullaby"
1948		"My Guitar

* * *

FRED FISHER

Fred Fisher was born and educated in Germany, and served in both the German navy and the French Foreign Legion. He came to the United States in 1900 when he was twenty-five years old. Four years later, his first hit "Ev'ry Little Bit Helps" (lyric by George Whiting) was published. He began his songwriting career in Chicago and then moved to New York City where he became manager of the Harms, Inc. music publishing firm. He collaborated with lyricist Alfred Bryan to create one of 1910's most popular novelty numbers "Come, Josephine, in My Flying Machine." Five years later, he had become successful enough to found his own publishing company. In addition to Bryan, Fisher worked frequently with lyricist Joseph McCarthy with whom he wrote the 1917 hit "They Go Wild, Simply Wild Over Me." Although basically a composer, he supplied both the words and music for his most lasting song "Chicago (That Toddlin' Town)." Fisher also composed background scores for silent motion pictures. In 1940, he collaborated with his twenty-five year old daughter, Doris, on the song "Whispering Grass." It provided The Ink Spots with a best-selling record. Fred Fisher died two years later at the age of sixty-seven.

Year	Production Title	Popular Songs
1904		"Ev'ry Little Bit Helps"
1906		"If the Man in the Moon Were a Coon" "I've Said My Last Farewell"
1907		"And a Little Bit More" "Under the Matzos Tree"
1908		"My Brudda Sylvest"
1909		"In Sunny Italy"
1910		"Come, Josephine, in My Flying Machine" "Oh! You Chicken" "Any Little Girl That's a Nice Little Girl Is the Right Little Girl for Me"

Year	Production Title	Popular Songs
1910		"Gee, but It's Great to Meet a Friend from Your Home Town"
1911		"After That I Want a Little More" "Make Me Love You Like I Never Loved Before" "If Every Hour Were a Day" "First You Get the Money, Then You Get the Flat, Then It's Time Enough to Get the Girl" "Yiddisha Luck and Irisha Love"
1912		"When I Get You Alone To-night" "Big Blond Baby" "Roll Me Around Like a Hoop, My Dear"
1913	THE ZIEGFELD FOLLIES	Peg O' My Heart (HP-1) "I'm on My Way to Mandalay"
1914	THE BELLE OF BOND STREET	Who Paid the Rent for Mrs. Rip Van Winkle? "When It's Moonlight on the Alamo" "There's a Little Spark of Love Still Burning" "I Want to Go to Tokio"
1915		"Siam" "There's a Broken Heart for Every Light on Broadway" "Norway"
1916		"Ireland Must Be Heaven for My Mother Came from There" "There's a Little Bit of Bad in Every Good Little Girl" "You Can't Get Along with 'em or without 'em"
1917		"They Go Wild, Simply Wild, Over Me"

Year	Production Title	Popular Songs
1917		"Night Time in Little Italy" "Lorraine, My Beautiful Alsace, Lorraine"
1918		"Happiness"
1919		"Dardanella" "Ballyho Bay" "Goodbye, Teddy Roosevelt (You Were a Real American)"
1920	ED WYNN CARNIVAL KISSING TIME TICK-TACK-TOE	Rose of Spain Oui, Oui, Marie "Daddy, You've Been a Mother to Me"
1921		"I Found a Rose in the Devil's Garden" "When the Honeymoon Was Over"
1922		"Chicago (That Toddlin' Town)" "That Red Head Gal"
1924		"Savannah" "And the Band Played On"
1925		"I Want You to Want Me to Want You"
1927		"Fifty Million Frenchmen (Can't Be Wrong)" "When the Morning Glories Wake Up in the Morning"
1928	My Man	I'd Rather Be Blue "There Ain't No Sweet Man (Worth the Salt of My Tears)" "Happy Days and Lonely Nights"
1929	So This Is College Wonder of Women Hollywood Revue of 1929 Madonna of Avenue A	I Don't Want Your Kisses Ich Liebe Dich (I Love You)

Year	Production Title	Popular Songs
1930	Their Own Desire Children of Pleasure Chasing Rainbows	Blue Is the Night Dust Girl Trouble
1931		"I'm All Dressed Up with a Broken Heart"
1935		"Georgia Rockin' Chair"
1936		"Your Feet's Too Big"
1938	Angels with Dirty Faces	Angels with Dirty Faces
1939		"Two Fools in Love"
1940		"That's When Your Heart-aches Begin" "Whispering Grass"

* * *

ARTHUR FREED

The public remembers lyricist Arthur Freed as one of MGM's top producers rather than as the writer of "I Cried for You," "Temptation" and "Alone." Freed hailed from Charleston, South Carolina where he was born in 1894. After high school graduation, he worked as a song plugger in Chicago until Minnie Marx recognized his talent and put him in a vaudeville act with her sons. Freed served in the Army in World War I and then earned a living writing for floor shows staged in Broadway cafes. He was twenty-nine when his lyrics for "I Cried for You" brought him attention as a songwriter. He next achieved a reputation as a producer by staging plays in Southern California in the late 1920's. Freed's first assignment at MGM was as lyricist on the 1929 film "Broadway Melody" which was the first musical to be selected as the Best Picture of the Year. During his more than 40 years with the studio, he collaborated with composer Nacio Herb Brown on dozens of films in which such stars as Ramon Navarro, Joan Crawford, Marion Davies, Jean Harlow, Norma Shearer, Eleanor Powell, Jeanette MacDonald, Mickey Rooney and Judy Garland appeared. His popular songs included "Singin' in the Rain," "All I Do Is Dream of You" and "You Are My Lucky Star." Freed became a full-fledged movie producer in 1939. Among his best-known films were "Meet Me In St. Louis," "Easter Parade" and "Annie Get Your Gun." Arthur Freed's screen musicals "An American in Paris" and "Gigi" won the Best Picture "Oscars" in 1951 and 1958.

He also won a nomination for his 1940 song "Our Love Affair."
Freed died in 1973 at the age of seventy-nine.

Year	Production Title	Popular Songs
1920	SILKS AND SATINS	
1921		"When Buddha Smiles"
1922		"After Every Party"
1923		"I Cried for You" (HP)
1929	Broadway Melody	Broadway Melody You Were Meant for Me The Wedding of the Painted Doll The Love Boat
	Hollywood Revue of 1929 The Pagan Untamed Marianne	Singin' in the Rain Pagan Love Long The Chant of the Jungle Blondy
		"Here Comes the Sun"
1930	Lord Byron of Broadway	Should I? The Woman in the Shoe A Bundle of Old Love Letters
	Montana Moon Those Three French Girls Good News A Lady's Morals	The Moon Is Low You're Simply Delish
		"It Looks Like Love"
1932	Blondie of the Follies	It Was So Beautiful
		"Fit as a Fiddle" "It's Winter Again" "Come Out, Come Out, Wherever You Are"
1933	Going Hollywood	Temptation We'll Make Hay While the Sun Shines Our Big Love Scene After Sundown
	The Barbarian Hold Your Man Stage Mother Peg O' My Heart College Coach	Love Songs of the Nile Hold Your Man Beautiful Girl

Year	Production Title	Popular Songs
1934	Sadie McKee	All I Do Is Dream of You
	Student Tour	A New Moon Is Over My Shoulder
		From Now On
	Hollywood Party	
	Hide-Out	
	Riptide	
1935	Broadway Melody of 1936	You Are My Lucky Star (HP-1)
		Broadway Rhythm (HP)
		Sing Before Breakfast
		I've Got a Feelin' You're Foolin' (HP)
		On a Sunday Afternoon
	A Night at the Opera	Alone (HP-1)
	China Seas	
1936	San Francisco	Would You? (HP)
	After the Thin Man	Smoke Dreams
	The Devil Is a Sissy	
1937	Broadway Melody of 1938	Everybody Sing
		Yours and Mine (HP)
		Sun Showers
		I'm Feelin' Like a Million
1939	Babes in Arms	Good Morning (HP)
	The Ice Follies of 1939	
1940	Strike Up the Band	Our Love Affair (AN) (HP)
	Two Girls on Broadway	My Wonderful One, Let's Dance
1945	Yolanda and the Thief	Coffee Time
		Yolanda
1946	Ziegfeld Follies	This Heart of Mine
1950	Pagan Love Song	The Sea of the Moon
1952	Singin' in the Rain	Make 'em Laugh

* * *

CLIFF FRIEND

    Composer/lyricist Cliff Friend was born and raised on a farm in Cincinnati, Ohio. He planned to be a concert pianist and studied at the Cincinnati Conservatory of Music. He gave up that ambition after a three year bout with tuberculosis, and became a vaudeville artist. His stage career culminated in an international tour in which he performed as Harry Richman's accompanist in most of the capital cities of the world. One of his first popular songs was the comedy number "You Tell Her--I Stutter" with lyrics by Billy Rose. Friend frequently shared his credits with other composers and three of his biggest hits--"June Night," "Mama Loves Papa" and "Hello, Bluebird"--were written in collaboration with Abel Baer. In 1937, he and Dave Franklin created the sensational novelty number "The Merry-Go-Round Broke Down" which became the theme song for Warner Bros. "Looney Tunes" featuring cartoon favorites "Porky Pig," "Bugs Bunny" and "Daffy Duck." Friends' songs were first heard by movie audiences in 1930. He was also a frequent contributor to the Broadway revues staged by George White. His timely song "We Did It Before and We Can Do It Again" was introduced by Eddie Cantor in the stage production "Banjo Eyes" just two weeks after the United States entered World War II. Cliff Friend was nearing his seventies when he composed "Old Man Time" which was included in an album recorded by comic Jimmy Durante. Friend died in 1974 at the age of eighty.

Year	Production Title	Popular Songs
1919		"Strava-Nada"
1920		"Naughty Eyes"
1921	BOMBO THE PASSING SHOW MIDNIGHT ROUNDERS	
1922		"You Tell Her--I Stutter" "O-oo Ernest, Are You Earnest with Me?" "Lovesick Blues" "California"
1923		"Chili Bom Bom" "Blue Hoosier Blues"
1924		"June Night" "Mama Loves Papa" "There's Yes Yes in Your Eyes" (HP) "Let Me Linger Longer in Your Arms" "Where the Lazy Daisies Grow"

Year	Production Title	Popular Songs
1924		"Where the Dreamy Wabash Flows"
		"When the One You Love Loves You"
		"Big Butter and Egg Man"
1925	BIG BOY	How I Love You (I'm Tellin' the Birds, I'm Tellin' the Bees)
		"Then I'll Be Happy"
		"Let It Rain! Let It Pour!"
1926		"Hello, Bluebird"
		"Tamiami Trail"
		"Oh, If I Only Had You"
		"Elsie Schultzenheim"
		"I Told Them All About You"
1927	PIGGY	"Whisper Song (When the Pussy Willow Whispers to the Catnip)"
		"Give Me a Night in June"
1928	WHOOPEE	My Blackbirds Are Bluebirds Now
		"It Goes Like This"
		"You're a Real Sweetheart"
1929	GEORGE WHITE'S SCANDALS	Bottoms Up
		Bigger and Better Than Ever
		"Bashful Baby"
		"Same Old Moon (Same Old June, but Not the Same Old You)"
		"Satisfied"
		"I'll Close My Eyes to the Rest of the World"
1930	The Cuckoos	
	The Golden Calf	
	The Dancers	
	Last of the Duanes	
	Let's Go Places	
	On the Level	

Year	Production Title	Popular Songs
1931	EARL CARROLL'S VANITIES Palmy Days	My Baby Said Yes, Yes "Freddie, the Freshman" "At Last I'm Happy" "I Wanna Sing About You"
1932	GEORGE WHITE'S MUSIC HALL VARIETIES The Crooner	Sweethearts Forever "You've Got Me in the Palm of Your Hand" "Let's Have a Party" "Just Because You're You" "Neath the Silv'ry Moon"
1934	Many Happy Returns Bachelor of Arts Down to Their Last Yacht	The Sweetest Music This Side of Heaven "Freckle Face, You're Beautiful" "What's Good for the Goose (Is Good for the Gander)" "South American Joe" "The Lights Are Low (the Music Is Sweet)"
1935	George White's Scandals	Hunkadola
1936	Happy Go Lucky	"When My Dream Boat Comes Home" (HP) "The Broken Record" (HP) "Wah-hoo" (HP) "Wake Up and Sing" "Cut Where the Blue Begins" "It's the Gypsy in Me"
1937	Hit Parade	"You Can't Stop Me from Dreaming" (HP-1) "The Merry-Go-Round Broke Down" (HP) "Never Should Have Told You" "Everything You Said Came True" "Two Dreams Got Together"

Year	Production Title	Popular Songs
1938		"There's a Brand New Picture in My Picture Frame" "Will You Remember Tonight Tomorrow?"
1939	The Ice Follies of 1939	"I Must See Annie Tonight" (HP) "I'm Building a Sailboat of Dreams" (HP) "Concert in the Park" "You Don't Know How Much You Can Suffer"
1940		"Trade Winds" (HP-1) "Confucius Say"
1941	BANJO EYES	We Did It Before and We Can Do It Again "Below the Equator"
1944	Hi, Beautiful Shine on Harvest Moon	Don't Sweetheart Me (HP) Time Waits for No One (HP) "Gonna Build a Big Fence Around Texas"
1946		"You Put a Song in My Heart"
1947		"Lone Star Moon"
1949		"Two Little, New Little, Blue Little Eyes"
1950		"You Missed the Boat" "You're Gettin' a Good Girl" "You Are My Love"
1961		"Old Man Time"

* * *

RUDOLF FRIML

Rudolf Friml was born in Czechoslavakia in 1879. His first

composition--a selection for piano--was published when he was only ten.   After graduation from the Prague Conservatory, Friml spent eight years performing in piano recitals in Europe.   He made his American debut as soloist in New York's Carnegie Hall in 1904, and then spent several years appearing with the country's leading symphonies.

Friml's career as a popular music composer began as the result of a tempermental dispute between two leading theatrical personalities.   Composer Victor Herbert had been engaged to write the music for "The Firefly."   Herbert withdrew when leading lady, Emma Trentini, refused to travel from New York to Philadelphia to discuss the score.   Producer Arthur Hammerstein persuaded Friml to take over Herbert's assignment.   The success of "The Firefly" established Friml as the leading contender for Herbert's throne.   Most Broadway musicals were still patterned after European operettas and Friml continued in the traditions of that form. "The Firefly" was followed by "High Jinks" in 1913, "The Peasant Girl" and "Katinka" in 1915, and 11 more productions (including the 1921 edition of "The Ziegfeld Follies") before he scored with the first of his three most successful operettas.

His greatest triumph was in 1924 when "Rose-Marie" ran for 527 performances--the longest run achieved by any musical that year.   It was so popular that four road companies were formed to tour the country.   In addition to the show's title song, the score introduced the classic "Indian Love Call."   "Rose-Marie" was in the twelfth month of its run when "The Vagabond King" premiered in 1925 and ran for 511 performances.   Friml celebrated his forty-sixth birthday that same year by becoming a United States citizen. His last success was "The Three Musketeers" in 1928.   Operetta was becoming less and less popular and the majority of theatregoers preferred the modern rhythms and sophisticated lyrics of such songwriters as George Gershwin, DeSylva, Brown and Henderson, and Cole Porter.   The last two Friml operettas produced on Broadway were "Luana" (1930) and "Music Hath Charms" (1934).   Each closed in less than a month.   The remainder of his career was spent in California where he was an occasional contributor to motion pictures.   His most famous work, "Rose-Marie," was filmed for the second time in 1936, and "The Firefly" reached the screen the following year.   For the film version of "The Firefly," Friml collaborated with Herbert Stothart, Robert Wright, and Chet Forrest in adapting his earlier composition "Chansonette" into the tremendously popular "Donkey Serenade."

Ten years passed between the film "The Firefly" and Friml's next major effort--the 1947 motion picture "Northwest Outpost." Then, in 1954, MGM filmed "Rose-Marie" for the third time and engaged Friml to compose additional songs with lyrics by Paul Francis Webster.   Friml also worked with lyricist Johnny Burke on new songs for the 1956 remake of "The Vagabond King."   In December of 1969, ASCAP staged a special tribute in Manhattan's

Shubert Theatre to celebrate the ninetieth birthday of operetta's
Grand Old Man.   Rudolf Friml died three years later at the Hollywood Presbyterian Hospital.

Year	Production Title	Popular Songs
1912	THE FIREFLY	Giannina Mia When a Maid Comes Knock- ing at Your Heart The Dawn of Love Sympathy Love Is Like a Firefly
1913	HIGH JINKS	The Bubble Something Seems Tingle-ing- eling Not Now but Later Love's Own Kiss
1915	KATINKA	Tis the End, So Farewell Allah's Holiday I Want to Marry a Male Quartette Katinka Rackety Coo! My Paradise
	THE PEASANT GIRL	
1917	YOU'RE IN LOVE KITTY DARLIN'	You're in Love
1918	SOMETIME	Sometime Any Kind of Man
	GLORIANNA	
1919	TUMBLE INN LITTLE WHOPPER	
1921	JUNE LOVE THE ZIEGFELD FOLLIES	Dear Love, My Love Bring Back My Blushing Rosie
1922	THE BLUE KITTEN	Cutie "L'Amour, Toujours, L'Amour (Love Everlast- ing)"
1923	CINDERS DEW DROP INN	"In Love with Love"
1924	ROSE-MARIE	Rose-Marie

Year	Production Title	Popular Songs
1924	ROSE-MARIE	Indian Love Call The Mounties Totem Tom Tom The Door of My Dreams Pretty Things "On the Blue Lagoon"
1925	THE VAGABOND KING	Song of the Vagabonds Only a Rose Some Day Huguette Waltz Love Me Tonight Love for Sale Tomorrow Nocturne
1926	NO FOOLIN' THE WILD ROSE	Florida, the Moon and You We'll Have a Kingdom The Wild Rose
1927	THE WHITE EAGLE	Give Me One Hour Gather the Rose The Regimental Song One Golden Hour
1928	THE THREE MUSKETEERS	Ma Belle March of the Musketeers Your Eyes With Red Wine
1930	9:15 REVUE LUANA Lottery Bride	
1934	MUSIC HATH CHARMS	
1936	Rose-Marie	
1937	The Firefly Music for Madame	Donkey Serenade
1947	Northwest Outpost	
1954	Rose-Marie	I Have the Love
1956	The Vagabond King	
1965		"Somewhere in My Heart"

GEORGE GERSHWIN

    Although George Gershwin was thoroughly exposed to clas-
sical music through piano lessons he received as a child, the two
composers who most interested him were popular song writers
Jerome Kern and Irving Berlin. Gershwin was born in Brooklyn
in 1898, and cut his high school education short to take a job as
pianist in a music publishing firm. He was eighteen years old
when his first song was published in 1916. He quit his job as a
song plugger to work as an accompanist for vaudeville performers,
and rehearsal pianist for Broadway musicals. He succeeded in
having his songs interpolated into Sigmund Romberg's score for
"The Passing Show" and E. Ray Goetz' "Hitchy-Koo." In 1919,
Gershwin's music attracted the attention of Alex Aarons whose father was a theatrical producer. The elder Aarons engaged the
young songwriter to write the complete score for the book musical
"La, La Lucille." That same year, Gershwin collaborated with
lyricist Irving Caesar on the song "Swanee" which was introduced
in a stage show at a movie theatre. Al Jolson interpolated the
number in his revival of "Sinbad" and it proved to be the turning
point in Gershwin's career. The song sold two million recordings,
more than a million copies of sheet music, and was the most financially profitable of all the songs Gershwin was ever to write.

    In 1919, one of Florenz Ziegfeld's stars left "The Follies"
to produce his own revue. The reception accorded dancer George
White's "Scandals" encouraged him to continue with the new enter-
prise and he hired George Gershwin as composer for the second
edition. Gershwin stayed with "George White's Scandals" for five
editions in which his "I'll Build a Stairway to Paradise" and "Somebody Loves Me" were introduced. During this period he also contributed songs to a dozen other Broadway attractions. He parted
company with the "Scandals" in 1924--the year he first publicly
performed his "Rhapsody in Blue" in New York's Aeolian Hall.
The composition attracted world-wide attention. Composer Arthur
Schwartz has called it "the most influential, as well as the most
played, orchestral composition of this century."

    The Gershwin family was blessed with two talented sons.
George's older brother Ira was a verse and lyric writer. Although
the brothers had collaborated as early as 1918, it wasn't until
1924 that they became full-time partners. From 1924 through
1931, George and Ira Gershwin's songs were heard in such outstanding Broadway productions as "Lady, Be Good" (1924), "Oh,
Kay!" (1926), "Funny Face" (1927), "Strike Up the Band" (1930),
and "Of Thee I Sing" (1931). From these shows came the Gershwin classics "Fascinatin' Rhythm," "Someone to Watch Over Me,"
"'S Wonderful," "Embraceable You," and "I Got Rhythm." George
spent part of 1928 in Europe studying classical music. On his return, his impressions of Paris were conveyed in the tone poem
"An American in Paris" which was used as a ballet in the 1929
production "Show Girl." After several years in preparation, Gersh-

win's all-Negro folk opera "Porgy and Bess" opened in New York.
It was not a success and closed in only four months. In retrospect,
historian Stanley Green has said that "More than any other work,
it is the one that is most universally accepted as a truly American form of opera."

George Gershwin composed his first motion picture score
for the 1931 release "Delicious" starring Janet Gaynor. In 1936,
he and Ira succumbed to Hollywood offers and settled in California.
Their first year on the West Coast saw their song "They Can't
Take That Away from Me" nominated for the "Oscar." Before the
second year ended, George was dead. While working on his score
for "The Goldwyn Follies," the thirty-eight year old genius col-
lapsed. On July 11, 1937, he died of a brain tumor.

George Gershwin's career spanned only 21 years yet during
that time he created music for more diverse entertainment forms
than any other popular song writer--stage, screen, ballet, concert
hall and opera. In 1945, Hollywood released Gershwin's film biography "Rhapsody in Blue." Two years later, several of his unpublished songs were heard in the film musical "The Shocking Miss
Pilgrim." "An American in Paris" with a score composed of
Gershwin standards was selected as the Best Picture of 1951.
"Porgy and Bess" began to receive its long overdue recognition
when it was selected by the State Department to represent the nation in a 1953 international tour. It became the first opera by an
American-born composer ever staged in the home of grand opera--
the La Scala Opera House. Gershwin received Italy's highest
award to foreign composers--an honorary membership in Rome's
Academy of Santa Cecilia. Additional posthumous honors paid him
include the Gold Medallion Award bestowed on world famous composers by the Union Bank of Switzerland, a Chicago elementary
school bearing his name, a street in Hull, England, named "Gershwin Avenue," and a United States postage stamp commemorating
the 75th anniversary of his birth.

Year	Production Title	Popular Songs
1916	THE PASSING SHOW	
1918	LADIES FIRST	The Real American Folk Song
	HITCHY-KOO	You-oo, Just You
	HALF PAST EIGHT	
	(closed in tryout)	
1919	GOOD MORNING, JUDGE	I Was So Young
	LA, LA LUCILLE	Nobody but You
	THE LADY IN RED	
	MORRIS GEST'S MIDNIGHT WHIRL	
		"Swanee"
		"Come to the Moon"

Year	Production Title	Popular Songs
1920	GEORGE WHITE'S SCANDALS	Scandal Walk
	THE SWEETHEART SHOP	Waiting for the Sun to Come Out
	ED WYNN CARNIVAL	
	BROADWAY BREVITIES	
	DERE MABLE (closed in tryout)	
1921	GEORGE WHITE'S SCANDALS	Drifting Along with the Tide
	A DANGEROUS MAID (closed in tryout)	Boy Wanted
	BLUE EYES	
	SNAPSHOTS OF 1921	
	THE BROADWAY WHIRL	
	THE PERFECT FOOL	"Swanee Rose"
		"Yan-kee"
		"No One Else but That Girl of Mine"
1922	THE FRENCH DOLL	Do It Again
	FOR GOODNESS SAKE	Tra La La
	SPICE OF 1922	The Yankee Doodle Blues
	GEORGE WHITE'S SCANDALS	I'll Build a Stairway to Paradise
		I Found a Four Leaf Clover
	OUR NELL	
1923	GEORGE WHITE'S SCANDALS	Life of a Rose
		Let's Be Lonesome Together
	LITTLE MISS BLUEBEARD	I Won't Say I Will
	NIFTIES OF 1923	Nashville Nightingale
	THE DANCING GIRL	
	THE RAINBOW (London)	
1924	SWEET LITTLE DEVIL	Virginia, Don't Go Too Far
		Someone Who Believes in You
	GEORGE WHITE'S SCANDALS	Somebody Loves Me
		Rose of Madrid
	LADY, BE GOOD!	Oh, Lady, Be Good!
		Fascinatin' Rhythm
		The Half of It Dearie Blues
		So Am I
		Hang on to Me
		Little Jazz Bird
	PRIMROSE (London)	"The Man I Love"

Year	Production Title	Popular Songs
1925	TELL ME MORE!	Why Do I Love You? Tell Me More Kickin' the Clouds Away
	TIP-TOES	That Certain Feeling Looking for a Boy Sweet and Lowdown Lady Luck Nightie Night Three Times a Day These Charming People
	SONG OF THE FLAME	Cossack Love Song Song of the Flame
1926	OH, KAY!	Someone to Watch Over Me Maybe Do-Do-Do Clap Yo' Hands Dear Little Girl
	AMERICANA	
1927	FUNNY FACE	'S Wonderful My One and Only He Loves and She Loves The Babbitt and the Bromide Let's Kiss and Make Up Funny Face
	STRIKE UP THE BAND (closed in tryout)	
1928	ROSALIE	How Long Has This Been 　　Going On? Say So Oh Gee! Oh Joy!
	TREASURE GIRL	Feeling I'm Falling K-ra-zy for You Oh, So Nice Got a Rainbow Where's the Boy? Here's 　　the Girl
1929	SHOW GIRL	Liza Do What You Do So Are You "In the Mandarin's Orchid 　　Garden"
1930	STRIKE UP THE BAND	I've Got a Crush on You Soon Strike Up the Band

Year	Production Title	Popular Songs
1930	GIRL CRAZY	Embraceable You
		I Got Rhythm
		Bidin' My Time
		But Not for Me
		Boy, What Love Has Done to Me
		Could You Use Me?
		Sam and Delilah
	9:15 REVUE	
1931	OF THEE I SING	Who Cares?
		Love Is Sweeping the Country
		Of Thee I Sing
	Delicious	Blah, Blah, Blah
		Delishious
1932	Girl Crazy	
1933	PARDON MY ENGLISH	Isn't It a Pity?
		The Lorelei
		My Cousin in Milwaukee
	LET 'EM EAT CAKE	Mine
1935	PORGY AND BESS	Summertime
		I Got Plenty O' Nuttin'
		Bess, You Is My Woman Now
		It Ain't Necessarily So
		I Loves You, Porgy
		There's a Boat That's Leavin' Soon for New York
1936	THE SHOW IS ON	By Strauss
		"King of Swing"
1937	Shall We Dance	They Can't Take That Away from Me (AN) (HP)
		Let's Call the Whole Thing Off (HP)
		I've Got Beginner's Luck
		They All Laughed
		Slap That Bass
		Shall We Dance?
	A Damsel in Distress	Nice Work If You Can Get It (HP)
		A Foggy Day
		Things Are Looking Up
		I Can't Be Bothered Now

Year	Production Title	Popular Songs

Posthumous:

1938	The Goldwyn Follies	Love Walked In (HP-1) Our Love Is Here to Stay I Was Doing All Right
1939		"Dawn of a New Day"
1947	The Shocking Miss Pilgrim	For You, for Me, Forever- more (HP) Changing My Tune Aren't You Kinda Glad We Did?

* * *

IRA GERSHWIN

Ira Gershwin ranks third among Broadway's most successful lyricists. For two years after the death of his brother George, Ira was virtually nonproductive. Beginning in 1924, the Gershwins had worked as a team on 16 musicals produced on Broadway through 1936. Ira had supplied the words to such popular songs as "The Man I Love," "Oh, Lady, Be Good!," "Maybe," "Funny Face," "How Long Has This Been Going On?," "Strike Up the Band," "But Not for Me," "Mine," and "Bess, You Is My Woman Now"-- all with music by George Gershwin.

Ira was two years older than his brother and began his professional career writing with other composers, frequently using the pen name of "Arthur Francis." One of Ira's first hits, "Oh Me, Oh My, Oh You," boasted music by Vincent Youmans. Among his other successes were "Cheerful Little Earful" (music by Harry Warren), "Let's Take a Walk Around the Block" (music by Harold Arlen) and "I Can't Get Started" (music by Vernon Duke). Ira sometimes worked with co-lyricists such as Billy Rose, E. Y. Harburg, DuBose Heywood, and Gus Kahn with whom he shared credit for "Liza."

Ira Gershwin received the first Pulitzer Prize for Drama ever awarded to a musical comedy for his lyrics to "Of Thee I Sing" (1931). The Gershwin brothers' work in Hollywood in 1936 and 1937 produced the favorites "A Foggy Day," "Nice Work If You Can Get It," "Let's Call the Whole Thing Off" and "They All Laughed." Their last film, "The Goldwyn Follies," was released in 1938--the year after George's death from a brain tumor. It wasn't until 1941 that Ira Gershwin's name again appeared on a production. Working with German-born composer Kurt Weill, Ira

wrote the lyrics for the musical "Lady in the Dark" which was acclaimed as a milestone in Broadway history.   He also worked
with Weill on the unsuccessful "Firebrand of Florence" and the
film musical "Where Do We Go from Here?"   Other composers
with whom he collaborated were Jerome Kern, Arthur Schwartz
and Burton Lane.   He provided Judy Garland with one of her most
memorable lyrics--"The Man That Got Away" which she introduced
in the remake of "A Star Is Born" in 1954.   A book of Ira Gershwin's work titled "Lyrics on Several Occasions" was published in
1959.   He received Academy Award nominations for "They Can't
Take That Away from Me," "Long Ago and Far Away" and "The
Man That Got Away."

Year	Production Title	Popular Songs
1918	LADIES FIRST	The Real American Folk Song
	HALF PAST EIGHT (closed in tryout)	
1920	THE SWEETHEART SHOP	Waiting for the Sun to Come Out
1921	TWO LITTLE GIRLS IN BLUE	Oh Me, Oh My, Oh You Dolly
	A DANGEROUS MAID (closed in tryout)	Boy Wanted
1922	FOR GOODNESS SAKE	Tra La La
	GEORGE WHITE'S SCANDALS	I'll Build a Stairway to Paradise
	PINS AND NEEDLES	
	MOLLY DARLING	
1923	LITTLE MISS BLUEBEARD	I Won't Say I Will
	NIFTIES OF 1923	
	THE GREENWICH VILLAGE FOLLIES	
1924	LADY, BE GOOD!	Fascinatin' Rhythm
		Oh, Lady Be Good!
		Little Jazz Bird
		The Half of It Dearie Blues
		Hang on to Me
		So Am I
	BE YOURSELF	
	TOP HOLE	
	THE FIREBRAND (play)	
	PRIMROSE (London)	"The Man I Love"
1925	TELL ME MORE!	Kickin' the Clouds Away

Year	Production Title	Popular Songs
1925	TELL ME MORE!	Why Do I Love You?
		Tell Me More
	TIP-TOES	That Certain Feeling
		Sweet and Lowdown
		Looking for a Boy
		Lady Luck
		Nightie Night
		These Charming People
		Three Times a Day
1926	AMERICANA	Sunny Disposish
	OH, KAY!	Someone to Watch Over Me
		Maybe
		Do-Do-Do
		Clap Yo' Hands
		Dear Little Girl
1927	FUNNY FACE	'S Wonderful
		He Loves and She Loves
		My One and Only
		The Babbitt and the Bromide
		Let's Kiss and Make Up
		Funny Face
	STRIKE UP THE BAND (closed in tryout)	
1928	ROSALIE	How Long Has This Been Going On?
		Say So
		Oh Gee! Oh Joy!
	TREASURE GIRL	Got a Rainbow
		Where's the Boy? Here's the Girl
		Feeling I'm Falling
		Oh, So Nice
		K-ra-zy for You
	THAT'S A GOOD GIRL (London)	The One I'm Looking For
1929	SHOW GIRL	Liza
		Do What You Do
		So Are You
		"In the Mandarin's Orchid Garden"
1930	STRIKE UP THE BAND	I've Got a Crush on You
		Soon
		Strike Up the Band
	THE GARRICK GAIETIES	I'm Only Human After All

Year	Production Title	Popular Songs
1930	GIRL CRAZY	Embraceable You
		I Got Rhythm
		Bidin' My Time
		But Not for Me
		Boy, What Love Has Done to Me
		Could You Use Me?
		Sam and Delilah
	SWEET AND LOW	Cheerful Little Earful
		Sweet So-and-So
	9:15 REVUE	
1931	OF THEE I SING	Who Cares?
		Love Is Sweeping the Country
		Of Thee I Sing
	THE SOCIAL REGISTER (play)	The Key to My Heart
	BILLY ROSE'S CRAZY QUILT	
	Delicious	Blah, Blah, Blah
		Delishious
1932	Girl Crazy	
1933	PARDON MY ENGLISH	Isn't It a Pity?
		My Cousin in Milwaukee
		The Lorelei
	LET 'EM EAT CAKE	Mine
1934	LIFE BEGINS AT 8:40	Let's Take a Walk Around the Block
		Fun to Be Fooled
		You're a Builder-Upper
		What Can You Say in a Love Song?
		Shoein' the Mare
1935	PORGY AND BESS	I Got Plenty O' Nuttin'
		Bess, You Is My Woman Now
		It Ain't Necessarily So
		I Loves You, Porgy
		There's a Boat That's Leavin' Soon for New York
1936	THE ZIEGFELD FOLLIES	I Can't Get Started
		Island in the West Indies
		That Moment of Moments
	THE SHOW IS ON	By Strauss

Year	Production Title	Popular Songs
1937	Shall We Dance?	They Can't Take That Away from Me (AN) (HP)
		Let's Call the Whole Thing Off (HP)
		I've Got Beginner's Luck
		They All Laughed
		Slap That Bass
		Shall We Dance?
	A Damsel in Distress	Nice Work If You Can Get It (HP)
		A Foggy Day
		Things Are Looking Up
		I Can't Be Bothered Now
1938	The Goldwyn Follies	Love Walked In (HP-1)
		Our Love Is Here to Stay
		I Was Doing All Right
		Spring Again
1939		"Dawn of a New Day"
1941	LADY IN THE DARK	My Ship
		The Saga of Jenny
		This Is New
		Tschaikowsky
		"Honorable Moon"
1943	The North Star	
1944	Cover Girl	Long Ago and Far Away (AN) (HP-1)
		Sure Thing
1945	THE FIREBRAND OF FLORENCE	
	Where Do We Go from Here?	All at Once
1946	PARK AVENUE	There's No Holding Me
1947	The Shocking Miss Pilgrim	For You, For Me, Forevermore (HP)
		Changing My Tune
		Aren't You Kinda Glad We Did?
1949	The Barkleys of Broadway	My One and Only Highland Fling (HP)
		You'd Be Hard to Replace

Year	Production Title	Popular Songs
1953	Give a Girl a Break	Applause, Applause It Happens Every Time
1954	A Star Is Born	The Man That Got Away (AN) It's a New World Here's What I'm Here For
	The Country Girl	The Search Is Through
1964	Kiss Me, Stupid	

* * *

L. WOLFE GILBERT

L. Wolfe Gilbert was an infant when his Russian parents emigrated to the United States. They settled in Philadelphia, Pennsylvania, where their son attended public school. He began a singing career as an amateur night contestant and then progressed to vaudeville and cafe engagements. In 1912, Gilbert's lyrics were heard in two Broadway productions, and he collaborated with composer Lewis Muir on one of the most durable popular songs ever written--"Waiting for the Robert E. Lee." Among his four dozen hits that followed were "Ramona" (music by Mabel Wayne), "Jeannine, I Dream of Lilac Time" (music by Nathaniel Shilkret), and "The Peanut Vendor" (co-lyricist Marion Sunshine, music by Moises Simon). During the 1930's and 1940's, he worked on over 30 film musicals at Paramount, United Artists, Fox, and RKO studios, and appeared frequently on radio shows. L. Wolfe Gilbert died in 1970 at the age of eighty-three.

Year	Production Title	Popular Songs
1912	WHIRL OF SOCIETY BROADWAY TO PARIS	
		"Waiting for the Robert E. Lee" "Hitchy-Koo" "Here Comes My Daddy Now" "Ragging the Baby to Sleep" "Take Me to That Swanee Shore"
1913		"Mammy Jinny's Jubilee" "You Did, You Know You Did"
1914		"If I Had a Gal, I Had a Pal"

Year	Production Title	Popular Songs
1915		"My Sweet Adair" "By Heck" "I Love You--That's One Thing I Know"
1916		"My Own Iona" "Hawaiian Sunshine"
1917		"Lily of the Valley" "Oriental Nights" "Are You from Heaven?"
1918		"Singapore"
1920		"Dance-o-Mania"
1922		"Down Yonder" (HP)
1925	CHAUVE-SOURIS	I Miss My Swiss O, Katharina! "Don't Wake Me Up, Let Me Dream"
1926		"Hello, Aloha!--How Are You?"
1927		"Ramona" "Lucky Lindy" "When You're with Somebody Else"
1928	Marriage by Contract	"Jeannine, I Dream of Lilac Time" "Chiquita" "Gypsy" "If You Believed in Me"
1929	Lucky Boy Molly and Me Romance of the Rio Grande South Sea Rose Two Men and a Maid Girl from Havana Love, Live and Laugh Mississippi Gambler	My Mother's Eyes In the Land of Make Believe "The Right Kind of Man" "My Angeline"
1930	Happy Days	

Year	Production Title	Popular Songs
1930	Paramount on Parade The Texan Love Among the Millionaires Cameo Kirby True to the Navy	"Chimes of Spring"
1931	THE SINGING RABBI Road to Singapore Sit Tight	African Lament "The Peanut Vendor" "Mama Inez" "Marta" "Mama Don't Want No Peas and Rice and Cocoanut Oil" "Maria, My Own" "Poor Kid" "Green Eyes"
1932	Hat Check Girl Painted Woman	
1933	Roman Scandals I Loved You Wednesday Terror of Tiny Town	
1935	The Nitwits	
1937	Off to the Races	"Mio Rio de Janeiro"
1938	The Cowboy and the Lady	
1939	Eternally Yours Winter Carnival	
1940	My Son, My Son	
1942		"I Laughed at Love" "My Little Dream Girl"
1943		"Shades of Night"
1944	Beautiful but Broke	
1945	Eadie Was a Lady	
1949	Alimony	

Year	Production Title	Popular Songs
1956		"(I'm Happy When I'm Singing) A Weepin' and Wailin' Song"

* * *

MACK GORDON

Mack Gordon was Hollywood's most successful lyricist. One hundred and fifteen of his songs written for motion pictures were hits! He ranks second in the number (38) of his songs to place on "Your Hit Parade," and ties with lyricist Sammy Cahn for Third Place in the number (11) that led the "Parade."

Gordon was born in Warsaw, Poland in 1904, and was brought to the United States as a child. He attended public schools in New York City, and was a boy soprano in minstrel shows. Before becoming a full-time songwriter, Gordon was a vaudeville comic and singer. His first hit "Ain'tcha?" was published in 1929.

After six stage musicals featuring his songs, the twenty-nine year old lyricist arrived in Hollywood. His first year on the West Coast, working with composer Harry Revel, he wrote the hits "Did You Ever See a Dream Walking?," "You're My Past, Present and Future" and the Walter Winchell-inspired "An Orchid to You." The names of Gordon and Revel appeared in the screen credits for as many as eight films a year. Among Gordon's most memorable lyrics of the 1930's were "Love Thy Neighbor," "Take a Number from One to Ten," "Here Comes Cookie," "Goodnight My Love" and "Never in a Million Years." The dissolution of his partnership with Revel had no effect on Mack Gordon's success. Working with composer Harry Warren at Fox Studios, he supplied the words for a score of hits that included "Down Argentina Way," "Chattanooga Choo-Choo," "I Had the Craziest Dream," "My Heart Tells Me," "The More I See You," and the 1943 Academy Award winner "You'll Never Know." He was still an active creator at the time of his death in 1959. Mack Gordon's work was featured in 81 motion pictures over a period of 29 years. Nine of his songs were "Oscar" nominees.

Year	Production Title	Popular Songs
1929	Pointed Heels Song of Love	Ain'tcha?
1930	SMILES Swing High	Time on My Hands
1931	THE ZIEGFELD FOLLIES	Help Yourself to Happiness

Year	Production Title	Popular Songs
1931	THE ZIEGFELD FOLLIES FAST AND FURIOUS EVERYBODY'S WELCOME	Cigars, Cigarettes "Such Is Life, Such Is Love"
1932	SMILING FACES MARCHING BY	"Underneath the Harlem Moon" "I Played Fiddle for the Czar" "Listen to the German Band" "A Boy and a Girl Were Dancing" "And So to Bed"
1933	Broadway Thru a Keyhole Sitting Pretty White Woman Design for Living	You're My Past, Present and Future Doin' the Uptown Lowdown Did You Ever See a Dream Walking? You're Such a Comfort to Me Good Morning Glory "An Orchid to You" "It's within Your Power" "It Was a Night in June" "A Tree Was a Tree" "There's a Bluebird at My Window"
1934	The Gay Divorcee We're Not Dressing Shoot the Works College Rhythm	Don't Let It Bother You Love Thy Neighbor Once in a Blue Moon May I? She Reminds Me of You Good Night, Lovely Little Lady With My Eyes Wide Open I'm Dreaming Were Your Ears Burning, Baby? Stay as Sweet as You Are Take a Number from One to Ten College Rhythm Let's Give Three Cheers for Love

Year	Production Title	Popular Songs
1934	She Loves Me Not	Straight from the Shoulder I'm Hummin', I'm Whistlin', I'm Singin'
	The Old-Fashioned Way Here Comes the Groom	
1935	Love in Bloom	Here Comes Cookie (HP) My Heart Is an Open Book Got Me Doin' Things
	Paris in the Spring Two for Tonight	Paris in the Spring (HP-1) From the Top of Your Head to the Tip of Your Toes (HP) Without a Word of Warning (HP) Takes Two to Make a Bargain I Wish I Were Aladdin Two for Tonight
	Stolen Harmony	Would There Be Love?
1936	Collegiate	I Feel Like a Feather in the Breeze (HP) You Hit the Spot (HP)
	Poor Little Rich Girl	When I'm with You (HP-1) Oh, My Goodness You've Gotta Eat Your Spinach, Baby But Definitely
	Stowaway	Goodnight My Love (HP-1) One Never Knows (Does One?) You Gotta S-M-I-L-E to Be H-A Double P-Y
	The Princess Comes Across	"A Star Fell Out of Heaven" (HP) "To Mary, with Love"
1937	Head Over Heels in Love	Through the Courtesy of Love May I Have the Next Romance with You? Looking Around Corners for You
	You Can't Have Everything	Please Pardon Us, We're in Love Afraid to Dream (HP) The Loveliness of You You Can't Have Everything Danger--Love at Work

Year	Production Title	Popular Songs
1937	Wake Up and Live	Never in a Million Years (HP)
		There's a Lull in My Life (HP)
		Wake Up and Live
		I'm Bubbling Over
		It's Swell of You
	Love and Hisses	Sweet Someone (HP)
		I Wanna Be in Winchell's Column
		Broadway's Gone Hawaiian
	Ali Baba Goes to Town	I've Got My Heart Set on You
	This Is My Affair	I Hum a Waltz
	Everybody Dance	
	Thin Ice	
1938	In Old Chicago	In Old Chicago
	My Lucky Star	I've Got a Date with a Dream (HP)
		Could You Pass in Love?
	Love Finds Andy Hardy	Meet the Beat of My Heart
	Sally, Irene and Mary	Sweet as a Song (HP)
	Josette	Where in the World? (HP)
		In Any Language
	Rebecca of Sunnybrook Farm	An Old Straw Hat
	Thanks for Everything	Thanks for Everything (HP)
	I'll Give a Million	
	Hold That Co-ed	
1939	Rose of Washington Square	I Never Knew Heaven Could Speak (HP)
	Tailspin	
	The Rains Came	"Speaking of Heaven" (HP)
1940	Down Argentina Way	Down Argentina Way (AN) (HP)
		Two Dreams Met (HP)
	Tin Pan Alley	You Say the Sweetest Things, Baby
	Young People	I Wouldn't Take a Million
	Star Dust	Secrets in the Moonlight
	Johnny Apollo	This Is the Beginning of the End
	Little Old New York	In an Old Dutch Garden (HP)
	Lillian Russell	
1941	Sun Valley Serenade	Chattanooga Choo-Choo (AN) (HP-1)

Year	Production Title	Popular Songs
1941	Sun Valley Serenade	I Know Why
		It Happened in Sun Valley
	That Night in Rio	I Yi Yi Yi Yi
		Chica Chica Boom Chic
	Week-End in Havana	Tropical Magic
	Great American Broadcast	Long Ago Last Night
1942	Orchestra Wives	I've Got a Gal in Kalamazoo (AN) (HP-1)
		Serenade in Blue (HP)
		At Last (HP)
	Springtime in the Rockies	I Had the Craziest Dream (HP)
	Iceland	There Will Never Be Another You (HP)
	Song of the Islands	
	Son of Fury	
1943	Hello, Frisco, Hello	You'll Never Know (AA) (HP-1)
	Sweet Rosie O'Grady	My Heart Tells Me (HP-1)
		"Let's Sing a Song About Susie"
1944	Sweet and Lowdown	I'm Making Believe (AN) (HP)
	Pin-Up Girl	Time Alone Will Tell
		Once Too Often
	Irish Eyes Are Smiling	
1945	The Dolly Sisters	I Can't Begin to Tell You (AN) (HP-1)
	Diamond Horseshoe	The More I See You (HP-1)
		I Wish I Knew (HP)
		In Acapulco
1946	Three Little Girls in Blue	You Make Me Feel So Young
		Somewhere in the Night (HP)
		On the Boardwalk in Atlantic City
	The Razor's Edge	Mam'selle (HP-1)
		"This Is Always" (HP)
1947	Mother Wore Tights	You Do (AN) (HP)
		Kokomo, Indiana
	Daisy Kenyon	

Year	Production Title	Popular Songs
1948	When My Baby Smiles at Me	By the Way What Did I Do?
1949	Come to the Stable	Through a Long and Sleepless Night (AN) Everytime I Meet You
	The Beautiful Blonde from Bashful Bend	
	It Happens Every Spring	It Happens Every Spring
1950	Wabash Avenue	Wilhelmina (AN) Baby, Won't You Say You Love Me?
	Summer Stock	If You Feel Like Singing, Sing Friendly Star
	Under My Skin	
1951	Call Me Mister	I Just Can't Do Enough for You
	I Love Melvin	A Lady Loves
1953	The Girl Next Door	Nowhere Guy
1954	Young at Heart	You, My Love
1957	Bundle of Joy	All About Love
1958		"You Will Find Your Love in Paris"

* * *

OSCAR HAMMERSTEIN

Because of the phenomenal commercial success Oscar Hammerstein enjoyed during his later years as composer Richard Rodgers' collaborator, his work before the production of "Oklahoma!" in 1943 is sometimes minimized.

Oscar Hammerstein was born in New York City in 1895 and was introduced to show business as a child. Both his grandfather and an uncle were successful producers, and his father managed the Victoria Theatre. After attending Columbia's Law School (where he wrote lyrics for the Varsity Show of 1916), he left college to become a stage manager. His first professional writing effort, the 1919 play "The Light," was followed the next year by the musical "Always You." It was at this point that Hammerstein began collaborating with thirty-seven year old lyricist/librettist Otto Harbach

who already had more than a dozen Broadway musicals behind him.
During the next seven years, Harbach and Hammerstein's success-
es included "Wildflower" (the longest-running musical of 1923),
"Rose-Marie," "Sunny" (the longest-running musical of 1925), and
"The Desert Song" (the longest-running musical of 1926). Among
their popular songs from these productions were "Rose-Marie,"
"Who?," and "Blue Heaven."

In 1927, Hammerstein completed his first major assignment
without Harbach--the book and lyrics for the legendary "Show Boat."
From that time on, he worked without another lyricist. "Show
Boat" (music by Jerome Kern) was hailed as the greatest artistic
achievement in musical theatre history. Hammerstein's lyrics included such standards as "Ol' Man River," "Only Make Believe,"
"Why Do I Love You?" and "Can't Help Lovin' Dat Man." The
production was still running when "The New Moon" had its premiere. Its score, with music by Sigmund Romberg, introduced
"Lover, Come Back to Me" and "Stouthearted Men." During the
Thirties, Hammerstein supplied the lyrics for Kern's "Music in
the Air" and Romberg's "May Wine" before becoming one of Holly-
wood's busiest writers. His memorable film songs included "When
I Grow Too Old to Dream," "I'll Take Romance" and "A Mist Is
Over the Moon" which was nominated for an "Oscar" in 1938. In
1939, Oscar Hammerstein worked on Broadway on "Very Warm for
May." The show failed but Kern and Hammerstein's "All the
Things You Are" became a hit. Two years later, they won the
Academy Award for "The Last Time I Saw Paris."

Before forty-seven year old Oscar Hammerstein became
partners with Richard Rodgers, he had more than 80 hit songs, 28
stage musicals, and an "Oscar" to his credit! Richard Rodgers
was also at the top of his profession when their historic collaboration began. When his partner of 24 years, lyricist Lorenz Hart,
declined to work on a new project, Rodgers turned to Hammerstein. The 1943 project turned out to be "Oklahoma!" which broke
all long-run records for a Broadway musical and remained champion until "My Fair Lady" overtook it 18 years later. Hammerstein's second triumph of 1943 was his adaptation of the opera
"Carmen." Hammerstein moved the story's action to the southern
United States during World War II, made "Carmen" a worker in a
parachute factory, and transformed Bizet's torreador into a prize-
fighter. The all-Negro "Carmen Jones" chalked up a run of 502
performances.

The second Rodgers and Hammerstein production, "Carousel,"
opened in 1945 and many critics acclaimed it as greater than "Ok-
lahoma!" Its score included Hammerstein's lyric "You'll Never
Walk Alone." The year of "Carousel's" premiere saw the Academy
Award presented to Rodgers and Hammerstein's "It Might as Well
Be Spring." The succession of their successful Broadway musicals
included "South Pacific" (which won the Pulitzer Prize for Drama),
"The King and I," "Flower Drum Song" and "The Sound of Music."

Rodgers and Hammerstein produced several of their own shows and Irving Berlin's 1946 hit "Annie Get Your Gun." They also created the television special "Cinderella" in 1957.

Working without Rodgers, Oscar Hammerstein won Academy nominations for "All Through the Day" (1946) and "A Kiss to Build a Dream On" (1951). His 40 years in the theatre ended with his death in 1960 at the age of sixty-five. He was the most successful Broadway lyricist in history.

Year	Production Title	Popular Songs
1920	ALWAYS YOU TICKLE ME JIMMIE	
1922	QUEEN O' HEARTS	You Need Someone, Someone Needs You
	DAFFY DILL	
1923	WILDFLOWER	Wildflower Bambalina
	MARY JANE MCKANE	Toodle-Oo
1924	ROSE-MARIE	Rose-Marie Indian Love Call The Mounties Door of My Dreams Totem Tom Tom Pretty Things
	ROUND THE TOWN	
1925	SUNNY	Who? D'ye Love Me? Sunny Two Little Bluebirds Let's Say Good Night Till It's Morning
	SONG OF THE FLAME	Cossack Love Song Song of the Flame
1926	THE WILD ROSE	We'll Have a Kingdom One Golden Hour The Wild Rose
	THE DESERT SONG	Blue Heaven (The Desert Song) The Riff Song One Alone Romance It One Flower Grows Alone in Your Garden

Year	Production Title	Popular Songs
1927	SHOW BOAT	Only Make Believe Ol' Man River Can't Help Lovin' Dat Man Why Do I Love You? Life Upon the Wicked Stage You Are Love
	THE GOLDEN DAWN	
1928	THE NEW MOON	Lover, Come Back to Me Stouthearted Men Softly, as in a Morning Sunrise One Kiss Wanting You Marianne
	RAINBOW	I Want a Man Hay, Straw The One Girl
1929	SWEET ADELINE	Why Was I Born? Don't Ever Leave Me Here Am I 'Twas Not So Long Ago
1930	BALLYHOO	I'm One of God's Children Who Hasn't Got Wings No Wonder I'm Blue
	Viennese Nights	You Will Remember Vienna I Bring a Love Song
	Song of the West	
1931	FREE FOR ALL EAST WIND Children of Dreams	Not That I Care
1932	MUSIC IN THE AIR	The Song Is You I've Told Ev'ry Little Star In Egern on the Tegern See And Love Was Born We Belong Together There's a Hill Beyond a Hill
1934	THREE SISTERS (London)	Lonely Feet
1935	MAY WINE	Dance, My Darlings Just Once Around the Clock I Built a Dream One Day Somebody Ought to Be Told Something New Is in My Heart

Year	Production Title	Popular Songs
1935	The Night Is Young	When I Grow Too Old to Dream (HP)
		The Night Is Young
	Roberta	I Won't Dance (HP)
	Sweet Adeline	We Were So Young
	Reckless	Reckless
1936	Show Boat	I Have the Room Above
		I Still Suits Me
	Give Us This Night	
1937	High, Wide and Handsome	Can I Forget You?
		The Folks Who Live on the Hill
		High, Wide and Handsome
	I'll Take Romance	I'll Take Romance
1938	GENTLEMEN UNAFRAID (St. Louis)	Your Dream
	The Lady Objects	A Mist Is Over the Moon (AN)
		That Week in Paris
	The Great Waltz	One Day When We Were Young
1939	VERY WARM FOR MAY	All the Things You Are (HP-1)
		All in Fun
		In the Heart of the Dark
		That Lucky Fellow
		Heaven in My Arms
		"The Sweetest Sight That I Have Seen"
1940	AMERICAN JUBILEE (New York World's Fair)	Tennessee Fish Fry
		How Can I Ever Be Alone?
1941	SUNNY RIVER	
	Lady Be Good	The Last Time I Saw Paris (AA)
1943	OKLAHOMA!	People Will Say We're in Love (HP-1)
		Oh, What a Beautiful Mornin' (HP)
		The Surrey with the Fringe on Top
		Oklahoma!

Year	Production Title	Popular Songs
1943	OKLAHOMA!	Out of My Dreams I Cain't Say No
	CARMEN JONES	
1945	CAROUSEL	If I Loved You (HP-1) June Is Bustin' Out All Over You'll Never Walk Alone What's the Use of Wond'rin?
	State Fair	It Might as Well Be Spring (AA) (HP-1) It's a Grand Night for Singing That's for Me (HP) Isn't It Kinda Fun?
1946	SHOW BOAT (revival) HAPPY BIRTHDAY (play)	Nobody Else but Me I Haven't Got a Worry in the World
	Centennial Summer	All Through the Day (AN) (HP-1)
1947	ALLEGRO	The Gentleman Is a Dope So Far (HP) A Fellow Needs a Girl You Are Never Away
1949	SOUTH PACIFIC	Some Enchanted Evening (HP-1) A Wonderful Guy (HP) Bali Ha'i (HP) There Is Nothing Like a Dame Younger Than Springtime (HP) Happy Talk I'm Gonna Wash That Man Right Out of My Hair A Cockeyed Optimist
1951	THE KING AND I	Hello, Young Lovers I Whistle a Happy Tune Getting to Know You We Kiss in a Shadow I Have Dreamed
	The Strip	A Kiss to Build a Dream On (AN)
1953	ME AND JULIET Main Street to Broadway	No Other Love (HP-1)

Year	Production Title	Popular Songs
1955	PIPE DREAM	All at Once You Love Her Everybody's Got a Home but Me
1957	Cinderella (TV)	Do I Love You Because You're Beautiful?
1958	FLOWER DRUM SONG	You Are Beautiful I Enjoy Being a Girl Love, Look Away
1959	THE SOUND OF MUSIC	The Sound of Music My Favorite Things Do Re Mi Climb Ev'ry Mountain

* * *

OTTO HARBACH

With the exception of "I Won't Dance," all of Otto Harbach's hit songs were introduced in Broadway musicals. In addition to his lyrics, Harbach also functioned as the book writer for most of his 37 stage productions. He was born in Salt Lake City, Utah, in 1873, and was the son of Danish immigrants. After graduating from Knox College in Illinois, he taught English at a university in Washington. In 1901, he moved to New York to do post-graduate work at Columbia but was soon forced to drop out in order to support himself. Harbach sold insurance and then went to work as a newspaper reporter and advertising copywriter. After his daytime job, he worked with composer Karl Hoschna and it took the two of them six years to convince Broadway producers that they were ready for an assignment. The team's big break was "The Three Twins" in which "Cuddle Up a Little Closer" was introduced. Harbach wrote both the book and lyrics and the show ran for eight months. "Madame Sherry" and four other productions followed before Hoschna's death in 1911. The next year, Harbach began collaborating with composer Rudolf Friml with whom he created "Giannina Mia" ("The Firefly"--1912). In addition to Hoschna and Friml, Harbach worked with composer Louis Hirsch on "Going Up" and "Mary" in which the hit "The Love Nest" was heard.

One of Harbach's producers was Arthur Hammerstein whose nephew Oscar was just beginning his career as a lyricist and playwright. Harbach formed a partnership with Oscar Hammerstein (who was 20 years his junior) and the pair became one of the most successful teams of lyricists in Broadway history. Their musical "Wildflower" was the sensation of 1923. It was followed by such

hits as "Rose-Marie," "Sunny" and "The Desert Song." The popular music standards introduced in these productions included "Indian Love Call," "Who?" and "One Alone." In 1928, Harbach and
Hammerstein dissolved their partnership. Three years later, Harbach collaborated with composer Jerome Kern on "The Cat and the
Fiddle." Harbach's most famous work proved to be his lyrics for
"Smoke Gets in Your Eyes" from the 1933 musical "Roberta." In
the mid-Thirties, Harbach's career went into a decline. His last
produced work was "Gentlemen Unafraid" which was staged at the
St. Louis Municipal Opera in 1938. Otto Harbach survived Oscar
Hammerstein by three years. He died in 1963 at the age of ninety.

Year	Production Title	Popular Songs
1908	THREE TWINS	Cuddle Up a Little Closer
1910	MADAME SHERRY	Every Little Movement The Smile She Means for Me The Birth of Passion
	BRIGHT EYES	
1911	THE GIRL OF MY DREAMS	Doctor Tinkle Tinker Every Girl Loves Me but the Girl I Love
	DR. DELUXE THE FASCINATING WIDOW	
1912	THE FIREFLY	Giannina Mia When a Maid Comes Knocking at Your Heart Sympathy The Dawn of Love Love Is Like a Firefly
1913	HIGH JINKS	The Bubble Not Now but Later Something Seems Tingle-ing-eling Love's Own Kiss
1914	SUZI	
1915	KATINKA	Allah's Holiday I Want to Marry a Male Quartette Tis the End, So Farewell Katinka Rackety Coo!
1917	YOU'RE IN LOVE GOING UP	You're in Love Going Up

Year	Production Title	Popular Songs
1917	GOING UP	Everybody Ought to Know How to Do the Tickle Toe If You Look in Her Eyes
1919	TUMBLE INN THE LITTLE WHOPPER	
1920	MARY	The Love Nest Mary Waiting
	TICKLE ME JIMMIE	
1921	THE O'BRIEN GIRL	Learn to Smile
1922	THE BLUE KITTEN	Cutie
1923	WILDFLOWER	Bambalina Wildflower
	JACK AND JILL	
1924	ROSE-MARIE	Totem Tom Tom Door of My Dreams Pretty Things Rose-Marie Indian Love Call The Mounties
	BETTY LEE	
1925	NO, NO NANETTE	No, No Nanette I've Confessed to the Breeze
	SUNNY	Who? Sunny D'ye Love Me? Two Little Bluebirds Let's Say Good Night Till It's Morning
	SONG OF THE FLAME	Cossack Love Song Song of the Flame
1926	THE WILD ROSE	We'll Have a Kingdom One Golden Hour The Wild Rose
	THE DESERT SONG	The Riff Song Blue Heaven (The Desert Song) One Alone Romance One Flower Grows Alone in My Garden It

Year	Production Title	Popular Songs
1926	CRISS CROSS	You Will, Won't You?
		In Araby with You
	OH, PLEASE	I Know That You Know
1927	LUCKY	Dancing the Devil Away
		The Same Old Moon
	THE GOLDEN DAWN	
1928	GOOD BOY	
1931	THE CAT AND THE FIDDLE	A New Love Is Old
		One Moment Alone
		She Didn't Say Yes
		The Night Was Made for Love
		I Watch the Love Parade
		Try to Forget
		Poor Pierrot
1933	ROBERTA	Smoke Gets in Your Eyes
		The Touch of Your Hand
		Yesterdays
		You're Devastating
1935	Roberta	I Won't Dance (HP)
1936	FORBIDDEN MELODY	
1938	GENTLEMEN UNAFRAID (St. Louis)	Your Dream

* * *

E. Y. HARBURG

E. Y. Harburg was a graduate of New York City College.
He turned to songwriting as a profession when his electrical appliance merchandising firm failed after the 1929 stock market
crash. He was then in his early thirties. Already behind him
were credits in two Broadway musicals, and the film "Applause"
in which the legendary Helen Morgan had introduced his "What
Wouldn't I Do for That Man?" (music by Jay Gorney). Six more
Broadway revues followed including the 1932 edition of "Americana."
That year found the United States deep in the throes of the depression that followed the Wall Street panic. Men who had once held
executive positions in business and industry were reduced to selling
apples on street corners and waiting in block-long lines for handouts of soup. Harburg captured their plight in his lyric for "Bro-

ther, Can You Spare a Dime?" which became an anthem of the
Depression.   The same year the song was introduced in "Americana," Harburg collaborated with composer Vernon Duke on the
classic "April in Paris. "

The composer with whom Harburg is most closely identified
is Harold Arlen.   Their association began in the early Thirties
and continued for more than three decades.   The team composed
songs for Dick Powell and Al Jolson at Warner Bros. , and supplied the scores for the Broadway successes "Life Begins at 8:40"
(1934) and "Hooray for What" (1937).   They were awarded the 1939
"Oscar" for "Over the Rainbow" which became Judy Garland's
theme and is included on ASCAP's list of the 16 most popular songs
of all time.   Harburg also received Academy Award nominations
for "Happiness Is a Thing Called Joe" and "More and More."   His
masterpiece is the long-run stage musical "Finian's Rainbow"
(1947) on which he collaborated with composer Burton Lane and
also co-authored the book.

In addition to Arlen, Duke and Lane, Harburg has worked
with Arthur Schwartz, Jerome Kern and Jule Styne.   In 1961, he
set his lyrics to the melodies of classical composer Jacques Offen-
bach for Broadway's "The Happiest Girl in the World. "   The following year, his talents were reunited with those of Judy Garland
and Harold Arlen on the animated feature film "Gay Purr-ee. "
Harburg was seventy-five years old when he created the revue "I
Got a Song" in 1974.   The show took its title from a number of
the same name introduced in Harburg and Arlen's long-run musical
"Bloomer Girl" and featured dozens of songs written by Harburg
over his 50 year career.   E. Y. Harburg was born in New York
City in 1898.

Year	Production Title	Popular Songs
1926	QUEEN HIGH	
1929	EARL CARROLL'S SKETCH BOOK	Kinda Cute
	Applause	What Wouldn't I Do for That Man?
1930	THE GARRICK GAIETIES	I'm Only Human After All Too, Too Divine
	EARL CARROLL'S VANITIES THE VANDERBILT REVUE Roadhouse Nights The Sap from Syracuse Queen High	
		"I'm Yours"
1931	BILLY ROSE'S CRAZY QUILT	

Year	Production Title	Popular Songs
1931	THE ZIEGFELD FOLLIES	
	SHOOT THE WORKS	
		"If I Didn't Have You"
1932	BALLYHOO	Thrill Me
	AMERICANA	Brother, Can You Spare a Dime?
		Satan's Li'l Lamb
		Whistling for a Kiss
	WALK A LITTLE FASTER	April in Paris
		Speaking of Love
		Where Have We Met Before?
		That's Life
	THE GREAT MAGOO	It's Only a Paper Moon
	(play)	(HP)
1933	Moonlight and Pretzels	Ah, but Is It Love?
		There's a Little Bit of You in Ev'ry Love Song
		Moonlight and Pretzels
	Take a Chance	New Deal Rhythm
		"Isn't It Heavenly?"
1934	THE ZIEGFELD FOLLIES	What Is There to Say?
		I Like the Likes of You
		Suddenly
		Water Under the Bridge
	LIFE BEGINS AT 8:40	Let's Take a Walk Around the Block
		You're a Builder-Upper
		Fun to Be Fooled
		What Can You Say in a Love Song?
		Shoein' the Mare
	NEW FACES	
	CONTINENTAL VARIETIES	
	Count of Monte Cristo	The World Is Mine
		"Then I'll Be Tired of You"
1936	THE SHOW IS ON	Song of the Woodman
		Long as You Got Your Health
	The Singing Kid	You're the Cure for What Ails Me
		I Love to Sing-a
	Stage Struck	Fancy Meeting You
		In Your Own Quiet Way
	Gold Diggers of 1937	Let's Put Our Heads Together

Year	Production Title	Popular Songs
1936	Gold Diggers of 1937	Speaking of the Weather
		"Last Night When We Were Young"
1937	HOORAY FOR WHAT	In the Shade of the New Apple Tree Moanin' in the Mornin' Down with Love I've Gone Romantic on You God's Country
		"The Legend of Niagara"
1939	The Wizard of Oz	Over the Rainbow (AA) (HP-1) We're Off to See the Wizard Ding, Dong, the Witch Is Dead
	At the Circus	Lydia, the Tattooed Lady Two Blind Loves
1940	HOLD ON TO YOUR HATS	There's a Great Day Coming Manana Don't Let It Get You Down The World Is in My Arms Would You Be So Kindly?
1941	Babes on Broadway	"Honorable Moon"
1942	Ship Ahoy	Poor You Last Call for Love I'll Take Tallulah Buds Won't Bud
	Cairo Panama Hattie Rio Rita	
1943	Cabin in the Sky	Happiness Is a Thing Called Joe (AN) Life's Full o' Consequence And Russia Is Her Name
	Song of Russia Dubarry Was a Lady Presenting Lily Mars Thousands Cheer	
1944	BLOOMER GIRL	Evelina (HP) Right as the Rain The Eagle and Me I Got a Song

Year	Production Title	Popular Songs
1944	Can't Help Singing	More and More (AN) (HP) Any Moment Now Can't Help Singing
	Cover Girl Hollywood Canteen Meet the People Kismet	
1945	BLUE HOLIDAY The Affairs of Susan	Free and Equal Blues
1946	California Centennial Summer	
1947	FINIAN'S RAINBOW	How Are Things in Glocca Morra? (HP) Old Devil Moon When I'm Not Near the Girl I Love If This Isn't Love Look to the Rainbow Something Sort of Grandish
1951	FLAHOOLEY	The World Is Your Balloon Here's to Your Illusions
1957	JAMAICA	Take It Slow, Joe Cocoanut Sweet
1961	THE HAPPIEST GIRL IN THE WORLD	
1962	Gay Purr-ee	Little Drops of Rain
1963	I Could Go on Singing	I Could Go on Singing "Silent Spring"
1968	DARLING OF THE DAY	
1974	I GOT A SONG (closed in tryout)	

* * *

LORENZ HART

Lorenz Hart was born in New York City in 1895 and wrote

his first lyric for a Richard Rodgers' melody when he was twenty-two years old. During the first eight years of their collaboration, Rodgers and Hart wrote for varsity shows at Columbia University and other amateur productions. Their songs were heard in the Broadway productions "A Lonely Romeo" (1919), "Poor Little Ritz Girl" (1920) and "The Melody Man" (1924) but it took the first edition of "The Garrick Gaieties" in 1925 to push the two songwriters over the top. Even in his first major hit song "Manhattan," Hart exhibited a talent for unusual rhymes seldom equalled by any lyric writer. After its success, his songs "The Girl Friend," "Mountain Greenery," "Thou Swell," "You Took Advantage of Me" and "I've Got Five Dollars" added to his reputation for inventiveness. Hart began writing for films in 1930 and created "Mimi" for Maurice Chevalier, "Hallelujah, I'm a Bum" for Al Jolson, and "Soon" for Bing Crosby. He also supplied new lyrics for the 1934 screen adaptation of "The Merry Widow." While in Hollywood, Rodgers and Hart composed a song titled "Prayer" for a Jean Harlow film but it was cut from the picture before it was released. Hart wrote a different lyric and it was heard in "Manhattan Melodrama" as "The Bad in Every Man." Still dissatisfied, Hart came up with a third set of words and "Blue Moon" became one of the team's best-known songs.

Lorenz Hart resumed his Broadway career in 1935 and provided the lyrics for such Richard Rodgers' melodies as "Little Girl Blue," "My Funny Valentine," "Have You Met Miss Jones?," "Spring Is Here," "This Can't Be Love" and "Bewitched." By 1942, his work had been heard in 32 Broadway productions, three musicals staged in London, and 18 motion pictures. Hart's talent never diminished and the year of his death he wrote one of his most comic lyrics for "To Keep My Love Alive." It was added to the 1943 Broadway revival of "A Connecticut Yankee" which opened five days before he died at the age of only forty-eight.

Year	Production Title	Popular Songs
1919	A LONELY ROMEO	Any Old Place with You
1920	POOR LITTLE RITZ GIRL	
1924	THE MELODY MAN (play)	
1925	THE GARRICK GAIETIES	Manhattan Sentimental Me
	DEAREST ENEMY	Here in My Arms Bye and Bye
	JUNE DAYS	
1926	THE GIRL FRIEND	The Blue Room The Girl Friend Why Do I?

Year	Production Title	Popular Songs
1926	THE GARRICK GAIETIES PEGGY-ANN BETSY LIDO LADY (London)	Mountain Greenery Where's That Rainbow? A Tree in the Park A Little Birdie Told Me So
1927	A CONNECTICUT YANKEE ONE DAM THING AFTER ANOTHER (London)	My Heart Stood Still Thou Swell I Feel at Home with You
1928	SHE'S MY BABY PRESENT ARMS CHEE-CHEE	A Baby's Best Friend You Took Advantage of Me Do I Hear You Saying I Love You? Blue Ocean Blues Moon of My Delight I Must Love You The Tartar Song
1929	SPRING IS HERE HEADS UP LADY FINGERS	With a Song in My Heart Yours Sincerely . Why Can't I? Baby's Awake Now A Ship Without a Sail Why Do You Suppose? My Man Is on the Make
1930	SIMPLE SIMON EVERGREEN (London) Follow Thru	Ten Cents a Dance Send for Me He Was Too Good to Me Dancing on the Ceiling
1931	AMERICA'S SWEETHEART BILLY ROSE'S CRAZY QUILT The Hot Heiress	I've Got Five Dollars Like Ordinary People Do
1932	Love Me Tonight The Phantom President	Lover Isn't It Romantic? Mimi
1933	Hallelujah, I'm a Bum Dancing Lady	You Are Too Beautiful

Year	Production Title	Popular Songs
1934	Nana	That's Love
	The Merry Widow	
	Hollywood Party	
	Manhattan Melodrama	
	Evergreen	"Blue Moon"
1935	Mississippi	It's Easy to Remember (HP)
		Soon (HP-1)
		Down by the River
	JUMBO	Little Girl Blue
		Over and Over Again
		The Most Beautiful Girl in the World
		My Romance
	SOMETHING GAY (play)	
1936	ON YOUR TOES	There's a Small Hotel (HP)
		Glad to Be Unhappy
		On Your Toes
		It's Got to Be Love
		Quiet Night
	THE SHOW IS ON	
	Dancing Pirate	Are You My Love?
1937	BABES IN ARMS	Where or When (HP)
		The Lady Is a Tramp
		My Funny Valentine
		Johnny One Note
		I Wish I Were in Love Again
		All at Once
	I'D RATHER BE RIGHT	Have You Met Miss Jones?
		I'd Rather Be Right
1938	I MARRIED AN ANGEL	I Married an Angel (HP)
		Spring Is Here
		I'll Tell the Man in the Street
	THE BOYS FROM SYRACUSE	Falling in Love with Love
		This Can't Be Love (HP)
		Sing for Your Supper
	Fools for Scandal	How Can You Forget?
		There's a Boy in Harlem
1939	TOO MANY GIRLS	I Didn't Know What Time It Was (HP)
		Love Never Went to College

Year	Production Title	Popular Songs
1940	HIGHER AND HIGHER	It Never Entered My Mind
		From Another World
		Ev'ry Sunday Afternoon
	PAL JOEY	Bewitched (HP-1)
		I Could Write a Book
		Zip
	Too Many Girls	You're Nearer
	Boys from Syracuse	
1941	They Met in Argentina	
1942	BY JUPITER	Wait Till You See Her
		Everything I've Got
		Nobody's Heart
		Careless Rhapsody
1943	A CONNECTICUT YANKEE (revival)	To Keep My Love Alive
	Stage Door Canteen	

* * *

RAY HENDERSON

Composer Ray Henderson was a native of Buffalo, New York, where he was born in 1896. He received his musical training at the Chicago Conservatory of Music, and began his career plugging songs for a music publisher, playing the piano in dance bands, and accompanying vaudeville performers. Henderson was twenty-six when he wrote his first hit "Georgette" introduced in "The Greenwich Village Follies." In 1925, he appeared to have cornered the popular music market when ten of his songs were among the nation's favorites. That same year he began collaborating with lyricist Lew Brown (with whom he had already written several successes) and B. G. DeSylva. The team of DeSylva, Brown and Henderson created the scores for three editions of "George White's Scandals" and such book musicals as "Good News," "Manhattan Mary" and "Flying High." Among their songs introduced on Broadway were "Lucky Day," "The Varsity Drag," "Button Up Your Overcoat" and "Without Love." Their biggest film success was the 1929 release "Sunny Side Up" starring Janet Gaynor and Charles Farrell. After the trio dissolved their partnership in 1930, Henderson continued to supply music for Brown's lyrics and their "Life Is Just a Bowl of Cherries" was one of the anthems of the American Depression. After the Broadway hit "Strike Me Pink" in 1933, Brown and Henderson went their separate ways. One of the composers' most memorable songs, "Animal Crackers in My Soup," was performed by moppet Shirley Temple in the 1935 film "Curly Top." Hender-

son survived both DeSylva and Brown living to the age of seventy-
four. The songwriters were saluted in the 1956 motion picture
"The Best Things in Life Are Free." Ray Henderson died in
1970.

Year	Production Title	Popular Songs
1922	THE GREENWICH VILLAGE FOLLIES	Georgette "I Thought I'd Die"
1923	THE ZIEGFELD FOLLIES	"Annabelle" "That Old Gang of Mine" "Why Did I Kiss That Girl?" "Counterfeit Bill from Louisville"
1924		"Follow the Swallow" "I Wonder Who's Dancing with You Tonight?" "Peter Pan, I Love You" "You're in Love with Everyone but the One Who's in Love with You"
1925	BIG BOY GEORGE WHITE'S SCANDALS	It All Depends on You I Want a Lovable Baby "Alabamy Bound" "I'm Sitting on Top of the World" "'Bam 'Bam, 'Bamy Shore" "If I Had a Girl Like You" "Keep Your Skirts Down, Mary Ann" "Dummy Song (I'll Take the Legs from Some Old Table)" "Don't Bring Lulu" "Five Foot Two, Eyes of Blue" (HP)
1926	GEORGE WHITE'S SCANDALS	The Birth of the Blues Black Bottom Lucky Day The Girl Is You and the Boy Is Me "Bye, Bye Blackbird" "I'm in Love with You, That's Why"

Year	Production Title	Popular Songs
1926		"Too Many Parties and Too Many Pals"
1927	GOOD NEWS	The Best Things in Life Are Free (HP)
		Lucky in Love
		Just Imagine
		The Varsity Drag
		Good News
		The Girls of Pi Beta Phi
	MANHATTAN MARY	Manhattan Mary
		Broadway
		The Five Step
		It Won't Be Long Now
	ARTISTS AND MODELS	Here Am I--Broken Hearted
		"Just a Memory"
		"Magnolia"
		"Cover Me Up with Sunshine"
		"So Blue"
		"South Wind"
		"Without You, Sweetheart"
		"I Wonder How I Look When I'm Asleep?"
		"The Church Bells Are Ringing for Mary"
1928	GEORGE WHITE'S SCANDALS	I'm on the Crest of a Wave
		What D'ya Say?
		Pickin' Cotton
		American Tune
	HOLD EVERYTHING	You're the Cream in My Coffee
		Don't Hold Everything
	THREE CHEERS	Maybe This Is Love
		Pompanola
	The Singing Fool	Sonny Boy
		"For Old Time's Sake"
		"That's Just My Way of Forgetting You"
		"Together" (HP)
		"The Song I Love"
		"Sorry for Me"
1929	FOLLOW THRU	Button Up Your Overcoat
		My Lucky Star
		You Wouldn't Fool Me, Would You?
		Follow Thru
		I Want to Be Bad

Year	Production Title	Popular Songs

1929 GEORGE WHITE'S
        SCANDALS
      Sunny Side Up

(I'm a Dreamer) Aren't We
  All?
Sunny Side Up
If I Had a Talking Picture
  of You
Turn on the Heat

      Say It with Songs

Used to You
Why Can't You?
I'm in Seventh Heaven
Little Pal

      In Old Arizona

My Tonia

"My Sin"

1930 FLYING HIGH

Without Love
Wasn't It Beautiful While It
  Lasted?
Thank Your Father
Red Hot Chicago
Good for You, Bad for Me

      Just Imagine

(There's Something About
  an) Old-Fashioned Girl
(I Am the Words) You
  Are the Melody

      Happy Days

"Don't Tell Her What Hap-
  pened to Me"
"(I am the Words) You Are
  the Melody"

1931 GEORGE WHITE'S
        SCANDALS

Life Is Just a Bowl of Cher-
  ries
My Song
The Thrill Is Gone
This Is the Missus
That's Why Darkies Were
  Born

      Indiscreet

Come to Me
If You Haven't Got Love

"You Try Somebody Else"
"One More Time"

1932 HOT-CHA!

You Can Make My Life a
  Bed of Roses
There I Go Dreaming Again

1933 STRIKE ME PINK

Let's Call It a Day
Strike Me Pink

1934 SAY WHEN

When Love Comes Swinging
  Along

Year	Production Title	Popular Songs
1934	SAY WHEN George White's Scandals	Say When (Oh, You) Nasty Man Hold My Hand My Dog Loves Your Dog
1935	GEORGE WHITE'S SCANDALS Curly Top George White's 1935 Scandals	I'm the Fellow Who Loves You Life Begins at Sweet Sixteen Animal Crackers in My Soup When I Grow Up The Simple Things in Life "Every Once in Awhile"
1940		"Up the Chimney Go My Dreams"
1941		"Don't Cry, Cherie"
1942		"There Are Rivers to Cross"
1943	THE ZIEGFELD FOLLIES	Love Songs Are Made in the Night
1944		"On the Corner of Dream Street and Main" "Let Us All Sing Auld Lang Syne"
1948		"An Old Sombrero (and an Old Spanish Shawl)"

* * *

EDWARD HEYMAN

Twenty-three year old Edward Heyman shared the success
of his first hit with composer Johnny Green and lyricists Robert
Sour and Frank Eyton. The song was the classic "Body and Soul"
introduced by Libby Holman in the 1930 Broadway revue "Three's
a Crowd." Heyman was born in New York City in 1907. He started writing lyrics for college musicals when he was an undergraduate at the University of Michigan. He worked frequently with
Johnny Green who set his lyrics for "Out of Nowhere" and "I Cover
the Waterfront" to music. The lyricist alternated between stage
and screen work and, from 1930 through 1936, his work was heard

in eight Broadway productions and ten motion pictures. Among his
biggest successes during that time were "Drums in My Heart,"
"My Silent Love," and "You Oughta Be in Pictures." He served in
the Air Force during World War II. After 13 years of writing for
films, Heyman returned to Broadway in 1950 with composer Victor
Young with whom he had written the "Oscar"-contending title song
for the 1945 release "Love Letters." Their stage musical "Pardon
Our French" was a financial failure. In 1954, Heyman became the
producer for an English-speaking theatre group which performed in
Mexico for several years.

Year	Production Title	Popular Songs
1929	Vagabond Lover	
1930	THREE'S A CROWD	Body and Soul
1931	HERE GOES THE BRIDE Monkey Business	Hello, My Lover, Goodbye Ho-Hum "Out of Nowhere" (HP) "I Don't Want Love"
1932	THROUGH THE YEARS EARL CARROLL'S VANITIES	Drums in My Heart Through the Years Kinda Like You You're Everywhere My Darling "My Silent Love" "Rain, Rain, Go Away" "I Wanna Be Loved"

1933	MURDER AT THE VANITIES
	
	SHE LOVES ME NOT
	(play)
	Song of Songs
		Weep No More, My Baby
		Me for You Forever
		After All, You're All I'm
		    After
		Jonny
		
		"I Cover the Waterfront"
		"This Is Romance"
		"Two Buck Tim from Tim-
		    buctoo"
		"You're Mine, You"
		"Shame on You"

1934	CAVIAR Bachelor of Arts	My Heart Is an Open Book Easy Come, Easy Go "You Oughta Be in Pictures" "Blame It on My Youth" "Carefree"

Year	Production Title	Popular Songs
1935	Curly Top Sweet Surrender	When I Grow Up
1936	THE ZIEGFELD FOLLIES That Girl from Paris Anything Goes Dizzy Dames The First Baby	Seal It with a Kiss Love and Learn (HP) Moonburn "Mutiny in the Parlor" "Darling, Not Without You" "For Sentimental Reasons"
1937		"Boo Hoo" (HP-1) "Alibi Baby" "It's High Time I Got the Lowdown on You" "To Love You and to Lose You"
1938		"They Say" (HP) "Have You Forgotten So Soon?" (HP) "Let Me Whisper" (HP)
1939	Let Freedom Ring	"Melancholy Lullaby" "My Love for You"
1940	The Border Legion	"The Sky Fell Down"
1942		"Fun to Be Free"
1943	So Proudly We Hail	
1945	Love Letters The Great John L Delightfully Dangerous	Love Letters (AN) (HP)
1946	The Strange Love of Martha Ivers The Searching Wind	Strange Love
1947	Northwest Outpost Magic Town Living in a Big Way	
1948	The Kissing Bandit On an Island with You	If I Steal a Kiss "Bluebird of Happiness" (HP)

Year	Production Title	Popular Songs
1950	PARDON OUR FRENCH	
1952	One Minute to Zero The Fabulous Senorita Thunderbirds	When I Fall in Love
1955		"Blue Star"
1961		"No More Shadows"
1963	David and Lisa	The More I See of Lisa
		"All Yours"

* * *

BOB HILLIARD

Bob Hilliard averaged better than two hit songs a year before his career was cut short by his death at the age of fifty-three. His first successful lyric was "The Coffee Song" published in 1946. The following year, the Broadway revue "Angel in the Wings" introduced Hilliard's "Civilization" (music by Carl Sigman). "Dear Hearts and Gentle People," which he wrote with composer Sammy Fain, was one of the most-recorded songs of 1949 and was Number One on "Your Hit Parade" for seven weeks. Hilliard was represented on Broadway in the 1950's by songs in "Michael Todd's Peep Show" and "Hazel Flagg." That same decade, he collaborated with composer David Mann on the novelty calypso "Somebody Bad Stole de Wedding Bell." Hilliard provided the words for several of Burt Bacharach's early hits. In 1965, he contributed lyrics to the Off-Broadway musical "Wet Paint." Bob Hilliard was born in New York City in 1918, and died in 1971.

Year	Production Title	Popular Songs
1946		"The Coffee Song" (HP)
1947	ANGEL IN THE WINGS	Civilization (HP-1) The Big Brass Band from Brazil Once Around the Moon The Thousand Islands Song "Passing Fancy" "Pancho Maximilian Hernan- deez (The Best President We Ever Had)"

Year	Production Title	Popular Songs
1947		"Red Silk Stockings and Green Perfume" "Mention My Name in Sheboygan"
1948		"Bouquet of Roses" "My Fair Lady" "A Strawberry Moon"
1949		"Dear Hearts and Gentle People" (HP-1) "Careless Hands" (HP) "These Will Be the Best Years of Our Lives" "Cheap Cigars"
1950	MICHAEL TODD'S PEEP SHOW	Stay with the Happy People "Dearie" (HP) "Boutonniere"
1951	Alice in Wonderland	I'm Late Alice in Wonderland "Be My Life's Companion" (HP) "Shanghai" (HP)
1952	Something to Live For	"Don't Ever Be Afraid to Go Home"
1953	HAZEL FLAGG	How Do You Speak to an Angel? Every Street's a Boulevard in Old New York Everybody Loves to Take a Bow "Downhearted" "Send My Baby Back to Me"
1954	Living It Up	Money Burns a Hole in My Pocket That's What I Like "Somebody Bad Stole de Wedding Bell" "I'm in Favor of Friendship"

Year	Production Title	Popular Songs
1955		"(In the) Wee Small Hours (of the Morning)"
		"Sailor Boys Have Talk to Me in English"
		"Zambezi"
1956		"English Muffins and Irish Stew"
		"Moonlight Gambler" (HP)
		"Wrong Joe"
		"From the Candy Store on the Corner (To the Chapel on the Hill)"
		"In the Middle of the House"
1957		"A Poor Man's Roses (or a Rich Man's Gold?)"
1958		"The Waiting Game"
		"The Only Man on the Island"
1959		"Sitting in the Back Seat"
1960		"My Little Corner of the World"
		"A Kookie Little Paradise"
		"The King of Holiday Island"
1961		"Tower of Strength"
		"(Don't Go) Please Stay"
		"You're Following Me"
		"Summertime Lies"
1962		"Our Day Will Come"
		"Any Day Now"
		"Don't You Believe It"
1963		"My Summer Love"
		"Everyday's a Holiday"
		"Young Wings Can Fly"
1964		"Baby, Come Home"
		"Imagination Is a Magic Dream"
1965	WET PAINT (Off Broadway)	

* * *

AL HOFFMAN

Minsk, Russia was the birthplace of composer Al Hoffman whose family emigrated to Seattle, Washington, in 1908. His first musical instrument was a pedal organ. His interest changed from classical and religious compositions to popular music when he learned to play percussions in high school. After graduation, Hoffman worked as a drummer in West Coast bands and then organized his own orchestra which played in Manhattan speakeasies during Prohibition. He was twenty-eight years old when he composed the music for four songs which attained popularity in 1930. They were followed by "Heartaches," "I Apologize," "I Saw Stars," "Why Don't You Practice What You Preach?," and "Little Man, You've Had a Busy Day." His reputation landed him a contract with Gaumont British studios in 1934, and he spent three years writing the music for such hits as "Everything's in Rhythm with My Heart" and "She Shall Have Music" which were introduced in two of the 18 English films to which he contributed. He frequently shared his credits with composer Jerry Livingston who was his collaborator on three of his biggest commercial successes: "Mairzy Doats," "Chi-Baba, Chi-Baba" and "A Dream Is a Wish Your Heart Makes." His primary lyricists were Maurice Sigler and Mack David. Al Hoffman was nominated for an Academy Award for "Bibbidi-Bobbidi-Boo" from Walt Disney's "Cinderella" (1949). His last hit, "O Dio Mio," was published in 1960--the year he died at the age of fifty-eight.

Year	Production Title	Popular Songs
1929		"In the Hush of the Night"
1930		"On a Blue and Moonless Night"
		"Roses Are Forget-Me-Nots"
		"I Don't Mind Walkin' in the Rain"
		"Good Evenin'"
1931		"Heartaches" (HP-1)
		"I Apologize" (HP)
		"Oh, What a Thrill to Hear It from You"
		"Makin' Faces at the Man in the Moon"
1932		"If You Haven't Got a Girl"
		"Auf Wiedersehn, My Dear"
		"It's Winter Again"
		"Fit as a Fiddle"
		"Happy-Go-Lucky You (and Broken-Hearted Me)"
		"Sweet Muchacha"

Year	Production Title	Popular Songs

1933   College Coach

"Black-Eyed Susan Brown"
"Roll Up the Carpet"
"Come Out, Come Out,
    Wherever You Are"
"Two Buck Tim from Tim-
    buctoo"

1934   Marie Galante

"I Saw Stars"
"Why Don't You Practice
    What You Preach?"
"Little Man, You've Had a
    Busy Day"
"Jimmy Had a Nickel"
"Who Walks in When I Walk
    Out?"
"Your Guess Is Just as
    Good as Mine"
"You're in My Power"

1935   First a Girl

Everything's in Rhythm with
    My Heart
I Can Wiggle My Ears
Say the Word and It's Yours

Come Out of the Pantry

Everything Stops for Tea
From One Minute to Another

Hyde Park Corner
Car of Dreams
A Fire Has Been Arranged
Limelight
Stormy Weather

"Black Coffee"

1936   THIS'LL MAKE YOU
        WHISTLE (London)

I'm in a Dancing Mood (HP)
Crazy with Love
There Isn't Any Limit to
    My Love

GOING GREEK (London)
HIDE AND SEEK (London)
Jack of All Trades

Where There's You There's
    Me

When Knights Were Bold

Let's Put Some People to
    Work

Squibs
Peg of Old Drury

"There's Always a Happy
    Ending"

1937   Gangway

Gangway
Lord and Lady Whoozis

Year	Production Title	Popular Songs
1937	She Shall Have Music	She Shall Have Music (HP) My First Thrill
	Good Morning, Boys Take My Tip London Melody O. H. M. S. Sunset in Vienna	
1938	Listen, Darling	On the Bumpy Road to Love "I Ups to Her and She Ups to Me" "After Looking at You"
1939		"Romance Runs in the Family"
1940		"Apple Blossoms and Chapel Bells" (HP)
1941		"The Story of a Starry Night"
1942	Get Hep to Love	"Put, Put, Put Your Arms Around Me"
1943		"What's the Good Word, Mr. Bluebird?" (HP) "Close to You"
1944		"Mairzy Doats" (HP-1) "Goodnight, Wherever You Are" (HP) "She Broke My Heart in Three Places" "I Must Have One More Kiss, Kiss, Kiss" "Fuzzy Wuzzy"
1945		"I'm a Big Girl Now" "Promises"
1946		"I Had Too Much to Dream Last Night"
1947	Rose of Santa Rosa	"Chi-Baba, Chi-Baba" (HP) "Give Me Something to Dream About"

Year	Production Title	Popular Songs
1948		"Don't You Love Me Anymore?" "There's a Barber in the Harbor of Palermo"
1949	Cinderella	Bibbidi-Bobbidi-Boo (AN) (HP) A Dream Is a Wish Your Heart Makes So This Is Love "There's No Tomorrow" (HP)
1950	Montana	"If I Knew You Were Coming I'd've Baked a Cake" (HP-1) "I'm Gonna Live Till I Die" "One-Finger Melody" "Night Wind" "Me and My Imagination"
1951	Alice in Wonderland	The Unbirthday Song
1952		"Takes Two to Tango" "Dennis the Menace"
1953		"Roo, Roo Kangaroo"
1954	20,000 Leagues Under the Sea Heat Wave	"Papa Loves Mambo" (HP) "Gilly Gilly Ossenfeffer Katzenellen Bogen by the Sea" "I Can't Tell a Waltz from a Tango"
1955		"Don't Stay Away Too Long" "Santo Natale" "Where Will the Dimple Be?"
1956		"Allegheny Moon" (HP) "Hot Diggity" (HP) "Mama, Teach Me to Dance"
1957		"Mi Casa, Su Casa (My House Is Your House)"

Year	Production Title	Popular Songs
1957		"Ivy Rose" "You're Cheatin' Yourself"
1958		"Oh, Oh, I'm Falling in Love Again" "Secretly" "Are You Really Mine?" "Torero" "Moon-Talk" "Hawaiian Wedding Song"
1959		"La Plume de Ma Tante"
1960		"O Dio Mio"

* * *

GUS KAHN

Gus Kahn is the second of the nation's most successful popular song writers. His career spanned 35 years--24 of which were during Tin Pan Alley's heyday. He was five years old when his family came to America from their home in Coblenz, Germany. He grew up in Chicago, Illinois, where he attended public schools. After working as a clerk in a mail order house, he broke into show business writing special material for vaudeville artists. He was only twenty years old when he collaborated with composer Egbert Van Alstyne on the 1906 hit "My Dreamy China Lady." His next partner was composer Grace LeBoy whom he married. Beginning in 1916, Kahn's lyrics were heard in a dozen Broadway productions including the annual "Passing Show" revues in which his "Pretty Baby" (music by Tony Jackson and Egbert Van Alstyne) and "Carolina in the Morning" (music by Walter Donaldson) were heard. During the 1920's, as many as 15 of Kahn's songs became national favorites in a single year! Among them were "Ain't We Got Fun?," "My Buddy," "It Had to Be You," "I'll See You in My Dreams" and "Yes Sir, That's My Baby." Ruth Etting and Eddie Cantor introduced two Kahn standards in the 1928 Florenz Ziegfeld production "Whoopee": "Love Me or Leave Me" and "Makin' Whoopee."

Although Gus Kahn's songs were included in film musicals during the first year of sound, his career in Hollywood really got underway in 1933. He collaborated that year with lyricist Edward Eliscu and composer Vincent Youmans on the score for the first film in which Ginger Rogers and Fred Astaire were teamed--"Flying Down to Rio." Among the film's distinguished songs were "The Carioca" which was nominated for the "Oscar." During the

next eight years, more than 50 motion pictures introduced such
classics as "One Night of Love," "Thanks a Million," "San Francisco," "Love Me Forever" and "You Stepped Out of a Dream."
Kahn worked with more successful composers than any other lyricist and his collaborators included such masters as Walter Donaldson, Harry Warren, George Gershwin, Richard Whiting, Jimmy
McHugh, Rudolf Friml, Nacio Herb Brown, Isham Jones, and Sigmund Romberg.   During his lengthy career, Gus Kahn averaged
five hits a year! He was still one of Hollywood's busiest lyricists
when he died in 1941 at the age of fifty-five.   Ten years later,
Danny Thomas portrayed Kahn in the film biography "I'll See You
in My Dreams."

Year	Production Title	Popular Songs
1906		"My Dreamy China Lady"
1907		"I Wish I Had a Girl"
1913		"Moonlight on the Mississip-pi" "Sunshine and Roses" "I'm on the Jury"
1914		"On the Good Ship Mary Ann" "Everybody Rag with Me" "Oh, How He Could Sing an Irish Song"
1915		"Memories"
1916	THE PASSING SHOW	Pretty Baby "Just a Word of Sympathy"
1917	GOOD NIGHT, PAUL	Sailin' Away on the Henry Clay "'n Everything" "Some Sunday Morning" "Where the Morning Glories Grow" "Along the Way to Waikiki"
1918	SINBAD	I'll Say She Does You Ain't Heard Nothin' Yet
1919	ZIEGFELD MIDNIGHT FROLIC	Baby "Your Eyes Have Told Me So"

Year	Production Title	Popular Songs
1919		"My Isle of Golden Dreams"
1920	THE PASSING SHOW	
1921	BOMBO	Toot, Toot, Tootsie
		"Ain't We Got Fun?"
		"Biminy Bay"
1922	THE PASSING SHOW	Carolina in the Morning
		"My Buddy"
		"On the Alamo"
		"Broken-Hearted Melody"
		"Dixie Highway"
1923		"Swingin' Down the Lane"
		"Beside a Babbling Brook"
		"Sittin' in a Corner"
		"Worried"
		"No, No Nora"
		"Mindin' My Business"
		"When Lights Are Low"
1924		"It Had to Be You" (HP)
		"I'll See You in My Dreams"
		"Nobody's Sweetheart"
		"The One I Love Belongs to Somebody Else"
		"Spain"
		"Charley, My Boy"
		"When You and I Were Seventeen"
		"Gotta Getta Girl"
		"The Little Old Clock on the Mantel"
		"Where Is That Old Girl of Mine?"
		"Why Couldn't It Be Poor Little Me?"
		"I Need Some Petting"
		"Old Pal"
1925	HOLKA POLKA	"Yes Sir, That's My Baby"
		"Isn't She the Sweetest Thing?"
		"I Never Knew"
		"Sometime"
		"My Sweetie Turned Me Down"

GUS KAHN   295

Year	Production Title	Popular Songs

1925

"That Certain Party"
"Ukulele Lady"
"Alone at Last"
"Dreamer of Dreams"
"Got No Time"
"I Wonder Where My Baby
   Is Tonight?"
"Kentucky's Way of Sayin'
   Good Mornin'"
"The Midnight Waltz"
"When I Dream of the Last
   Waltz with You"
"Ida, I Do"

1926   KITTY'S KISSES

"Bashful"
"For My Sweetheart"
"Just a Bird's-Eye View of
   My Old Kentucky Home"
"Let's Talk About My Sweet-
   ie"
"Oh, If I Only Had You"
"There Ain't No Maybe in
   My Baby's Eyes"
"Barcelona"
"But I Do--You Know I Do"
"Drifting Apart"

1927

"Coquette"
"Chlo-e"
"Baby Feet Go Pitter Patter"
"My Ohio Home"
"Persian Rug"
"If You See Sally"
"Collette"
"Sing Me a Baby Song"
"Dixie Vagabond"
"He's the Last Word"
"Oh, What a Pal Was 'Whoo-
   zis'"
"You Said Good Night but
   Meant Goodbye"
"Who's That Knocking at
   My Door?"

1928   WHOOPEE

Makin' Whoopee
Love Me or Leave Me
I'm Bringing a Red, Red
   Rose

RAINBOW

Year	Production Title	Popular Songs
1928	Hit of the Show	

"Ready for the River"
"Indian Cradle Song"
"I'm Sorry, Sally"
"Beloved"
"Where the Shy Little Vio-
    lets Grow"
"Last Night I Dreamed You
    Kissed Me"
"Ten Little Miles from
    Town"
"You're in Style When You're
    Wearing a Smile"
"You Tell Me Your Dream"
"She's Wonderful"
"Little Boy Blue Jeans"
"Little Orphan Annie"

1929   SHOW GIRL

Liza
Do What You Do
So Are You

"Here We Are"
"When You Come to the
    End of the Day"

1930   Whoopee

My Baby Just Cares for Me

"Around the Corner"
"Sweetheart of My Student
    Days"
"The One I Love Can't Be
    Bothered with Me"
"Where the Golden Daffodils
    Grow"
"Hangin' on the Garden Gate"
"The Waltz You Saved for
    Me"
"Was I to Blame for Falling
    in Love with You?"

1931   Holy Terror

"Guilty" (HP)
"Dream a Little Dream of
    Me"
"Building a House for You"
"Old Playmate"
"The Hour of Parting"
"I'm Thru with Love"
"Now That You're Gone"

Year	Production Title	Popular Songs
1931		"In the Little Church in the Valley" "You Gave Me Everything but Love"
1932		"A Little Street Where Old Friends Meet" "Goofus" "You're Telling Me" "Lovable" "A Million Dreams" "So at Last It's Come to This" "The Voice in the Old Village Choir" "I'll Never Be the Same" "Evening" "Think of Me" "Someone to Care For" "Lazy Day" "Twas Only a Summer Night's Dream"
1933	Flying Down to Rio Peg O' My Heart The Prizefighter and the Lady The White Sister Storm at Daybreak	The Carioca (AN) Orchids in the Moonlight Flying Down to Rio Music Makes Me Sweetheart Darlin' You've Got Everything "What Have We Got to Lose?" "Kalua Lullaby"
1934	One Night of Love Bottoms Up Stingaree Riptide Kid Millions Operator 13 Hollywood Party Caravan Gay Bride The Merry Widow Forsaking All Others Laughing Boy	One Night of Love Waitin' at the Gate for Katy Tonight Is Mine Riptide An Earful of Music Okay, Toots When My Ship Comes In Sleepy Head Once in a Lifetime I've Had My Moments Ha-Cha-Cha

Year	Production Title	Popular Songs
1934		"Rhythm of the Raindrops" "Dancing in the Moonlight" "How Can It Be a Beautiful Day?"
1935	Thanks a Million	Thanks a Million (HP) I'm Sitting High on a Hill-top (HP) Sugar Plum New O'leans I've Got a Pocketful of Sunshine
	Love Me Forever Escapade The Girl Friend Mutiny on the Bounty Naughty Marietta Reckless Last of the Pagans	Love Me Forever (HP) You're All I Need (HP-1) Two Together
		"Clouds" "Footloose and Fancy Free" (HP)
1936	San Francisco Her Master's Voice Let's Sing Again Love on the Run Rose-Marie Small Town Girl	San Francisco With All My Heart Let's Sing Again (HP) Gone
		"I've Got a Heavy Date"
1937	A Day at the Races	All God's Chillun Got Rhythm Tomorrow Is Another Day (HP) Blue Venetian Waters A Message from the Man in the Moon
	They Gave Him a Gun Maytime Three Smart Girls	A Love Song of Long Ago Farewell to Dreams My Heart Is Singing Someone to Care for Me
	Music for Madame Captains Courageous The Bride Wore Red	
		"Josephine"
1938	Girl of the Golden West	Who Are We to Say? Soldiers of Fortune Shadows on the Moon

Year	Production Title	Popular Songs
1938	Everybody Sing	The One I Love (Will Come Along Some Day)
1939	Honolulu	Honolulu This Night Will Be My Souvenir
	Idiot's Delight Broadway Serenade Bridal Suite Balalaika	How Strange
1940	Spring Parade	Waltzing in the Clouds (AN) When April Sings It's Foolish but It's Fun
	Lillian Russell The Golden Fleecing Bittersweet Go West Two Girls on Broadway	Blue Lovebird (HP)
1941	Ziegfeld Girl The Chocolate Soldier	You Stepped Out of a Dream "Day Dreaming" (HP)
Posthumous: 1942		"Sometimes" (HP)

* * *

BERT KALMAR

Although lyricist Bert Kalmar's name is almost always linked with that of composer Harry Ruby, Kalmar was a successful song-writer for six years before he collaborated with Ruby. When he was only ten years old, Kalmar ran away from home to join a tent show as a boy magician. He eventually became a dancing comedian in burlesque and vaudeville--a career from which he was forced to retire due to a serious knee injury. When he was twenty-seven years old, he wrote the lyric to his first hit "In the Land of Harmony" (1911). Kalmar teamed with Harry Ruby in 1917 and, after half a dozen Broadway musicals, the pair moved to Hollywood in 1930. Kalmar's most famous lyric, "Three Little Words," was written during his first year on the Coast. He was particularly adept at comic lyrics--many of which were heard in the early films of the Marx Brothers and Wheeler and Woolsey. Groucho Marx adopted Kalmar's "Hooray for Captain Spaulding" as his theme song. Kalmar returned to Broadway for the production "High Kickers" in

1941, and died six years later at the age of sixty-three. In 1951,
he received a posthumous "Oscar" nomination for "A Kiss to Build
a Dream On." The song was written years earlier and was a
success only after Oscar Hammerstein reworked the lyric. Bert
Kalmar was portrayed by Fred Astaire in the 1950 film "Three
Little Words."

Year	Production Title	Popular Songs
1911		"In the Land of Harmony"
1912		"The Ghost of a Violin"
1913		"Where Did You Get That Girl?"
1914		"Moonlight on the Rhine"
1915	MAID IN AMERICA	I've Been Floating Down the Old Green River
		"Hello, Hawaii, How Are You?"
		"If You Can't Get a Girl in the Summertime, You Can't Get a Girl at All"
		"Every Morning You Hear Them Say Good Night Again"
1916		"Since Maggie Dooley Learned the Hooley Hooley"
1917		"When Those Sweet Hawaiian Babies Roll Their Eyes"
		"The More I See of Hawaii, the Better I Like New York"
		"He Sits Around"
1918	LADIES FIRST	
1919		"Oh, What a Pal Was Mary"
		"Take Me to the Land of Jazz"
		"You Said It"
		"All the Quakers Are Shoulder Shakers--Down in Quaker Town"
		"Take Your Girlie to the Movies"

Year	Production Title	Popular Songs
1920	THE ZIEGFELD FOLLIES	I'm a Vamp from East Broadway
	BROADWAY BREVITIES	
		"Snoops, the Lawyer"
		"So Long, Oo-Long"
		"Timbuctoo"
		"Where Do They Go When They Row, Row, Row?"
1921	THE MIDNIGHT ROUNDERS	My Sunny Tennessee
	SNAPSHOTS OF 1921	
		"Mandy 'n' Me"
		"She's Mine, All Mine"
1922	THE GREENWICH VILLAGE FOLLIES	Beautiful Girls
		"The Sheik of Avenue B"
		"I Gave You Up Just Before You Threw Me Down"
1923	HELEN OF TROY, NEW YORK	I Like a Big Town
		It Was Meant to Be
		Happy Ending
		"Who's Sorry Now?" (HP)
		"The Window Cleaners"
1924	NO OTHER GIRL	You Flew Away from the Nest
1925	PUZZLES OF 1925	
1926	THE RAMBLERS	All Alone Monday
	TWINKLE, TWINKLE	
1927	LUCKY	Dancing the Devil Away
		The Same Old Moon
	FIVE O'CLOCK GIRL	Thinking of You (HP)
		Up in the Clouds
1928	GOOD BOY	I Wanna Be Loved by You (HP)
	ANIMAL CRACKERS	Hooray for Captain Spaulding
		Watching the Clouds Roll By
1929	TOP SPEED	Keep Your Undershirt On
		What Would I Care?
		"Over and Over Again"
1930	Check and Double Check	Three Little Words

Year	Production Title	Popular Songs
1930	The Cuckoos Animal Crackers	I Love You So Much
1931		"Nevertheless" (HP-1) "I'm So Afraid of You"
1932	Horsefeathers The Kid from Spain Manhattan Parade	Everyone Says "I Love You" Look What You've Done What a Perfect Combination
1933	Duck Soup	
1934	Hips, Hips Hooray Kentucky Kernels Happiness Ahead	Keep on Doin' What You're Doin' Tired of It All Keep Romance Alive One Little Kiss
1935	Bright Lights Thanks a Million	
1936	Walking on Air	
1938	Everybody Sing Cocoanut Grove 	 "When You Dream About Hawaii"
1939	The Story of Vernon and Irene Castle	Only When You're in My Arms
1940	Go West	
1941	HIGH KICKERS	
1947		"The Egg and I" "Go West, Young Man"

Posthumous:

| 1951 | The Strip | A Kiss to Build a Dream
On (AN) |

* * *

JEROME KERN

The melodies of Jerome Kern served as models for a genera-

tion of songwriters who were in their teens at the time his early
Broadway musicals were being performed.   In those days, musical
comedies were no more than a series of songs, written to achieve
popularity on their own, and only loosely connected by spoken dialogue.   Any song that might increase the success of a show was
added to it--no matter how extraneous it actually was.

Jerome Kern was born in New York in 1885.   His first song
to be heard on Broadway was in the 1902 production "The Silver
Slipper" when Kern was only seventeen.   Three years later, he obtained the degree of Master of Music at Heidelberg University, and
began working as a rehearsal pianist.   During rehearsals of "The
Earl and the Girl, " Kern interested the producer in using one of
his songs and the result was his first major hit--"How'd You Like
to Spoon with Me?"

From 1905 to 1912, Kern had more than 50 of his songs
featured in two dozen Broadway musicals whose basic scores were
by other composers.   The initial show for which Kern received
sole composing credit was "The Red Petticoat" (1912).   His real
break came in 1914 when several of his songs were added to "The
Girl from Utah, " and "They Didn't Believe Me" marked him as a
melody writer of great promise.

In 1915, Kern composed the score for a production that was
greeted as an innovation in musical comedy form.   The show was
"Nobody Home, " and it opened in the tiny Princess Theatre which
seated less than 300 persons.   The size of the theatre necessitated
scaling down the customary lavish sets used in musicals and limit-
ing their number.   The proximity of the audience to the stage also
required more realism than usual in the production design.   In addition, the show's humor resulted from situations written into the
story instead of from comic routines having no connection with the
plot.   The outcome was one of the first intelligent and believable
musical comedies ever presented.   Three more Princess Theatre
musicals followed: "Very Good, Eddie, " "Oh, Boy!, " and "Oh,
Lady! Lady!"   While most musicals were imitations of European
operettas and their stories generally involved romances between
commoners and the royalty of mythical kingdoms, the books for the
Princess shows dealt with simple, modern ideas, and ordinary
American men and women.

Kern enjoyed his biggest success to date with Florenz Ziegfeld's 1920 production "Sally, " starring Marilyn Miller.   It was the
third musical comedy since 1900 to run for more than 500 performances.   Its success was repeated five years later when "Sunny"
(also starring Miss Miller) became the fourth musical to run for
more than 500 performances.

Twenty-five years after his first song was interpolated into
another composer's score, Kern wrote his masterpiece.   In 1927,
he collaborated with Oscar Hammerstein on an adaptation of Edna

Ferber's novel "Show Boat" which dealt with the ill-fated love affair between the daughter of a Mississippi river boat captain and
a dashing ne'er-do-well gambler. A major character in the story
was a mulatto girl who was in love with a white man. The music,
dances, and comedy in "Show Boat" were inseparable from the
show's book and the production was hailed as the most artistic musical accomplishment of the time. It also made a star of a wistful
young singer named Helen Morgan who introduced "Bill" (written
nine years earlier for "Oh, Lady! Lady!") and "Can't Help Lovin'
Dat Man." "Show Boat" was filmed in 1929, revived on the New
York stage in 1932, refilmed in 1936, revived again on Broadway
in 1946, filmed for the third time in 1951, and presented in Manhattan for the fourth time in 1966! It's now included in the permanent repertory of the New York City Opera Company. The original production ran for 575 performances.

    "Show Boat" was followed by "Sweet Adeline," "Ripples,"
"The Cat and the Fiddle," "Music in the Air" and "Roberta." The
year "Roberta" had its premiere, the motion picture industry discovered the cure for its declining box office when Warner Bros.
hit the jackpot with its musicals "Forty-Second Street" and "Gold
Diggers of 1933." Other studios followed suit, and adaptations of
Kern's "The Cat and the Fiddle" and "Music in the Air" reached
the screen in 1934. Kern then accepted an offer from RKO and
Broadway's loss became Hollywood's gain. Kern's "Lovely to Look
At" from the film version of "Roberta" was nominated for an Aca-
demy Award in 1935. The following year, he won the "Oscar" for
"The Way You Look Tonight."

    Kern planned to return to Broadway with the musical comedy
"Gentlemen Unafraid" but it was abandoned after a production at the
St. Louis Municipal Opera. "Very Warm for May" marked his return in 1939 and his score included one of his most famous melod-
ies--"All the Things You Are." It was the last new Broadway musical to feature the melodies of the celebrated composer.

    By 1941, Nazi troops had invaded France and the United
States was approaching its entry into World War II. Jerome Kern
and Oscar Hammerstein composed a ballad expressing the sadness
and dismay felt by millions at the German conquest of Paris. The
song, "The Last Time I Saw Paris," was an immediate hit and
was interpolated into the 1941 motion picture "Lady Be Good." Although not actually written for the film this song earned Jerome
Kern his second "Oscar." Controversy over the selection resulted
in a ruling by the Academy of Motion Picture Arts and Sciences
that future nominees for "Best Song" must have been written ex-
pressly for the film in which they were performed. Kern received
additional nominations for "Dearly Beloved," "Long Ago and Far
Away" and "More and More." In addition to Oscar Hammerstein,
Kern's frequent lyricists included such notable talents as P. G.
Wodehouse, Otto Harbach, B. G. DeSylva, Dorothy Fields, Johnny
Mercer and E. Y. Harburg.

In 1945, Kern traveled to New York for rehearsals of a revival of "Show Boat," and to discuss plans for a new production
based on the career of sharpshooter Annie Oakley.   While in New
York, he became the second musical comedy composer in history
to receive the honor of membership in the National Institute of
Arts and Letters.   The trip was Kern's last.   He suffered a stroke
and died in November of 1945 at the age of sixty.   The year after
his death, the film "Centennial Summer" introduced Kern's "All
Through the Day" which was nominated for the "Oscar."   He was
second only to Richard Rodgers in the number of his musical comedy songs that achieved popularity.   He contributed to 86 stage
productions--the largest number to feature any composer's work.
Arthur Schwartz has called Jerome Kern "the daddy of modern
musical comedy music."

Year	Production Title	Popular Songs
1902	THE SILVER SLIPPER	
1903	THE BEAUTY AND THE BATH (London)	Mister Chamberlain
1904	MR. WIX OF WICKHAM	
1905	THE EARL AND THE GIRL	How'd You Like to Spoon with Me?
	THE CATCH OF THE SEASON THE BABES AND THE BARON	
1906	THE LITTLE CHERUB MY LADY'S MAID THE RICH MR. HOGGENHEIMER	
1907	THE ORCHID FASCINATING FLORA THE DAIRYMAIDS THE GAY WHITE WAY	
1908	A WALTZ DREAM THE GIRLS OF GOTTENBURG FLUFFY RUFFLES	
1909	KITTY GREY THE GAY HUSSARS THE DOLLAR PRINCESS THE GIRL AND THE WIZARD	
1910	THE KING OF CADONIA THE ECHO OUR MISS GIBBS	

Year	Production Title	Popular Songs
1911	THE HEN PECKS LA BELLE PAREE LITTLE MISS FIX-IT THE SIREN THE KISS WALTZ	
1912	THE GIRL FROM MONTMARTRE THE RED PETTICOAT	
1913	OH, I SAY! THE DOLL GIRL LIEBER AUGUSTIN THE MARRIAGE MARKET	I Can't Forget Your Eyes
1914	THE GIRL FROM UTAH THE LAUGHING HUSBAND	They Didn't Believe Me Same Sort of Girl The Land of Let's Pretend I'd Like to Wander with Alice in Wonderland You're Here and I'm Here
1915	NOBODY HOME MISS INFORMATION VERY GOOD, EDDIE 90 IN THE SHADE A MODERN EVE COUSIN LUCY	The Magic Melody You Know and I Know In Arcady Some Sort of Somebody Babes in the Wood On the Shore at Le Lei Wi Nodding Roses Isn't It Great to Be Married? I've Got to Dance
1916	THE ZIEGFELD FOLLIES GO TO IT MISS SPRINGTIME	Have a Heart
1917	HAVE A HEART LOVE O' MIKE OH, BOY!	And I'm All Alone Honeymoon Inn You Said Something I Wonder Why Drift with Me Till the Clouds Roll By You Never Knew About Me Nesting Time in Flatbush Rolled into One An Old-Fashioned Wife Ain't It a Grand and Glorious Feeling?

Year	Production Title	Popular Songs
1917	LEAVE IT TO JANE	The Siren's Song
		Leave It to Jane
		Cleopatterer
		The Sun Shines Brighter
		The Crickets Are Calling
		Just You Watch My Step
	THE RIVIERA GIRL	A Bungalow in Quogue
	MISS 1917	Go, Little Boat
		The Land Where Good Songs Go
	THE ZIEGFELD FOLLIES	
1918	OH, LADY! LADY!	Moon Song
		Oh, Lady! Lady!
		Before I Met You
		Our Little Love Nest
	TOOT TOOT!	
	ROCK-A-BYE BABY	
	HEAD OVER HEELS	
	THE CANARY	
1919	SHE'S A GOOD FELLOW	
	THE LADY IN RED	
1920	THE NIGHT BOAT	Left All Alone Again Blues
		Whose Baby Are You?
	SALLY	Look for the Silver Lining
		The Church 'Round the Corner
		Whip-poor-will
		Wild Rose
		Sally
		Lorelei
	HITCHY-KOO	
1921	GOOD MORNING, DEARIE	Ka-Lu-A
		Good Morning, Dearie
		Blue Danube Blues
	THE ZIEGFELD FOLLIES	
1922	THE BUNCH AND JUDY	
	CABARET GIRL (London)	
1923	STEPPING STONES	Once in a Blue Moon
		Raggedy Ann
		In Love with Love
	THE BEAUTY PRIZE (London)	
1924	SITTING PRETTY	

Year	Production Title	Popular Songs
1924	DEAR SIR PETER PAN	
1925	SUNNY	Who? D'ye Love Me? Sunny Two Little Bluebirds Let's Say Good Night Till It's Morning
	THE CITY CHAP	
1926	CRISS CROSS	In Araby with You You Will, Won't You?
1927	SHOW BOAT	Ol' Man River Only Make Believe Bill Can't Help Lovin' Dat Man Why Do I Love You? You Are Love Life Upon the Wicked Stage
	LUCKY	
1928	BLUE EYES (London)	
1929	SWEET ADELINE	Why Was I Born? Don't Ever Leave Me Here Am I 'Twas Not So Long Ago
1930	RIPPLES	
1931	THE CAT AND THE FIDDLE	She Didn't Say Yes Try to Forget I Watch the Love Parade Poor Pierrot A New Love Is Old One Moment Alone The Night Was Made for Love
1932	MUSIC IN THE AIR	The Song Is You I've Told Ev'ry Little Star In Egern on the Tegern See There's a Hill Beyond a Hill And Love Was Born We Belong Together
1933	ROBERTA	Smoke Gets in Your Eyes Yesterdays

Year	Production Title	Popular Songs
1933	ROBERTA	The Touch of Your Hand You're Devastating I'll Be Hard to Handle
1934	THREE SISTERS (London)	Lonely Feet
1935	Roberta	Lovely to Look At (AN) (HP-1) I Won't Dance (HP)
	I Dream Too Much	I Dream Too Much Jockey on the Carousel I Got Love I'm the Echo
	Sweet Adeline Reckless	We Were So Young Reckless
1936	Swing Time	The Way You Look Tonight (AA) (HP-1) A Fine Romance (HP) Pick Yourself Up Bojangles of Harlem The Waltz in Swing Time Never Gonna Dance
	Show Boat	I Still Suits Me I Have the Room Above
1937	High, Wide and Handsome	The Folks Who Live on the Hill Can I Forget You? High, Wide and Handsome
	When You're in Love	Our Song
1938	GENTLEMEN UNAFRAID (St. Louis)	Your Dream
	MAMBA'S DAUGHTERS (play)	Lonesome Walls
	Joy of Living	You Couldn't Be Cuter (HP) Just Let Me Look at You
1939	VERY WARM FOR MAY	All the Things You Are (HP-1) All in Fun That Lucky Fellow In the Heart of the Dark Heaven in My Arms "The Sweetest Sight That I Have Seen"
1940	One Night in the Tropics	Remind Me

Year	Production Title	Popular Songs
1941	Lady Be Good	The Last Time I Saw Paris (AA)
		"Day Dreaming" (HP)
1942	You Were Never Lovelier	Dearly Beloved (AN) (HP)
		I'm Old-Fashioned
		You Were Never Lovelier
		"Windmill Under the Stars"
1943	Song of Russia	And Russia Is Her Name
1944	Cover Girl	Long Ago and Far Away (AN) (HP-1)
		Sure Thing
	Can't Help Singing	More and More (AN) (HP)
		Any Moment Now
		Can't Help Singing

Posthumous:

1946	SHOW BOAT (revival)	Nobody Else but Me
	Centennial Summer	All Through the Day (AN) (HP-1)
		In Love in Vain (HP)
		Up with the Lark

* * *

TED KOEHLER

     Lyricist Ted Koehler's biggest hits were written with composer Harold Arlen. Koehler was born in Washington, D. C. in 1894. After high school graduation, he worked as a photo-engraver, and played the piano in silent movie houses. His first hit song, "Dreamy Melody," was published in 1922. Koehler was thirty-five years old when he collaborated with Harold Arlen on "Get Happy" which was introduced in the "9:15 Revue" (1930). The team wrote for revues staged at Harlem's Cotton Club where such popular songs as "Stormy Weather," "Between the Devil and the Deep Blue Sea," "I Love a Parade" and "I've Got the World on a String" were first heard. Koehler also worked with composers Jimmy McHugh and Burton Lane on motion picture scores during the 1930's and 1940's. He received two Academy Award nominations in 1944 and another in 1945. Ted Koehler died in 1973 at the age of seventy-eight.

Year	Production Title	Popular Songs
1922		"Dreamy Melody"

Year	Production Title	Popular Songs
1923		"When Lights Are Low"
1929		"Baby--Oh, Where Can You Be?" "Gladly"
1930	9:15 REVUE EARL CARROLL'S VANITIES	Get Happy Hittin' the Bottle The March of Time "Linda"
1931		"Between the Devil and the Deep Blue Sea" "Kickin' the Gong Around" "I Love a Parade" "Wrap Your Troubles in Dreams" "Tell Me with a Love Song"
1932	EARL CARROLL'S VANITIES	I Gotta Right to Sing the Blues "I've Got the World on a String" "My Best Wishes" "Minnie the Moocher's Wedding Day" "Music, Music, Everywhere"
1933		"Stormy Weather" "Happy as the Day Is Long" "Stay on the Right Side of the Road" "Raisin' the Rent" "Calico Days"
1934	SAY WHEN Let's Fall in Love	When Love Comes Swinging Along Say When Let's Fall in Love Love Is Love Anywhere This Is Only the Beginning "Out in the Cold Again" "Here Goes (a Fool)" "As Long as I Live" "Ill Wind" "Breakfast Ball"
1935	King of Burlesque	I've Got My Fingers Crossed

Year	Production Title	Popular Songs
1935	King of Burlesque	Lovely Lady Spreadin' Rhythm Around I'm Shooting High (HP) Whose Big Baby Are You?
	Curly Top	Animal Crackers in My Soup The Simple Things in Life
	Every Night at Eight	It's Great to Be in Love Again
		"Truckin'" (HP) "Cotton"
1936	Dimples	Picture Me Without You Hey, What Did the Bluejay Say?
	Happy Go Lucky	
1937	Artists and Models	Stop, You're Breakin' My Heart (HP)
	23½ Hours Leave The King and the Chorus Girl The Big Show	
		"Let's Waltz for Old Time's Sake"
1938	Start Cheering	"I Can't Face the Music (Without Singing the Blues)" "Feelin' High and Happy"
1939	Love Affair	Sing, My Heart
		"Don't Worry 'Bout Me" (HP) "If I Were Sure of You" "What Goes Up Must Come Down"
1940	Hullabaloo	We've Come a Long Way Together
1941		"When the Sun Comes Out" "Good for Nothin' Joe"
1942		"Every Night About This Time" "The Moment I Laid Eyes on You"

Year	Production Title	Popular Songs
1943	Stormy Weather	There's No Two Ways About Love
1944	Hollywood Canteen	Sweet Dreams, Sweetheart (AN) (HP) What Are You Doin' the Rest of Your Life?
	Up in Arms	Now I Know (AN) Tess's Torch Song
	Rainbow Island	"More Now Than Ever"
1945	San Antonio	Some Sunday Morning (AN) (HP)
	Weekend at the Waldorf Pillow to Post	And There You Are (HP)
1946	Janie Gets Married	"Me and the Blues"
1947	Escape Me Never My Wild Irish Rose Cheyenne	Love for Love
1948	Race Street	

* * *

BURTON LANE

The majority of composer Burton Lane's melodies have been created for motion pictures. Lane was born in New York City in 1912 and went to work as a pianist for the Remick Music Corporation when he was only fifteen. He was discovered by producer J. J. Shubert who hired him to write the music for the 1929 edition of "The Greenwich Village Follies" but the show was never produced. Lane's name finally appeared in a Playbill in 1930 when his songs were featured in the revues "Three's a Crowd" and "Earl Carroll's Vanities." During the next two years, he placed numbers in another edition of the "Vanities," "The Third Little Show" and the revue "Americana."

From 1933 through 1939, Burton Lane wrote songs for almost three dozen films starring such luminaries as Eddie Cantor, Jack Benny, Bing Crosby, Maurice Chevalier and Bob Hope. The occasion of Al Jolson's return to Broadway was important enough to lure Lane away from the sound stages. Working with lyricist E. Y. Harburg, Lane created the score for his first book musical "Hold

on to Your Hats." The show appeared headed for a long run when
the star became ill and the production was forced to close. It
proved to be Jolson's last Broadway musical. Lane went back to
the West Coast to supply songs for another dozen motion pictures
and to receive his first "Oscar" nomination for "How About You?"
introduced by Judy Garland in the 1941 release "Babes on Broadway."

   Burton Lane has E. Y. Harburg to thank for what became
Lane's masterpiece. Harburg conceived the idea for the brilliant
"Finian's Rainbow" and had to persuade a reluctant Lane to compose the show's score. The production opened in 1947 and was one
of the biggest hits of the decade chalking up a two year run!
Lane's music included "How Are Things in Glocca Morra?" and
five other songs that became standards. Lane has collaborated
with many of the nation's top lyricists. In addition to Harburg, his
melodies have boasted words by Ira Gershwin, Al Dubin and Frank
Loesser. In 1957, Lane became partners with the nation's most
successful woman lyric writer Dorothy Fields and the team provided the score for the television musical "Junior Miss." After almost 18 years of self-imposed exile from Broadway, Lane returned
to the legitimate stage to take over as composer on "I Picked a
Daisy" after veteran Richard Rodgers withdrew from the project.
By the time the production opened in 1965, its title had been
changed to "On a Clear Day You Can See Forever." It received a
lukewarm reception from the critics but Lane's music won unani-
mous praise.

Year	Production Title	Popular Songs
1930	EARL CARROLL'S VANITIES THREE'S A CROWD	
1931	EARL CARROLL'S VANITIES	Heigh Ho, the Gang's All Here Have a Heart Love Came into My Heart
	THE THIRD LITTLE SHOW	
1932	AMERICANA	
1933	Dancing Lady Turn Back the Clock	Everything I Have Is Yours Tony's Wife "Look Who's Here"
1934	Bottoms Up Kid Millions Palooka	Little Did I Dream Your Head on My Shoulder Like Me a Little Bit Less (Love Me a Little Bit More)

Year	Production Title	Popular Songs
1934	Strictly Dynamite	
	The Band Plays On	
	Coming Out Party	
	Long Lost Father	
1935	Folies Bergere	You Took the Words Right Out of My Mouth
	Shadow of Doubt	Beyond the Shadow of a Doubt
	Here Comes the Band	
	Reckless	
	The Perfect Gentleman	
1936	College Holiday	
	Every Saturday Night	
		"Guess Who?"
		"Tain't No Use"
1937	Artists and Models	Stop, You're Breakin' My Heart (HP)
	Champagne Waltz	When Is a Kiss Not a Kiss?
	Double or Nothing	Smarty
	Swing High, Swing Low	Swing High, Swing Low
	Her Husband Lies	No More Tears
	Hideaway Girl	
	King of Gamblers	
	Wells Fargo	
	Partners of the Plains	
1938	Cocoanut Grove	Says My Heart (HP-1)
	College Swing	Moments Like This
		How'dja Like to Love Me? (HP)
	Spawn of the North	I Wish I Was the Willow
	Love on Toast	I Want a New Romance
1939	Some Like It Hot	The Lady's in Love with You (HP)
	She Married a Cop	I'll Remember
	St. Louis Blues	Blue Nightfall
	Cafe Society	
	Flight at Midnight	
1940	HOLD ON TO YOUR HATS	There's a Great Day Coming Mañana
		Don't Let It Get You Down
		The World Is in My Arms
		Would You Be So Kindly?
1941	Babes on Broadway	How About You? (AN) (HP)
	Dancing on a Dime	I Hear Music

Year	Production Title	Popular Songs
1941	Las Vegas Nights World Premiere	
1942	Ship Ahoy	Poor You Last Call for Love I'll Take Tallulah
	Panama Hattie Her Cardboard Lover	
1943	DuBarry Was a Lady	Madame, I Love Your Crepe Suzette I Dug a Ditch in Wichita
	Thousands Cheer Presenting Lily Mars	
1944	LAFFING ROOM ONLY Hollywood Canteen	Feudin' and Fightin' (HP-1) What Are You Doin' the Rest of Your Life?
	Rainbow Island	
1945	Pillow to Post	
1947	FINIAN'S RAINBOW	How Are Things in Glocca Morra? (HP) Old Devil Moon When I'm Not Near the Girl I Love If This Isn't Love Look to the Rainbow Something Sort of Grandish
	This Time for Keeps	
1951	Royal Wedding	Too Late Now (AN) Open Your Eyes I Left My Hat in Haiti You're All the World to Me How Could You Believe Me When I Said I Loved You When You Know I've Been a Liar All My Life?
1952	JOLLYANNA (Los Angeles)	
1953	Give a Girl a Break	It Happens Every Time Applause, Applause
1955	Jupiter's Darling	
1957	Junior Miss (TV)	
1965	ON A CLEAR DAY YOU CAN SEE FOREVER	What Did I Have That I Don't Have?

Year	Production Title	Popular Songs
1965	ON A CLEAR DAY YOU CAN SEE FOREVER	Come Back to Me On a Clear Day You Can See Forever
1970	On a Clear Day You Can See Forever	

* * *

EDGAR LESLIE

Edgar Leslie was twenty-two years old when his comedy song "The Police Won't Let Mariuch-a Dance Unless She Move da Feet" became a hit in 1907. Two years later, he collaborated with young and unknown entertainer/songwriter Irving Berlin to create the novelty ditty "Sadie Salome, Go Home." The 1913 Broadway revue "The Pleasure Seekers" included Leslie's warning to early owners of Model "T" automobiles: "He'd Have to Get Under (Get Out and Get Under)." His most famous lyrics proved to be those written for "For Me and My Gal" and "Among My Souvenirs." When he was fifty, Leslie began working with composer Joseph Burke and their songs "Moon Over Miami," "On Treasure Island," "In a Little Gypsy Tea Room," and "A Little Bit Independent" all made the Number One spot on "Your Hit Parade" in the single year 1935! Leslie's 1915 success "America, I Love You" (music by Archie Gottler) was revived during World War II. Edgar Leslie was born in Stamford, Connecticut, in 1885, and died in 1976 at the age of ninety.

Year	Production Title	Popular Songs
1907		"The Police Won't Let Mariuch-a Dance Unless She Move da Feet"
1908		"I'm a Yiddish Cowboy"
1909	THE SILVER STAR	"Sadie Salome, (Go Home)" "Lonesome" "I Didn't Go Home at All" "Way Down in Cotton Town" "Be Jolly, Molly" "Good Luck, Mary"
1910		"I'm Awfully Glad I'm Irish" "That Italian Rag"

Year	Production Title	Popular Songs
1911		"When Ragtime Rosie Ragged the Rosary" "Lord, Have Mercy on a Married Man"
1912	BROADWAY TO PARIS	"Oh, You Little Rascal"
1913	THE PLEASURE SEEKERS	He'd Have to Get Under (Get Out and Get Under) "Oh, You Million Dollar Doll" "Salvation Nell" "Down in Monkeyville"
1914		"Moonlight on the Rhine" "California and You" "On the Steps of the Great White Capitol" "The 20th Century Rag" "Put It On, Take It Off (Wrap It Up, Take It Home)"
1915		"America, I Love You" "Hello, Hawaii, How Are You?" "In the Gold Fields of Nevada" "When You Were a Baby and I Was a Kid Next Door"
1916	BETTY	"Since Maggie Dooley Learned the Hooley Hooley" "Rolling Stones--All Come Rolling Home Again"
1917		"For Me and My Gal" (HP) "Let's All Be Americans Now"
1918		"When Alexander Takes His Ragtime Band to France" "Come on, Papa" "The Dixie Volunteers"
1919		"Oh, What a Pal Was Mary" "Take Me to the Land of Jazz"

Year	Production Title	Popular Songs
1919		"All the Quakers Are Shoulder Shakers--Down in Quaker Town" "Down by the Meadow-Brook" "Take Your Girlie to the Movies"
1920		"What-cha Gonna Do When There Ain't No Jazz?" "In Sweet September"
1922		"Rose of the Rio Grande" "On the 'Gin, 'Gin, 'Ginny Shore" "Blue (and Broken-Hearted)" "Don't Feel Sorry for Me" "Oogie Oogie Wa Wa (Means 'I Want a Mama' to an Eskimo)"
1923		"Dirty Hands, Dirty Face" "Home in Pasadena"
1925		"I'll Take Her Back If She Wants to Come Back" "Masculine Women! Feminine Men!"
1927		"Among My Souvenirs"
1928		"Me and the Man in the Moon" "My Inspiration Is You"
1929	Hot for Paris	"Kansas City Kitty" "My Troubles Are Over" "Reaching for Someone" "Mistakes"
1930	Cameo Kirby	Romance "Reminiscing" "I Remember You from Somewhere" "'Tain't No Sin" "When Kentucky Bids the World 'Good Morning'" "Football Freddie, My Collegiate Man"

Year	Production Title	Popular Songs
1931	Road to Singapore	
		"By the River Sainte Marie" "I'm an Unemployed Sweet- heart" "When the Shepherd Leads His Flock Back Home"
1932	The Big Broadcast	Crazy People
		"Just a Little Home for the Old Folks" "You've Got Me in the Palm of Your Hand"
1933		"The Moon Was Yellow" "I Wake Up Smiling"
1934		"Lovely" "Were You Foolin'?" "And I Still Do"
1935		"Moon Over Miami" (HP-1) "On Treasure Island" (HP-1) "In a Little Gypsy Tea Room" (HP-1) "A Little Bit Independent" (HP-1)
1936	THE ZIEGFELD FOLLIES	Midnight Blue
		"Robins and Roses" (HP) "Cling to Me" (HP) "A Little Rendezvous in Honolulu"
1937		"It Looks Like Rain in Cher- ry Blossom Lane" (HP-1) "Getting Some Fun Out of Life" "Moonlight on the Highway"
1938		"At a Perfume Counter" (HP) "Sailing at Midnight"
1939		"Rainbow Valley"
1942	When Johnny Comes Marching Home	We Must Be Vigilant
1949		"Lost in a Dream"

SAMUEL M. LEWIS

Sam Lewis left his job as a runner for a Wall Street brokerage firm to sing in cafes in his home town of New York City. He was almost thirty in 1914 when he wrote the lyrics for the classic "When You're a Long, Long Way from Home" (music by George Meyer). Two years later, he became partners with lyricist Joe Young with whom he shared credit for dozens of his hits. Al Jolson and Eddie Cantor helped popularize such Lewis and Young successes as "Rock-a-Bye Your Baby with a Dixie Melody," "My Mammy," "I'm Sitting on Top of the World," "How Ya Gonna Keep 'em Down on the Farm?" and "Dinah." In addition to his early collaboration with composer George Meyer, Lewis wrote words for the melodies of Walter Donaldson, Harry Warren, and J. Fred Coots. Although his songs were heard in several Broadway and Hollywood musicals, most of his work achieved popularity without the benefit of a theatrical showcase. Sam Lewis died in 1959 at the age of seventy-four.

Year	Production Title	Popular Songs
1912		"That Mellow Melody"
1913		"That Naughty Melody"
1914		"When You're a Long, Long Way from Home"
1915		"Put Me to Sleep with an Old-Fashioned Melody" "My Mother's Rosary" "There's a Little Lane without a Turning" "My Little Girl"
1916	ROBINSON CRUSOE JR.	Where Did Robinson Crusoe Go with Friday on a Saturday Night?
	STEP THIS WAY	If I Knock the "L" Out of Kelly
	FOLLOW ME	When the Girls Grow Older, They Grow a Little Bolder
		"Way Down in Iowa I'm Going to Hide Away" "Arrah, Go On (I'm Gonna Go Back to Oregon)" "Come on and Baby Me"
1917	THE PASSING SHOW	Meet Me at the Station, Dear

<u>Year</u>	Production Title	<u>Popular Songs</u>
1917		"In San Domingo" "Huckleberry Finn" "I'm All Bound 'Round with the Mason Dixon Line"
1918	SINBAD	Rock-a-Bye Your Baby with a Dixie Melody Hello, Central, Give Me No Man's Land How'd You Like to Be My Daddy? Why Do They All Take the Night Boat to Albany? "Just a Baby's Prayer at Twilight" "Oh, How I Wish I Could Sleep Till My Daddy Comes Home"
1919		"How Ya Gonna Keep 'em Down on the Farm?" "I'll Be Happy When the Preacher Makes You Mine" "You're a Million Miles from Nowhere (When You're One Little Mile from Home)" "Daddy Long Legs" "Don't Cry, Frenchy, Don't Cry" "My Barney Lies Over the Ocean--Just the Way He Lied to Me" "Desert Gold" "Who Played Poker with Pocahontas When John Smith Went Away?" "Upstairs and Down"
1920		"Old Pal, Why Don't You Answer Me?" "I'd Love to Fall Asleep and Wake Up in My Mammy's Arms" "Singin' the Blues (Till My Daddy Comes Home)"
1921		"My Mammy"

Year	Production Title	Popular Songs
1921		"Tuck Me to Sleep in My Old 'Tucky Home" "Cry Baby Blues"
1922		"Hello, Hello, Hello"
1923		"Lovey Came Back"
1924		"Dinah" "Put Away a Little Ray of Golden Sunshine for a Rainy Day" "In Shadowland" "Cover Me Up with the Sunshine of Virginia" "In a Little Rendezvous"
1925		"I'm Sitting on Top of the World" "Five Foot Two, Eyes of Blue" (HP)
1926	AMERICANA	"In a Little Spanish Town" "Take in the Sun, Hang Out the Moon"
1927	LADY DO	"There's a Cradle in Caroline" "Keep Sweeping the Cobwebs Off the Moon" "High-High-High Up in the Hills"
1928	Stepping High	"Revenge" "I Ain't Got Nobody" "Laugh, Clown, Laugh" "King for a Day" "Happy Go Lucky Lane" "In My Bouquet of Memories" "Just a Little Way Away from Home"
1929	Wolf Song Looping the Loop	Mi Amado "I Used to Love Her in the Moonlight"

Year	Production Title	Popular Songs
1929		"I Kiss Your Hand, Madame" "Then You've Never Been Blue" "Absence Makes the Heart Grow Fonder"
1930	Spring Is Here	Crying for the Carolines Have a Little Faith in Me "Song of the Fool"
1931		"Too Late" "Just Friends"
1932		"Lawd, You Made the Night Too Long" "Street of Dreams"
1933		"One Minute to One" "This Time It's Love" "Lost in Your Arms" "We Were the Best of Friends"
1934		"For All We Know" "Am I to Blame?"
1935	EARL CARROLL'S SKETCH BOOK	"I Believe in Miracles" "It Never Dawned on Me" "A Beautiful Lady in Blue" (HP) "Things Might Have Been So Diff'rent"
1936		"Gloomy Sunday" "Now or Never" "Close to Me" "I'm a Fool for Loving You" "Love, What Are You Doing to My Heart?" "Half of Me Wants to Be Good" "That's Life, I Guess"
1938		"Don't Wake Up My Heart" "A Garden in Granada"
1939		"The Last Two Weeks in July"

Year	Production Title	Popular Songs
1940		"What's the Matter with Me?"
1941		"A Tale of Two Cities"
1944	The Fighting Seabees	
1947		"I Can't Believe It Was All Make Believe Last Night"
1951		"Got Her Off My Hands (but Can't Get Her Off My Mind)"

* * *

JERRY LIVINGSTON

Composer Jerry Livingston began playing the piano while a high school student in his home town of Denver, Colorado. His first score was composed for a production staged at the University of Arizona where he received his higher education. After college, he toured the country with a dance orchestra before settling in New York City. He was twenty-three when his "When It's Darkness on the Delta" established him as a composer of promise in 1932. Livingston's most popular song was the 1944 novelty ditty "Mairzy Doats." His biggest hits were written in collaboration with composer Al Hoffman, and Mack David supplied the lyrics for many of them. Livingston has written more themes for television programs than any other popular song writer. His melodies have announced such popular series as "Surfside 6," "Hawaiian Eye," "77 Sunset Strip," "Bourbon Street Beat" and "Roaring Twenties." Livingston has received "Oscar" nominations for his songs "Bibbidi-Bobbidi-Boo," "The Hanging Tree" and "The Ballad of Cat Ballou." In 1973, he collaborated with Mack David on the unsuccessful Broadway musical "Molly."

Year	Production Title	Popular Songs
1932		"When It's Darkness on the Delta"
1933		"It's the Talk of the Town" "Under a Blanket of Blue" "It's Sunday Down in Caroline"
1934		"In Other Words We're Through"

Year	Production Title	Popular Songs
1934		"Learning" "Ol' Pappy"
1935		"Star Gazing" "I've Got an Invitation to a Dance" "Where There's Smoke There's Fire" "In a Blue and Pensive Mood"
1936	HOLLYWOOD REVELS OF 1936	"Moonrise on the Lowlands"
1937		"You're Looking for Romance" "The Shag" "Oh, Oh, What Do You Know About Love?"
1938		"Sixty Seconds Got Together" (HP) "Just a Kid Named Joe" "Sweet Stranger"
1939		"You're Letting the Grass Grow Under Your Feet" "That's All, Brother" "Blue and Sentimental" "I'd Give a Million Tomorrows (For Just One More Yesterday)"
1941		"The Story of a Starry Night"
1942	Get Hep to Love	"Put, Put, Put Your Arms Around Me"
1943	BRIGHT LIGHTS OF 1944 Stage Door Canteen	"What's the Good Word, Mr. Bluebird?" (HP) "Close to You"
1944		"Mairzy Doats" (HP-1) "She Broke My Heart in Three Places" "Goodnight, Wherever You Are" "Fuzzy Wuzzy"

JERRY LIVINGSTON   327

Year	Production Title	Popular Songs
1945		"I'm a Big Girl Now" "Promises" "I Had Too Much to Dream Last Night"
1947	Rose of Santa Rosa	"Chi-Baba, Chi-Baba" (HP) "Give Me Something to Dream About"
1948		"Don't You Love Me Anymore?" "There's a Barber in the Harbor of Palermo"
1949	Cinderella	Bibbidi-Bobbidi-Boo (AN) (HP) A Dream Is a Wish Your Heart Makes So This Is Love
1950	Montana At War with the Army	"My Destiny" "I've Got a Sunday Feeling in My Heart" "Dreamin' Is My Business"
1951	Sailor Beware Alice in Wonderland Teresa	I Like It, I Like It The Unbirthday Song
1952	Jumping Jacks The Stooge Glory Alley	
1953	Scared Stiff Those Redheads from Seattle	
1955		"Wake the Town and Tell the People" (HP)
1956	Jack and the Beanstalk (TV)	"The Twelfth of Never"
1957		"Shenandoah Rose"
1958		"Bluebell"

Year	Production Title	Popular Songs
1959	The Hanging Tree 77 Sunset Strip (TV) Lawman (TV) Bronco (TV) Bourbon Street Beat (TV) Hawaiian Eye (TV) Alaskans (TV) Room for One More (TV)	The Hanging Tree (AN)
1960	Sergeant Rutledge Guns of the Timberland Roaring Twenties (TV) Surfside 6 (TV)	Captain Buffalo
1962	Follow That Dream	"Young Emotions" "Adios, Amigo"
1963	For Those Who Think Young	
1965	Cat Ballou	The Ballad of Cat Ballou (AN)
1973	MOLLY	

* * *

FRANK LOESSER

Frank Loesser was one of a select group of ten popular song writers to have been awarded the distinguished Pulitzer Prize for Drama. He was born in New York City in 1910, and wrote his first song at the age of six. When he was sixteen, he dropped out of New York City College and worked as an office boy, a roving reporter, and a process server.

Loesser began his musical career as a writer of lyrics only and his first published song, "In Love with a Memory of You," went on sale in 1931. A contract with RKO Studios followed but none of his work reached the screen. During the next few years, he wrote material for vaudeville and radio performers and finally became a performer himself--at a night club on New York's Fifty-Second Street. His first hit song was "I Wish I Were Twins" (1934). Several of the songs Loesser sang in his act, written with Irving Actman, were featured in the 1936 Broadway revue "The Illustrator's Show." His lyrics won him another Hollywood contract and the following year Samuel Goldwyn's "The Hurricane" was released featuring Loesser's "Moon of Mana Koora" (music by Alfred

Newman). Loesser's Hollywood career lasted almost a dozen
years. Melodies with his lyrics became a regular feature on the
Saturday night broadcasts of "Your Hit Parade." Year after year,
his songs turned up among the top ten from coast-to-coast and
were frequently in the Number One Spot. He received his first
Academy Award nomination for "Dolores" in 1941.

World War I found Loesser serving as a Private First Class
in the Army's Special Services Division where he wrote sketches
and songs for all-soldier shows. It was while working in this capacity that Loesser wrote his first song without a collaborator to
furnish the music. It was published in 1942 and sold more than
two million records and a million copies of sheet music. "Praise
the Lord and Pass the Ammunition" was one of the most outstanding songs of the war. In 1945, the United States Infantry commissioned him to compose a song glorifying their branch of the service and the result was "The Ballad of Rodger Young."

Loesser returned to civilian life in 1946 and resumed his
career as one of Hollywood's most prominent songwriters. In
1948, he ventured his luck on Broadway and was one of the few
composers whose initial try at the legitimate stage was an unqualified success! "Where's Charley?" ran for 21 months and earned
a million dollar profit on a $200,000 investment.

In addition to his 1941 "Oscar" nomination, Loesser was
nominated for "They're Either Too Young or Too Old" (1943), "I
Wish I Didn't Love You So" (1947) and "Thumbelina" (1952). His
only win was for "Baby, It's Cold Outside" from the 1949 film
"Neptune's Daughter."

After "Where's Charley?", Loesser went to work on "Guys
and Dolls" which was based on a Damon Runyon short story. Loesser's familiarity with the colorful figures that inhabited the Broadway area made him a natural selection to compose songs to be
sung by such Runyon characters as "Big Jule," "Harry, the Horse"
and "Nicely-Nicely Johnson." "Guys and Dolls" opened in 1950 and
grossed $12,000,000!

Loesser's third musical comedy was "The Most Happy Fella."
In addition to composing the songs, which ran the gamut from show
tunes to operatic arias, he wrote the book which he adapted from
the play "They Knew What They Wanted." The integration of Loesser's book, music and lyrics was so complete that the production
required almost no dialogue. "The Most Happy Fella" is considered to be his masterpiece and ran for 676 performances. In addition to his success as a songwriter and author, Loesser also owned
The Frank Music Corporation, and was a founder of Frank Productions, Incorporated which presented Meredith Willson's "The Music
Man."

In 1960, all of Loesser's resources were combined for the
production "Greenwillow." The show was presented in association

with Frank Productions, Inc. The music and lyrics were by Frank
Loesser, and he also co-authored the book. The Frank Music
Corp. published the score and produced the original cast record
album.   But the diverse efforts of Loesser on behalf of the musical failed to insure its success and "Greenwillow" ran for only
three months. Its failure was almost forgotten the following year
when "How To Succeed in Business Without Really Trying" opened.
The show became the twelfth longest-running musical in Broadway
history and won Frank Loesser the Pulitzer Prize for Drama.
"How to Succeed" was the last Loesser musical produced on Broadway.   His next venture, "Pleasures and Palaces," received such
poor notices when it opened in Detroit, Michigan in 1965 that the
production was never brought into New York.   Four years later,
the prize-winning composer of four of the theatre's most memorable musicals died of lung cancer at the age of fifty-nine.

Year	Production Title	Popular Songs
1934		"I Wish I Were Twins" "Junk Man"
1936	THE ILLUSTRATOR'S SHOW	
1937	The Hurricane Vogues of 1938 Blossoms on Broadway Flight for Your Lady	Moon of Mana Koora Lovely One
1938	Cocoanut Grove College Swing	Says My Heart (HP-1) I Fall in Love with You Every Day (HP) Moments Like This How'dja Like to Love Me? (HP)
	Sing You Sinners Thanks for the Memory Spawn of the North A Song Is Born (short subject) Freshman Year Men with Wings Stolen Heaven	Small Fry (HP) Two Sleepy People (HP) I Wish I Was the Willow Heart and Soul (HP)
1939	Man About Town St. Louis Blues Destry Rides Again Hawaiian Nights The Gracie Allen Murder Case	Strange Enchantment (HP) That Sentimental Sandwich I Go for That Blue Nightfall The Boys in the Back Room You've Got That Look Little Joe, the Wrangler Hey, Good Lookin' Snug as a Bug in a Rug

Year	Production Title	Popular Songs
1939	Some Like It Hot	The Lady's in Love with You (HP)
	Cafe Society Heritage of the Desert Invitation to Happiness Island of Lost Men Zaza	
1940	Buck Benny Rides Again	Say It (HP) My! My!
	Johnny Apollo Moon Over Burma Seven Sinners Typhoon A Night at Earl Carroll's The Farmer's Daughter North West Mounted Police The Quarterback Seventeen Youth Will Be Served	Moon Over Burma I've Been in Love Before Palms of Paradise
1941	Las Vegas Nights Kiss the Boys Goodbye	Dolores (AN) Sand in My Shoes Kiss the Boys Goodbye I'll Never Let a Day Pass By That's How I Got My Start
	Mr. Bug Goes to Town	We're the Couple in the Castle (HP)
	Glamour Boy Aloma of the South Seas	The Magic of Magnolias The White Blossoms of Tah-ni
	Sailors on Leave Dancing on a Dime Hold Back the Dawn World Premiere Caught in the Draft Sis Hopkins	Since You I Hear Music
1942	Priorities on Parade	You're in Love with Some-one Else
	Seven Days' Leave	Can't Get Out of This Mood A Touch of Texas I Get the Neck of the Chicken
	Sweater Girl	I Don't Want to Walk without You (HP-1) I Said No
	The Forest Rangers True to the Army	Jingle, Jangle, Jingle (HP-1)

Year	Production Title	Popular Songs
1942	Beyond the Blue Horizon Reap the Wild Wind This Gun for Hire Tortilla Flat	
		"Praise the Lord and Pass the Ammunition" (HP) "Hello, Mom"
1943	Thank Your Lucky Stars	They're Either Too Young or Too Old (AN) (HP) The Dreamer How Sweet You Are (HP) Love Isn't Born
	Happy Go Lucky	Let's Get Lost (HP-1) Murder, He Says Happy Go Lucky Sing a Tropical Song
	Tornado	
		"What Do You Do in the Infantry?" "Skirts" "Have I Stayed Away Too Long?"
1944	Christmas Holiday	Spring Will Be a Little Late This Year
	See Here, Private Hargrove	In My Arms (HP)
		"Sad Bombardier" "First Class Private Mary Brown" "One Little WAC"
1945	Duffy's Tavern	Leave Us Face It (We're in Love)
		"The Ballad of Rodger Young" "Wave to Me, My Lady"
1947	The Perils of Pauline	I Wish I Didn't Love You So (AN) (HP-1) Rumble, Rumble, Rumble Papa, Don't Preach to Me
	Variety Girl	Tallahassee (HP)
		"Bloop-Bleep" "What Are You Doing New Year's Eve?" "A Tune for Humming"

Year	Production Title	Popular Songs
1948	WHERE'S CHARLEY?	Once in Love with Amy My Darling, My Darling (HP) Make a Miracle The New Ashmolean Marching Society and Students Conservatory Band "Feathery Feelin'" "The Last Thing I Want Is Your Pity"
1949	Neptune's Daughter Red, Hot and Blue Roseanna McCoy	Baby, It's Cold Outside (AA) (HP) Now That I Need You "On a Slow Boat to China" (HP-1)
1950	GUYS AND DOLLS Let's Dance	If I Were a Bell Luck Be a Lady Guys and Dolls I've Never Been in Love Before My Time of Day I'll Know A Bushel and a Peck (HP-1) "Hoop-Dee-Doo" (HP)
1952	Hans Christian Andersen	Thumbelina (AN) Wonderful Copenhagen No Two People The Inch Worm Anywhere I Wander
1953		"Just Another Polka"
1955	Guys and Dolls	A Woman in Love (HP)
1956	THE MOST HAPPY FELLA	Standing on the Corner (HP) Warm All Over Joey, Joey, Joey
1960	GREENWILLOW	Never Will I Marry Summertime Love
1961	HOW TO SUCCEED IN BUSINESS WITHOUT REALLY TRYING	I Believe in You

Year	Production Title	Popular Songs
1965	PLEASURES AND PALACES (closed in tryout)	

* * *

HERB MAGIDSON

Lyricist Herb Magidson's first hit song, "Is There Anything Wrong in That?," was published in 1928 when he was twenty-two years old. Although his lyrics were heard in four Broadway revues from 1928 through 1950, most of his popular songs were written for motion pictures or published as independent numbers. Magidson was the first lyricist to receive an "Oscar" when the Academy of Motion Picture Arts and Sciences established its Best Song category in 1934. He won for "The Continental" which Fred Astaire and Ginger Rogers introduced in their second film "The Gay Divorcee." The song's composer, Con Conrad, was the first of Magidson's regular partners in Hollywood. The second was Allie Wrubel with whom he wrote such hits of the 1930's as "Roses in December," "Music, Maestro, Please" and "The Masquerade Is Over." Two of Magidson's most popular World War II lyrics were "Say a Pray'r for the Boys Over There" and "I'll Buy That Dream" both of which were nominated for Academy Awards. Herb Magidson is a native of Braddock, Pennsylvania, where he was born in 1906. He attended the University of Pittsburgh and worked for a New York music publisher during his early career.

Year	Production Title	Popular Songs
1928	EARL CARROLL'S VANITIES	
		"Is There Anything Wrong in That?"
1929	Show of Shows Forward Pass Tiger Rose	Singin' in the Bathtub H'lo, Baby The Day You Fall in Love
1930	TATTLE TALES (closed in tryout) No, No Nanette Little Johnny Jones College Lovers	My Impression of You
1931	Bright Lights	
1932	GEORGE WHITE'S MUSIC HALL VARIETIES	

Year	Production Title	Popular Songs
1932		"Hummin' to Myself" "I Beg Your Pardon, Made- moiselle" "The Organ Grinder"
1933		"Black-Eyed Susan Brown"
1934	The Gay Divorcee	The Continental (AA) A Needle in a Haystack
	Gift of Gab	Talking to Myself Blue Sky Avenue
		"'Fraidy Cat" "I Knew You When"
1935	Here's to Romance	Here's to Romance (HP) Midnight in Paris
	George White's 1935 Scandals Reckless King Solomon of Broadway	According to the Moonlight
1936	Hats Off	Twinkle, Twinkle, Little Star Where Have You Been All My Life?
	I'd Give My Life Every Saturday Night	"'Tain't No Use"
1937	Life of the Party	Roses in December (HP) Let's Have Another Cigarette
	Music for Madame	"Gone with the Wind" (HP)
1938	Radio City Revels	Good Night, Angel (HP) There's a New Moon Over the Old Mill
		"Music, Maestro, Please" (HP-1)
1939	GEORGE WHITE'S SCANDALS	Something I Dreamed Last Night
		"The Masquerade Is Over" (HP)
1940		"I'm Stepping Out with a Memory Tonight" (HP)

Year	Production Title	Popular Songs
1940		"I Can't Love You Anymore (Anymore Than I Do)" (HP) "An Old, Old Castle in Scotland"
1941		"Beau Night in Hotchkiss Corners"
1942	Priorities on Parade	Conchita, Marquita, Lolita, Pepita, Rosita, Juanita Lopez
	Sleepytime Gal	Barrelhouse Bessie from Basin Street I Don't Want Anybody at All (If I Can't Have You)
1943	Hers to Hold	Say a Pray'r for the Boys Over There (AN) "A Pink Cocktail for a Blue Lady"
1944	Music in Manhattan	
1945	Sing Your Way Home	I'll Buy That Dream (AN) (HP-1)
1946	Do You Love Me?	 "Linger in My Arms a Little Longer, Baby" (HP)
1947	Song of the Thin Man	 "I'll Dance at Your Wedding" (HP)
1948		"Enjoy Yourself (It's Later Than You Think)" (HP)
1949	Make Mine Laughs	
1950	MICHAEL TODD'S PEEP SHOW	Violins from Nowhere

* * *

JOSEPH McCARTHY

Summerville, Massachusetts, was the home town of lyricist

JOSEPH McCARTHY 337

Joseph McCarthy. During the early years of his career, he sang
in Boston cafes and was a music publisher in that city. "That
Dreamy Italian Waltz" (1910) started him on the road to success
as a popular song writer. His stage musicals from 1912 through
1928 included "Irene" (which was the first Broadway musical to
break the long-run record held for 26 years by "A Trip to Chinatown"), "Kid Boots" and "Rio Rita." His songs were also heard
in four editions of "The Ziegfeld Follies." Composer Harry Tierney was McCarthy's collaborator on most of his Broadway efforts.
Joseph McCarthy's motion picture songs failed to achieve the popularity of his earlier work. He died at the age of fifty-five--three
years after the film version of his biggest hit "Irene" was released
in 1940.

Year	Production Title	Popular Songs
1910		"That Dreamy Italian Waltz" "In All My Dreams I Dream of You"
1911		"That Long Lost Chord" "When Broadway Was a Pasture" "My Little Lovin' Honey Man"
1912	THE WALL STREET GIRL	"When I Got You Alone Tonight" "You Made Me Love You" "That's How I Need You" "Love, Honor and Obey"
1913		"I Miss You Most of All" "I'm Crying Just for You" "Melinda's Wedding Day" "There's a Wireless Station Down in My Heart" "While They Were Dancing Around"
1914		"There's a Little Spark of Love Still Burning" "I Want to Go to Tokio"
1915		"Norway" "If We Can't Be the Same Old Sweethearts" "Beatrice Fairfax"
1916		"What Do You Want to Make Those Eyes at Me For?" "Ireland Must Be Heaven for My Mother Came from There"

Year	Production Title	Popular Songs
1916		"There's a Garden in Old Italy" "Sweet Cider Time When You Were Mine"
1917		"They Go Wild, Simply Wild, Over Me" "Night Time in Little Italy"
1918	OH, LOOK! EVERYTHING MISS SIMPLICITY	I'm Always Chasing Rainbows (HP) "I Found the End of the Rainbow"
1919	THE ZIEGFELD FOLLIES IRENE THE ROYAL VAGABOND	My Baby's Arms Alice Blue Gown (HP) Irene Castle of Dreams "Ballyho Bay"
1920	KISSING TIME AFGAR THE ZIEGFELD FOLLIES	Oui, Oui, Marie Why Don't You?
1921	THE BROADWAY WHIRL	 "Saw Mill River Road"
1922	UP SHE GOES GLORY	Journey's End Let's Kiss and Make Up Lady Luck, Smile on Me
1923	THE ZIEGFELD FOLLIES KID BOOTS	Take, Oh Take, Those Lips Away Someone Loves You After All Keep Your Eye on the Ball If Your Heart's in the Game
1924	THE ZIEGFELD FOLLIES ANNIE DEAR	Adoring You
1927	RIO RITA	Rio Rita The Ranger's Song Following the Sun Around You're Always in My Arms The Kinkajou

Year	Production Title	Popular Songs
1927	RIO RITA	If You're in Love You'll Waltz Sweetheart, We Need Each Other
	CROSS MY HEART	
1929		"Through"
1930	High Society Blues	I'm in the Market for You High Society Blues Just Like in a Story Book
	Man Trouble Let's Go Places	
1931		"Sing Song Girl"
1933		"Underneath the Arches" (HP)
1935		"My Dream Is in My Arms"
1938	Listen, Darling Freshman Year	Ten Pins in the Sky "How Little I Knew" "Naturally"
1940	BILLY ROSE'S AQUACADE (New York World's Fair) Irene	You Think of Everything (HP) You've Got Me Out on a Limb

Posthumous:

| 1947 | | "Come Back to Sorrento" |

* * *

JIMMY McHUGH

Jimmy McHugh is second only to Harry Warren as the most successful composer of popular motion picture songs. The nearly five dozen films on which he worked introduced 86 songs that became favorites. Although the motion picture industry honored five of his melodies with "Oscar" nominations, none of them emerged the victor.

McHugh was born in Boston, Massachusetts, in 1894. After graduation from high school, he worked as a plumber's helper, re-

hearsal pianist at the Boston Opera House, and song plugger for
the local branch of Irving Berlin's music publishing firm.   He was
twenty-two years old when his first hit song "Carolina, I'm Coming Back to You" went on sale in 1916.   Four years later, McHugh
moved to New York City where he composed melodies featured in
floor shows at Harlem's Cotton Club.   In 1924, he collaborated
with lyricists Irving Mills and Gene Austin on one of the year's
biggest songs--"When My Sugar Walks Down the Street."   He began his partnership with lyricist Dorothy Fields in 1927 and their
score for "Blackbirds" (1928) introduced the classic "I Can't Give
You Anything but Love."   It was soon followed by "On the Sunny
Side of the Street" and "Exactly Like You."   From 1929 through
1939, McHugh supplied songs for such screen luminaries as Alice
Faye, Shirley Temple, Bobby Breen and Deanna Durbin.   Irene
Dunne introduced McHugh's first Academy Award-nominated song
"Lovely to Look At" in the 1935 release "Roberta."

In 1939, Jimmy McHugh accepted producer Michael Todd's
offer to compose the score for the Broadway revue "Streets of
Paris" which featured Portuguese singer Carmen Miranda.   Mc-
Hugh's "South American Way" became her trademark.   The following year, his songs were heard in another revue which closed after
only 44 performances.   McHugh then resumed his career as one of
Hollywood's most sought after composers.   During World War II,
he worked at Paramount, RKO and Twentieth Century-Fox on musicals starring Betty Hutton, Frank Sinatra and Vivian Blaine.   Mc-
Hugh was a diligent war worker and raised $28,000,000 during a
Beverly Hills bond rally in 1945.   The accomplishment won him a
presidential citation.   During his long residence in Southern California, McHugh formed a close friendship with Hearst newspaper
columnist Louella Parsons for whom he wrote the song "Louella"
in 1957.

McHugh's film songs were written in collaboration with such
outstanding lyricists as Frank Loesser, Johnny Mercer and Harold
Adamson.   In 1961, he and Adamson dedicated their "The First
Lady Waltz" to Jacqueline Kennedy.   Jimmy McHugh died in Beverly
Hills eight years later at the age of seventy-four.

Year	Production Title	Popular Songs
1916		"Carolina, I'm Coming Back to You"
1921		"Emaline"
1922		"When You and I Were Young Maggie Blues" "Immigration Rose"
1924		"When My Sugar Walks Down the Street"

Year	Production Title	Popular Songs
1924		"What Has Become of Hinky Dinky Parley Voo?" "I Don't Care What You Used to Be, I Know What You Are Today"
1925	SKY HIGH	"The Lonesomest Girl in Town" "Everything Is Hotsy Totsy Now"
1926		"My Dream of the Big Parade" "There's a New Star in Heaven Tonight--Rudolph Valentino" "I Don't Mind Being All Alone When I'm All Alone with You"
1927		"I Can't Believe That You're in Love with Me"
1928	BLACKBIRDS	I Can't Give You Anything but Love Diga-Diga-Doo I Must Have That Man Doin' the New Lowdown Porgy Baby!
	HELLO, DADDY	Let's Sit and Talk About You Futuristic Rhythm In a Great Big Way Out Where the Blues Begin
1929	The Time, the Place and the Girl	Collegiana
1930	THE INTERNATIONAL REVUE	On the Sunny Side of the Street Exactly Like You I'm Feeling Blue
	THE VANDERBILT REVUE Love in the Rough	Blue Again Button Up Your Heart Go Home and Tell Your Mother One More Waltz

Year	Production Title	Popular Songs
1931	SHOOT THE WORKS SINGIN' THE BLUES	How's Your Uncle? Singin' the Blues It's the Darndest Thing Cuban Love Song
	Cuban Love Song Flying High	
1932	Meet the Baron	
		"Goodbye Blues"
1933	RADIO CITY MUSIC HALL (opening stage show)	Hey! Young Fella Happy Times With a Feather in My Cap
	Dancing Lady The Prizefighter and the Lady	My Dancing Lady Lucky Fella
		"Don't Blame Me" "Dinner at Eight"
1934	Fugitive Lovers	
		"Thank You for a Lovely Evening" "Lost in a Fog" "Serenade for a Wealthy Widow"
1935	Roberta	Lovely to Look At (AN) (HP-1) I Won't Dance (HP)
	Every Night at Eight	I'm in the Mood for Love (HP-1) I Feel a Song Comin' On It's Great to Be in Love Again Speaking Confidentially
	Hooray for Love	Hooray for Love You're an Angel I'm Livin' in a Great Big Way I'm in Love All Over Again
	King of Burlesque	I've Got My Fingers Crossed I'm Shooting High (HP) Lovely Lady Spreadin' Rhythm Around Whose Big Baby Are You?
	The Nitwits	Music in My Heart
		"Every Little Moment" (HP)
1936	Dimples	Picture Me Without You Hey, What Did the Bluejay Say?

JIMMY McHUGH   343

Year	Production Title	Popular Songs

1936 Banjo on My Knee   There's Something in the Air
                                  Where the Lazy River Goes By

      Her Master's Voice   With All My Heart
      Let's Sing Again   Let's Sing Again (HP)
      The Voice of Bugle Ann

1937 Hitting a New High   I Hit a New High
                                  This Never Happened Before
                                  Let's Give Love Another Chance

      Top of the Town   Where Are You? (HP)
                                  Blame It on the Rhumba
                                  Top of the Town
                                  Jamboree
                                  That Foolish Feeling
      You're a Sweetheart   You're a Sweetheart (HP-1)
                                  My Fine Feathered Friend
                                  Broadway Jamboree
      Merry-Go-Round of 1938 You're My Dish
                                  More Power to You
      When Love Is Young   When Love Is Young
      Breezing Home

1938 That Certain Age   My Own (AN) (HP)
                                  You're as Pretty as a Picture
      Mad About Music   I Love to Whistle (HP)
                                  Chapel Bells
                                  Serenade to the Stars
      Youth Takes a Fling   For the First Time
      Devil's Party
      Reckless Living
      Road to Reno

1939 STREETS OF PARIS   South American Way
                                  Is It Possible?
                                Rendezvous Time in Paree
      The Family Next Door
      Rio

1940 KEEP OFF THE GRASS Clear Out of This World
                                  A Latin Tune, a Manhattan Moon and You
                                On the Old Park Bench
      You'll Find Out   I'd Know You Anywhere (AN)
                                  You've Got Me This Way
                                  I've Got a One Track Mind
                                  The Bad Humor Man

Year	Production Title	Popular Songs
1940	Buck Benny Rides Again	Say It (HP)
		My! My!
	Two Girls on Broadway	
1941	You're the One	You're the One
		I Could Kiss You for That
1942	Seven Days' Leave	Can't Get Out of This Mood
		A Touch of Texas
		I Get the Neck of the Chicken
1943	Hers to Hold	Say a Pray'r for the Boys Over There (AN)
	Higher and Higher	I Couldn't Sleep a Wink Last Night (AN) (HP-1)
		A Lovely Way to Spend an Evening (HP)
		The Music Stopped
	Happy Go Lucky	Let's Get Lost (HP-1)
		Murder, He Says
		Sing a Tropical Song
		Happy Go Lucky
	Around the World	Candlelight and Wine
		Don't Believe Everything You Dream
		"Comin' in on a Wing and a Prayer" (HP-1)
1944	Four Jills in a Jeep	How Blue the Night (HP)
		You Send Me
		How Many Times Do I Have to Tell You?
	Something for the Boys	In the Middle of Nowhere
		I Wish We Didn't Have to Say Goodbye
		Wouldn't It Be Nice?
	Two Girls and a Sailor	In a Moment of Madness
	The Princess and the Pirate	
1945	Nob Hill	I Don't Care Who Knows It (HP)
		I Walked in with My Eyes Wide Open
	Doll Face	Here Comes Heaven Again
		Dig You Later--A Hubba-Hubba-Hubba

Year	Production Title	Popular Songs
1945	Doll Face	Somebody's Walkin' in My Dreams
	Bring on the Girls	
1946	Do You Love Me?	
1947	Smash-Up	Life Can Be Beautiful (HP) I Miss That Feeling
	Calendar Girl Hit Parade of 1947	
1948	AS THE GIRLS GO	You Say the Nicest Things, Baby I Got Lucky in the Rain There's No Getting Away from You
	A Date with Judy If You Knew Susie	It's a Most Unusual Day
1951	His Kind of Woman	
1954		"Dream, Dream, Dream"
1955		"The Star You Wished Upon Last Night"
1956	STRIP FOR ACTION (closed in tryout)	Too Young to Go Steady Love Me as Though There Were No Tomorrow I Just Found Out About Love
1958	Home Before Dark	
1959	A Private's Affair	Warm and Willing
1960	Where the Hot Wind Blows!	Where the Hot Wind Blows!

* * *

JOHNNY MERCER

The third most successful lyricist in motion picture history--and the fourth most successful popular song writer in America after Tin Pan Alley--is Johnny Mercer. Mercer received the second highest number of "Oscar" nominations for Best Song (18) and tied with Sammy Cahn and Jimmy Van Heusen as the winner for four of the coveted statuettes. He holds the record for the most songs (14) that occupied the Number One spot on "Your Hit Parade," and is third in the total number (36) of his songs that placed on the Parade.

After finishing high school in Virginia, Johnny Mercer decided to go on the stage and traveled to New York with the Savannah Little Theatre Group to participate in an acting competition. He had written his first song when he was 15, and continued writing lyrics while trying to make headway as an actor. Fortune winked at Mercer the actor but smiled on Mercer the songwriter, and one of his songs was heard in the Broadway revue "The Garrick Gaieties" in 1930. In addition to being an actor and lyricist, Mercer had another ace up his sleeve--he sang. Orchestra leader Paul Whiteman thought enough of Mercer's vocal ability to hire him as a band singer. Whiteman performed an even greater service by introducing him to Hoagy Carmichael whose hit songs already included the classic "Stardust." Mercer's collaboration with Carmichael began in 1932, and the following year "Lazybones" became Mercer's biggest success to date. The song attracted the attention of Hollywood, and Warner Bros. used one of his songs in the 1933 release "College Coach." Four years later, Mercer signed a contract with Warner's, and from 1937 through 1939 his songs were heard in a dozen of its films which introduced such hits as "Hooray for Hollywood," "Have You Got Any Castles, Baby?," "Too Marvelous for Words," and "Jeepers Creepers" which earned Mercer his first "Oscar" nomination in 1938. Mercer was only twenty-nine years old!

While writing for motion pictures and the popular music trade, Johnny Mercer contributed to the Broadway theatre. His work was heard in both the 1936 and 1939 editions of the all-Negro revue "Blackbirds," and the 1940 book musical "Walk with Music." During the Forties, Mercer worked in Hollywood with composers Harold Arlen and Jerome Kern with whom he wrote the Academy Award contenders "Blues in the Night," "That Old Black Magic," "Dearly Beloved," "My Shining Hour," and "Ac-cent-tchu-ate the Positive." It was the 1946 envelope that finally contained Mercer's name as the winner for "On the Atchison, Topeka and the Santa Fe" (music by Harry Warren). That same year, Mercer and Arlen supplied the score for Broadway's "St. Louis Woman."

Johnny Mercer was an accomplished musician who worked with other composers only by choice. In addition to the complete score for the 1951 stage success "Top Banana," he wrote both words and music for such popular songs as "I'm an Old Cowhand," "The Strip Polka," "Dream," and the "Oscar"-nominated "Something's Gotta Give." One of Mercer's most unusual successes was his adaptation of the French song "Autumn Leaves" which became a national favorite in 1955. It was followed by his greatest Broadway triumph "Li'l Abner" which ran for a year and a half. Mercer collected his three additional "Oscars" for "In the Cool,

Cool, Cool of the Evening" (1951), "Moon River" (1961), and
"Days of Wine and Roses" (1962).   The last two songs were written with composer Henri Mancini during their ten year partnership.
Mercer's last nomination was for "Life Is What You Make It" in
1971.

At the age of sixty-five, Mercer was far from retirement.
His stage musical "Good Companions" (music by Andre Previn)
opened in London in 1974 and ran for five months.   The next year,
he was operated on for a brain tumor--an operation from which
he never recovered.   The reknowned lyricist/composer died in
1976.   Johnny Mercer's screen credits include over 65 films in
which 87 hit songs were introduced!

Year	Production Title	Popular Songs
1930	THE GARRICK GAIETIES	Out of Breath and Scared to Death of You
1932	AMERICANA	Satan's Li'l Lamb Would'ja for a Big Red Apple? Whistling for a Kiss "After Twelve O'Clock" "While We Danced at the Mardi Gras" "It's About Time" "Thanksgivin'"
1933	TATTLE TALES College Coach	"Lazybones" "You Have Taken My Heart" "It Might Have Been a Diff'rent Story"
1934	Transatlantic Merry-Go-Round	If I Had a Million Dollars "P.S. I Love You" (HP) "Here Come the British" "Pardon My Southern Accent" "When a Woman Loves a Man" "Fare-Thee-Well to Harlem" "Moon Country (Is Home to Me)"
1935	To Beat the Band	I Saw Her at Eight O'Clock Eeny, Meeny, Meiny, Mo (HP) If You Were Mine

Year	Production Title	Popular Songs
1935	Old Man Rhythm	I Never Saw a Better Night
		"I'm Building Up to an Aw- ful Letdown" (HP) "Dixieland Band" "Down 't Uncle Bill's"
1936	BLACKBIRDS Rhythm on the Range	I'm an Old Cowhand (HP)
		"Goody, Goody" (HP-1) "Jamboree Jones" "Dream-Awhile" "Lost" (HP-1) "Peter Piper" "Welcome Stranger"
1937	Varsity Show	Have You Got Any Castles, Baby? (HP) We're Working Our Way Through College Love Is on the Air Tonight You've Got Something There Moonlight on the Campus
	Hollywood Hotel	Hooray for Hollywood I'm Like a Fish Out of Water I've Hitched My Wagon to a Star Let That Be a Lesson to You Silhouetted in the Moonlight Can't Teach My Old Heart New Tricks
	The Singing Marine Ready, Willing and Able	Night Over Shanghai Too Marvelous for Words (HP) Just a Quiet Evening Sentimental and Melancholy
		"Bob White (What'cha Gonna Swing Tonight?)" (HP) "Love Is a Merry-Go-Round"
1938	Going Places	Jeepers Creepers (AN) (HP-1) Say It with a Kiss Mutiny in the Nursery
	Hard to Get	You Must Have Been a Beautiful Baby (HP-1)

Year	Production Title	Popular Songs
1938	Cowboy from Brooklyn	Ride, Tenderfoot, Ride I'll Dream Tonight I've Got a Heartful of Music
	Garden of the Moon	The Girl Friend of the Whirling Dervish Confidentially Love Is Where You Find It Garden of the Moon
	Gold Diggers in Paris	Daydreaming All Night Long (HP) "Could Be" (HP) "The Weekend of a Private Secretary" "Something Tells Me"
1939	BLACKBIRDS Naughty but Nice	Hooray for Spinach In a Moment of Weakness
	Wings of the Navy	"And the Angels Sing" (HP-1) "Day In, Day Out" (HP-1) "(Gotta Get Some) Shut Eye" (HP) "I Thought About You" "You Grow Sweeter as the Years Go By" "You and Your Love" "Make with the Kisses" "Cuckoo in the Clock" "Blue Rain" "Show Your Linen, Miss Richardson"
1940	WALK WITH MUSIC	The Rhumba Jumps Ooh, What You Said I Walk with Music Way Back in 1939 A.D.
	Second Chorus You'll Find Out	Love of My Life (AN) I'd Know You Anywhere (AN) You've Got Me This Way I've Got a One Track Mind The Bad Humor Man
	Let's Make Music	"Fools Rush In" (HP-1) "Mister Meadowlark" "On Behalf of the Visiting Firemen"

Year	Production Title	Popular Songs
1941	Blues in the Night	Blues in the Night (AN) (HP-1) This Time the Dream's on Me Says Who? Says You, Says I!
	You're the One	I Could Kiss You for That You're the One
	Navy Blues	In Waikiki You're a Natural
	Birth of the Blues	"G. I. Jive" "The Air-Minded Executive"
1942	Star Spangled Rhythm	That Old Black Magic (AN) (HP) Hit the Road to Dreamland
	You Were Never Lovelier	Dearly Beloved (AN) (HP) I'm Old-Fashioned You Were Never Lovelier
	The Fleet's In	Tangerine (HP) I Remember You (HP) Not Mine If You Build a Better Mousetrap Arthur Murray Taught Me Dancing in a Hurry
	All Through the Night Captains of the Clouds	"Skylark" (HP) "The Strip Polka" "Windmill Under the Stars" "Mandy Is Two"
1943	The Sky's the Limit	My Shining Hour (AN) (HP) One for My Baby The Old Music Master
	True to Life Riding High They Got Me Covered	"Trav'lin' Light"
1944	Here Come the Waves	Ac-cent-tchu-ate the Positive (AN) (HP-1) I Promise You Let's Take the Long Way Home (HP)
	To Have and Have Not	How Little We Know "Dream" (HP-1) "When Love Walks By"

JOHNNY MERCER

Year	Production Title	Popular Songs
1944		"You've Got Me Where You Want Me"
1945	Out of This World	Out of This World (HP) June Comes Around Every Year
		"Laura" (HP-1)
1946	ST. LOUIS WOMAN	Come Rain or Come Shine (HP) Anyplace I Hang My Hat Is Home Legalize My Name It's a Woman's Prerogative
	The Harvey Girls	On the Atchison, Topeka and the Santa Fe (AA) (HP) Wait and See (HP)
		"And So to Bed"
1947	Dear Ruth	"Midnight Sun" "Every So Often"
1948	Mr. Peabody and the Mermaid	
1949	TEXAS LI'L DARLIN'	The Big Movie Show in the Sky
	Always Leave Them Laughing Make Believe Ballroom	
1950	The Petty Girl	Fancy Free
		"When the World Was Young"
1951	TOP BANANA Here Comes the Groom	In the Cool, Cool, Cool of the Evening (AA) (HP)
	My Favorite Spy	"The Bilboa Song" "Here's to My Lady"
1952	Belle of New York	When I'm Out with the Belle of New York
	Everything I Have Is Yours	"The Glow Worm" (HP-1) "Early Autumn"

Year	Production Title	Popular Songs
1953	Dangerous When Wet	
1954	Seven Brides for Seven Brothers	When You're in Love
1955	Daddy Long Legs	Something's Gotta Give (AN) (HP-1)
	Timberjack	
	I'll Cry Tomorrow	"Autumn Leaves" (HP-1)
1956	LI'L ABNER	
	You Can't Run Away from It	You Can't Run Away from It
1958	Bernadine	Bernadine
	Love in the Afternoon	
	Merry Andrew	"Satin Doll"
1959	SARATOGA	
		"I Wanna Be Around"
1960	Facts of Life	The Facts of Life (AN)
		"Two of a Kind"
1961	Breakfast at Tiffany's	Moon River (AA)
1962	Days of Wine and Roses	The Days of Wine and Roses (AA)
	Hatari	Just for Tonight
	How the West Was Won	"Once Upon a Summertime"
1963	Charade	Charade (AN)
	Love with the Proper Stranger	Love with the Proper Stranger
1964	FOXY	Talk to Me, Baby
	The Pink Panther	It Had Better Be Tonight
	The Americanization of Emily	Emily
	Man's Favorite Sport	
1965	The Great Race	The Sweetheart Tree (AN)
		"Summer Wind"
1966	Moment to Moment	Moment to Moment
	Not with My Wife You Don't	

JOHNNY MERCER

Year	Production Title	Popular Songs
1967	Barefoot in the Park	
1968	Rosie	
1969	Darling Lili	Whistling Away in the Dark (AN)
1971	Kotch	
1973	The Long Goodbye	
1974	THE GOOD COMPANIONS (London)	

* * *

BOB MERRILL

     Bob Merrill was born in New Jersey in 1921 and grew up in Pennsylvania. He was a teenaged actor and impersonator before being inducted into the Army during World War II. After he was discharged, Merrill moved to the West Coast and tried his hand at writing for radio and motion pictures while employed as a dialogue director at Columbia Studios. He found his true vocation as a songwriter when he was twenty-four years old and hit the commercial jackpot in 1950 with "If I Knew You Were Comin', I'd've Baked a Cake" written in collaboration with Al Hoffman and Clem Watts. During the next six years, Merrill wrote dozens of popular songs while working as a television producer. He had trouble realizing his ambition to become a Broadway composer because of his reputation as a writer of nonsense ditties such as "The Doggie in the Window" and "Mambo Italiano." Merrill finally interested producer George Abbott in a musical version of Eugene O'Neill's Pulitzer Prize-winning play "Anna Christie." Retitled "New Girl in Town," it opened in 1957 and made a star of dancer Gwen Verdon."

     Merrill's success in the theatre was phenomenal since he had no formal musical education. When he began writing, he was unable to read music and composed his tunes on a xylophone using a self-devised numbering system. "New Girl in Town" was followed by "Take Me Along" (adapted from O'Neill's play "Ah, Wilderness"). Merrill's third hit in a row was the stage version of the film "Lili" called "Carnival." His next assignment brought him the greatest success of his career to date. Although he had proven himself equally capable as both composer and lyricist, he agreed to function as lyricist only for the musical "Funny Girl." The show's story was about Ziegfeld comedienne Fanny Brice and her hectic marriage to gambler Nicky Arnstein. "Funny Girl" opened

in 1964 and ran for three years! Merrill then returned to working
without a musical collaborator and composed the score for "Holly
Golightly." It closed before reaching Broadway. He fared little
better with his score for "Henry, Sweet Henry" which managed to
make it to Manhattan but lasted for less than three months.

    Bob Merrill received an Academy Award nomination for the
lyrics to the title song added to the film version of "Funny Girl"
in 1968.   Three years later, he rejoined "Funny Girl" composer
Jule Styne and suffered another disaster when their "Prettybelle"
expired in Boston.   Merrill and Styne's 1972 Broadway offering
"Sugar" (based on the film "Some Like It Hot") was a modest success.

Year	Production Title	Popular Songs
1947		"Why Does It Have to Rain on Sunday?"
1948		"Not Much (Funny)"
1949		"Lover's Gold" (HP) "Fools Paradise" "Chicken Song (I Ain't Gonna Take It Sittin' Down)"
1950		"If I Knew You Were Comin', I'd've Baked a Cake" (HP-1) "Candy and Cake" (HP-1) "So Long, Sally" "I'm Bashful" "You Don't Have to Be a Baby to Cry" "Me and My Imagination"
1951		"Belle, Belle, My Liberty Belle" "Sparrow in the Tree Top" (HP) "Let Me In"
1952		"My Truly, Truly Fair" (HP) "Pittsburgh, Pennsylvania" "Walkin' to Missouri" "Feet Up (Pat Him on the Po-Po)" "'Cause I Love Ya (That's a-Why)"
1953		"The Doggie in the Window" (HP-1)

Year	Production Title	Popular Songs
1953		"Butterflies"
1954		"Mambo Italiano" "Make Yourself Comfortable" (HP) "Honeycomb" (HP) "Tina Marie" (HP)
1955		"Where Will the Dimple Be?"
1956		"A Sweet Old-Fashioned Girl" "Miracle of Love"
1957	NEW GIRL IN TOWN	Sunshine Girl Did You Close Your Eyes?
1958		"When the Boys Talk About the Girls"
1959	TAKE ME ALONG	Staying Young Take Me Along
1960		"Oh, Oh, Rosie" "The Sheik of Chicago (Mustafa)"
1961	CARNIVAL	Love Makes the World Go 'Round
1962	The Wonderful World of the Brothers Grimm Mr. Magoo's Christmas Carol (TV)	Above the Stars
1964	FUNNY GIRL	People You Are Woman, I Am Man Don't Rain on My Parade "Absent-Minded Me"
1965	The Dangerous Christmas of Red Riding Hood (TV)	
1966	HOLLY GOLIGHTLY (closed in tryout)	
1967	HENRY, SWEET HENRY	
1968	Funny Girl	Funny Girl (AN)

Year	Production Title	Popular Songs
1971	PRETTYBELLE (closed in tryout)	
1972	SUGAR	

* * *

GEORGE W. MEYER

Composer George Meyer was born in Boston, Massachusetts, where he attended Roxbury High School. He worked as an electrician, and as an accountant in department stores in Boston and New York. His first job in the music business was as a song plugger. He was twenty-five years old when three of his songs became popular in 1909. From that time through the late 1940's, Meyer's more than five dozen hits included "For Me and My Gal," "When You're a Long, Long Way from Home" and "There Are Such Things." He worked frequently with lyricists Jack Drislane, Alfred Bryan, Sam Lewis and Joe Young. Meyer died in 1959 at the age of seventy-five.

Year	Production Title	Popular Songs
1909		"Lonesome" "I'm Awfully Glad I Met You" "You Taught Me How to Love You, Now Teach Me to Forget"
1910		"Somebody Else, It's Always Somebody Else" "I've Got Your Number" "Cupid's I.O.U."
1911		"That Was Before I Met You" "Bring Back My Golden Dream" "Honey-Love" "A Girlie Was Made to Love" "A Ring on Your Finger Is Worth Two on the Phone" "There's a Dixie Girl Who's Longing for a Yankee Doodle Boy" "Brass Band Ephraham Jones"
1912		"Dear Old Rose"

Year	Production Title	Popular Songs
1912		"That Mellow Melody" "In Dixie Land with Dixie Lou" "Oh, You Little Rascal"
1913		"That Naughty Melody"
1914		"When You're a Long, Long Way from Home"
1915		"My Mother's Rosary" "There's a Little Lane Without a Turning"
1916	ROBINSON CRUSOE JR.	Where Did Robinson Crusoe Go with Friday on a Saturday Night? "Since Maggie Dooley Learned the Hooley Hooley" "Way Down in Iowa I'm Going to Hide Away" "If You Were the Only Girl" "Long Live the Ladies" "Come on and Baby Me"
1917		"For Me and My Gal" (HP) "Bring Back My Daddy to Me" "Let's All Be Americans Now"
1918		"Everything Is Peaches Down in Georgia" "Just Like Washington Crossed the Delaware" "If He Can Fight Like He Can Love, Good Night, Germany" "In the Land of Beginning Again" "You'll Find Old Dixieland in France"
1919		"Anything Is Nice If It Comes from Dixie Land" "Johnny's in Town"
1920		"Hiawatha's Melody of Love"

358

Year	Production Title	Popular Songs
1920		"Now I Lay Me Down to Sleep" "Beautiful Anna Bell Lee" "The Hen and the Cow" "They'll Never Miss the Wine in Dixieland"
1921	SNAPSHOTS OF 1921	"Tuck Me to Sleep in My Old 'Tucky Home'" "Cry Baby Blues"
1923		"Sittin' in a Corner"
1924	DIXIE TO BROADWAY	Mandy, Make Up Your Mind I'm a Little Blackbird Looking for a Bluebird Dixie Dreams "Cover Me Up with the Sunshine of Virginia"
1925		"Brown Eyes, Why Are You Blue?" "Row! Row! Rosie"
1926		"Her Beaus Are Only Rainbows" "Someone Is Losin' Susan" "For Baby and Me"
1929	Drag Footlights and Fools Girl from Woolworth's Her Private Life Broadway Babies Careers Hard to Get Two Weeks Off	My Song of the Nile If I Can't Have You
1930	Maybe It's Love The Matrimonial Bed	Maybe It's Love "To Whom It May Concern"
1931	Blonde Crazy	"I'm Sure of Everything but You"
1933		"We Were the Best of Friends"

Year	Production Title	Popular Songs
1935		"Quicker Than You Can Say Jack Robinson" "I'm Growing Fonder of You" "I Believe in Miracles"
1937		"It's Raining Sunshine" "I Wouldn't Change You for the World"
1938		"Don't Wake Up My Heart"
1943		"There Are Such Things" (HP-1)
1947		"If I Only Had a Match"
1948		"In a Little Book Shop"
1950		"The Story of Annie Laurie"
Posthumous:		
1961		"Looks Like a Beautiful Day"

* * *

JOSEPH MEYER

Joseph Meyer is one of the few successful composers who were born on the West Coast. His father, a merchant in Modesto, California, financed his violin studies in Paris. When he returned from abroad, Meyer clerked for a haberdasher, and played with an orchestra in a San Francisco tavern. After Army service during World War I, he was set up in a wholesale dry goods business of his own. A year later, he abandoned merchandising and moved to New York. Meyer was twenty-eight years old when he enjoyed his first success with his 1922 hit "My Honey's Lovin' Arms." The following year, he supplied the music for Al Jolson and B. G. De-Sylva's lyric "California, Here I Come." Among the popular songs he created for more than a dozen Broadway musicals were "A Cup of Coffee, a Sandwich and You," "Crazy Rhythm" and "Sweet So-and-So." His only outstanding film score was written for the 1935 release "George White's Scandals." Joe Meyer's last hit song, "No Fool Like an Old Fool," went on sale in 1958.

Year	Production Title	Popular Songs
1922	RAYMOND HITCHCOCK'S PINWHEEL	

Year	Production Title	Popular Songs
1922		"My Honey's Lovin' Arms" "Ji Ji Boo"
1923	BATTLING BUTTER	"California, Here I Come"
1924		"As Long as I've Got My Mammy" "Born and Bred in Old Kentucky"
1925	BIG BOY	If You Knew Susie Hello, 'Tucky
	CHARLOT'S REVUE	A Cup of Coffee, a Sandwich and You
	GAY PAREE	Sugar Plum
		"Clap Hands, Here Comes Charley" "Headin' for Louisville"
1926	SWEETHEART TIME	"Falling in Love"
1927	JUST FANCY	"Blue River"
1928	HERE'S HOWE	Crazy Rhythm Imagination
	THAT'S A GOOD GIRL (London)	The One I'm Looking For
	Show Girl	Buy, Buy for Baby
		"Golden Gate" "Happy Go Lucky Lane"
1929	WAKE UP AND DREAM LADY FINGERS Wolf of Wall Street	Fancy Our Meeting
1930	SWEET AND LOW JONICA	Sweet So-and-So
	Remote Control Way Out West Those Three French Girls Life of the Party Dancing Sweeties	Just a Little Closer Singing a Song to the Stars You're Simply Delish
1931	WONDER BAR SHOOT THE WORKS Possessed	How Long Will It Last?

JOSEPH MEYER

Year	Production Title	Popular Songs
1932		"Whose Arms Are You in Tonight?"
1933		"Isn't It Heavenly?"
1934	THE ZIEGFELD FOLLIES	"I Wish I Were Twins" "Junk Man"
1935	George White's 1935 Scandals	According to the Moonlight It's an Old Southern Custom Hunkadola
1936		"Mickey Mouse's Birthday Party"
1937		"And Then They Called It Love" "It's High Time I Got the Lowdown on You"
1938		"Hurry Home" (HP)
1940		"Love Lies" "Cherry Blossoms on Capitol Hill" "Watching the Clock" "Busy as a Bee, I'm Buzz, Buzz, Buzzin'"
1944		"But I Did"
1946		"Passe"
1949		"Meadows of Heaven"
1953		"Idle Gossip"
1958		"No Fool Like an Old Fool"

* * *

IRVING MILLS

Irving Mills was composer Duke Ellington's most frequent lyricist, and was at one time his manager. Mills received his education in New York City public schools. He was twenty-eight years old when his song "Lovesick Blues" (music by Cliff Friend) became

a best-seller in 1922.   Six years later, he began his collaboration
with Ellington and, over a period of ten years, supplied the words
for such popular songs as "Mood Indigo," "Sophisticated Lady,"
"Solitude" and "I Let a Song Go Out of My Heart."   In addition to
his songwriting, Mills frequently conducted studio orchestras during
recording sessions, and worked as a talent scout.   He also wrote
the classic "Minnie, the Moocher" (music by Cab Calloway) and
the 1943 hit "Straighten Up and Fly Right" (music by Nat Cole).
Mills shared the lyric credits on several of his successes with Al
Dubin, Eddie DeLange and Mitchell Parish.

Year	Production Title	Popular Songs
1922		"Lovesick Blues"
1923		"The House of David Blues"
1924		"When My Sugar Walks Down the Street" "What Has Become of Hinky, Dinky Parlay Voo?"
1925		"Washboard Blues" "Nobody Knows What a Red-headed Mama Can Do" "Everything Is Hotsy Totsy Now" "The Lonesomest Girl in Town"
1926		"There's a New Star in Heaven Tonight--Rudolph Valentino" "I Don't Mind Being All Alone When I'm All Alone with You" "When Banana Skins Are Falling, I'll Come Sliding Back to You"
1927		"There'll Come a Time When You'll Need Me"
1930	Check and Double Check	Ring Dem Bells "Double Check Stomp"
1931		"Minnie, the Moocher" "Mood Indigo" "Blues in My Heart"
1932		"It Don't Mean a Thing If It Ain't Got That Swing"

Year	Production Title	Popular Songs
1932		"Someone Stole Gabriel's Horn"
1933		"Sophisticated Lady" "Blue Interlude" "Skrontch"
1934		"Solitude" "Moon Glow" (HP-1) "Sidewalks of Cuba" "'Long About Midnight" "Lonesome Nights"
1935		"In a Sentimental Mood" "Like a Bolt from the Blue" "Devil in the Moon" "I'm a Hundred Percent for You" "Blue Lou" "Down South Camp Meetin'"
1936	The Singing Kid	"Organ Grinder's Swing" (HP) "You're Not the Kind" (HP) "I'll Never Tell You I Love You"
1937		"Caravan" "Mr. Ghost Goes to Town" "You're My Desire" "Scattin' at the Kit Kat" "Clouds in My Heart" "Azure" "Black Butterfly"
1938		"I Let a Song Go Out of My Heart" (HP-1) "Prelude to a Kiss" "Dusk on the Desert" "If You Were in My Place (What Would You Do?)" "If Dreams Come True" "There's Something About an Old Love" "Harmony in Harlem" "Lost in Meditation" "Please Forgive Me" "Pyramid" "Steppin' into Swing Society"

Year	Production Title	Popular Songs
1939		"Riverboat Shuffle" "Blame It on My Last Affair" "Gal from Joe's" "Grievin'" "Boy Meets Horn"
1940		"Slow Freight"
1941	Sundown	
1943	Here Comes Elmer Stormy Weather	Straighten Up and Fly Right There's No Two Ways About Love "That Ain't Right"
1945		"Remember When" (HP) "I Left a Good Deal in Mobile"
1947		"Indigo Echoes" "T. T. on Toast" "I Don't Know Why I Love You So"

* * *

SIDNEY D. MITCHELL

Sidney Mitchell was born in Baltimore, Maryland, in 1888. He attended Cornell University and worked as a reporter for a Baltimore newspaper before joining the staff of a New York publishing firm. Mitchell wrote the lyrics to his first hit song, "Would You Rather Be a Colonel with an Eagle on Your Shoulder or a Private with a Chicken on Your Knee" when he was thirty years old. It was introduced by Ziegfeld star Eddie Cantor in the 1918 edition of "The Follies." Mitchell was among the first lyricists to be called to Hollywood where he worked primarily for Fox Studios until his death in 1942. His films included Judy Garland's first feature-length picture "Pigskin Parade" and "One in a Million" which introduced champion figure skater Sonja Henie. The composers with whom he worked most frequently were Con Conrad, Lew Pollack, and Louis Alter. Sidney Mitchell's lyric for "A Melody from the Sky" received a 1936 "Oscar" nomination.

Year	Production Title	Popular Songs
1918	THE ZIEGFELD FOLLIES	Would You Rather Be a Colonel with an Eagle on Your Shoulder or a Private with a Chicken on Your Knee?
		"Mammy's Chocolate Soldier"
1920		"Now I Lay Me Down to Sleep"
1921	SNAPSHOTS OF 1921 THE GREENWICH VILLAGE FOLLIES	Saturday
1922		"I'm Always Stuttering" "Tenement Rose"
1923		"Ain't You Ashamed?" "She Wouldn't Do (What I Asked Her To)"
1925		"To Be Loved"
1926		"Sugar"
1929	Broadway	Hittin' the Ceiling Sing a Little Love Song
	Fox Movietone Follies of 1929	That's You, Baby Big City Blues Breakaway Look What You've Done to Me Walking with Susie
	Cock-Eyed World	"Why Can't I Be Like You?"
1930	Maybe It's Love Happy Days	Maybe It's Love Crazy Feet Mona
	Life of the Party Let's Go Places The Matrimonial Bed	"To Whom It May Concern"
1931	Blonde Crazy Road to Singapore	
1933	Broadway Bad Wine, Women and Song	

Year	Production Title	Popular Songs
1934	I Like It That Way	I Like It That Way
	Down to Their Last Yacht	
	He Was Her Man	
	Social Register	
	Goodbye Love	
1935	The Eagle's Brood	
1936	Trail of the Lonesome Pine	A Melody from the Sky (AN) (HP-1)
		Twilight on the Trail
	Laughing Irish Eyes	All My Life
	Sing, Baby, Sing	You Turned the Tables on Me (HP)
	Pigskin Parade	The Balboa
		You Do the Darnd'st Things, Baby
		It's Love I'm After
	Captain January	At the Codfish Ball
		Early Bird
	One in a Million	Who's Afraid of Love?
		One in a Million
	Follow Your Heart	Follow Your Heart
	Sitting on the Moon	
	Dancing Feet	
1937	Seventh Heaven	Seventh Heaven
	Life Begins in College	Why Talk About Love?
	Thin Ice	
	Heidi	
	Love Is News	
1938	Rebecca of Sunnybrook Farm	Alone with You
		The Toy Trumpet
	Kentucky Moonshine	Moonshine Over Kentucky
	In Old Chicago	
	Three Blind Mice	
		"A Love Like Ours"
1940	Nobody's Children	
1941		"Thanks for the Boogie Ride"

* * *

JAMES V. MONACO

Jimmy Monaco was six years old when his parents came to

the United States from Italy in 1891.   He began his theatrical
career playing the piano in Chicago and New York saloons where
he became known as "Ragtime Jimmy."   His major break as a
composer came when "Oh, You Circus Day" (lyrics by Edna Less-
ing) was interpolated into the 1912 Broadway revue "Hanky Panky."
That same year, "Row, Row, Row" (lyrics by William Jerome)
was the hit of "The Ziegfeld Follies" and competed for sheet music
sales with "You Made Me Love You" (lyrics by Joseph McCarthy).
ASCAP includes "You Made Me Love You" as one of 16 songs on
its All-Time Hit Parade announced in 1964.   Monaco was forty-
five years old when he joined his contemporaries in Hollywood
where he wrote songs for half a dozen films and led his own dance
orchestra.   In 1936, he signed a contract with Paramount and
formed a partnership with lyricist Johnny Burke.   The team supplied the scores for eight Bing Crosby films including "Road to
Singapore" which began the famous Crosby-Hope series.   Their
hits included "My Heart Is Taking Lessons," "I've Got a Pocketful
of Dreams," "Too Romantic" and "Only Forever" which won Monaco his first "Oscar" nomination in 1940.   He lost his collaborator when Burke began working with Jimmy Van Heusen.   Monaco
continued at other studios where he garnered three more Academy
nominations.   Jimmy Monaco died of a heart ailment in 1945 while
the country was enjoying his newest hit "I Can't Begin to Tell You."
He was sixty years old.   One of Monaco's earliest film songs,
"Crazy People," was used as George Burns and Gracie Allen's
theme for several years.

Year	Production Title	Popular Songs
1911		"Oh, Mr. Dream Man"
1912	HANKY PANKY	Oh, You Circus Day
	THE ZIEGFELD FOLLIES	Row, Row, Row
		"You Made Me Love You"
		"Mister Fortune Tellin' Man"
		"At the Ragtime Ball"
1913		"I Miss You Most of All"
		"I'm Crying Just for You"
		"There's a Wireless Station Down in My Heart"
		"While They Were Dancing Around"
1914		"Pigeon Walk"
1915		"If We Can't Be the Same Old Sweethearts"
		"Beatrice Fairfax"
1916	ROBINSON CRUSOE JR.	You're a Dog Gone Danger-ous Girl

Year	Production Title	Popular Songs
1916		"What Do You Want to Make Those Eyes at Me For?" "The Honolulu Blues" "Honolulu, America Loves You"
1920	AFGAR	Caresses "In Sweet September" "All That I Want Is You"
1921	THE ZIEGFELD FOLLIES SNAPSHOTS OF 1921	Now I Know
1922		"You Know You Belong to Somebody Else"
1923		"Dirty Hands, Dirty Face" "Cross Word Mamma, You Puzzle Me"
1924		"Me and the Boy Friend" "The Only Only One"
1925		"I'll Take Her Back If She Wants to Come Back" "Masculine Women! Feminine Men!" "We're Back Together Again"
1926		"Just a Smile"
1927	DELMAR'S REVELS	"Red Lips, Kiss My Blues Away" "I'll Take Care of Your Cares"
1928		"Me and the Man in the Moon"
1929		"Through" "My Troubles Are Over"
1930	The Golden Calf Let's Go Places On the Level The Dancers	
1931	Holy Terror	Lonesome Lover

Year	Production Title	Popular Songs
1931	Road to Singapore	
		"I'm an Unemployed Sweet-heart"
1932	The Big Broadcast	Crazy People
		"You've Got Me in the Palm of Your Hand"
1933		"You're Gonna Lose Your Gal"
		"It Might Have Been a Diff'rent Story"
		"Baby"
		"Longing"
1934		"'Fraidy Cat"
1935		"Out of the Frying Pan into the Fire"
1938	Doctor Rhythm	My Heart Is Taking Lessons
		On the Sentimental Side (HP)
		This Is My Night to Dream
	Sing, You Sinners	I've Got a Pocketful of Dreams (HP-1)
		Laugh and Call It Love
		Don't Let That Moon Get Away
1939	The Star Maker	An Apple for the Teacher (HP)
		A Man and His Dream (HP)
		Go Fly a Kite (HP)
		Still the Bluebird Sings
	East Side of Heaven	Hang Your Heart on a Hickory Limb
		East Side of Heaven
		Sing a Song of Sunbeams
		That Sly Old Gentleman from Featherbed Lane
1940	Road to Singapore	Too Romantic (HP)
		Sweet Potato Piper
	If I Had My Way	Meet the Sun Half-way
		April Played the Fiddle
		I Haven't Time to Be a Millionaire
	Rhythm on the River	Only Forever (AN) (HP-1)
		That's for Me

Year	Production Title	Popular Songs
1940	Rhythm on the River	When the Moon Comes Over Madison Square Ain't It a Shame About Mame? "Six Lessons from Madame LaZonga" (HP)
1941	Week-End in Havana	
1942		"Ev'ry Night About This Time"
1943	Stage Door Canteen	We Mustn't Say Goodbye (AN)
1944	Sweet and Lowdown	I'm Making Believe (AN) (HP)
	Pin-Up Girl	Once Too Often Time Alone Will Tell
	Irish Eyes Are Smiling	"More Now Than Ever"
1945	The Dolly Sisters	I Can't Begin to Tell You (AN) (HP-1)

Posthumous:

| 1948 | | "Crying for Joy" |

* * *

MITCHELL PARISH

Mitchell Parish is responsible for the lyrics to one of the four most-recorded songs of all time--"Stardust." In addition to that 1929 classic, many of his other lyrics stand by themselves as poetry. Parish attended both Columbia and New York University but dropped out of college to work as a special material writer for Mills Music, Inc. Included in his early popular songs are "Sweet Lorraine," "Hands Across the Table," "Stars Fell on Alabama," and "Does Your Heart Beat for Me?" which became the theme of the Russ Morgan Orchestra. He is also the author of the words to the Glenn Miller Orchestra theme "Moonlight Serenade." Seven of his songs made "Your Hit Parade" in the single year of 1939, and two of them occupied the Number One spot. Parish's specialty has been adding lyrics to successful instrumental compositions. He converted two movements of Peter DeRose's piano solo "Deep Purple" into "Lilacs in the Rain" and "Deep Purple." He also add-

ed words to Hoagy Carmichael's "Riverboat Shuffle" and several of
Leroy Anderson's best-known orchestral works.   Mitchell Parish's
lyrics have been featured in seven Broadway musicals including
two of the first ice revues.   He was born in Shreveport, Louisiana,
in 1900.

Year	Production Title	Popular Songs
1922	CHAUVE-SOURIS	
1927		"Bells of Avalon"
1928		"Sweet Lorraine" (HP)
1929		"Stardust"
1930		"Is That Religion?"
1931		"Corrine Corrina"
1932		"Take Me in Your Arms" "Cabin in the Cotton" "Sentimental Gentleman from Georgia" "The Scat Song"
1933	BLACKBIRDS Turn Back the Clock	Christmas Night in Harlem Turn Back the Clock "Sophisticated Lady" "One Morning in May" "Down a Carolina Lane" "You Excite Me"
1934	CONTINENTAL VARIETIES Girl from Missouri	Hands Across the Table "Stars Fell on Alabama" "It Happens to the Best of Friends" "Evenin'" "Emaline" "Sidewalks of Cuba" "Georgia's Gorgeous Gal" "La Cucaracha"
1935		"A Blues Serenade" "Louisiana Fairy Tale" "I'm a Hundred Percent for You" "Like a Bolt from the Blue"
1936		"Organ Grinder's Swing" (HP) "Does Your Heart Beat for Me?"

Year	Production Title	Popular Songs
1937		"Sophisticated Swing" "Mr. Ghost Goes to Town" "Blue September"
1938		"Don't Be That Way" (HP) "Who Blew Out the Flame?" (HP) "It's Wonderful" (HP)
1939	BLACKBIRDS	"Deep Purple" (HP-1) "Stairway to the Stars" (HP-1) "Lilacs in the Rain" (HP) "The Lamp Is Low" (HP) "Annabelle" (HP) "Moonlight Serenade" (HP) "The Moon Is a Silver Dollar" (HP) "Riverboat Shuffle"
1940	EARL CARROLL'S VANITIES IT HAPPENS ON ICE	The Starlit Hour (HP) Angel The Moon Fell in the River "Let Me Love You Tonight" (HP) "Orchids for Remembrance"
1941	ICE-CAPADES	I Hear America Singing "Orange Blossom Lane" (HP) "Baby, When You Ain't There" "I'm Satisfied"
1942		"All I Need Is You" "Closer and Closer" "Evening Star"
1943	Crazy House	"Never a Day Goes By"
1945		"American Waltz" "The Blond Sailor"
1947		"Did the Moon Tap on Your Window Last Night?" "Fiddle Faddle"

Year	Production Title	Popular Songs
1948		"Mademoiselle de Paree" "The Blue Skirt Waltz"
1950		"All My Love" (HP-1) "Tzena, Tzena, Tzena" (HP) "Sleigh Ride" "Serenata" "Syncopated Clock" "Promenade"
1951		"Blue Tango" (HP-1) "Belle of the Ball"
1952	Ruby Gentry	Ruby (HP)
1954		"Dream, Dream, Dream"
1956		"Moonlight Love"
1958		"Volare"
1959		"Ciao, Ciao, Bambino"
1960		"Love Me Some More"
1962		"The Sinner" "Lazy Rhapsody"

* * *

COLE PORTER

Cole Porter was the son of a wealthy Indiana farmer. Born in 1891, he learned to play the piano as a child and wrote his first composition when he was eight years old. After undergraduate work at Worcester Academy, Porter pursued his higher education at Yale where six musicals featuring his songs were produced. He left Yale to study at the Harvard Law School, and it was during this period that two of his songs were introduced in Broadway productions. When he was twenty-three, Porter wrote his first complete Broadway score for "See America First" in conjunction with a Cambridge classmate. It was so poorly received that it ran for only 15 performances. Almost immediately after its failure, Porter dropped out of college and joined the French Army in which he served during the First World War. After the Armistice, Porter had his first commercial hit when his "Old-Fashioned Garden" became popular. Despite its success, he still refused to take composing seriously.

In 1919, Porter inherited a fortune and married socialite
Linda Lee Thomas who was regarded as one of the world's most
beautiful women.   The newlyweds' main interests were world travel, and parties which they hosted at their Paris apartment for
the many international celebrities of their acquaintance.   Among
the few songs Porter composed in the mid-1920's was "The Lazi-
est Gal in Town."   The year 1928 was the turning point in his
career.   He was persuaded by a Broadway producer visiting in
Europe to write songs for a production named after his adopted
city of Paris.   He was thirty-five when "Paris" opened and the
reception given his song "Let's Do It" finally convinced him to
pursue the career of a theatrical composer.   Once Porter began
writing in earnest, he became one of Broadway's most prolific
composers.   From 1928 through 1956 there was only one year in
which the theatre was without a Cole Porter show.   His scores
consistently produced songs which became standards and he was
unsurpassed as a writer of witty, sophisticated, and often risqué
lyrics.   His lyrics were close to true poetry and have been published in book form.

"Paris" was followed in quick succession by "Fifty Million
Frenchmen," a New York production of his London revue "Wake
Up and Dream," "The New Yorkers" and "Gay Divorcee" starring
Fred Astaire.   Astaire introduced Porter's "Night and Day" and
the song is one of 16 listed on ASCAP's All-Time Hit Parade.
Porter enjoyed one of his greatest successes with "Anything Goes"
in 1934.   Five of its songs became national favorites and eventually achieved the status of popular music standards.   "You're the
Top" and "I Get a Kick Out of You" were Porter at his most in-
ventive.   "Anything Goes" ran for a year to become the longest-
running musical of 1934.   The composer shared credit for the
long-run hit with singer Ethel Merman.   Porter's intricate lyrics
needed to be heard from the last row of the balcony and Miss
Merman's brassy voice had no trouble traveling the distance.
"Anything Goes" was the first of five Porter and Merman musicals.
It had been playing for 11 months when his next effort "Jubilee"
had its premiere and added "Begin the Beguine" to the ASCAP list
of 16 All-Time Hits.

The first Porter song heard on the silver screen was in the
1929 Gertrude Lawrence feature "Battle of Paris."   In 1936, he
composed his first complete score for an original motion picture
and the film made a star of dancer Eleanor Powell.   Although the
executives at MGM Studios failed to impress the composer, the
Southern California climate did and he became so enamoured of
the area that he maintained a home in the Pacific Palisades for
many years.

The second Porter-Merman collaboration was the 1936 production "Red, Hot and Blue" which introduced "It's De-Lovely."
The following year, he wrote his second film musical, "Rosalie,"
and was partially crippled when he was thrown from a horse.

During his lifetime he underwent numerous operations to correct the injury but it was eventually necessary to amputate one leg. The pain endured by Porter had no noticeable effect on his productivity and the year after the accident, he had two new shows on Broadway including "Leave It to Me" in which Mary Martin introduced "My Heart Belongs to Daddy."

The Porter-Merman combination continued to click: "DuBarry Was a Lady" was the longest-running musical of 1939; "Panama Hattie" opened in 1940 and ran even longer; and "Something for the Boys" entertained World War II audiences for a solid year. Between his Merman musicals Porter composed the score for "Let's Face It" which made a star of Danny Kaye. In 1944, Porter's "Don't Fence Me In" (written nine years earlier for an unproduced film) held the Number One spot on "Your Hit Parade" for eight weeks. That same year, Porter entered into a short-lived decline. After 16 years of hit shows, he was disappointed in the receptions given "Mexican Hayride," "The Seven Lively Arts," and "Around the World in 80 Days" and wondered if his prime creative years had passed. The worry was dispelled when "Kiss Me, Kate" opened in 1948. The critics hailed it as the greatest musical accomplishment in the history of American musical comedy. Then Rodgers and Hammerstein's "South Pacific" had its premiere and "Kiss Me, Kate" was quickly relegated to second place.

Anxious to regain his crown, Porter went to work on "Out of This World" but the critics turned their thumbs down and the show closed in five months. Just how wrong critics can be was proven when Porter's 1953 effort "Can-Can" was reviewed. Most of them pronounced the show's score as not up to Porter's usual excellence. The show ran for over two years and introduced "C'est Magnifique," "I Am in Love," "Allez-Vous-En," "It's All Right with Me" and "I Love Paris"--all of which became popular music standards!

During the last ten years of Porter's career, he composed the score for the hit Broadway musical "Silk Stockings," the film "High Society" and the television spectacular "Aladdin." Cole Porter died in Santa Monica, California in October 1964 at the age of seventy-one leaving a legacy of scores written for more than 40 Broadway and Hollywood productions. The show business tradepaper Variety includes six of his songs on its list of the 100 Most Popular Songs of All Time: "Night and Day," "Begin the Beguine," "Just One of Those Things," "What Is This Thing Called Love?," "I Get a Kick Out of You" and "I've Got You Under My Skin." Four of Porter's film songs were nominated for the Academy Award but none of them were winners.

Year	Production Title	Popular Songs
1915	HANDS UP	
	MISS INFORMATION	

Year	Production Title	Popular Songs
1916	SEE AMERICA FIRST	I've a Shooting-box in Scotland
1918	VERY GOOD, EDDIE (England) TELLING THE TALE (England)	
1919	HITCHY-KOO BUDDIES	Old-Fashioned Garden
1920	AS YOU WERE A NIGHT OUT (London)	
1922	MAYFAIR & MONTMARTRE (London) HITCHY-KOO (closed in tryout)	
1924	THE GREENWICH VILLAGE FOLLIES	I'm in Love Again Two Little Babes in the Wood
1927		"The Laziest Gal in Town" "Weren't We Fools?"
1928	PARIS IN THE OLD DAYS AND TODAY (Paris)	Let's Do It Let's Misbehave Don't Look at Me That Way
1929	FIFTY MILLION FRENCHMEN WAKE UP AND DREAM Battle of Paris	You Do Something to Me Find Me a Primitive Man You Don't Know Paree You've Got That Thing I Worship You Paree, What Did You Do to Me? What Is This Thing Called Love? Looking at You Which? They All Fall in Love
1930	THE NEW YORKERS VANDERBILT REVUE	Love for Sale I Happen to Like New York Let's Fly Away Where Have You Been? I'm Getting Myself Ready for You

Year	Production Title	Popular Songs
1932	GAY DIVORCEE	Night and Day I've Got You on My Mind After You How's Your Romance?
1933	NYMPH ERRANT (London)	Experiment Nymph Errant How Could We Be Wrong?
1934	ANYTHING GOES	I Get a Kick Out of You Anything Goes You're the Top All Through the Night Blow, Gabriel, Blow "Miss Otis Regrets"
1935	JUBILEE	Begin the Beguine Just One of Those Things Why Shouldn't I? Me and Marie A Picture of Me Without You
1936	RED, HOT AND BLUE!	It's De-Lovely (HP-1) Down in the Depths Ridin' High Red, Hot and Blue!
	O MISTRESS MINE (London - play) Born to Dance	I've Got You Under My Skin (AN) (HP) Easy to Love (HP) Hey, Babe, Hey!
1937	Rosalie	Rosalie (HP-1) In the Still of the Night (HP) Who Knows? I've a Strange New Rhythm in My Heart Close
1938	YOU NEVER KNOW LEAVE IT TO ME	At Long Last Love (HP) Get Out of Town (HP) My Heart Belongs to Daddy Most Gentlemen Don't Like Love From Now On
1939	DUBARRY WAS A LADY	Do I Love You? (HP) Friendship

Year	Production Title	Popular Songs
1939	DUBARRY WAS A LADY	When Love Beckoned It Was Written in the Stars Kaiti Went to Haiti Well, Did You Evah?
	THE MAN WHO CAME TO DINNER (play) The Sun Never Sets	
1940	PANAMA HATTIE	Let's Be Buddies Make It Another Old-Fashion- ed, Please I've Still Got My Health
	Broadway Melody of 1940	I've Got My Eyes on You (HP) I Concentrate on You
1941	LET'S FACE IT	Everything I Love (HP) Ace in the Hole
	You'll Never Get Rich	Since I Kissed My Baby Goodbye (AN)
	Break the News	
1943	SOMETHING FOR THE BOYS Something to Shout About	Something for the Boys You'd Be So Nice to Come Home To (AN) (HP)
1944	MEXICAN HAYRIDE	I Love You (HP-1) Sing to Me, Guitar
	SEVEN LIVELY ARTS	Ev'rytime We Say Goodbye (HP) Only Another Boy and Girl
	Hollywood Canteen	Don't Fence Me In (HP-1)
1946	AROUND THE WORLD IN 80 DAYS	Pipe-Dreaming
1948	KISS ME, KATE	Wunderbar Why Can't You Behave? So in Love (HP) Always True to You in My Fashion Too Darn Hot Were Thine That Special Face Another Op'ning, Another Show Where Is the Life That Late I Led?
	The Pirate	Love of My Life Be a Clown You Can Do No Wrong

COLE PORTER   379

Year	Production Title	Popular Songs
1949	Adam's Rib	
1950	OUT OF THIS WORLD	I Am Loved Nobody's Chasing Me Use Your Imagination Where, Oh Where?
1953	CAN-CAN	I Love Paris (HP) C'est Magnifique (HP) It's All Right with Me Allez-Vous-En, Go Away I Am in Love
	Kiss Me, Kate	From This Moment On
1955	SILK STOCKINGS	All of You Without Love Paris Loves Lovers
1956	High Society	True Love (AN) (HP)
1957	Les Girls Silk Stockings	Ca, C'est l'Amour
1958	Aladdin (TV)	Come to the Supermarket

* * *

RALPH RAINGER

Composer Ralph Rainger was the son of a New York City merchant. While enrolled at the Damrosch Institute of Musical Arts, he was persuaded by his father to forego music in favor of the legal profession. Rainger drove trucks, labored on farms, and worked as a door-to-door salesman to earn his way through law school. After graduation, he abandoned his legal practice and supported himself as a vaudeville accompanist and rehearsal pianist. His melodies were first heard on Broadway in "Queen High" when he was twenty-five years old. The following year he formed a partnership with Edgar Fairchild and the team performed as duo-pianists in several Broadway musicals. The success of his song "Moanin' Low" brought him offers from Hollywood and, together with lyricist Leo Robin, Rainger wrote songs for over 50 films starring such Paramount luminaries as Bing Crosby, W. C. Fields, Jack Benny and Carole Lombard. His music for "Thanks for the Memory" won the 1938 "Oscar" and the song became Bob Hope's theme. His earlier "Oscar" nominee "Love in Bloom" was already Jack Benny's trademark. Rainger moved from Paramount to Twentieth Century-Fox in the early 1940's but his work at that stu-

dio failed to equal his earlier accomplishments. Ralph Rainger
was killed in an airplane crash in 1942 at the age of only forty-
one.

Year	Production Title	Popular Songs
1926	QUEEN HIGH	
1929	THE LITTLE SHOW	Moanin' Low
1930	9:15 REVUE Be Yourself Queen High Sea Legs	When a Woman Loves a Man "Got a Man on My Mind"
1931	Along Came Youth	"Is This the Music of Love?"
1932	The Big Broadcast This Is the Night Big City Blues Million Dollar Legs	Please Here Lies Love This Is the Night
1933	TATTLE TALES A Bedtime Story Torch Singer She Done Him Wrong International House Way to Love Cradle Song Midnight Club Three-Cornered Moon	I'll Take an Option on You In the Park in Paree Look What I've Got Give Me Liberty or Give 　Me Love A Guy What Takes His 　Time
1934	She Loves Me Not Shoot the Works Here Is My Heart Little Miss Marker The Trumpet Blows We're Not Dressing Come on Marines Good Dame	Love in Bloom (AN) Take a Lesson from the 　Lark June in January With Every Breath I Take Here Is My Heart I'm a Black Sheep Who's 　Blue Low-Down Lullaby

Year	Production Title	Popular Songs
1934	Wharf Angel	
	Kiss and Make Up	
1935	Big Broadcast of 1936	I Wished on the Moon (HP)
		Miss Brown to You
		Why Dream?
		Double Trouble
	Rumba	
	Four Hours to Kill	
	Millions in the Air	
	Ruggles of Red Gap	
1936	Rose of the Rancho	If I Should Lose You
		Thunder Over Paradise
		Little Rose of the Rancho
	Palm Springs	The Hills of Old Wyoming
		I Don't Want to Make History (I Just Want to Make Love) (HP)
	Big Broadcast of 1937	Here's Love in Your Eye (HP)
		You Came to My Rescue
		La Bomba
	Three Cheers for Love	Long Ago and Far Away
		Where Is My Heart?
	Poppy	A Rendezvous with a Dream (HP)
	College Holiday	I Adore You
	Rhythm on the Range	
1937	Waikiki Wedding	Blue Hawaii (HP)
		Sweet Is the Word for You (HP)
		In a Little Hula Heaven
	Blossoms on Broadway	Blossoms on Broadway (HP)
	Ebb Tide	Ebb Tide (HP)
	Easy Living	Easy Living
	Swing High, Swing Low	(If It Isn't Pain) Then It Isn't Love
	Artists and Models Abroad	What Have You Got That Gets Me? (HP)
		You're Lovely Madame
	Hideaway Girl	
	Souls at Sea	
1938	Give Me a Sailor	What Goes on Here in My Heart? (HP)
		A Little Kiss at Twilight
	The Texans	Silver on the Sage

Year	Production Title	Popular Songs
1938	Big Broadcast of 1938	Thanks for the Memory (AA) (HP-1) You Took the Words Right Out of My Heart (HP) Mama, That Moon Is Here Again (HP)
	Tropic Holiday Romance in the Dark Her Jungle Love	
1939	Gulliver's Travels	Faithful Forever (AN) (HP) Bluebirds in the Moonlight
	Paris Honeymoon	I Have Eyes (HP) You're a Sweet Little Headache (HP) The Funny Old Hills Joobalai The Wind at My Window
	Nice Goin' Never Say Die $1000 a Touchdown	
1940		"Just a-Whistlin', Just a-Whittlin', and a-Watchin' the World Go By"
1941	Moon Over Miami	Loveliness and Love You Started Something
	Tall, Dark and Handsome	Wishful Thinking Hello, Ma! I Done It Again
	Rise and Shine A Yank in the R.A.F. Cadet Girl	
1942	My Gal Sal	Here You Are (HP) Oh, the Pity of It All
	Footlight Serenade Tales of Manhattan	

Posthumous:

| 1943 | Coney Island
Riding High
Colt Comrades | |

* * *

DON RAYE

Don Raye won a Virginia state dancing championship in 1924

when he was fifteen years old. The title led to vaudeville engagements in the United States and Europe after which he created a
night club act in which he played the piano and sang his own songs.
In 1935, he collaborated with composer Saul Chaplin and lyricist
Sammy Cahn on the hit "Rhythm in My Nursery Rhymes." Raye
resumed his studies in 1937 at New York University and also went
to work for a music publisher in Manhattan. He became associated
with The Andrews Sisters in 1939 when his song "Well All Right!"
became a juke box favorite. During the early 1940's, he supplied
the vocal trio with their hits "Rhumboogie," "Pig Foot Pete" and
"The Boogie Woogie Bugle Boy." During the same period, the
Will Bradley Orchestra achieved national popularity largely on the
strength of Raye's "Beat Me Daddy (Eight to the Bar)", "Scrub Me
Mama, with a Boogie Beat" and "Down the Road a Piece." The
Harry James Orchestra adopted Raye's "The Music Makers" as its
theme. Raye also provided singer Ella Mae Morse with her initial
successes "Mr. Five by Five" and "Cow Cow Boogie." He writes
both words and music but has frequently collaborated with other
artists such as Gene DePaul and Hughie Prince. His most unusual partner was actor Robert Mitchum with whom he wrote "Ballad of Thunder Road" (1958). Even in the 1970's, Don Raye's work
was making stars and Bette Midler made the best-seller charts
with her multi-track recorded imitation of The Andrews Sisters'
"Boogie Woogie Bugle Boy." Raye was born in Washington, D.C.
in 1909.

Year	Production Title	Popular Songs
1935		"Rhythm in My Nursery Rhymes" (HP)
1937		"For Dancers Only"
1939		"Well All Right!" "Yodelin' Jive" "Why Begin Again? (Pastel Blue)" "Just for a Thrill" "She Had to Go and Lose It at the Astor"
1940	Argentine Nights	Rhumboogie Hit the Road "Beat Me Daddy (Eight to the Bar)" "Scrub Me, Mama, with a Boogie Beat" "Your Red Wagon" "I Love You Much Too Much" "This Is My Country" "Do You Call That a Buddy?"

Year	Production Title	Popular Songs
1941	Buck Privates	Boogie Woogie Bugle Boy (AN)
		Bounce Me, Brother, with a Solid Four
	In the Navy	Gimme Some Skin
	Keep 'em Flying	Pig Foot Pete (AN)
		You Don't Know What Love Is
	Ride 'em Cowboy	I'll Remember April
	Hellzapoppin'	Watch the Birdie
	Moonlight in Hawaii	
	San Antonio Rose	
		"The Music Makers"
		"Down the Road a Piece"
1942	Behind the Eight Ball	Mr. Five by Five (HP)
	Who Done It?	
	When Johnny Comes Marching Home	
	Almost Married	
	Pardon My Sarong	
		"He's My Guy" (HP)
1943	I Dood It	Star Eyes (HP)
	What's Buzzin' Cousin?	Ain't That Just Like a Man?
	Crazy House	
	Hi'ya, Chum	
	Larceny with Music	
		"Cow Cow Boogie"
1944	Broadway Rhythm	Irresistible You
		Milkman, Keep Those Bottles Quiet (HP)
	Hi, Good Lookin'	
	Lost in a Harem	
	Stars on Parade	
1946	Wake Up and Dream	
		"House of Blue Lights"
		"Hey, Mr. Postman"
1948	A Date with Judy	Judaline
	A Song Is Born	A Song Is Born
		Daddy-O (I'm Gonna Teach You Some Blues)
	Race Street	
	So Dear to My Heart	
	Enchantment	
1949	Ichabod and Mr. Toad	
	The Big Sombrero	

DON RAYE   385

Year	Production Title	Popular Songs
1950		"Domino" (HP) "Jing-a-Ling, Jing-a-Ling"
1951	Alice in Wonderland	
1954		"They Were Doin' the Mambo" (HP) "Traveling Down a Lonely Road" "Too Little Time"
1958	Thunder Road	Ballad of Thunder Road
1960		"I'm Looking Out the Window"
1963		"Yet ... I Know"
1965		"Gentle Is My Love"

* * *

ANDY RAZAF

Andy Razaf attended public school in Washington, D.C. Although he succeeded in placing a song in the 1913 edition of Broadway's "The Passing Show" when he was only eighteen, eleven years passed before Razaf's work won nationwide recognition. In addition to the four stage musicals to which he contributed, he also wrote for night club revues. His biggest hits--"Ain't Misbehavin'," "Honeysuckle Rose," and "Lonesome Me"--were written in collaboration with reknowned jazz pianist Thomas "Fats" Waller. Razaf was awarded a citation by the Government for his extensive efforts during World War II bond drives. After suffering a severe stroke in 1950, he became a newspaper columnist. Andy Razaf was seventy-eight years old when he died in 1973.

Year	Production Title	Popular Songs
1913	THE PASSING SHOW	
1924		"No One Can Toddle Like My Cousin Sue"
1925		"Anybody Here Want to Try My Cabbage?"
1926		"Mama Stayed Out the Whole Night Long"

Year	Production Title	Popular Songs
1926		"My Special Friend Is Back in Town" "Nobody but My Baby Is Gettin' My Love"
1928	KEEP SHUFFLIN'	Willow Tree "Dusky Stevedore" "Louisiana" "Take Your Tomorrow (and Give Me Today)" "When" "Dip Your Brush in the Sunshine" "Lonesome Swallow" "My Handy Man Ain't Handy Anymore"
1929	HOT CHOCOLATES	Ain't Misbehavin' What Did I Do to Be So Black and Blue? Sweet Savannah Sue "Honeysuckle Rose" "S'posin'" "My Fate Is in Your Hands" "Zonky" "My Baby Sure Knows How to Love" "The Way I Feel Today"
1930	BLACKBIRDS	Memories of You You're Lucky to Me "Blue, Turning Grey Over You" "On Revival Day" "Porter's Love Song to a Chambermaid"
1931		"Concentratin' on You"
1932		"Keepin' Out of Mischief Now" "Doin' What I Please" "If It Ain't Love" "Lonesome Me" "Strange as It Seems"
1933		"Ain'tcha Glad?" "Deep Forest" "Mississippi Basin"

Year	Production Title	Popular Songs
1934		"How Can You Face Me?"
1935		"Rhythm Lullaby"
1936		"Stompin' at the Savoy" "Christopher Columbus" "Big Chief DeSota" "You're Everything Sweet" "Stealin' Apples" "Make Believe Ballroom" "Milkman's Matinee"
1937		"I Can't Break the Habit of You" "Alligator Crawl" "Havin' a Ball" "I'm Gonna Move on the Outskirts of Town"
1938		"The Joint Is Jumpin'" "Patty Cake, Patty Cake (Baker Man)" "Yancey Special"
1940		"In the Mood" (HP) "A Lover's Lullaby" (HP) "Black Maria"
1942		"Twelfth St. Rag" (HP) "Massachusetts" "Knock Me a Kiss"
1944		"That's What I Like 'bout the South"

* * *

HARRY REVEL

London-born Harry Revel began playing piano in a Paris band when he was only fifteen. After several years of touring the continent with dance orchestras, he composed the score for an operetta produced in Berlin. Other stage musicals followed including London's "Charlot's Revue" in 1927. Two years later, Revel went to New York where he met the lyricist with whom he is usually identified--Mack Gordon. Their songs were featured in five Broadway musicals before they moved to the West Coast where they became one of the three most successful songwriting teams in

motion picture history.   Paramount was the first studio to benefit
by the music of Revel.   From 1933 through 1936, his popular
songs included "Love Thy Neighbor," "With My Eyes Wide Open
I'm Dreaming," "Paris in the Spring" and "You Hit the Spot." He
then moved to Fox Studios to compose for its top musical star
Alice Faye.   Miss Faye introduced such Revel hits as "Goodnight
My Love," "You Can't Have Everything," "Sweet Someone" and "I
Never Knew Heaven Could Speak."   When the partnership of Gordon
and Revel was dissolved at the outset of World War II, the team
had contributed to more than three dozen films in seven years.   Revel became active in organizing recreation centers for servicemen
and staging shows for their entertainment.   How important Gordon
was to Revel became evident during the 1940's.   Revel collaborated
with lyricists Mort Greene and Paul Francis Webster on songs for
18 motion pictures but only five of them achieved popularity.   In
1945, he supplied the music for the unsuccessful Broadway production "Are You with It?" Harry Revel was sixty-three when he died
in 1958.

Year	Production Title	Popular Songs
1927	CHARLOT'S REVUE (London)	
1931	THE ZIEGFELD FOLLIES	Cigars, Cigarettes Help Yourself to Happiness
	FAST AND FURIOUS EVERYBODY'S WELCOME	
		"Such Is Life, Such Is Love"
1932	MARCHING BY SMILING FACES	
		"Underneath the Harlem Moon" "Listen to the German Band" "I Played Fiddle for the Czar" "And So to Bed" "A Boy and a Girl Were Dancing"
1933	Sitting Pretty	Did You Ever See a Dream Walking? Good Morning Glory You're Such a Comfort to Me
	Broadway Thru a Keyhole	You're My Past, Present and Future Doin' the Uptown Lowdown
	White Woman Design for Living	
		"An Orchid to You" "It Was a Night in June"

Year	Production Title	Popular Songs
1933		"It's Within Your Power" "A Tree Was a Tree" "There's a Bluebird at My Window"
1934	The Gay Divorcee We're Not Dressing	Don't Let It Bother You Love Thy Neighbor Once in a Blue Moon May I? Good Night, Lovely Little Lady She Reminds Me of You
	Shoot the Works	With My Eyes Wide Open I'm Dreaming Were Your Ears Burning, Baby?
	College Rhythm	Stay as Sweet as You Are Take a Number from One to Ten College Rhythm Let's Give Three Cheers for Love
	She Loves Me Not	Straight from the Shoulder I'm Hummin', I'm Whistlin', I'm Singin'
	The Old-Fashioned Way Here Comes the Groom	
1935	Love in Bloom	My Heart Is an Open Book Got Me Doin' Things
	Paris in the Spring Two for Tonight	Paris in the Spring (HP-1) From the Top of Your Head to the Tip of Your Toes (HP) Without a Word of Warning (HP) Takes Two to Make a Bargain Two for Tonight I Wish I Were Aladdin
	Stolen Harmony	Would There Be Love?
1936	Collegiate	You Hit the Spot (HP) I Feel Like a Feather in the Breeze (HP)
	Poor Little Rich Girl	When I'm with You (HP-1) Oh, My Goodness You've Gotta Eat Your Spinach, Baby But Definitely

Year	Production Title	Popular Songs
1936	Stowaway	Goodnight My Love (HP-1)
		One Never Knows (Does One?)
		You Gotta S-M-I-L-E to be H-A Double P-Y
	The Princess Comes Across	"A Star Fell Out of Heaven" (HP)
		"To Mary, with Love"
1937	Head Over Heels in Love	Through the Courtesy of Love
		May I Have the Next Romance with You?
		Looking Around Corners for You
	You Can't Have Everything	Afraid to Dream (HP)
		The Loveliness of You
		You Can't Have Everything
		Please Pardon Us, We're in Love
		Danger--Love at Work
	Wake Up and Live	Never in a Million Years (HP)
		There's a Lull in My Life (HP)
		I'm Bubbling Over
		Wake Up and Live
		It's Swell of You
	Love and Hisses	Sweet Someone (HP)
		Broadway's Gone Hawaiian
		I Wanna Be in Winchell's Column
	Ali Baba Goes to Town	I've Got My Heart Set on You
	This Is My Affair	I Hum a Waltz
	Everybody Dance	
	Thin Ice	
1938	In Old Chicago	In Old Chicago
	My Lucky Star	I've Got a Date with a Dream (HP)
		Could You Pass in Love?
	Love Finds Andy Hardy	Meet the Beat of My Heart
	Sally, Irene and Mary	Sweet as a Song (HP)
	Josette	Where in the World? (HP)
		In Any Language
	Thanks for Everything	Thanks for Everything (HP)

Year	Production Title	Popular Songs
1938	Rebecca of Sunnybrook Farm I'll Give a Million Hold That Co-ed	An Old Straw Hat
1939	Rose of Washington Square	I Never Knew Heaven Could Speak (HP)
	The Rains Came Tailspin	
1940	Moon Over Burma	
1941	Four Jacks and a Jill	You Go Your Way
1942	The Mayor of 44th Street	When There's a Breeze on Lake Louise (AN) Heavenly, Isn't It?
	Call Out the Marines The Big Street Joan of Ozark Sing Your Worries Away Moonlight Masquerade Beyond the Blue Horizon Here We Go Again	
1943	Hit the Ice It Ain't Hay	I'd Like to Set You to Music
1944	Minstrel Man	Remember Me to Carolina (AN)
	Ghost Catchers	
1945	ARE YOU WITH IT? The Stork Club The Dolly Sisters	Just Beyond the Rainbow
1947	It Happened on Fifth Avenue	
1950		"Jet"
1952	The Half-Breed	

* * *

LEO ROBIN

Leo Robin is second only to Mack Gordon as Hollywood's

most successful lyricist. Robin was born in Pennsylvania in 1900.
After attending the University of Pittsburgh Law School, he worked
as a newspaper reporter, publicity agent, and social worker. Robin was twenty-five years old when Broadway audiences first heard
his lyrics in "By the Way." Two years later, he and Clifford
Grey supplied the words for "Hallelujah!" from Vincent Youmans'
score for "Hit the Deck." Robin was hired by Paramount in 1929,
and the first composer with whom he worked was Richard Whiting.
Among their memorable film songs were "Louise," "Beyond the
Blue Horizon," "I Can't Escape from You" and "(I'd Love to Spend)
One Hour with You" which Eddie Cantor adopted as the theme song
for his weekly broadcast. Robin then collaborated with Ralph Rainger and Robin and Rainger soon ranked with Al Dubin and Harry
Warren and Mack Gordon and Harry Revel as one of Hollywood's
three greatest songwriting teams. The first in Paramount's "Big
Broadcast" series, released in 1932, featured Bing Crosby's rendition of Robin's lyric "Please." Crosby also introduced such Robin and Rainger classics as "Love in Bloom," "June in January"
and "Blue Hawaii." The high point in Robin's film career was the
Academy Award he received for his lyric "Thanks for the Memory."

After Ralph Rainger was killed in an airplane crash in 1942,
Robin collaborated with composers Harry Warren, Jerome Kern,
Arthur Schwartz, and Harold Arlen to create such hits as "No
Love, No Nothin'," "In Love in Vain," "Oh, but I Do" and "For
Every Man There's a Woman." In 1949, he supplied the lyrics
for one of Broadway's most successful musical comedies "Gentlemen Prefer Blondes" in which Carol Channing introduced "Diamonds
Are a Girl's Best Friend." Robin's work has been featured in
over 115 motion pictures. In 1936 and 1937, his output averaged
one film per month! Leo Robin's songs have been nominated for
a total of ten "Oscars."

Year	Production Title	Popular Songs
1925	BY THE WAY	
1926	BUBBLING OVER	"My Cutey's Due at Two to Two Today"
1927	HIT THE DECK	Hallelujah! Why, Oh, Why?
	ALLEZ-OOP JUDY A LA CARTE JUST FANCY	"Paree!"
1928	HELLO YOURSELF	I Want the World to Know
1929	Innocents of Paris	Louise

Year	Production Title	Popular Songs
1929	Innocents of Paris	Wait Till You See Ma Cherie
		It's a Habit of Mine
	Syncopation	Jericho
	Dance of Life	True Blue Lou
	Pointed Heels	I Have to Have You
	Wild Party	
	Fashions in Love	
	The Kibitzer	
	The Man I Love	
	Close Harmony	
	River of Romance	
	Why Bring That Up?	
1930	Paramount on Parade	All I Want Is Just One
		Come Back to Sorrento
	Monte Carlo	Beyond the Blue Horizon
		Give Me a Moment, Please
		Always in All Ways
		She'll Love Me and Like It
	Playboy of Paris	My Ideal (HP)
		It's a Great Life If You
		Don't Weaken
	Vagabond King	If I Were King
	Dangerous Nan McGrew	
	Derelict	
	Dangerous Paradise	
	Morocco	
	Devil's Holiday	
1931	SHOOT THE WORKS	
	Monkey Business	
	Dude Ranch	
		"Prisoner of Love" (HP)
		"Have You Forgotten (the
		Thrill?)"
1932	The Big Broadcast	Please
		Here Lies Love
	One Hour with You	(I'd Love to Spend) One
		Hour with You
		We Will Always Be Sweet-
		hearts
	Blonde Venus	
	Trouble in Paradise	
1933	TATTLE TALES	I'll Take an Option on You
	Bedtime Story	In the Park in Paree
		Look What I've Got
	Torch Singer	Give Me Liberty or Give
		Me Love

Year	Production Title	Popular Songs
1933	My Weakness	Gather Lip Rouge While You May
	Alice in Wonderland International House Way to Love Cradle Song Midnight Club Three-Cornered Moon	
1934	She Loves Me Not Shoot the Works	Love in Bloom (AN) Take a Lesson from the Lark
	Here Is My Heart	June in January With Every Breath I Take Love Is Just Around the Corner Here Is My Heart
	Little Miss Marker	I'm a Black Sheep Who's Blue Low-Down Lullaby
	You Belong to Me	When He Comes Home to Me
	The Trumpet Blows Come on Marines Wharf Angel Kiss and Make Up Good Dame We're Not Dressing	
1935	The Big Broadcast of 1936	Miss Brown to You Why Dream? Double Trouble
	Here Comes Cookie Four Hours to Kill One Hour Late The Crusades Rumba Millions in the Air	
1936	Rhythm on the Range	I Can't Escape from You (HP) The House Jack Built for Jill
	Rose of the Rancho	If I Should Lose You Thunder Over Paradise Little Rose of the Rancho
	Palm Springs	The Hills of Old Wyoming I Don't Want to Make

Year	Production Title	Popular Songs
1936		History (I Just Want to Make Love) (HP)
	The Jungle Princess	Moonlight and Shadows (HP)
	Poppy	A Rendezvous with a Dream (HP)
	The Big Broadcast of 1937	You Came to My Rescue Here's Love in Your Eye (HP) La Bomba
	Three Cheers for Love	Where Is My Heart? Long Ago and Far Away
	Anything Goes	My Heart and I Sailor Beware
	College Holiday The Moon's Our Home Preview Murder Mystery The Princess Comes Across It's a Great Life	I Adore You
1937	Artists and Models	Whispers in the Dark (AN) (HP-1)
	Waikiki Wedding	Blue Hawaii (HP) Sweet Is the Word for You (HP) In a Little Hula Heaven
	Blossoms on Broadway Ebb Tide Easy Living Swing High, Swing Low	Blossoms on Broadway (HP) Ebb Tide (HP) Easy Living (If It Isn't Pain) Then It Isn't Love
	Artists and Models Abroad	What Have You Got That Gets Me? (HP) You're Lovely Madame
	Souls at Sea Angel Champagne Waltz Hideaway Girl Make Way for Tomorrow	
1938	The Big Broadcast of 1938	Thanks for the Memory (AA) (HP-1) You Took the Words Right Out of My Heart (HP) Mama, That Moon Is Here Again (HP)
	Give Me a Sailor	What Goes on Here in My Heart? (HP) A Little Kiss at Twilight

Year	Production Title	Popular Songs
1938	The Texans Tropic Holiday Romance in the Dark Her Jungle Love	Silver on the Sage
1939	Gulliver's Travels Paris Honeymoon St. Louis Blues Nice Goin' $1000 a Touchdown Never Say Die	Faithful Forever (AN) (HP) Bluebirds in the Moonlight I Have Eyes (HP) You're a Sweet Little Head- ache (HP) The Funny Old Hills Joobalai Kinda Lonesome The Wind at My Window
1940		"Just a-Whistlin', Just a- Whittlin', and a-Watchin' the World Go By"
1941	Moon Over Miami Tall, Dark and Handsome Rise and Shine A Yank in the RAF Cadet Girl	Loveliness and Love You Started Something Wishful Thinking Hello, Ma! I Done It Again
1942	My Gal Sal Footlight Serenade Tales of Manhattan	Here You Are (HP) Oh, the Pity of It All
1943	Wintertime Coney Island Riding High Colt Comrades	Later Tonight
1944	The Gang's All Here Greenwich Village	No Love, No Nothin' (HP) A Journey to a Star
1945	Wonder Man	So-o-o-o-o in Love (AN)
1946	The Time, the Place and the Girl Centennial Summer	A Gal in Calico (AN) (HP-1) Oh, but I Do (HP) A Rainy Night in Rio Through a Thousand Dreams In Love in Vain (HP)

Year	Production Title	Popular Songs
1946	Centennial Summer	Up with the Lark
		"One Love"
1947	Something in the Wind	Something in the Wind The Turntable Song
1948	Casbah	For Every Man There's a Woman (AN) It Was Written in the Stars What's Good About Goodbye? Hooray for Love
	That Lady in Ermine	This Is the Moment (AN)
1949	GENTLEMEN PREFER BLONDES	Diamonds Are a Girl's Best Friend A Little Girl from Little Rock Bye, Bye Baby Just a Kiss Apart
1951	Meet Me After the Show	It's a Hot Night in Alaska Betting on a Man
	Two Tickets to Broadway	
1952	Just for You	Zing a Little Zong (AN) A Flight of Fancy I'll Si, Si Ya in Bahia
	Macao	
1953	Small Town Girl	My Flaming Heart (AN)
	Latin Lovers	A Little More of Your Amor
1954	THE GIRL IN PINK TIGHTS	Lost in Loveliness In Paris and in Love
1955	My Sister Eileen	
1957	Ruggles of Red Gap (TV)	Ride on a Rainbow

* * *

RICHARD RODGERS

For the first two decades of his career, Richard Rodgers'
name was inseparable from that of lyricist Lorenz Hart. Songs
by Rodgers and Hart were featured in 29 musicals staged on
Broadway. After Hart's death, Richard Rodgers' name became

equally well associated with that of lyricist/librettist Oscar Hammerstein.   The outstanding success of Rodgers and Hammerstein's
nine Broadway musicals made theirs the most financially profitable
songwriting partnership in the history of popular music.

        Richard Rodgers was born in 1902 on Long Island, New
York and wrote his first melody at the age of fourteen.   Three
years later he began collaborating with Lorenz Hart.   Their first
song heard by a Broadway audience was in the 1919 production "A
Lonely Romeo."   The following year, the team was hired to compose the complete score for "Poor Little Ritz Girl" but most of
their work was dropped before the show opened.   They continued
writing for amateur theatricals and received their first break when
the New York Theatre Guild engaged them to write for its revue
"The Garrick Gaieties."   Rodgers' melodies were heard in as
many as four productions a year during the Twenties.   Among the
most notable were "The Girl Friend" (1926), "A Connecticut Yankee" (1927), "Present Arms" (1928), "Spring Is Here" (1929) and
"Simple Simon" (1930).   The scores for these five musicals included such hits as "The Blue Room," ."Thou Swell," "You Took Advantage of Me," "With a Song in My Heart" and "Ten Cents a
Dance."

        After his first original film score in 1931, Rodgers sup-
plied Hollywood studios with "Lover," "You Are Too Beautiful" and
"It's Easy to Remember" introduced by Maurice Chevalier, Jeanette
MacDonald, Al Jolson and Bing Crosby.   After four years on the
West Coast, Rodgers and Hart returned to Broadway to create the
score for Billy Rose's spectacle "Jumbo."   It was the last production staged in New York's historic Hippodrome.   In 1936, Rodgers
wrote the music for the ballet "Slaughter on Tenth Avenue" which
was a major segment of the hit "On Your Toes."   It was followed
by "Babes in Arms" which boasted no less than five songs that became standards including "Where or When" and "The Lady Is a
Tramp."   In retrospect, Rodgers and Hart's "Pal Joey" is considered a milestone in musical comedy history but it was not popular
when it was originally presented in 1940.   The characters of a
lecherous middle-aged married woman and the young hustler she
sponsored as a night club proprietor shocked critics and public
alike.   The last new Rodgers and Hart show was "By Jupiter"
(1942).   Lorenz Hart died the following year.

        Shortly before Hart's death, Richard Rodgers began colla-
borating with Oscar Hammerstein on a musical titled "Away We
Go."   By the time it opened in 1943, it was called "Oklahoma!"
The show's integration of songs, dances, humor and plot caused
the critics to hail it as the greatest musical comedy ever written.
The public supported this opinion and kept the show running for
five years.   The original production cost $83,000 and grossed
seven million!   It was the first to have almost its entire score
recorded by the original cast and over one million albums were
sold.   The score included the classics "People Will Say We're
in Love," "Oh, What a Beautiful Mornin'" and "The Surrey with

the Fringe on Top." Rodgers next triumph was an Academy Award
for his music to "It Might as Well Be Spring" from the 1945 release "State Fair."

"Oklahoma!" was followed by "Carousel" (1945), "Allegro"
(1947), and "South Pacific" (1949). "South Pacific" became the
third musical in history to win the Pulitzer Prize for Drama. Its
score included "A Wonderful Guy," "Some Enchanted Evening,"
and "Bali Ha'i." Rodgers' success with Hammerstein continued
through the Fifties with their best work being "The King and I"
(1951) and "The Sound of Music" (1959). Oscar Hammerstein died
the year after "The Sound of Music" opened.

Richard Rodgers' "No Strings" had its Broadway premiere
in 1962. The composer also wrote the lyrics for the show. Not
only were they adequate, but his song "The Sweetest Sounds" became a national favorite. Rodgers also supplied his own lyrics
for the 1962 remake of the film "State Fair" and the 1967 television production "Androcles and the Lion." His 1970 stage musical
"Two by Two" received mixed reviews but managed a respectable
run due to the drawing power of its star Danny Kaye.

Rodgers was seventy-four when his most recent effort, titled
"Rex," was presented in 1976. It closed in less than two months
at a loss of $750,000. Richard Rodgers is still the most success-
ful composer in the history of the American theatre.

Year	Production Title	Popular Songs
1919	A LONELY ROMEO	Any Old Place with You
1920	POOR LITTLE RITZ GIRL	
1924	THE MELODY MAN (play)	
1925	THE GARRICK GAIETIES	Manhattan
		Sentimental Me
		April Fool
		An Old-Fashioned Girl
	DEAREST ENEMY	Here in My Arms
		Bye and Bye
	JUNE DAYS	
1926	THE GIRL FRIEND	The Blue Room
		The Girl Friend
		Why Do I?
	THE GARRICK GAIETIES	Mountain Greenery
	PEGGY-ANN	Where's That Rainbow?
		A Tree in the Park
		A Little Birdie Told Me So
	BETSY	
	LIDO LADY (London)	

Year	Production Title	Popular Songs
1927	A CONNECTICUT YANKEE	My Heart Stood Still Thou Swell I Feel at Home with You
	ONE DAM THING AFTER ANOTHER (London)	
1928	SHE'S MY BABY PRESENT ARMS	A Baby's Best Friend You Took Advantage of Me Do I Hear You Saying I Love You? Blue Ocean Blues
	CHEE-CHEE	Moon of My Delight The Tartar Song I Must Love You
1929	SPRING IS HERE	With a Song in My Heart Yours Sincerely Baby's Awake Now Why Can't I?
	HEADS UP	A Ship Without a Sail Why Do You Suppose? My Man Is on the Make
	LADY FINGERS	
1930	SIMPLE SIMON	Ten Cents a Dance He Was Too Good to Me Send for Me
	EVERGREEN (London) Follow Thru	Dancing on the Ceiling
1931	AMERICA'S SWEETHEART BILLY ROSE'S CRAZY QUILT The Hot Heiress	I've Got Five Dollars Like Ordinary People Do
1932	Love Me Tonight	Lover Isn't It Romantic? Mimi
	The Phantom President	
1933	Hallelujah, I'm a Bum Dancing Lady	You Are Too Beautiful
1934	Nana Manhattan Melodrama Hollywood Party Evergreen	That's Love "Blue Moon"
1935	JUMBO	Little Girl Blue My Romance

Year	Production Title	Popular Songs
1935	JUMBO	The Most Beautiful Girl in the World Over and Over Again
	SOMETHING GAY (play) Mississippi	It's Easy to Remember (HP) Soon (HP-1) Down by the River
1936	ON YOUR TOES	There's a Small Hotel (HP) Glad to Be Unhappy It's Got to Be Love Quiet Night On Your Toes
	THE SHOW IS ON Dancing Pirate	Are You My Love?
1937	BABES IN ARMS	Where or When (HP) The Lady Is a Tramp My Funny Valentine Johnny One Note I Wish I Were in Love Again All at Once
	I'D RATHER BE RIGHT	Have You Met Miss Jones? I'd Rather Be Right
1938	I MARRIED AN ANGEL	Spring Is Here I Married an Angel (HP) I'll Tell the Man in the Street
	THE BOYS FROM SYRACUSE	This Can't Be Love (HP) Falling in Love with Love Sing for Your Supper
	Fools for Scandal	How Can You Forget? There's a Boy in Harlem
1939	TOO MANY GIRLS	I Didn't Know What Time It Was (HP) Love Never Went to College
1940	HIGHER AND HIGHER	It Never Entered My Mind Ev'ry Sunday Afternoon From Another World
	PAL JOEY	Bewitched (HP-1) I Could Write a Book Zip
	Too Many Girls Boys from Syracuse	You're Nearer
1941	They Met in Argentina	

Year	Production Title	Popular Songs
1942	BY JUPITER	Wait Till You See Her Nobody's Heart Careless Rhapsody Everything I've Got
1943	OKLAHOMA!	People Will Say We're in Love (HP-1) Oh, What a Beautiful Mornin' (HP) The Surrey with the Fringe on Top Out of My Dreams Oklahoma! I Cain't Say No
	A CONNECTICUT YANKEE (revival)	To Keep My Love Alive.
	Stage Door Canteen	
1945	CAROUSEL	If I Loved You (HP-1) June Is Bustin' Out All Over You'll Never Walk Alone What's the Use of Wond'rin'?
	State Fair	It Might as Well Be Spring (AA) (HP-1) It's a Grand Night for Singing That's for Me (HP) Isn't It Kinda Fun?
1946	HAPPY BIRTHDAY (play)	I Haven't Got a Worry in the World
1947	ALLEGRO	The Gentlemen Is a Dope So Far (HP) A Fellow Needs a Girl You Are Never Away
1949	SOUTH PACIFIC	Some Enchanted Evening (HP-1) A Wonderful Guy (HP) Bali Ha'i (HP) I'm Gonna Wash That Man Right Out of My Hair Happy Talk Younger Than Springtime (HP) There Is Nothing Like a Dame A Cockeyed Optimist

Year	Production Title	Popular Songs
1951	THE KING AND I	Hello, Young Lovers I Whistle a Happy Tune Getting to Know You We Kiss in a Shadow I Have Dreamed
1953	ME AND JULIET Main Street to Broadway	No Other Love (HP-1)
1955	PIPE DREAM	All at Once You Love Her Everybody's Got a Home but Me
1957	Cinderella (TV)	Do I Love You Because You're Beautiful?
1958	FLOWER DRUM SONG	You Are Beautiful I Enjoy Being a Girl Love, Look Away
1959	THE SOUND OF MUSIC	The Sound of Music My Favorite Things Do Re Mi Climb Ev'ry Mountain
1962	NO STRINGS State Fair	The Sweetest Sounds No Strings Loads of Love
1965	DO I HEAR A WALTZ? The Sound of Music	Do I Hear a Waltz? Take the Moment Someone Like You
1967	Androcles and the Lion (TV)	
1970	TWO BY TWO	
1976	REX	

* * *

SIGMUND ROMBERG

Sigmund Romberg was born in Nagy Kaniga, Hungary, in 1887, and came to the United States when he was twenty-two years old. Although he had studied engineering in Vienna, his real in-

terest was in music and he was an accomplished violinist and
pianist.   His first job in America was in a pencil factory but he
soon quit to become a piano player in a restaurant.   In 1911, ragtime music swept the country and Romberg became interested in
the new rhythm.   He decided to try his hand at writing ragtime
instrumentals which were performed for the pleasure of the cafe's
dancing customers.   The compositions were so successful that
three of them, including "Leg of Mutton," were published in 1913.
A year earlier, Romberg had become a United States citizen.

Among the customers at the restaurant where Romberg
worked were the Shubert Brothers--then one of the theatre's foremost producing teams.   The brothers had lost one of their leading
staff composers and hired the young Hungarian to replace him.
Romberg's first assignments were the Shubert's 1914 extravaganza
"The Whirl of the World" and their annual revue "The Passing
Show."   His first real opportunity came when the Shuberts decided
to produce the European operetta "The Blue Paradise."   The producers were dissatisfied with the original music and assigned Romberg to rework the score and write additional melodies.   The result included the composer's outstanding "Auf Wiedersehn."

"The Blue Paradise" was the longest-running musical of
1915 and was followed by ten more Romberg scores, most of
which were written in conjunction with other composers.   His second major success was the 1917 Shubert production "Maytime."
This time the composer took full credit for the music which included "Will You Remember?"   During its year-long run, "Maytime"
achieved the distinction of playing in two theatres across the street
from each other.   In 1921, Romberg was represented by three
Broadway productions, the most popular of which was "Blossom
Time."   The operetta, based on the life of classical composer
Franz Schubert, was originally produced in Germany.   Just as
they had done with their earlier import, "The Blue Paradise,"
the Shuberts discarded the original score and had Romberg create
a new one.   His songs were adapted from Schubert's most famous
themes and the result was so successful that four companies were
formed to tour the United States while the production was still on
Broadway.   "Blossom Time" became the longest-running musical
of 1921.   Historian David Ewen points out that Romberg made
over $100,000 in royalties from "The Song of Love" while Schu-
bert himself received around a total of $500 for his entire output
of compositions during his lifetime!   Despite the show's success,
Romberg was unable to end his association with the Shubert Brothers and remained a staff composer.   In this capacity, he was required to write for any Shubert production the brothers desired--
regardless of his opinion of their projects.   After "Blossom Time,"
Romberg contributed melodies to almost a dozen Shubert productions in the span of only three years.

The production that finally made Romberg independent of
the Shuberts was "The Student Prince" which opened in 1924 and

ran for a year and a half to become the biggest hit of his career.
Again, Romberg was the composer of the year's longest-running
musical. He achieved this distinction for the third time two years
later with "The Desert Song." The Romberg score that introduced
the most hits was the 1928 offering "The New Moon." From this
single operetta came "Lover, Come Back to Me," "Stouthearted
Men," "One Kiss," "Softly, as in a Morning Sunrise" and "Want-
ing You."

Romberg settled in Hollywood in the 1930's and wrote for
motion pictures. The most popular of his film songs was "When
I Grow Too Old to Dream." During the early years of the Second
World War, the composer toured the country in "An Evening with
Sigmund Romberg" in which he conducted a concert orchestra in
performances of his own work and other light music. The year
the war ended brought him the last success of his career--"Up in
Central Park." His musical "My Romance" was produced in 1948
but closed in a few months.

Sigmund Romberg died in 1951 at the age of sixty-four. He
left behind an incomplete score for a production about the early
days of the musical theatre. The work was completed by Don
Walker and three years after Romberg's death "The Girl in Pink
Tights" had its premiere. It was a financial failure.

Year	Production Title	Popular Songs
1914	THE PASSING SHOW THE WHIRL OF THE WORLD DANCING AROUND	Omar Khayyam
1915	THE BLUE PARADISE A WORLD OF PLEASURE MAID IN AMERICA HANDS UP RUGGLES OF RED GAP	Auf Wiedersehn Fascination
1916	FOLLOW ME HER SOLDIER BOY ROBINSON CRUSOE JR. THE PASSING SHOW THE GIRL FROM BRAZIL THE SHOW OF WONDERS	I Want to Be Good but My Eyes Won't Let Me Mother
1917	MAYTIME THE PASSING SHOW MY LADY'S GLOVE DOING OUR BIT OVER THE TOP	Will You Remember? The Road to Paradise Jump Jim Crow

Year	Production Title	Popular Songs
1918	SINBAD FOLLOW THE GIRL THE PASSING SHOW THE MELTING OF MOLLY	
1919	THE MAGIC MELODY	The Little Church 'Round the Corner
	MONTE CRISTO JR. THE PASSING SHOW	
1920	POOR LITTLE RITZ GIRL	
1921	LOVE BIRDS	I Love to Go Swimmin' with Wimmin' Two Little Lovebirds
	BLOSSOM TIME	Serenade Song of Love Tell Me Daisy My Springtime Thou Art Three Little Maids
	BOMBO	
1922	THE BLUSHING BRIDE THE LADY IN ERMINE THE ROSE OF STAMBOUL THE SPRINGTIME OF YOUTH	Mister and Missus When Hearts Are Young
1923	THE DANCING GIRL THE PASSING SHOW	
1924	THE STUDENT PRINCE	Deep in My Heart, Dear Serenade The Drinking Song Golden Days Just We Two
	ARTISTS AND MODELS INNOCENT EYES MARJORIE THE PASSING SHOW ANNIE DEAR	Tomorrow's Another Day
1925	LOUIS THE 14TH PRINCESS FLAVIA	Edelweiss
1926	THE DESERT SONG	Blue Heaven (The Desert Song) One Alone The Riff Song Romance One Flower Grows Alone in My Garden

Year	Production Title	Popular Songs
1926	THE DESERT SONG	It
1927	MY MARYLAND	Silver Moon Mother The Boys in Grey Your Land and My Land
	CHERRY BLOSSOMS MY PRINCESS THE LOVE CALL	
1928	THE NEW MOON	Lover, Come Back to Me Stouthearted Men One Kiss Wanting You Softly, as in a Morning Sunrise Marianne
	ROSALIE	
1930	NINA ROSA	Your Smiles, Your Tears Serenade of Love Nina Rosa
	Viennese Nights	You Will Remember Vienna I Bring a Love Song
1931	EAST WIND Children of Dreams	
1933	MELODY	You Are the Song Give Me a Roll on the Drum
1935	MAY WINE	Just Once Around the Clock Dance, My Darlings I Built a Dream One Day Something New Is in My Heart Somebody Ought to Be Told
	The Night Is Young	When I Grow Too Old to Dream (HP) The Night Is Young
1936	FORBIDDEN MELODY	
1937	They Gave Him a Gun Maytime	A Love Song of Long Ago Farewell to Dreams
1938	Girl of the Golden West	Who Are We to Say? Soldiers of Fortune Shadows on the Moon

Year	Production Title	Popular Songs
1939	Balalaika Broadway Serenade Let Freedom Ring	
1941	SUNNY RIVER	
1945	UP IN CENTRAL PARK	Close as Pages in a Book It Doesn't Cost You Any- thing to Dream When You Walk in the Room April Snow
1948	MY ROMANCE	
1950		"Zing Zing, Zoom Zoom" (HP)
1951	Faithfully Yours	Faithfully Yours

Posthumous:

1954	THE GIRL IN PINK TIGHTS	Lost in Loveliness In Paris and in Love

* * *

BILLY ROSE

Billy Rose's activities as a producer of stage musicals have overshadowed his reputation as a lyricist. Rose began attracting attention as a teenager when he was named the World's Champion Shorthand Writer. A few years later, his first song "Ain't Nature Grand?" made its appearance in music stores. In the early 1920's, he specialized in comic lyrics for such songs as "Barney Google," "You Tell Her--I Stutter," and "Does the Spearmint Lose Its Flavor on the Bedpost Overnight?" During Prohibition, Rose operated a speakeasy called The Back Stage Club which featured singer Helen Morgan. By the time the Depression began, his string of popular hits included "A Cup of Coffee, a Sandwich, and You," "Me and My Shadow," "More Than You Know," "Without a Song," "Don't Bring Lulu," and "Back in Your Own Backyard." He worked with such top composers as Joe Meyer, Dave Dreyer, Vincent Youmans, Harry Warren and Harold Arlen, and shared credit for some of his lyrics with Al Dubin, Edward Eliscu, Ira Gershwin, Mort Dixon and E. Y. Harburg. His career as a producer got under full steam with "Billy Rose's Crazy Quilt" in 1931 and the Rodgers and Hart musical "Jumbo" in 1935. "Jumbo" was followed by the Great Lakes Exposition in Cleveland, Ohio (1938) and "Billy Rose's Aquacade" staged at the World's Fair in New York in 1940.

Rose opened his Manhattan cabaret The Diamond Horseshoe in 1940 and it became one of the most famous night spots in the country. His theatrical productions continued with Oscar Hammerstein's "Carmen Jones" (1943) and Cole Porter's "Seven Lively Arts" (1944). Billy Rose advanced from the lower class New York City home in which he was born in 1899 to owner of extensive properties which included Manhattan's Ziegfeld Theatre and a lavish estate on Long Island. He was also a collector of valuable oil paintings and other museum pieces. Billy Rose died in 1966 at the age of sixty-seven. In 1975, Rose was portrayed in the film "Funny Lady." The facts of his career and his marriage to Fanny Brice were considerably distorted, and audiences were given the impression that he single-handedly wrote all the music and lyrics for the popular music standards performed in the picture.

Year	Production Title	Popular Songs
1921		"Ain't Nature Grand?"
1922		"Barney Google" "You Tell Her--I Stutter" "You Gotta See Mama Every Night"
1923		"That Old Gang of Mine" "Come On, Spark Plug" "Twelve O'Clock at Night" "Somebody Else Took You Out of My Arms"
1924	BE YOURSELF	Cooking Breakfast for the One I Love "I Wonder Who's Dancing with You Tonight?" "Follow the Swallow" "Does the Spearmint Lose Its Flavor on the Bedpost Overnight?" "I Can't Get the One I Want" "Mah Jong" "She's Everybody's Sweetheart" "Worried"
1925	CHARLOT'S REVUE	A Cup of Coffee, a Sandwich and You "Don't Bring Lulu"

Year	Production Title	Popular Songs
1925		"Clap Hands, Here Comes Charley" "In the Middle of the Night" "If I Had a Girl Like You" "Swanee Butterfly" "Where Is My Old Girl Tonight?" "Dummy Song (I'll Take the Legs from Some Old Table)"
1926		"Poor Papa--He's Got Nuthin' at All" "Tonight You Belong to Me" (HP) "There's a Little White House" "Say It with a Red, Red Rose" "Too Many Parties and Too Many Pals"
1927	DELMAR'S REVELS PADLOCKS OF 1927	Me and My Shadow "Here Comes the Showboat" "Four Walls" "Barbara" "Fifty Million Frenchmen (Can't Be Wrong)" "When the Morning Glories Wake Up in the Morning"
1928	My Man	I'd Rather Be Blue If You Want the Rainbow "Back in Your Own Backyard" "Hello, Montreal" "Right or Wrong, I Love You" "There's a Rainbow 'Round My Shoulder" "Golden Gate"
1929	GREAT DAY EARL CARROLL'S SKETCH BOOK	More Than You Know Without a Song Great Day Happy Because I'm in Love

BILLY ROSE 411

Year	Production Title	Popular Songs
1929	Applause	I've Got a Feeling I'm Fall-ing
	Noah's Ark	"I Got a 'Code' in My 'Doze'" "Building a Nest for Mary" "Evangeline" "Happy Days and Lonely Nights" "I'm Ka-razy for You"
1930	SWEET AND LOW	Would You Like to Take a Walk? Cheerful Little Earful Overnight He's Not Worth Your Tears
	King of Jazz Be Yourself	It Happened in Monterey When a Woman Loves a Man
1931	BILLY ROSE'S CRAZY QUILT	I Found a Million Dollar Baby "I'm for You One Hundred Percent"
1932	THE GREAT MAGOO (play)	It's Only a Paper Moon (HP) "I Wanna Be Loved"
1933		"There's a Home in Wyo-min'"
1934	THE ZIEGFELD FOLLIES	Suddenly The House Is Haunted "Got the Jitters" "Have a Little Dream on Me"
1936	CASA MANANA (Ft. Worth)	The Night Is Young and You're So Beautiful (HP)
	Once in a Blue Moon	
1937		"Gone with the Dawn" "The Sun Will Shine Tonight"
1940	BILLY ROSE'S AQUACADE (New York World's Fair)	You Think of Everything (HP) Yours for a Song You're Too Good to Be True

Year	Production Title	Popular Songs
1942		"Only a Moment Ago"
1948		"Crying for Joy"

* * *

HARRY RUBY

Harry Ruby was a member of the Jet Set of his generation. He and his wife, film actress Eileen Percy, were regular guests at the lavish parties hosted by movie star Marion Davies at both her Santa Monica beach mansion and at William Randolph Hearst's castle at San Simeon, California. Ruby was born in New York City in 1895, and began working as a piano player in nickelodeons and cafes just after receiving his high school diploma. While performing in vaudeville as part of a trio which included Harry Cohn (who eventually became the head of Columbia Studios), he met song and dance man Bert Kalmar. Kalmar was part owner of a music publishing business and hired the twenty-two year old Ruby as a staff pianist. From that time until lyricist Kalmar's death in 1947, the two men wrote most of their songs together. After half a dozen Broadway successes which introduced such Ruby melodies as "All Alone Monday," "I Wanna Be Loved by You" and "Thinking of You," the team moved to Hollywood. Their first year in the film capitol saw the release of "Check and Double Check" in which their most famous song, "Three Little Words," was featured. Harry Ruby returned to Broadway in 1941 to supply numbers for the Sophie Tucker revue "High Kickers." Ten years later his melody "A Kiss to Build a Dream On" was nominated for the "Oscar." The song had been written by Kalmar and Ruby years earlier and gained success after Oscar Hammerstein reworked the lyric. Red Skelton portrayed Harry Ruby in the 1950 film musical "Three Little Words." The noted composer died at the age of seventy-nine in 1974.

Year	Production Title	Popular Songs
1917		"He Sits Around" "When Those Sweet Hawaiian Babies Roll Their Eyes"
1918	LADIES FIRST	"Come On, Papa" "The Dixie Volunteers"
1919		"And He'd Say Oo-la, La, Wee, Wee" "Daddy Long Legs"

Year	Production Title	Popular Songs
1919		"What'll We Do on a Saturday Night--When the Town Goes Dry?"
1920	THE ZIEGFELD FOLLIES	I'm a Vamp from East Broadway
	BROADWAY BREVITIES	"So Long, Oo-Long" "Timbuctoo" "Where Do They Go When They Row, Row, Row?"
1921	THE MIDNIGHT ROUNDERS SNAPSHOTS OF 1921	My Sunny Tennessee "She's Mine, All Mine" "Snoops, the Lawyer"
1922	THE GREENWICH VILLAGE FOLLIES	Beautiful Girls "I Gave You Up Just Before You Threw Me Down" "Sheik of Avenue B"
1923	HELEN OF TROY, NEW YORK	I Like a Big Town It Was Meant to Be Happy Ending
	NIFTIES OF 1923	"Who's Sorry Now?" (HP) "The Window Cleaners"
1924	NO OTHER GIRL	You Flew Away from the Nest
1925	PUZZLES OF 1925	
1926	THE RAMBLERS TWINKLE, TWINKLE	All Alone Monday
1927	LUCKY	The Same Old Moon Dancing the Devil Away
	FIVE O'CLOCK GIRL	Thinking of You (HP) Up in the Clouds
1928	GOOD BOY	I Wanna Be Loved by You (HP)
	ANIMAL CRACKERS	Watching the Clouds Roll By Hooray for Captain Spaulding
1929	TOP SPEED	Keep Your Undershirt On What Would I Care?

Year	Production Title	Popular Songs
1929		"Over and Over Again"
1930	Check and Double Check The Cuckoos Animal Crackers	Three Little Words I Love You So Much
1931		"Nevertheless" (HP-1) "I'm So Afraid of You"
1932	Horsefeathers The Kid from Spain Manhattan Parade	Everyone Says "I Love You" Look What You've Done What a Perfect Combination
1933	Duck Soup	
1934	Hips, Hips, Hooray Kentucky Kernels Happiness Ahead	Keep on Doin' What You're Doin' Tired of It All Keep Romance Alive One Little Kiss
1935	Bright Lights Thanks a Million	
1936	Walking on Air	
1938	Everybody Sing Cocoanut Grove	 "When You Dream About Hawaii"
1940	Go West	
1941	HIGH KICKERS	
1946	Wake Up and Dream Do You Love Me?	Give Me the Simple Life Do You Love Me?
1947	Carnival in Costa Rica	Another Night Like This "Go West, Young Man"
1949	ALONG FIFTH AVENUE	Maybe It's Because (HP)
1951	The Strip Take Care of My Little Girl	A Kiss to Build a Dream On (AN)
1957		"The Real McCoys"

BOB RUSSELL

     Although Bob Russell wrote film background scores and the
music for several popular songs, he generally worked as a lyricist.   Among his illustrious collaborators were Harry Warren,
Duke Ellington, Carl Sigman, Louis Alter and Peter DeRose.   Russell was born in Passaic, New Jersey, in 1914 and was educated
at Washington University.   He began his career writing advertising
copy for a film studio.   1940 was the milestone year in his career.
His work was heard in the Broadway revue "All in Fun, " and his
song "Frenesi" began a 19 week run on "Your Hit Parade" during
which it made the Number One spot three times.   The hits that
followed included "Maria Elena, " "Don't Get Around Much Anymore, "
"Do Nothin' Til You Hear from Me, " "Ballerina" and "You Came
a Long Way from St. Louis. "   He began writing for motion pictures in 1949 and received Academy Award nominations in 1967 and
1968.   Bob Russell died in 1970 at the peak of his career.

Year	Production Title	Popular Songs
1940	ALL IN FUN	"Frenesi" (HP-1) "Busy as a Bee, I'm Buzz, Buzz, Buzzing" "B-I Bi" "Watching the Clock"
1941		"Maria Elena" (HP-1) "Time Was" (HP) "Misirlou" "Babalu" "Warm Valley"
1942		"Don't Get Around Much Anymore" (HP-1) "Full Moon" (HP) "At the Crossroads" "Taboo" "Fooled"
1943		"Do Nothin' Til You Hear from Me" (HP) "Brazil" (HP-1) "Who Dat Up Dere?"
1944		"I Didn't Know About You" (HP) "No More"
1945	SHOOTIN' STAR (closed in tryout)	"Carnival"

Year	Production Title	Popular Songs
1947		"Ballerina" (HP-1)
1948		"You Came a Long Way from St. Louis" "Matinee" "It's Like Takin' Candy from a Baby"
1949	That Midnight Kiss	I Know, I Know, I Know "Crazy She Calls Me" "Circus"
1950	Ticket to Tomahawk	"No Other Love"
1951		"Would I Love You (Love You, Love You)" (HP) "Once" "Just When We're Falling in Love"
1952	Affair in Trinidad Sound Off Jack and the Beanstalk	I've Been Kissed Before Lady Love It's the Beast in Me
1953	The Blue Gardenia	Blue Gardenia "Half a Photograph"
1954	Meet Captain Kidd	
1956	The Naked Hills The Girl Can't Help It	"A Lonesome Cup of Coffee"
1958		"Interlude"
1962	A Matter of Who	
1963		"Cry Baby"
1964		"You Go Your Way"
1965		"The Color of Love"
1966		"A Banda"
1967	Banning	The Eyes of Love (AN)

Year	Production Title	Popular Songs
1968	For Love of Ivy	For Love of Ivy (AN)
1969	Smith!	
	Rascal	
		"He Ain't Heavy ... He's My Brother"

* * *

ARTHUR SCHWARTZ

Arthur Schwartz was introduced to show business at the age of fourteen when he played piano accompaniment for silent films in a Brooklyn movie house. He was born in New York in 1900. The first Broadway production to feature his music, "Dear Sir," opened in 1924 while Schwartz was earning his living as an attorney. After four more Broadway shows, he gave up law practice and became a full-time composer. From 1928 through 1937 his primary lyricist was Howard Dietz with whom he wrote such hits as "I Guess I'll Have to Change My Plan," "Something to Remember You By," "You and the Night and the Music" and "Alone Together." Historian Stanley Green has called the team's score for the 1931 hit "The Band Wagon" "possibly the finest ever written for a revue." It included Schwartz's most memorable melody "Dancing in the Dark." When Dietz's duties as a publicist for MGM caused him to work year-round for the studio, Schwartz collaborated with lyricist Al Stillman on the score for "Virginia" which opened New York's Center Theatre. The show closed in only two months. Lyricists Dorothy Fields, Oscar Hammerstein and Ira Gershwin were his next partners but none of their songs achieved the popularity of his work with Dietz.

Arthur Schwartz began contributing to films in 1930 and worked in Hollywood exclusively during World War II both as a songwriter and producer. His melodies for "They're Either Too Young or Too Old" (1943) and "A Gal in Calico" (1946) received Academy Award nominations. In 1948, Howard Dietz took a sabbatical from MGM and rejoined Schwartz on the score for the revue "Inside U.S.A." It was their longest-running hit (399 performances) and was also one of the last successful revues ever staged on Broadway. Schwartz supplied the music for the modestly successful Shirley Booth vehicles "A Tree Grows in Brooklyn" and "By the Beautiful Sea," and the television productions "High Tor" and "A Bell for Adano" during the 1950's. The Sixties found him working with Dietz again on "The Gay Life" and "Jennie" both of which failed on Broadway.

Arthur Schwartz has completed the score (both music and

lyrics) for a musical version of Dickens's novel "Nicholas Nickle-
by." The seventy-six year old composer turned vocalist in 1976
and cut an album of his own songs.

Year	Production Title	Popular Songs
1924	DEAR SIR	
1926	GRAND STREET FOLLIES QUEEN HIGH	
1927	THE NEW YORKERS	
1928	GOOD BOY	
1929	THE LITTLE SHOW	I Guess I'll Have to Change My Plan I've Made a Habit of You
	WAKE UP AND DREAM NED WAYBURN'S GAMBOLS GRAND STREET FOLLIES	She's Such a Comfort to Me
1930	SECOND LITTLE SHOW THREE'S A CROWD	Lucky Seven Something to Remember You By The Moment I Saw You Right at the Start of It
	PRINCESS CHARMING Follow the Leader Lottery Bride	
1931	THE BAND WAGON	Dancing in the Dark High and Low New Sun in the Sky I Love Louisa Hoops Confession
1932	FLYING COLORS	A Shine on Your Shoes Louisiana Hayride Alone Together A Rainy Day Fatal Fascination
1933	SHE LOVES ME NOT (play)	After All, You're All I'm After "Love Lost"
1934	REVENGE WITH MUSIC	If There Is Someone Love- lier Than You You and the Night and the Music

Year	Production Title	Popular Songs
1934	REVENGE WITH MUSIC	When You Love Only One Wand'rin Heart
	THUMBS UP Girl from Missouri	Born to Be Kissed
		"Then I'll Be Tired of You" "How High Can a Little Bird Fly?" "How Can We Be Wrong?"
1935	AT HOME ABROAD	Farewell, My Lovely What a Wonderful World Love Is a Dancing Thing Got a Bran' New Suit Loadin' Time
1936	That Girl from Paris	Seal It with a Kiss Love and Learn (HP)
1937	VIRGINIA	You and I Know (HP) An Old Flame Never Dies Goodbye, Jonah
	BETWEEN THE DEVIL	I See Your Face Before Me (HP) By Myself You Have Everything
	Under Your Spell	Under Your Spell
1939	STARS IN YOUR EYES	This Is It (HP) It's All Yours Just a Little Bit More I'll Pay the Check
1940	AMERICAN JUBILEE (New York World's Fair)	Tennessee Fish Fry How Can I Ever Be Alone?
1941	Navy Blues	In Waikiki You're a Natural
		"Honorable Moon"
1942	Cairo All Through the Night Crossroads	
1943	Thank Your Lucky Stars	They're Either Too Young or Too Old (AN) (HP) How Sweet You Are (HP) The Dreamer Love Isn't Born

Year	Production Title	Popular Songs
1946	PARK AVENUE The Time, the Place and the Girl	There's No Holding Me A Gal in Calico (AN) (HP-1) Oh, but I Do (HP) A Rainy Night in Rio Through a Thousand Dreams
1948	INSIDE U.S.A.	Haunted Heart (HP) Rhode Island Is Famous for You My Gal Is Mine Once More Blue Grass
1951	A TREE GROWS IN BROOKLYN Excuse My Dust	Make the Man Love Me Love Is the Reason Spring Has Sprung
1953	The Band Wagon Dangerous When Wet	That's Entertainment
1954	BY THE BEAUTIFUL SEA	More Love Than Your Love
1955	High Tor (TV) You're Never Too Young	When You're in Love
1956	A Bell for Adano (TV)	
1961	THE GAY LIFE	Magic Moment
1963	JENNIE	Before I Kiss the World Goodbye Waitin' for the Evening Train

* * *

JEAN SCHWARTZ

Jean Schwartz came to the United States from Budapest, Hungary, in 1888, when he was ten years old. He worked as an office boy and cashier before becoming a full-time pianist in a band that performed at New York's Coney Island. He progressed to demonstrating sheet music in a department store and finally became a song plugger for a major music publisher. Schwartz appeared in vaudeville with lyricist William Jerome and the two collaborated on such hits as "Bedelia," "Any Old Time at All," and their most famous song "Chinatown, My Chinatown." Jean Schwartz was one of the busiest composers on Broadway. His melodies were heard in 60 musicals in 27 years including the first edition of

Florenz Ziegfeld's "Follies." In 1912, his name appeared in the Playbills for no less than seven productions. Al Jolson introduced one of Schwartz's most lasting songs, "Rock-a-Bye Your Baby with a Dixie Melody" in the 1918 musical "Sinbad." During the 1930's, Schwartz composed "Au Revoir, Pleasant Dreams" which orchestra leader Ben Bernie used as his theme. Schwartz's wife was Rosie Dolly of the famous "Dolly Sisters." He died in 1956 at the age of seventy-eight.

Year	Production Title	Popular Songs
1901	THE STROLLERS	I'm Tired
	HOITY TOITY	When Mr. Shakespeare Comes to Town
	SLEEPING BEAUTY AND THE BEAST	Rip Van Winkle Was a Lucky Man
		Nursery Rhymes
		"Any Old Place I Can Hang My Hat Is Home Sweet Home to Me"
		"Don't Put Me Off at Buffalo Anymore"
		"It's All Right, Mayme"
1902	THE WILD ROSE	I'm Unlucky
	A CHINESE HONEYMOON	Mister Dooley
		"Since Sister Nell Heard Paderewski Play"
		"Back to the Woods"
		"Just Kiss Yourself Goodbye"
		"The Gambling Man"
1903	MR. BLUEBEARD	Hamlet Was a Melancholy Dane
	THE JERSEY LILY	Bedelia
	MOTHER GOOSE	
		"My Hula Lula Girl"
		"Why Don't You Go, Go, Go?"
1904	PIFF! PAFF!! POUF!!!	The Ghost That Never Walked
		Goodbye, My Own True Love
		Love, Love, Love
		"When You're Broke"
1905	SERGEANT BRUE	My Irish Molly O
	LIFTING THE LID	Oh, Marie
	THE WHITE CAT	Goodbye, Maggie Doyle
	A YANKEE CIRCUS ON MARS	

Year	Production Title	Popular Songs
1905	THE HAM TREE FRITZ IN TAMMANY HALL	 "My Guiding Star"
1906	THE RICH MR. HOGGEN- HEIMER THE LITTLE CHERUB	Any Old Time at All My Irish Rosie
1907	THE ZIEGFELD FOLLIES LOLA FROM BERLIN	Handle Me with Care "Miss Killarney"
1908	THE ZIEGFELD FOLLIES	When the Girl You Love Is Loving "Take Your Girl to the Ball Game" "Goodbye, Mr. Ragtime" "Love Days" "Kiss Your Minstrel Boy Goodbye" "Over the Hills and Far Away" "White Wash Man"
1909	THE SILVER STAR IN HAYTI	The Cooney Spooney Dance Franco-American Ragtime "The Hat My Father Wore on St. Patrick's Day" "Honey on Our Honeymoon" "I'm a Member of the Mid- night Crew" "Meet Me in Rose Time, Rosie"
1910	UP AND DOWN BROADWAY	Chinatown, My Chinatown "I'll Make a Ring Around Rosie" "Isn't It Exasperating, Sadie?"
1911	VERA VIOLETTA	Rum Tum Tiddle "Come Love, and Play Peek- a-Boo" "I'm Going Back to Reno" "Just Think of All the Money You Could Save" "Sarah's Hat"

Year	Production Title	Popular Songs
1912	MODEST SUZANNE OVER THE RIVER HOKEY-POKEY A WINSOME WIDOW THE WALL STREET GIRL MY BEST GIRL BROADWAY TO PARIS	
		"My Yellow Jacket Girl" "Honest True"
1913	THE PLEASURE SEEKERS	Sit Down, You're Rocking the Boat
	THE HONEYMOON EXPRESS THE PASSING SHOW	
		"When the Red, Red Roses Grow" "You Can't Get Away from It"
1914	OUR AMERICAN BOY WHEN CLAUDIA SMILES	I Love the Ladies
		"Back to the Carolina You Love"
1915	HANDS UP	I'm Simply Crazy Over You
		"Hello, Hawaii, How Are You?" "Goodbye, Virginia" "In Winky, Blinky Chinatown"
1916	FOLLOW ME	When the Girls Grow Older They Grow a Little Bolder
	BETTY	
		"I'm Going Back Home and Have a Wonderful Time"
1917	WORDS AND MUSIC	
		"I'm All Bound 'Round with the Mason Dixon Line"
1918	SINBAD	Rock-a-Bye Your Baby with a Dixie Melody Hello, Central, Give Me No Man's Land Why Do They All Take the Night Boat to Albany?
	THE PASSING SHOW	
		"Sahara"

Year	Production Title	Popular Songs
1919	MONTE CRISTO JR. SHUBERT GAIETIES HELLO, ALEXANDER THE PASSING SHOW	"I'm Goin' to Break That Mason-Dixon Line"
1920	THE MIDNIGHT ROUNDERS CENTURY REVUE	
1921	THE MIDNIGHT ROUNDERS TANGERINE THE PASSING SHOW	
1922	MAKE IT SNAPPY	"Tell Me What's the Matter, Lovable Eyes"
1923	DEW DROP INN THE PASSING SHOW ARTISTS AND MODELS TOPICS OF 1923	"Ev'ry Day Is Mother's Day"
1924	INNOCENT EYES	Innocent Eyes Garden of Love Organdy Days
	THE PASSING SHOW	
1927	A NIGHT IN SPAIN	
1928	SUNNY DAYS	
1930		"Au Revoir, Pleasant Dreams"
1931		"One Little Raindrop"
1933		"Little You Know" "Trouble in Paradise"
1934		"If I Didn't Care" "In a Little Red Barn (On a Farm Down in Indiana)"
1937	Make Way for Tomorrow	"Trust in Me" (HP)
1938		"There's Rain in My Eyes"

* * *

CARL SIGMAN

  Carl Sigman hails from Brooklyn, New York, where he was
born in 1909. He studied law at New York University, and was
awarded the Bronze Star for his service with the 82nd Airborne
Division during World War II. Sigman's first recognition as a
songwriter came with his 1940 hits "Love Lies" and "Pennsylvania
6-5000." His only Broadway musical has been "Angel in the Wings"
which introduced "Civilization (Bongo, Bongo, Bongo)" in 1947.
That same year he provided the music for Vaughan Monroe's best-
selling record "Ballerina." Sigman also writes lyrics and three
of his biggest successes were well-known melodies before he
added words to them: "It's All in the Game" was Charles B.
Dawe's famous "Melody," "What Now My Love" was a popular French song, and "Where Do I Begin?" was Francis Lai's
main theme from the 1970 motion picture "Love Story."

Year	Production Title	Popular Songs
1940		"Love Lies"
		"Pennsylvania 6-5000"
		"Celery Stalks at Midnight"
		"All Too Soon"
		"Watching the Clock"
		"Busy as a Bee, I'm Buzz, Buzz Buzzin'"
1941		"Cherry Blossoms on Capitol Hill"
1944		"Walter Winchell Rhumba"
1946		"Passe"
		"Talking Is a Woman"
		"If You Could See Me Now"
		"Put That Kiss Back Where You Found It"
1947	ANGEL IN THE WINGS	Civilization (HP-1)
		The Big Brass Band from Brazil
		The Thousand Islands Song
		Once Around the Moon
		"Ballerina" (HP-1)
1948		"Enjoy Yourself (It's Later Than You Think)" (HP)
		"Matinee"
		"My Fair Lady"
1949		"Hop-Scotch Polka"

Year	Production Title	Popular Songs
1949		"Twenty-four Hours of Sunshine" (HP) "Careless Hands" (HP) "The Blossoms on the Bough" "There's a Mile Between Esses in Smiles" "The Manuelo Tarantel" "Crazy She Calls Me"
1950		"My Heart Cries for You" (HP-1) "A Marshmallow World" (HP) "Buona Sera"
1951		"It's All in the Game" "If You Turn Me Down"
1952		"Don't Ever Be Afraid to Go Home"
1953	Stop, You're Killing Me She's Back on Broadway	"Ebb Tide" "Answer Me, My Love" (HP)
1954		"I Could Have Told You" "Funny Thing"
1955		"Arrividerci, Roma" "Dream Along with Me" "Believe in Me" "Summertime in Venice"
1956		"11th Hour Melody" "How Will I Remember You?"
1957	Band of Angels	"The Mountains Beyond the Moon" "Till" "The Day the Rains Came" "Souvenir of Italy"
1958		"The World Outside" "Willingly (Melodie Perdu)"
1959		"Six Boys and Seven Girls" "Right Now"

Year	Production Title	Popular Songs
1960		"I Belong to Your Heart"
1961		"Oceans of Love"
1962		"Addio, Addio"
1963		"Losing You"
1964		"Shangri-La" "You're My World"
1966		"What Now My Love?" "A Day in the Life of a Fool"
1967		"Lonely Is the Name" "The World We Knew (Over and Over)"
1968		"My Way of Life"

* * *

ABNER SILVER

New York-born Abner Silver studied law at New York University, and played the piano in dance orchestras. He enjoyed his first success in 1920 when the song "My Home Town Is a One Horse Town" (lyrics by Alex Gerber) became a big seller. It was followed by "I'm Goin' South" which Al Jolson introduced in the 1921 Broadway musical "Bombo." Silver's melodramatic "No! No! A Thousand Times No!!" (lyrics by Al Lewis and Al Sherman) was one of the most popular novelty numbers of 1934. During the late 1950's, the composer supplied songs for films starring singing sensation Elvis Presley. Abner Silver was sixty-one years old when his "My Love for You" became a hit in 1960. He died six years later.

Year	Production Title	Popular Songs
1920		"My Home Town Is a One Horse Town" "Spanish Love"
1921	BOMBO THE PASSING SHOW	I'm Goin' South Becky from Babylon "Which Hazel?"

Year	Production Title	Popular Songs
1922	SPICE OF 1922	Angel Child
		"Say It While Dancing"
1923		"Bebe"
		"When Will the Sun Shine for Me?"
1926		"(I Don't Believe It, but) Say It Again"
		"I Found a Roundabout Way to Heaven"
		"Elsie Schultzenheim"
1927	TAKE THE AIR	
		"C'est Vous, It's You"
		"Barbara"
		"Normandy"
1928	EARL CARROLL'S VANITIES Two Lovers	
		"Mary Ann"
1929	EARL CARROLL'S SKETCH BOOK GEORGE WHITE'S SCANDALS Sweetie	He's So Unusual
		"Bashful Baby"
		"(Step by Step) I'm Marching Home to You"
1930	Swing High Troupers Three Painted Faces	
1931		"I Hate Myself"
1932		"Pu-leeze, Mr. Hemingway!"
1933		"Farewell to Arms"
1934		"There Goes My Heart"
		"No! No! A Thousand Times No!!"
		"Isn't It a Shame?"
		"Cross-Eyed Kelly"
1935		"Chasing Shadows" (HP-1)

Year	Production Title	Popular Songs
1935		"Every Now and Then" (HP) "One Night in Monte Carlo" "Hypnotized"
1936	Sky's the Limit	"On the Beach at Bali Bali" (HP) "Darling, Not Without You" "For Sentimental Reasons"
1937		"The Mood That I'm In" "When the Mighty Organ Played 'Oh, Promise Me'"
1938		"Have You Forgotten So Soon?" (HP)
1939		"A New Moon and an Old Serenade" (HP) "An Old Curiosity Shop"
1940		"How Did He Look?" "There Shall Be No Night"
1942		"Are You Living, Old Man?"
1943	ARTISTS AND MODELS	"Little Did I Know" (HP) "And So Little Time"
1945		"After Awhile" (HP)
1948		"One Raindrop Doesn't Make a Shower"
1949		"How Green Was My Valley"
1950		"With These Hands" "Make Believe Land"
1952		"I Laughed at Love"
1955		"Don't Let Her Go"
1957	Jailhouse Rock	Young and Beautiful
1958	King Creole	Lover Doll
1960	G.I. Blues	What's She Really Like?

Year	Production Title	Popular Songs
1960	G. I. Blues	Tonight Is So Right for Love
		"My Love for You"

* * *

SAM H. STEPT

Sammy Stept's family emigrated to the United States from Odessa, Russia, when he was three years old. He studied classical music in Pittsburgh, Pennsylvania, and played the piano in his high school band. By the time he was twenty-three, Stept had his own small orchestra which entertained in Cleveland, Ohio, restaurants for five years. On his arrival in New York City, he worked as accompanist for Mae West and organized one of radio's first singing groups. Stept collaborated with lyricist Bud Green to write his first successful song "And That Ain't All" in 1919. Within ten years, he became his own publisher, wrote the hit "Please Don't Talk About Me When I'm Gone" (lyrics by Sidney Clare), and answered the call of Hollywood. His career as a motion picture composer was undistinguised and his assignments were generally on low budget films. During the early days of World War II, Stept's "Dear Mom," "I Came Here to Talk for Joe," "Don't Sit Under the Apple Tree" and "This Is Worth Fighting For" were all national favorites. His most successful Broadway musical was "Yokel Boy" in which "Comes Love" was introduced. His most frequent lyricists were Lew Brown and Charles Tobias. Sammy Stept was sixty-seven years old at the time of his death in 1964.

Year	Production Title	Popular Songs
1919		"And That Ain't All"
1925		"Underneath the Stars with You"
1927		"Mine, All Mine"
1928	Stepping High	I'll Always Be in Love with You
1929	Syncopation Lucky in Love Mother's Boy Nothing but the Truth	Do Something
		"That's My Weakness Now" "Good Little Bad Little You" "Congratulations"

Year	Production Title	Popular Songs
1930	Playing Around Show Girl in Hollywood Big Boy	
		"Please Don't Talk About Me When I'm Gone"
1931	Business Girl	
		"Why Did It Have to Be Me?"
1932	GEORGE WHITE'S MUSIC HALL VARIETIES	
		"I Beg Your Pardon, Ma- demoiselle" "The Organ Grinder"
1933	SHADY LADY	Swingy Little Thingy
1934	Baby Take a Bow	On Accounta I Love You
		"London on a Rainy Night"
1935	Here Comes the Band Bar 20 Rides Again The Eagle's Brood This Is the Life Hopalong Cassidy	
		"I'm Painting the Town Red" "Tiny Little Fingerprints"
1936	Laughing Irish Eyes Happy Go Lucky Dancing Feet Sitting on the Moon	All My Life
		"Breakin' in a Pair of Shoes"
1937	The Hit Parade $23\frac{1}{2}$ Hours Leave The Gold Racket Dodge City Trail The Big Show	Sweet Heartache
		"It Seems Like Old Times" "I Bet You Tell That to All the Girls" "I Want You for Christmas" "Let's Waltz for Old Time's Sake"
1938	Having Wonderful Time	My First Impression of You
		"A Love Like Ours"

Year	Production Title	Popular Songs
1939	YOKEL BOY	Comes Love (HP) Let's Make Memories To-night I Can't Afford to Dream
	That's Right--You're Wrong	
1940	Hullabaloo	We've Come a Long Way Together "A Prairie Fairy Tale" "Or Have I?"
1941	Secret of the Wastelands	"Dear Mom" "I Came Here to Talk for Joe" (HP)
1942	When Johnny Comes Marching Home Private Buckaroo	This Is Worth Fighting For (HP) Don't Sit Under the Apple Tree (HP-1)
1943		"I Have Faith, So Have You" "I've Had This Feeling Before"
1944	Stars on Parade Show Business	When They Ask About You (HP) "Bahia"
1945		"The Lord's Been Good to Me"
1946	Holiday in Mexico	"I Fall in Love with You Ev'ry Day"
1947		"Let's Go Back and Kiss the Girls Good Night Again" "Serenade to Love"
1948		"Next Time I Fall in Love" "Say Something Nice About Me, Baby"
1949		"And It Still Goes"
1950	MICHAEL TODD'S PEEP SHOW	A Brand New Rainbow in the Sky

Year	Production Title	Popular Songs
1950	MICHAEL TODD'S PEEP SHOW Indian Territory	Seems Like Yesterday
		"Spring Made a Fool of Me" "If You Should Leave Me" "Let Every Day Be Mother's Day"

* * *

AL STILLMAN

Al Stillman is a graduate of New York University. When the mammoth Radio City Music Hall opened in 1932, he was engaged to write special material for its stage shows and remained a member of its staff for several years. His first popular hit, "Song of the Blacksmith," was published the following year. Stillman was also in on the ground floor of the Center Theatre in Radio City and was the lyricist for its opening attraction "Virginia" in 1937. The score for the show included "An Old Flame Never Dies" (music by Arthur Schwartz). In 1940, Stillman wrote English lyrics for two Latin melodies which became popular as "I Want My Mama" and "The Breeze and I." Throughout the Forties, he supplied lyrics for several ice shows staged at the Center Theatre. The next decade found him collaborating with composer Robert Allen with whom he created such successes as "No, Not Much," "Chances Are" and "Teacher, Teacher." Al Stillman was born in New York City in 1906.

Year	Production Title	Popular Songs
1934		"Song of the Blacksmith" "How Can We Be Wrong?"
1935		"Cock-Eyed Mayor of Kaunakakai" "Tell Me That You Love Me" "It Must Have Been a Dream"
1936		"King of Swing" "Afterglow" "With Thee I Swing"
1937	VIRGINIA	An Old Flame Never Dies You and I Know (HP) Goodbye, Jonah
	When's Your Birthday?	

Year	Production Title	Popular Songs
1938	WHO'S WHO	
		"Bambina"
		"In My Little Red Book"
		"A Room with a View"
1939		"In the Middle of a Dream" (HP)
		"Many Dreams Ago"
		"The Shabby Old Cabby"
		"One-Two-Three Kick"
1940	EARL CARROLL'S VANITIES	I Want My Mama
	IT HAPPENS ON ICE	
		"The Breeze and I" (HP)
		"Say 'Si Si'"
		"Where Do You Keep Your Heart?"
1941		"Bless 'em All"
		"Taboo"
		"Now and Forever"
1942	STARS ON ICE	Juke Box Saturday Night
		"Lamp of Memory"
		"Sing, Everybody, Sing"
1944	She's a Sweetheart	
1945	Carnival in Costa Rica	
		"In the Middle of May"
		"Copacabana"
1947	ICETIME OF 1948	
1948	HOWDY, MR. ICE!	
		"Little Jack Frost Get Lost"
1949		"Who Do You Know in Heaven?"
1950	HOWDY, MR. ICE OF 1950	
	Harvey	
	Chain Lightning	
		"Don'cha Go 'Way Mad"
		"Happy Feet"
1951	Callaway Went Thataway	

Year	Production Title	Popular Songs
1952	USA Canteen (TV)	I Believe (HP-1)
1953		"You Alone" (HP) "My One and Only Heart"
1954		"Home for the Holidays" "There's Only One of You"
1955		"Moments to Remember" (HP)
1956		"Can You Find It in Your Heart?" "No, Not Much" (HP) "Who Needs You?"
1957	Lizzie	It's Not for Me to Say (HP) "Chances Are" (HP-1) "When I Am with You" "My Heart Reminds Me"
1958	Too Much, Too Soon	"Teacher, Teacher" "Enchanted Island" "If Dreams Come True"
1959	Happy Anniversary The FBI Story	Happy Anniversary "Every Step of the Way"
1962		"Meantime"
1963		"(I Love You and) Don't You Forget It" "The Little Boy"
1965		"Truly, Truly True"

* * *

JULE STYNE

London-born Jule Styne was a child prodigy who performed as a pianist with symphony orchestras when he was nine years old. His parents brought him to the United States in 1914. After an extensive musical education, he began playing in Chicago jazz bands.

He was twenty-two years old when his song "Sunday," written in
collaboration with Chester Conn, Ned Miller and Benny Kreuger,
became popular in 1927.   Four years later, Styne formed a dance
orchestra and worked as a performing musician until the mid-
Thirties.   He signed a contract as composer, arranger and vocal
coach for a motion picture studio in 1935, and his songs were
heard in a series of screen musicals starring Joan Davis and the
Ritz Brothers.   His talents were next employed by a smaller studio which specialized in low budget Westerns.   Gene Autry, Roy
Rogers and Judy Canova crooned his melodies in such epics as
"Back in the Saddle," "Bad Man of Deadwood," "Sheriff of Tomb-
stone" and "Sis Hopkins."   The initial film to produce hit songs
by Jule Styne was "Hit Parade of 1941" which introduced his first
Academy Award nominee "Who Am I?"   Styne's fortunes began
looking up in 1942 when his melodies "I Don't Want to Walk Without You" and "I've Heard That Song Before" became national favorites.   His primary lyricists during his Hollywood career were
Frank Loesser and Sammy Cahn.   He and Cahn made an effort to
establish themselves as Broadway songwriters in 1944 but their
production "Glad to See You" closed during its tryout.   Styne continued writing for films while girding himself for his next attack
on the legitimate stage.   When it came in 1947, the result was
"High Button Shoes" which ran for a year and a half!   The year
after its success, Styne received his sixth "Oscar" nomination for
"It's Magic" which Doris Day introduced in her first film.

    The production that firmly established Jule Styne as a lead-
ing Broadway composer was "Gentlemen Prefer Blondes" which
opened in 1949 and ran for two years.   The score for the show
(with lyrics by Leo Robin) was a major factor in making comedienne
Carol Channing the Toast of Broadway.   Four more stage musicals
followed during the early Fifties including "Peter Pan" in 1954.
The original production had floundered in its out-of-town tryouts
and Jule Styne and lyricists Betty Comden and Adolph Green were
enlisted to add new material.   After their work had been incorporated, the show opened in New York to critical acclaim and later
became a perennial on television.   The same year "Peter Pan"
triumphed, forty-nine year old Jule Styne finally won the Academy
Award for the title song of the film "Three Coins in the Fountain."
During the following decade, Styne supplied the music for such
outstanding Broadway musicals as "Bells Are Ringing," starring
Judy Holliday, "Gypsy", starring Ethel Merman, and his longest-
running hit "Funny Girl", starring Barbra Streisand.   After "Funny
Girl" in 1964, he suffered a string of five successive failures.
Although his "Hallelujah, Baby!" was selected as the Best Musical
of the Season, the award was little distinction since every musical
that opened in 1967 failed.   In 1972, Styne collaborated with Bob
Merrill on a stage adaptation of the movie "Some Like It Hot."
The musical version, titled "Sugar," received mixed reviews but
managed to run for a year.

    Over a span of 17 years, Jule Styne composed the music

for five productions which are listed among Broadway's longest-
running productions: "High Button Shoes, " "Gentlemen Prefer
Blondes, " "Bells Are Ringing, " "Gypsy" and "Funny Girl. " His
songs have been heard in more than 80 motion pictures which introduced ten songs nominated for "Oscars. "

Year	Production Title	Popular Songs
1927		"Sunday"
1938	Hold That Co-ed Straight, Place and Show Kentucky Moonshine	
1939	Pack Up Your Troubles Stop, Look and Love	
1940	The Hit Parade of 1941 Sing, Dance, Plenty Hot Girl from Havana The House Across the Bay Slightly Honorable Melody Ranch Melody and Moonlight	Who Am I? (AN) In the Cool of the Evening
1941	Sailors on Leave Angels with Broken Wings Puddin' Head Rookies on Parade Sis Hopkins Doctors Don't Tell Ice-Capades Rags to Riches Back in the Saddle Bad Man of Deadwood Down Mexico Way In Old Cheyenne Jessie James at Bay Nevada City Pals of the Pecos Ridin' on a Rainbow Sheriff of Tombstone The Singing Hill	Since You
1942	Youth on Parade Priorities on Parade	I've Heard That Song Before (AN) (HP-1) Conchita, Marquita, Lolita, Pepita, Rosita, Juanita Lopez You're in Love with Someone Else

Year	Production Title	Popular Songs
1942	Sweater Girl	I Don't Want to Walk Without You (HP-1) I Said No
	Sleepytime Gal	I Don't Want Anybody at All Barrelhouse Bessie from Basin Street
	Beyond the Blue Horizon The Powers Girl Ice-Capades Revue Johnny Doughboy The Old Homestead	
1943	Hit Parade of 1943 The Heat's On Larceny with Music Let's Face It Salute for Three Swing Your Partner Thumbs Up Henry Aldrich Swings It Shantytown	Change of Heart (AN)
1944	GLAD TO SEE YOU (closed in tryout) Follow the Boys Carolina Blues	Guess I'll Hang My Tears Out to Dry I'll Walk Alone (AN) (HP-1) There Goes That Song Again (HP) Poor Little Rhode Island
	Jam Session Step Lively	Vict'ry Polka Come Out, Come Out Wherever You Are And Then You Kissed Me (HP)
	Knickerbocker Holiday Janie	"It's Been a Long, Long Time" (HP-1) "Saturday Night (Is the Loneliest Night in the Week)" (HP)
1945	Anchors Aweigh	I Fall in Love Too Easily (AN) The Charm of You I Begged Her What Makes the Sunset?
	Tonight and Every Night The Stork Club	Anywhere (AN) "Let It Snow, Let It Snow, Let It Snow" (HP-1) "Can't You Read Between the Lines?" (HP)

Year	Production Title	Popular Songs
1946	Sweetheart of Sigma Chi Tars and Spars Cinderella Jones Earl Carroll's Sketch Book The Kid from Brooklyn	Five Minutes More (HP-1) I'm Glad I Waited for You When the One You Love Simply Won't Love Back I've Never Forgotten I Love an Old-Fashioned Song You're the Cause of It All "The Things We Did Last Summer" (HP)
1947	HIGH BUTTON SHOES It Happened in Brooklyn Ladies' Man	Papa, Won't You Dance with Me? I Still Get Jealous You're My Girl On a Sunday by the Sea Time After Time (HP) I Believe It's the Same Old Dream What Am I Gonna Do About You? I Gotta Gal I Love "We Knew It All the Time"
1948	Romance on the High Seas Two Guys from Texas Sons of Adventure Miracle of the Bells	It's Magic (AN) (HP-1) It's You or No One Every Day I Love You I Don't Care If It Rains All Night
1949	GENTLEMEN PREFER BLONDES It's a Great Feeling	Diamonds Are a Girl's Best Friend A Little Girl from Little Rock Bye, Bye Baby Just a Kiss Apart It's a Great Feeling (AN) (HP) Fiddle Dee Dee (HP) Blame My Absent-Minded Heart At the Cafe Rendezvous "Bop Goes My Heart"
1950	MICHAEL TODD'S PEEP SHOW	Stay with the Happy People

Year	Production Title	Popular Songs
1950	The West Point Story	
1951	TWO ON THE AISLE	If You Hadn't--but You Did Hold Me, Hold Me, Hold Me
	Meet Me After the Show	It's a Hot Night in Alaska Betting on a Man
	Two Tickets to Broadway Double Dynamite	
1952	Macao	
1953	HAZEL FLAGG	How Do You Speak to an Angel? Every Street's a Boulevard in Old New York Everybody Loves to Take a Bow
1954	PETER PAN	Never, Never Land Distant Melody
	Three Coins in the Fountain Living It Up	Three Coins in the Fountain (AA) (HP-1) Money Burns a Hole in My Pocket That's What I Like
1955	How to Be Very, Very Popular	
1956	BELLS ARE RINGING	Just in Time Long Before I Knew You The Party's Over
1957	Ruggles of Red Gap (TV)	Ride on a Rainbow
1958	SAY, DARLING	Dance Only with Me Something's Always Happening on the River
1959	GYPSY	Everything's Coming Up Roses Small World Let Me Entertain You
1960	DO RE MI Bells Are Ringing	Make Someone Happy
1961	SUBWAYS ARE FOR SLEEPING	Comes Once in a Lifetime I'm Just Taking My Time

Year	Production Title	Popular Songs
1962	Mr. Magoo's Christmas Carol (TV)	
1963	All the Way Home	
1964	FUNNY GIRL	People Don't Rain on My Parade You Are Woman, I Am Man
	FADE OUT-FADE IN What a Way to Go!	I Think That You and I Should Get Acquainted
		"Absent-Minded Me"
1965	The Dangerous Christmas of Red Riding Hood (TV)	
1967	HALLELUJAH, BABY!	
1968	DARLING OF THE DAY Funny Girl	Funny Girl (AN)
1970	LOOK TO THE LILIES	
1971	PRETTYBELLE (closed in tryout)	
1972	SUGAR	
1977	HELLZAPOPPIN' (closed in tryout)	

* * *

CHARLES TOBIAS

Harry, Charles, and Henry Tobias were all songwriters, but the more than 100 hit songs to which Charles contributed far exceeds that of either his older or younger brother. After finishing high school, he clerked in a men's clothing store and then worked as a song plugger for a music publishing firm in Boston. Tobias moved to New York City when he was twenty-two and decided to emulate his cousin-in-law Eddie Cantor by becoming a performer. His singing vaudeville act proved popular enough to earn him radio engagements in 1923. The previous year, he collaborated with his brother Harry and W. C. Polla on his first successful song "Girl of My Dreams."

Charles Tobias' outstanding lyrics of the 1930's included
"In the Valley of the Moon," "The Broken Record" and "Little
Lady Make-Believe." During the 1940's, he added "Trade Winds,"
"Rose O'Day" and "The Old Lamplighter" to his catalog of hits.
In 1954, Eddie Fisher adopted "May I Sing to You?" as his theme,
and 1963 found the Tobias number "Those Lazy, Hazy, Crazy
Days of Summer" high on popularity charts. The most lasting of
all his songs has been "Miss You" which he wrote in conjunction
with his two brothers in 1929. The composers with whom he
worked included Cliff Friend, Sammy Stept, and Nat Simon, and
among his co-lyricists were Haven Gillespie and Lew Brown.
Charles Tobias died in 1970 at the age of seventy-two.

Year	Production Title	Popular Songs
1922		"Girl of My Dreams"
1926		"Me Too (Ho, Ho, Ha, Ha)" "After My Laughter Came Tears" "Trudy"
1927		"A Dew-Dew-Dewy Day" "Just Another Day Wasted Away" "Everything's Made for Love"
1928	GOOD BOY	Don't Be Like That "Get Out and Get Under the Moon" "Giggling Gertie" "He's Tall, Dark and Handsome"
1929	KEEP IT CLEAN EARL CARROLL'S SKETCH BOOK Linda	"Ev'ry Day Away from You" "Gotta Great Big Date with a Little Bitta Girl" "Walking with My Sweetness Down Among the Sugar Cane" "I Can Get It for You Wholesale" "Miss You" (HP)
1930	The Cuckoos So Long Letty	

Year	Production Title	Popular Songs
1930		"When Your Hair Has Turned to Silver" "Somewhere in Old Wyoming"
1931		"Under Your Window Tonight" "I'm Just a Dancing Sweetheart" "You'll Be Mine in Apple Blossom Time" "One More Kiss Then Goodnight"
1932	EARL CARROLL'S VANITIES	"Somebody Loves You" "You'll Always Be the Same Sweetheart" "Whose Arms Are You in Tonight?"
1933		"In the Valley of the Moon" "Two Tickets to Georgia" "Goodnight, Little Girl of My Dreams" "Sing a Little Lowdown Tune"
1934	Gift of Gab	"An Old Water Mill" "Alice in Wonderland" "In an Old Log Cabin" "Throw Another Log on the Fire"
1935	EARL CARROLL'S SKETCH BOOK	Let's Swing It (HP) "Flowers for Madame" (HP) "A-Hunting We Will Go" "I'm Painting the Town Red" "Tiny Little Fingerprints"
1936		"The Broken Record" (HP) "Am I Gonna Have Trouble with You?" "Wake Up and Sing" "That Never-to-Be Forgotten Night" "It's the Gypsy in Me"

Year	Production Title	Popular Songs
1936		"Mickey Mouse's Birthday Party"
1937	You're a Sweetheart Life Begins in College	
		"It Seems Like Old Times" "Gee, but You're Swell" "I Want You for Christmas" "Love Marches On" "Here Comes the Girl" "I Bet You Tell That to All the Girls"
1938	HELLZAPOPPIN' Having Wonderful Time Start Cheering	My First Impression of You "Little Lady Make-Believe" (HP) "Is That the Way to Treat a Sweetheart?"
1939	YOKEL BOY	Comes Love (HP) Let's Make Memories To-night I Can't Afford to Dream "Start the Day Right"
1940	Forty Little Mothers	Little Curly Hair in a High Chair (HP) "Trade Winds" (HP-1) "Or Have I?" "A Prairie Fairy Tale" "I Hear Bluebirds"
1941	BANJO EYES	We Did It Before and We Can Do It Again "I Came Here to Talk for Joe" (HP) "Below the Equator"
1942	Private Buckaroo	Don't Sit Under the Apple Tree (HP-1) "Rose O'Day" (HP) "Wait for Me, Mary"
1943	She Has What It Takes	Moon on My Pillow

Year	Production Title	Popular Songs
1943	Forever and a Day	"I'm Sending X's to a Girl in Texas" "I Wish I Could Hide Inside This Letter" "You're Irish and You're Beautiful"
1944	Shine on Harvest Moon Hi, Beautiful Chip Off the Old Block	Time Waits for No One (HP) Don't Sweetheart Me (HP) "Just a Prayer Away" (HP) "There's a Lot of Moonlight Being Wasted"
1945	Patrick, the Great Saratoga Trunk	For the First Time (HP) As Long as I Live "No Can Do" (HP) "The Cocoanut Song" "Oh, Moytle" "White Orchids" "Her Bathing Suit Never Got Wet"
1946	Tomorrow Is Forever	Tomorrow Is Forever "The Old Lamplighter" (HP) "Coax Me a Little Bit" "I Used to Be Her One and Only"
1947	Song of Love Love and Learn Deep Valley	As Years Go By Would You Believe Me? "That's Where I Came In" "Home Is Where the Heart Is" "My Young and Foolish Heart"
1948		"No Longer" "I Remember Mama"
1949		"A Million Miles Away" "And It Still Goes" (HP) "Let Me Grow Old with You" "Merry Christmas Waltz" "The Rosewood Spinet" "The One Who Gets You"

Year	Production Title	Popular Songs
1950	The Daughter of Rosie O'Grady	"Zing Zing, Zoom Zoom" (HP) "You Missed the Boat" "The Bowling Song"
1951	On Moonlight Bay Faithfully Yours	Love Ya Faithfully Yours
1952	About Face	
1954		"May I Sing to You?" "The Mama Doll Song"
1955	A Man Called Peter	
1958	Kathy O'	
1962		"All Over the World"
1963		"Those Lazy, Hazy, Crazy Days of Summer" "Summer Green and Winter White" "That's What They Meant by the Good Old Summer-time"

* * *

HARRY TOBIAS

Harry Tobias is the second most successful of three brothers who became popular song writers. He was born in New York in 1895 and was educated in public schools in Worcester, Massachusetts. Harry wrote the lyrics for his first two hits in 1916, and the Tobias brothers were soon operating their own music publishing firm. After military service during World War I, he was active in real estate during the Florida land boom of the 1920's. His most famous song, "Miss You," was written in 1929 in collaboration with both Charles and Henry Tobias. During the Thirties and Forties, Harry Tobias supplied songs for three dozen motion pictures including "It's a Date" in which Deanna Durbin introduced "Love Is All."

Year	Production Title	Popular Songs
1916		"That Girl of Mine" "Take Me to My Alabam'"
1921	THE MIDNIGHT ROUNDERS	
1922		"Oo-oo Ernest, Are You Earnest with Me?" "Girl of My Dreams"
1928		"Giggling Gertie"
1929	EARL CARROLL'S SKETCH BOOK Linda	"Miss You" (HP) "Song of the Moonbeams" "Gotta Great Big Date with a Little Bitta Girl"
1930		"When It's Harvest Time" "The Wedding of the Birds"
1931		"Sweet and Lovely" (HP) "At Your Command" "I'm Sorry, Dear" "It's a Lonesome Old Town When You're Not Around" "All for the Love of Mike" "What Is It?" "I'm Gonna Get You" "Put Your Little Arms Around Me"
1932	Blondie of the Follies	
1933		"Here You Come with Love"
1934	Gift of Gab Countess of Monte Cristo	"Call of the Rockies" "Wild Honey" "The Daughter of Peggy O'Neill"
1935	The Old Homestead	"Rocky Mountain Express" "Paradise Valley"
1936	Devil on Horseback	So Divine Oh, Bella Mia

Year	Production Title	Popular Songs
1936	Trail Dust	Take Me Back to Those Wide Open Spaces
	One Rainy Afternoon With Love and Kisses Little Miss Nobody Dizzy Dames	
		"No Regrets" (HP)
1937	Sweetheart of the Navy Roll Along Cowboy	I Want You to Want Me On the Sunny Side of the Rockies
	The Barrier Meet the Boy Friend Criminal Lawyer Headin' East Swing While You're Able	
		"Sail Along, Silv'ry Moon" (HP) "Here Comes the Girl"
1938	Starlight Over Texas The Young in Heart	Starlight Over Texas
		"Lost and Found" "Chimes of Arcady"
1939	Made for Each Other Cafe Society	
1940	It's a Date Rancho Grande Shooting High Gaucho Serenade	Love Is All Swing of the Range
		"If It Wasn't for the Moon"
1941	Top Sergeant Mulligan	
1942		"Wait for Me, Mary" "I'll Keep the Lovelight Burning" "Rolleo Rolling Along"
1943	She Has What It Takes You're a Lucky Fellow, Mr. Smith Stormy Weather	
1944	Night Club Girl Sensations of 1945 I'm from Arkansas Winged Victory	

Year	Production Title	Popular Songs
1945	I'll Tell the World	
		"A Thousand Times a Day"
1946		"Go to Sleepy, Little Baby" "I Used to Be Her One and Only" "Bow Legged Cowboy"
1948	Moonrise	
		"No Longer"
1950		"Without Your Love" "The Bowling Song" "The Laundromat Song" "Ashes of Roses"
1951		"Star of Hope"

* * *

ROY TURK

Lyricist Roy Turk majored in architecture at a college in New York City. While serving in the Navy during World War I, he wrote special material which Nora Bayes and Sophie Tucker performed in their vaudeville acts. Turk turned professional songwriter when he was twenty-seven years old. Although his lyrics were featured in three Broadway musicals and eight motion pictures from 1922 through 1934, most of his hits became successes without being showcased in productions. Among his popular songs were "I'll Get By," "Mean to Me" and "Walkin' My Baby Back Home." He shared credit for the lyrics to "Where the Blue of the Night Meets the Gold of the Day" with Bing Crosby who used the song as his theme. The composer with whom Turk collaborated most often was Fred Ahlert. Roy Turk was forty-two when he died in 1934.

Year	Production Title	Popular Songs
1919		"Oh! How I Laugh When I Think How I Cried About You"
1920		"You Oughta See My Baby"
1921		"How Many Times"
1922	PLANTATION REVUE	

Year	Production Title	Popular Songs
1922		"Aggravatin' Papa" "I'll Be in My Dixie Home Again Tomorrow" "Just Because You're You (That's Why I Love You)"
1923	EARL CARROLL'S VANITIES	"Beale Street Mamma" "My Sweetie Went Away"
1924	DIXIE TO BROADWAY	Mandy, Make Up Your Mind Dixie Dreams I'm a Little Blackbird Looking for a Bluebird "From One 'Til Two (I Always Dream of You)" "Maybe She'll Write Me"
1925		I'm Gonna Charleston Back to Charleston"
1926		"Are You Lonesome Tonight?" "Gimme a Little Kiss, Will Ya, Huh?" "Someone Is Losin' Susan" "Two Ton Tessie"
1927		"Just Another Day Wasted Away" "After My Laughter Came Tears"
1928		"I'll Get By" (HP) "Evening Star"
1929	Port of Dreams Marianne Girl on the Barge	"Mean to Me" "I'll Never Ask for More" "The One That I Love Loves Me" "To Be in Love"
1930	Free and Easy In Gay Madrid Children of Pleasure	It Must Be You The "Free and Easy" Into My Heart The Whole Darned Thing's for You

Year	Production Title	Popular Songs
1930	Navy Blues	"Walkin' My Baby Back Home" (HP-1) "We're Friends Again"
1931	Blonde Crazy	"I Don't Know Why (I Just Do)" (HP) "Why Dance?" "Can't You See?"
1932	The Big Broadcast	Where the Blue of the Night Meets the Gold of the Day "Love, You Funny Thing" "Contented" "How Can You Say You Love Me?" "I'll Follow You" "You'll Get By" "I'm Still Without a Sweetheart with Summer Coming On"
1933		"I Couldn't Tell Them What to Do" "Blue Hours"
1934	Let's Talk It Over Cat's Paw	

* * *

JAMES VAN HEUSEN

While still in high school, Jimmy Van Heusen played the piano and sang on a local radio station in his home town of Syracuse, New York. He dropped out of Syracuse University in his sophomore year and supported himself working as an elevator operator, and as a staff pianist for a music publisher. He began making a name for himself as a composer with "There's a House in Harlem for Sale" in 1934. Four years later, three of his songs made "Your Hit Parade." In 1939, the curtain went up on Broadway's "Swingin' the Dream" in which "Darn That Dream" (lyrics by Eddie DeLange) was introduced. That same year, Van Heusen had 11 other hits including "Heaven Can Wait," "All I Remember Is You" and "Can I Help It" with lyrics by DeLange, and "Oh, You

Crazy Moon" and "Imagination" with lyrics by Johnny Burke. With his success, he became his own music publisher.

After contributing to "Billy Rose's Aquacade" staged at the New York World's Fair in 1940, twenty-seven year old Van Heusen signed with Paramount where he and Burke wrote songs for more than two dozen motion pictures. The Bing Crosby-Bob Hope "Road" series alone yielded such successes as "It's Always You," "Moonlight Becomes You," "Personality" and "But Beautiful." Van Heusen received his first "Oscar" for his music to "Swinging on a Star" from the 1944 release "Going My Way." He and Burke also supplied the score for the Broadway musicals "Nellie Bly" (1946) and "Carnival in Flanders" (1953) but neither was successful. In 1955, Van Heusen formed a partnership with lyricist Sammy Cahn and his career reached even greater heights. He collected television's "Emmy" award for the song "Love and Marriage" (1955) and won "Oscars" for "All the Way" (1957), "High Hopes" (1959) and "Call Me Irresponsible" (1963). In addition to his wins, his melodies have received nine other Academy Award nominations! In 1965 and 1966, he returned to Broadway for "Skyscraper" and "Walking Happy." Jimmy Van Heusen was born in 1913, and has created 120 hit songs in 41 years. He's the third most successful composer in film history.

Year	Production Title	Popular Songs
1934		"There's a House in Harlem for Sale"
1937		"If You're Ever in My Arms Again"
1938		"So Help Me" (HP) "Deep in a Dream" (HP) "Good for Nothin' but Love" (HP) "It's the Dreamer in Me" "This Is Madness" "Do You Wanna Jump, Children?" "When a Prince of a Fella Meets a Cinderella"
1939	SWINGIN' THE DREAM	Darn That Dream (HP-1) Peace, Brother "Heaven Can Wait" (HP-1) "Oh, You Crazy Moon" (HP) "All I Remember Is You" (HP) "Can I Help It?" (HP) "Speaking of Heaven" (HP)

Year	Production Title	Popular Songs
1939		"Blue Rain" "Shake Down the Stars" (HP) "I Thought About You" "Imagination" (HP-1) "Make with the Kisses"
1940	BILLY ROSE'S AQUACADE (New York World's Fair) Love Thy Neighbor	You Think of Everything (HP) Do You Know Why? Isn't That Just Like Love? Dearest, Darest I? "All This and Heaven Too" (HP) "Polka Dots and Moonbeams" "Looking for Yesterday" (HP) "Let's All Meet at My House"
1941	Playmates Road to Zanzibar	Humpty Dumpty Heart (HP) How Long Did I Dream? It's Always You (HP) Birds of a Feather
1942	Road to Morocco My Favorite Spy	Moonlight Becomes You (HP-1) Constantly Road to Morocco Ain't Got a Dime to My Name Got the Moon in My Pocket Just Plain Lonesome "Absent-Minded Moon"
1943	Dixie	Sunday, Monday or Always (HP-1) If You Please (HP)
1944	Going My Way Lady in the Dark And the Angels Sing Belle of the Yukon	Swinging on a Star (AA) (HP) The Day After Forever Going My Way Suddenly It's Spring It Could Happen to You (HP) Like Someone in Love Sleigh Ride in July (HP) "Nancy, with the Laughing Face"
1945	The Bells of St. Mary's	Aren't You Glad You're You? (AN) (HP)

Year	Production Title	Popular Songs
1945	Road to Utopia	Personality (HP) Welcome to My Dream It's Anybody's Spring Put It There, Pal
	The Great John L Duffy's Tavern	A Friend of Yours (HP) "Yah-Ta-Ta, Yah-Ta-Ta"
1946	NELLIE BLY Cross My Heart	Just My Luck That Little Dream Got No- where
	My Heart Goes Crazy	So Would I My Heart Goes Crazy
1947	Welcome Stranger	As Long as I'm Dreaming Smile Right Back at the Sun Country Style My Heart Is a Hobo
	Road to Rio	But Beautiful (HP) You Don't Have to Know the Language Apalachicola, Florida
	Variety Girl Magic Town	
1948	The Emperor Waltz Mystery in Mexico	
1949	Top o' the Morning A Connecticut Yankee in King Arthur's Court	You're in Love with Someone Once and for Always When Is Sometime? If You Stub Your Toe on the Moon
1950	Mr. Music	Life Is So Peculiar High on the List And You'll Be Home
	Riding High	Sunshine Cake Someplace on Anywhere Road "Early American"
1952	Road to Bali	Moonflowers To See You "Somewhere Along the Way" (HP)
1953	CARNIVAL IN FLANDERS Little Boy Lost	Here's That Rainy Day The Magic Window

Year	Production Title	Popular Songs
1954	Young at Heart	You, My Love
	Vera Cruz	
		"I Could Have Told You"
1955	The Tender Trap	(Love Is) The Tender Trap (AN)
	Not as a Stranger	Not as a Stranger
	Our Town (TV)	Love and Marriage (HP)
		The Impatient Years
		Look to Your Heart
		"How Can I Replace You?"
1956	Anything Goes	
	Pardners	
		"It's Better in the Dark"
		"My Dream Sonata"
1957	The Joker Is Wild	All the Way (AA) (HP-1)
1958	Some Came Running	To Love and Be Loved (AN)
	Indiscreet	Indiscreet
	Paris Holiday	
		"Only the Lonely"
		"Come Fly with Me"
1959	A Hole in the Head	High Hopes (AA)
		All My Tomorrows
	They Came to Cordura	They Came to Cordura
	Say One for Me	
	This Earth Is Mine	
	Journey to the Center of the Earth	
	Night of the Quarter Moon	
	Holiday for Lovers	
1960	High Time	The Second Time Around (AN)
	Wake Me When It's Over	Wake Me When It's Over
	Who Was That Lady?	
	The World of Suzie Wong	
	Ocean's Eleven	
	Let's Make Love	
1961	Pocketful of Miracles	Pocketful of Miracles (AN)
1962	COME ON STRONG (play)	
	Road to Hong Kong	Warmer Than a Whisper
	Boys' Night Out	The Boys' Night Out
1963	Papa's Delicate Condition	Call Me Irresponsible (AA)

Year	Production Title	Popular Songs
1963	Come Blow Your Horn Under the Yum Yum Tree Four for Texas My Six Loves Johnny Cool	
1964	Robin and the 7 Hoods	My Kind of Town (AN) Style I Like to Lead When I Dance
	Where Love Has Gone The Pleasure Seekers	Where Love Has Gone (AN) Everything Makes Music When You're in Love
	Honeymoon Hotel	"Love Is a Bore"
1965	SKYSCRAPER	I Only Miss Her When I Think of Her Everybody Has the Right to Be Wrong
		"September of My Years"
1966	WALKING HAPPY	What Makes It Happen? Walking Happy
1967	Thoroughly Modern Millie	Thoroughly Modern Millie (AN)
1968	Star!	Star! (AN)
1969	The Great Bank Robbery	
1971	Journey Back to Oz (TV)	

* * *

ALBERT VON TILZER

Albert Gumm was a product of Indianapolis, Indiana, where he was born in 1878. Like his older brother Harry, Albert was a self-taught pianist and assumed his brother's adopted name of Von Tilzer. Albert was twenty-two when he followed Harry to New York City. He supported himself working as a department store buyer while studying harmony. It took him only a year to interest a publisher in "Good Morning, Carrie" which was popularized in 1901. Seven years later, Albert wrote the music for one of the most famous songs in American history--"Take Me Out to the Ball

Game" (lyrics by Jack Norworth). The second of his most enduring melodies was "Put Your Arms Around Me, Honey" written in 1910 with lyricist Junie McCree. Among his frequent collaborators was Lew Brown who supplied the words for "I'm the Lonesomest Gal in Town" and "Oh, By Jingo." Von Tilzer's "I'll Be with You in Apple Blossom Time," published in 1920, was successfully revived by the Andrews Sisters in the late Thirties. His last success, "I'm Praying to St. Christopher," was written when he was seventy-two. Albert Von Tilzer died six years later.

Year	Production Title	Popular Songs
1901		"Good Morning, Carrie"
1903		"That's What the Daisy Said" "I Take Things Easy"
1904		"Teasing" "Tell Me with Your Eyes" "You Mustn't Pick Plums from My Plum Tree" "Bunker Hill"
1905		"The Moon Has His Eyes on You" "A Picnic for Two" "Goodbye, Sweetheart, Good-bye" "Have You Seen My Henry Brown?"
1906	ABOUT TOWN	"Just for Auld Lang Syne" "Bessie and Her Little Brown Bear"
1907		"Honey Boy"
1908	NEARLY A HERO	Since My Mother Was a Girl "Take Me Out to the Ball Game" "Smarty" "Bl_nd and P_g Spells Blind P̄ig" "The Story the Picture Blocks Told" "Good Evening, Caroline"
1909		"Carrie" "Take Me Up with You, Dearie"

Year	Production Title	Popular Songs
1909		"Nora Malone" "How Do You Do, Miss Josephine?"
1910		"Put Your Arms Around Me, Honey" (HP) "Oh, That Moonlight Glide" "I'll Get You Yet" "I Want Somebody to Flirt With"
1911	THE HAPPIEST NIGHT OF HIS LIFE	"The Song That Reaches Irish Hearts" "That College Rag" "On the New York, New Haven and Hartford"
1912		"I'm the Lonesomest Gal in Town" "Kentucky Sue" "Please Don't Take My Lovin' Man Away" "Pucker Up Your Lips, Miss Lindy" "Parisienne" "Here Comes the Bride That Took My Lovin' Man Away"
1915		"My Little Girl" "Floating Down the Mississippi River on My Way to New Orleans"
1916		"'Forever' Is a Long, Long Time" "It's the Irish in Your Eye, It's the Irish in Your Smile" "Put on Your Slippers and Fill Up Your Pipe" "Oh, How She Could Yacki, Hacki, Wicki, Wacki, Woo" "Down Where the Swanee River Flows"
1917	HITCHY-KOO	I May Be Gone for a Long, Long Time

Year	Production Title	Popular Songs
1917		"Au Revoir, but Not Good-bye, Soldier Boy" "Give Me the Moonlight, Give Me the Girl" "When the Moon Goes Down in Dixie" "Eve Wasn't Modest Till She Ate That Apple"
1918		"Waters of Venice--Floating Down the Sleepy Lagoon"
1919	LINGER LONGER LETTY	Oh, By Jingo "Chili Bean" "Wait Till You Get Them Up in the Air, Boys" "The Alcoholic Blues" "Dear Old Daddy Long Legs" "Somewhere Someone Is Waiting for Me"
1920	HONEY GIRL	"I'll Be with You in Apple Blossom Time" "I Used to Love You but It's All Over Now" "(Oh Gee! Say Gee! You Ought to See) My Gee Gee from the Fiji Isles" "When the Autumn Leaves Begin to Fall"
1921		"Dapper Dan" "I've Got the Travelling Choo Choo Blues" "Big Chief Wally Ho Wo (He'd Wiggle His Way to Her Wigwam)"
1922	THE GINGHAM GIRL	As Long as I Have You "Oh, How I Hate That Fellow Nathan"
1923	ADRIENNE	
1926		"My Cutey's Due at Two to Two Today"
1927	BYE, BYE BONNIE	

Year	Production Title	Popular Songs
1933	Rainbow Over Broadway	
1934	Gift of Gab	Don't Let This Waltz Mean Goodbye Somebody Looks Good
1935	Here Comes the Band	Roll Along Prairie Moon (HP) "Rocky Mountain Express"
1938	Rawhide	When a Cowboy Goes to Town
1939	Sundown on the Prairie	
1950		"I'm Praying to St. Christopher"

* * *

THOMAS WALLER

Thomas Waller is one of the few popular song writers whose name is known to the general public. His notoriety was due to his success as "Fats" Waller--one of the nation's leading Negro entertainers. Waller was born in New York in 1904, and learned to play the organ in the Baptist Church where his father was employed as the pastor. Waller began his career as a theatre organist in silent movie houses in the nation's capital. He also played jazz piano and frequently accompanied blues singer Bessie Smith. His talent as a vocalist earned him a featured spot in the 1928 Broadway revue "Keep Shufflin'," and his 1929 song hits "Ain't Misbehavin'" and "Honeysuckle Rose" (both with lyrics by Andy Razaf) established him as a leading popular music composer. During the Thirties, "Fats" Waller became a successful recording artist, was a frequent performer in motion pictures, and toured Europe with his own dance orchestra. In 1943, he supplied the score for the Broadway musical "Early to Bed." That same year, he died of pneumonia at the age of only thirty-eight.

Year	Production Title	Popular Songs
1924		"Bloody Razor Blues" "Bullet Wound Blues" "In Harlem's Araby"
1925		"Squeeze Me"

Year	Production Title	Popular Songs
1925		"Anybody Here Want to Try My Cabbage?"
1926	TAN TOWN TOPICS	Senorita Blues
		"Georgia Bo-Bo" "Old Folks' Shuffle"
1927		"I'm Goin' Huntin'" "There'll Come a Time When You'll Need Me"
1928	KEEP SHUFFLIN'	Willow Tree
		"The Whiteman Stomp"
1929	HOT CHOCOLATES	Ain't Misbehavin' What Did I Do to Be So Black and Blue? Sweet Savannah Sue
		"Honeysuckle Rose" "I've Got a Feeling I'm Falling" "My Fate Is in Your Hands" "Zonky"
1930		"Blue, Turning Grey Over You" "Keep a Song in Your Soul" "Rollin' Down the River"
1931		"Concentratin' on You" "I'm Crazy 'Bout My Baby" "Take It from Me"
1932		"Keepin' Out of Mischief Now" "You're My Ideal" "Strange as It Seems" "Sheltered by the Stars, Cradled by the Moon" "If It Ain't Love" "Doin' What I Please" "Lonesome Me"
1933		"Ain'tcha Glad?"
1934		"How Can You Face Me?"
1936		"Stealin' Apples"

Year	Production Title	Popular Songs
1937		"Our Love Was Meant to Be" "Alligator Crawl"
1938		"Patty Cake, Patty Cake (Baker Man)" "The Joint Is Jumpin'"
1940		"Black Maria"
1941		"All That Meat and No Potatoes"
1943	EARLY TO BED	There's a Man in My Life

* * *

HARRY WARREN

Brooklyn-born Harry Warren is the third most successful songwriter in America after Tin Pan Alley (only 10 percent of his hits were published before the demise of the Alley). He is also the most successful songwriter in the history of motion pictures. The more that 75 films to which he's contributed during his 45 year career in Hollywood have introduced 131 songs that achieved national popularity. It was not uncommon for three or four hits to emerge from a single Warren film score. He is first in the number (39) of songs that made "Your Hit Parade," and second in the number (12) that rose to the Number One position.

Warren taught himself to play several musical instruments and traveled as a drummer in a carnival band when he was only fifteen years old. He later worked as a stage hand in vaudeville theatres, and as a prop man for a movie studio in New York. His studio assignments increased to performing as an extra, playing music to put the silent screen players in the proper mood, and sometimes assisting the director. After serving in the Navy during World War I, Warren played the piano in New York cafes and became a song plugger for a music publishing firm. He was approaching thirty when he collaborated with lyricist Edgar Leslie on the 1922 hit "Rose of the Rio Grande." During the next decade, his successes included "Nagasaki," "Would You Like to Take a Walk?," "Crying for the Carolines," "Ooh! That Kiss," and "I Found a Million Dollar Baby." Among the lyricists with whom he worked during this period were Mort Dixon, Joe Young, Sam Lewis, and Billy Rose.

In 1932, Warren settled at Warner Bros. Studios with a new

collaborator--lyricist Al Dubin. For the next six years, Warren
and Dubin created dozens of popular film songs including "We're
in the Money," "You're Getting to Be a Habit with Me," "I'll
String Along with You," "I Only Have Eyes for You," "She's a
Latin from Manhattan," "Don't Give Up the Ship," and "Remember
Me?" The year Warren won his first "Oscar" for "Lullaby of
Broadway" (1935), 20 of his melodies were national favorites.   As
the Forties began, Warren started working with his second major
collaborator--Mack Gordon.   For five years, Warren and Gordon
supplied Fox Studios with such hits as "Down Argentina Way,"
"Chattanooga Choo-Choo," "I Had the Craziest Dream," the 1943
"Oscar"-winning "You'll Never Know," and "The More I See You."
Warren also set Johnny Mercer's lyric "On the Atchison, Topeka
and the Santa Fe" to music and collected his third "Oscar" for it.
In addition to his three winners, eight more of his songs have
been Academy Award contenders.   Harry Warren wrote only one
Broadway musical after he moved to Hollywood--the unsuccessful
"Shangri-La" in 1956.

Year	Production Title	Popular Songs
1922		"Rose of the Rio Grande"
1923		"Home in Pasadena"
1924		"The Only Only One"
1926		"I Love My Baby, My Baby Loves Me" "Where Do You Work-a John?" "You Gotta Know How to Love"
1927		"Away Down South in Heaven" "One Sweet Letter from You" "Clementine from New Orleans"
1928		"Nagasaki" "Where the Shy Little Violets Grow" "Old Man Sunshine--Little Boy Bluebird" "Hello, Montreal"
1929	Wolf Song	Mi Amado "Absence Makes the Heart Grow Fonder" "Here We Are"

Year	Production Title	Popular Songs
1929		"Where the Sweet Forget-Me-Nots Remember"
1930	SWEET AND LOW	Would You Like to Take a Walk?
		Cheerful Little Earful
		He's Not Worth Your Tears
	Spring Is Here	Crying for the Carolines
		Have a Little Faith in Me
		"The River and Me"
		"Reminiscing"
		"Tellin' It to the Daisies"
		"I Remember You from Somewhere"
		"Wasting My Love on You"
		"Gid-Ap Garibaldi"
		"Cover a Clover with Kisses"
1931	BILLY ROSE'S CRAZY QUILT	I Found a Million Dollar Baby
		Sing a Little Jingle
	THE LAUGH PARADE	You're My Everything
		Ooh! That Kiss
		The Torch Song
		"By the River Sainte Marie"
		"When the Shepherd Leads His Flock Back Home"
1932	The Crooner	Three's a Crowd
		"Too Many Tears"
		"Deep in Your Eyes"
		"Someone to Care For"
1933	Forty-Second Street	You're Getting to Be a Habit with Me
		Forty-Second Street
		Shuffle Off to Buffalo
		Young and Healthy
	Gold Diggers of 1933	We're in the Money (Gold Digger's Song)
		Pettin' in the Park
		The Shadow Waltz
		Remember My Forgotten Man
		I've Got to Sing a Torch Song
	Footlight Parade	Shanghai Lil
		Honeymoon Hotel

Year	Production Title	Popular Songs
1933	Roman Scandals	Keep Young and Beautiful
		No More Love
		Build a Little Home
1934	Wonder Bar	Don't Say Good Night
		Goin' to Heaven on a Mule
		Why Do I Dream Those Dreams?
		Wonder Bar
	Moulin Rouge	The Boulevard of Broken Dreams
		Song of Surrender
		Coffee in the Morning, Kisses at Night
	Twenty Million Sweethearts	I'll String Along with You
		Fair and Warmer
	Dames	I Only Have Eyes for You
1935	Gold Diggers of 1935	Lullaby of Broadway (AA) (HP-1)
		The Words Are in My Heart
		I'm Goin' Shoppin' with you
	Go into Your Dance	She's a Latin from Manhattan (HP)
		About a Quarter to Nine (HP)
		The Little Things You Used to Do
		Go into Your Dance
	Broadway Gondolier	The Rose in Her Hair (HP)
		Lulu's Back in Town (HP)
		Outside of You
		Sweet and Slow
	Shipmates Forever	Don't Give Up the Ship (HP)
		I'd Love to Take Orders from You
		I'd Rather Listen to Your Eyes
	Stars Over Broadway	Where Am I? (HP)
		You Let Me Down
	Page Miss Glory	Page Miss Glory (HP)
	In Caliente	Muchacha
	Sweet Music	Sweet Music
	Living on Velvet	Living on Velvet
1936	Gold Diggers of 1937	With Plenty of Money and You (HP-1)
		All's Fair in Love and War
	Cain and Mabel	I'll Sing You a Thousand Love Songs (HP-1)

Year	Production Title	Popular Songs
1936	Sing Me a Love Song	Summer Night
		The Little House That Love Built
	Hearts Divided	My Kingdom for a Kiss
	Colleen	
	Sons O' Guns	
	Stolen Holiday	
1937	Mr. Dodd Takes the Air	Remember Me? (AN) (HP-1)
		Am I Love?
	Melody for Two	September in the Rain (HP-1)
		Melody for Two
	The Singing Marine	I Know Now (HP)
		'Cause My Baby Says It's So (HP)
		The Song of the Marines (We're Shoving Right Off)
		Night Over Shanghai
		The Lady Who Couldn't Be Kissed
		You Can't Run Away from Love Tonight
	San Quentin	How Could You? (HP)
	Marked Woman	
1938	Going Places	Jeepers Creepers (AN) (HP-1)
		Say It with a Kiss
	Gold Diggers in Paris	Daydreaming All Night Long (HP)
		The Latin Quarter
		A Stranger in Paree
		I Wanna Go Back to Bali
		Put That Down in Writing
	Hard to Get	You Must Have Been a Beautiful Baby (HP-1)
	Garden of the Moon	The Girl Friend of the Whirling Dervish
		Confidentially
		Love Is Where You Find It
		Garden of the Moon
	Cowboy from Brooklyn	
		"Something Tells Me"
		"You're an Education"
1939	Naughty But Nice	Hooray for Spinach
		In a Moment of Weakness
	Honolulu	This Night Will Be My Souvenir
		Honolulu

Year	Production Title	Popular Songs
1939	Wings of the Navy	"Tears from My Inkwell" (HP)
1940	Down Argentine Way	Down Argentina Way (AN) (HP)
		Two Dreams Met (HP)
	Tin Pan Alley	You Say the Sweetest Things, Baby
	Young People	I Wouldn't Take a Million
		"Devil May Care" (HP)
1941	Sun Valley Serenade	Chattanooga Choo-Choo (AN) (HP-1)
		I Know Why
		It Happened in Sun Valley
	That Night in Rio	I Yi Yi Yi Yi
		Chica Chica Boom Chic
	Week-End in Havana	Tropical Magic
	Great American Broadcast	Long Ago Last Night
1942	Orchestra Wives	I've Got a Gal in Kalamazoo (AN) (HP-1)
		Serenade in Blue (HP)
		At Last (HP)
	Springtime in the Rockies	I Had the Craziest Dream (HP)
	Iceland	There Will Never Be Another You (HP)
1943	Hello, Frisco, Hello	You'll Never Know (AA) (HP-1)
	Sweet Rosie O'Grady	My Heart Tells Me (HP-1)
1944	The Gang's All Here	No Love, No Nothin' (HP)
		A Journey to a Star
		"You've Got Me Where You Want Me"
1945	Diamond Horseshoe	The More I See You (HP-1)
		In Acapulco
		I Wish I Knew (HP)
	Yolanda and the Thief	Coffee Time
		Yolanda
		"Carnival"
1946	The Harvey Girls	On the Atchison, Topeka and the Sante Fe (AA) (HP)

Year	Production Title	Popular Songs
1946	The Harvey Girls	Wait and See (HP)
	Ziegfeld Follies	This Heart of Mine
		"This Is Always" (HP)
		"Me and the Blues"
1947		"Every So Often"
1948	Summer Holiday	The Stanley Steamer
		Spring Isn't Everything
		"The First Time I Kissed You"
1949	My Dream Is Yours	Someone Like You (HP)
		My Dream Is Yours
	The Barkleys of Broadway	My One and Only Highland Fling (HP)
		You'd Be Hard to Replace
1950	Summer Stock	You, Wonderful You
		If You Feel Like Singing, Sing
		Friendly Star
	Pagan Love Song	The Sea of the Moon
1951	Texas Carnival	
1952	Just for You	Zing a Little Zong (AN)
		A Flight of Fancy
		I'll Si, Si Ya in Bahia
	The Belle of New York	When I'm Out with the Belle of New York
	Skirts Ahoy!	
1953	The Caddy	That's Amore (AN) (HP)
1955	Artists and Models	Inamorata
	Marty	
	The Legend of Wyatt Earp (TV)	
1956	SHANGRI-LA	
	The Birds and the Bees	
1957	An Affair to Remember	An Affair to Remember (AN)
1958	Separate Tables	Separate Tables
	Rock-A-Bye Baby	Dormi, Dormi, Dormi

Year	Production Title	Popular Songs
1959	These Thousand Hills	These Thousand Hills
1960	Cinderfella	Somebody
1961	The Ladies' Man	
1962	Satan Never Sleeps	Satan Never Sleeps
1964		"If You Ever Need Me"
1968	Rosie	

* * *

NED WASHINGTON

Ned Washington began his career as a Master of Ceremonies in vaudeville. He also functioned as a theatrical agent and wrote special material for stage performers. For the first six years of his songwriting career, he alternated between Broadway revues and motion pictures. He was twenty-seven when his lyrics were heard in the 1928 edition of "Earl Carroll's Vanities." The following year, he and co-lyricist Herb Magidson wrote the hit "Singin' in the Bathtub" (music by Michael Cleary) which was introduced in the film "The Show of Shows." In 1932, he collaborated with composer George Bassman on "I'm Gettin' Sentimental Over You" which became the theme song of the Tommy Dorsey Orchestra, and with Eugene Gifford on "Smoke Rings" which the Glen Gray Casa Loma Orchestra adopted as its signature. After "Blackbirds of 1933," Washington became a full-time Hollywood lyric writer.

It took Washington just six years after the Academy of Motion Picture Arts and Sciences established its Best Song category to win two "Oscars." The 1940 full-length cartoon "Pinocchio" netted him both the Best Song award for "When You Wish Upon a Star" (music by Leigh Harline) and the statuette for the Best Original Score. Two of his most frequent partners were composers Victor Young, with whom he wrote "Stella by Starlight" and "My Foolish Heart," and Dimitri Tiomkin with whom he created the 1952 "Oscar" winner "Do Not Forsake Me (High Noon)." Ned Washington was born in Scranton, Pennsylvania, in 1901 and died in 1976.

Year	Production Title	Popular Songs
1928	EARL CARROLL'S VANITIES	

Year	Production Title	Popular Songs
1929	Show of Shows	Singin' in the Bathtub
	Forward Pass	H'lo, Baby
	Tiger Rose	The Day You Fall in Love
1930	THE VANDERBILT REVUE	
	HELLO, PARIS	
	TATTLE TALES	My Impression of You
	(closed in tryout)	
	College Lovers	
	Lillies of the Field	
	No, No Nanette	
	Little Johnny Jones	
1931	Road to Singapore	
	Bright Lights	
		"I'm an Unemployed Sweet-heart"
		"Makin' Faces at the Man in the Moon"
		"It's Not Like That (C'est Pas Comme Ca)"
1932		"I'm Gettin' Sentimental Over You"
		"Smoke Rings"
		"My Love"
		"Can't We Talk It Over?"
		"Someone Stole Gabriel's Horn"
		"Waltzing in a Dream"
		"Got the South in My Soul"
		"Love Me Tonight"
		"My Romance"
		"Lazy Rhapsody"
1933	MURDER AT THE VANITIES	Sweet Madness
	BLACKBIRDS	A Hundred Years from To-day
		"(I Don't Stand) A Ghost of a Chance"
		"I'll Be Faithful"
		"I'd Be Telling a Lie"
		"Love Is the Thing"
		"Any Time, Any Day, Any-where"
		"Shadows on the Window"
		"Stay Out of My Dreams"
1934	Viva Villa!	La Cucaracha

Year	Production Title	Popular Songs
1934	Girl from Missouri	"London on a Rainy Night" "Love Me" "Your Love" "Give Me a Heart to Sing To"
1935	Here Comes the Band A Night at the Opera Kind Lady The Perfect Gentle- man	Headin' Home You're My Thrill Cosi Cosa
1936	Robin Hood of El Dorado	"Breakin' in a Pair of Shoes"
1937	The Hit Parade The Big Show Dodge City Trail	Sweet Heartache "I Want You for Chirstmas"
1938	Romance in the Dark Tropic Holiday	The Nearness of You (HP) The Lamp on the Corner Tonight Will Live
1939	All Women Have Secrets	
1940	Pinocchio A Night at Earl Carroll's Arise My Love	When You Wish Upon a Star (AA) (HP-1) Jiminy Cricket Give a Little Whistle I've Got No Strings One Look at You
1941	Dumbo I Wanted Wings	Baby Mine (AN)
1942	Saludos Amigos Reap the Wild Wind	Saludos Amigos (AN) Reap the Wild Wind
1943	For Whom the Bell Tolls Hands Across the Border Sleepy Lagoon	A Love Like This Hands Across the Border
1944	Brazil Passage to Marseilles	Rio de Janeiro (AN) Some Day I'll Meet You Again (HP)

Year	Production Title	Popular Songs
1944	Cowboy and the Senorita	
	Call of the South Seas	
		"Stella by Starlight"
1945	Mexicana	
		"Don't Let Me Dream"
1947	Green Dolphin Street	On Green Dolphin Street
	I Walk Alone	Don't Call It Love
	The Long Night	
1949	My Foolish Heart	My Foolish Heart (AN) (HP-1)
	Deadly Is the Female	Mad About You
	The Lucky Stiff	
	Mrs. Mike	
1950		"You're Not in My Arms Tonight"
1951	The Wild Blue Yonder	
		"A Woman's Intuition"
1952	High Noon	Do Not Forsake Me (High Noon) (AA)
	The Happy Time	
	The Greatest Show on Earth	
1953	Miss Sadie Thompson	Sadie Thompson's Song (Blue Pacific Blues) (AN)
		The Heat Is On
		Hear No Evil--See No Evil
	Return to Paradise	Return to Paradise
	Take the High Ground	
	So Big	
	Let's Do It Again	
	Bring Your Smile Along	
	A Prize of Gold	
1954	The High and the Mighty	The High and the Mighty (AN) (HP)
	The Adventures of Hajji Baba	Hajji Baba
1955	Strange Lady in Town	Strange Lady in Town
	The Man from Laramie	The Man from Laramie
	Timberjack	
	Wichita	
	Land of the Pharaohs	
1956	The Eddy Duchin Story	To Love Again

Year	Production Title	Popular Songs
1956	Cry in the Night Miracle in the Rain The Maverick Queen The Last Frontier	
1957	Wild Is the Wind Fire Down Below Pickup Alley Jeanne Eagels 3:10 to Yuma Gunfight at the O.K. Corral Night Passage Search for Paradise	Wild Is the Wind (AN) Fire Down Below
1958	The Roots of Heaven Rawhide (TV)	
1959	The Young Land These Thousand Hills Gunslinger (TV)	Strange Are the Ways of Love (AN) These Thousand Hills
1960	The Unforgiven Song without End	The Need for You Song without End
1961	Town without Pity The Guns of Navarone The Last Sunset	Town without Pity (AN) They Call It Love
1962	Advise and Consent	
1964	Circus World	A Circus World "The Fall of Love"
1965	Major Dundee Ship of Fools	
1968	Five Card Stud	

* * *

PAUL FRANCIS WEBSTER

Paul Francis Webster has written the third highest number of popular songs nominated for Academy Awards. Sixteen of his lyrics have been in the running since 1944, and three of them

emerged winners. He was born in New York City in 1907, and
attended both Cornell and New York University. During his early
career, he worked as an able-bodied seaman, and as a dance in-
structor in New York.

Webster's words have been set to the music of such noted
composers as Hoagy Carmichael, Harry Revel, and Sammy Fain.
He began writing for motion pictures in 1935 when he was twenty-
eight years old. Among his first assignments were songs introduced by boy soprano Bobby Breen. In 1941, he collaborated with
jazz-great Duke Ellington on the score for the all-Negro revue
"Jump for Joy" which originated in Los Angeles but was never
taken to Broadway. The show produced the classic "I Got It Bad
and That Ain't Good. " In 1951, Webster added lyrics to Juventino
Rosas' "Over the Waves" and it became the national favorite "The
Loveliest Night of the Year. "

Webster began his long association with composer Sammy
Fain in 1950, and the fifth year of their partnership brought him
the "Oscar" for "Secret Love. " Webster's two other Academy
Award winners are "Love Is a Many-Splendored Thing" (1955)
written with Fain, and "The Shadow of Your Smile" (1965) with music by Johnny Mandel. His most recent nomination was for "A
World That Never Was" from the 1976 film "Half a House. "

Year	Production Title	Popular Songs
1931		"Masquerade" "Two Little Blue Little Eyes"
1932		"The Whisper Waltz" "Me Minus You"
1933	MURDER AT THE VANITIES	"My Moonlight Madonna" "Reflections in the Water"
1934	KILL THAT STORY	Two Cigarettes in the Dark "Got the Jitters" "Water Under the Bridge" "In the Middle of a Kiss"
1935	Under the Pampas Moon Dressed to Thrill Our Little Girl	
1936	Rainbow on the River	Rainbow on the River A Thousand Dreams of You
1937	Make a Wish Vogues of 1938	

Year	Production Title	Popular Songs
1938	Breaking the Ice	Put Your Heart in a Song The Sunny Side of Things "Let's Tie the Old Forget-Me-Not"
1939	Fisherman's Wharf	
1940		"Up the Chimney Go My Dreams"
1941	JUMP FOR MOY (closed in tryout)	I Got It Bad and That Ain't Good (HP) Jump for Joy
1942	Seven Sweethearts Tales of Manhattan	"The Lamplighter's Serenade" "Lamp of Memory" "Lily of Laguna"
1943	Hit the Ice Thousands Cheer Presenting Lily Mars It Ain't Hay	I'd Like to Set You to Music
1944	Minstrel Man Ghost Catchers	Remember Me to Carolina (AN) "A Yankee Christmas"
1945	The Stork Club Johnny Angel How Do You Do	Doctor, Lawyer, Indian Chief (HP) Memphis in June "No More Toujours L'Amour" "Baltimore Oriole"
1946		"Things Have Changed"
1947	It Happened on Fifth Avenue	
1948		"Black Coffee" "Bubble-Loo"
1949		"How It Lies, How It Lies, How It Lies" (HP)

Year	Production Title	Popular Songs
1949		"Follow the Swallow to Hide-a-Way Hollow" "You Was" (HP) "The Three Rivers" "The Merry Christmas Polka"
1950	ALIVE AND KICKING A Life of Her Own	"Lock, Stock and Barrel"
1951	MY L.A. (Los Angeles) The Great Caruso	The Loveliest Night of the Year (HP)
1952	Invitation Because You're Mine The Merry Widow	Invitation "Watermelon Weather"
1953	Calamity Jane Blowing Wild His Majesty O'Keefe	Secret Love (AA) (HP-1)
1954	Lucky Me The Student Prince Rose Marie The Young at Heart	I Speak to the Stars I'll Walk with God I Have the Love There's a Rising Moon
1955	CATCH A STAR Love Is a Many-Splendored Thing Battle Cry Ain't Misbehavin' Sincerely Yours	 Love Is a Many-Splendored Thing (AA) (HP-1) Honey Babe (HP) A Little Love Can Go a Long, Long Way
1956	Friendly Persuasion Anastasia Giant The Revolt of Mamie Stover	Friendly Persuasion (Thee I Love) (AN) (HP) Anastasia There's Never Been Anyone Else but You "The Twelfth of Never"
1957	April Love Raintree County Let's Be Happy	April Love (AN) (HP-1) The Song of Raintree County

PAUL FRANCIS WEBSTER

Year	Production Title	Popular Songs
1957	Farewell to Arms Man on Fire Boy on a Dolphin	 "Padre" "Shenandoah Rose"
1958	A Certain Smile Marjorie Morningstar Gift of Love Mardi Gras Green Mansions	A Certain Smile (AN) A Very Precious Love (AN) The Gift of Love I'll Remember Tonight "Like Young" "Bluebell"
1959	Rio Bravo Imitation of Life Maverick (TV) Sugarfoot (TV)	
1960	CHRISTINE The Alamo Cimarron	 Green Leaves of Summer (AN) Ballad of the Alamo
1961	El Cid The Guns of Navarone Return to Peyton Place	Love Theme from El Cid (The Falcon and the Dove) (AN) Guns of Navarone
1962	Tender Is the Night Mutiny on the Bounty	Tender Is the Night (AN) Follow Me (AN)
1963	55 Days at Peking	So Little Time (AN)
1964	The Seventh Dawn 36 Hours	The Seventh Dawn "The Mood I'm In"
1965	The Sandpiper Joy in the Morning Sylvia	The Shadow of Your Smile (AA)
1966	An American Dream Made in Paris	A Time for Love (AN) "Somewhere My Love (Lara's Theme)"
1967	Three Bites of an Apple	

Year	Production Title	Popular Songs
1969	Heaven with a Gun	
1972	The Stepmother	
1975	Mr. Sycamore	
1976	Half a House	

* * *

RICHARD A. WHITING

  Composer Richard Whiting attended military school in Los Angeles and wanted to be a vaudeville performer. When he realized the shortcomings of his voice, he returned to his home town of Peoria, Illinois. He soon landed an office job in the Detroit branch of the Remick Music Corporation, and moonlighted playing the piano in a hotel orchestra. Whiting's first hit song was published in 1913 when he was twenty-two. Five years later, his "Till We Meet Again" (lyrics by Raymond Egan) sold more than five million copies. He was snapped up by Hollywood as soon as the "talkies" came in but managed to return to Broadway in the early 1930's for "Free for All" and "Take a Chance" in which Ethel Merman introduced his classic "Eadie Was a Lady." After working at Paramount and Fox Studios, Whiting enjoyed his greatest success writing for Warner Bros. where he turned out 17 hit songs in two years including the motion picture industry's theme "Hooray for Hollywood." Forty-seven year old Richard Whiting was at the peak of his career at the time of his death in 1938. Ten years later, Mrs. Eleanore Whiting discovered an unpublished melody titled "Sorry" which had been written about 1932. With lyrics added by Buddy Pepper, the song was popularized in 1949 through recordings by Bing Crosby, Frank Sinatra, Eddie Fisher and Richard Whiting's daughter Margaret.

Year	Production Title	Popular Songs
1913		"The Big Red Motor and the Little Blue Limousine"
1914		"I Wonder Where My Lovin' Man Has Gone?"
1915		"It's Tulip Time in Holland" "Down in the Old Neighborhood" "My American Beauty Rose"

Year	Production Title	Popular Songs
1916	ROBINSON CRUSOE JR.	Where the Black-Eyed Susans Grow
		"Mammy's Little Coal Black Rose"
		"(They Made It Twice as Nice as Paradise) and They Called It Dixieland"
1917		"Some Sunday Morning"
		"Where the Morning Glories Grow"
		"Along the Way to Waikiki"
1918		"Till We Meet Again"
1919	TOOT SWEET GEORGE WHITE'S SCANDALS A LONELY ROMEO	
1920		"Japanese Sandman"
1921		"Ain't We Got Fun?"
		"Biminy Bay"
		"When Shall We Meet Again?"
1922		"Song of Persia"
1923		"Everything Is KO in Kentucky"
		"Somebody's Wrong"
1924	ROUND THE TOWN	"Sleepy Time Gal"
1925		"Ukulele Lady"
		"Weary of Waiting for You"
		"Got No Time"
		"Sweet Child (I'm Wild About You)"
1926		"Breezin' Along with the Breeze"
		"Horses"
		"Precious"
1927		"Honey"
		"Tin Pan Parade
1928		"She's Funny That Way"

Year	Production Title	Popular Songs
1929	Innocents of Paris	Louise
		Wait Till You See Ma Cherie
		It's a Habit of Mine
	Dance of Life	True Blue Lou
	Sweetie	My Sweeter Than Sweet
	The Wolf Song	Yo Te Amo Means I Love
		You
	Pointed Heels	I Have to Have You
	Why Bring That Up?	
	Wild Party	
	The Man I Love	
	The Kibitzer	
	Close Harmony	
1930	Monte Carlo	Beyond the Blue Horizon
		Give Me a Moment, Please
		Always in All Ways
		She'll Love Me and Like It
	Safety in Numbers	My Future Just Passed
	Playboy of Paris	My Ideal (HP)
		It's a Great Life If You
		Don't Weaken
	Let's Go Native	It Seems to Be Spring
		My Mad Moment
	Paramount on Parade	All I Want Is Just One
	Dangerous Nan McGrew	
	Follow Thru	
	Dangerous Paradise	
1931	FREE FOR ALL	Not That I Care
	Monkey Business	
	Dude Ranch	
		"Guilty" (HP)
1932	TAKE A CHANCE	Eadie Was a Lady
		You're an Old Smoothie
		Turn Out the Light
	One Hour with You	(I'd Love to Spend) One Hour
		with You
	Red-Headed Woman	
1933	Adorable	My Heart's Desire
		Adorable
	My Weakness	Gather Lip Rouge While You
		May
	Rainbow Over Broadway	
	I Loved You Wednesday	
1934	Bright Eyes	On the Good Ship Lollipop
	Bottoms Up	Waitin' at the Gate for Katy

Year	Production Title	Popular Songs
1934	Transatlantic Merry- Go-Round 365 Nights in Hollywood Handy Andy She Learned About Sailors Call It Luck Bachelor of Arts	Rock and Roll It Was Sweet of You My Future Star Yes to You Roses in the Rain
1935	The Big Broadcast of 1936 Coronado Here Comes Cookie Four Hours to Kill The Crusades	Miss Brown to You Double Trouble Why Dream? How Do I Rate with You? You Took My Breath Away
1936	Sing, Baby, Sing Rhythm on the Range Anything Goes	When Did You Leave Hea- ven? (AN) (HP-1) I Can't Escape from You (HP) Sailor Beware "Peter Piper"
1937	Varsity Show Ready, Willing and Able Hollywood Hotel	Have You Got Any Castles, Baby? (HP) Moonlight on the Campus We're Working Our Way Through College You've Got Something There Love Is on the Air Tonight Too Marvelous for Words (HP) Sentimental and Melancholy Just a Quiet Evening I'm Like a Fish Out of Water Hooray for Hollywood Silhouetted in the Moonlight Can't Teach My Old Heart New Tricks Let That Be a Lesson to You I've Hitched My Wagon to a Star
1938	Cowboy from Brooklyn	Ride, Tenderfoot, Ride I've Got a Heartful of Music

Year	Production Title	Popular Songs
1938	Cowboy from Brooklyn	I'll Dream Tonight

Posthumous:

| 1949 | | "Sorry" |

* * *

HARRY M. WOODS

  Harry MacGregor Woods was born in North Chelmsford, Massachusetts, in 1896. He attended Harvard University and then became a New England farmer. His music came to the attention of publishers in 1921 when Al Jolson introduced "I'm Goin' South" (lyrics by Abner Silver) in the Broadway production "Bombo." During the next 11 years, Woods's successes included "Side by Side," "I'm Looking Over a Four Leaf Clover," "Try a Little Tenderness," and "When the Moon Comes Over the Mountain" which became Kate Smith's theme song. During the mid-Thirties, Woods spent three years in England writing for films which starred British favorite Jessie Matthews. Although he sometimes wrote his own words, he generally worked with such lyricists as Mort Dixon, Reginald Connelly, and Jimmy Campbell. Harry Woods was seventy-three at the time of his death in 1970.

Year	Production Title	Popular Songs
1921	BOMBO	I'm Goin' South
1923		"Long Lost Mama"
1925		"Paddlin' Madeline Home" "Where Is My Old Girl To-night?" "Spread a Little Sunshine as You Go" "Oh, How She Can Love" "What's a Fellow Gonna Do?" "Lullaby Lane"
1926		"When the Red, Red Robin Comes Bob-Bob Bobbin' Along" "Me Too (Ho, Ho, Ha, Ha)" "Poor Papa--He's Got Nuthin' at All" "Take in the Sun, Hang Out the Moon"

Year	Production Title	Popular Songs
1926		"Tenting Down in Tennes-see" "Who'd Be Blue?" "Your Flag and My Flag"
1927		"Side by Side" (HP) "I'm Looking Over a Four Leaf Clover" (HP-1) "Just Like a Butterfly That's Caught in the Rain" "Where the Wild Wild Flowers Grow" "Is It Possible?" "Moonbeam, Kiss Her for Me" "What Do I Care What Somebody Said?" "Since I Found You" "You're So Easy to Remember"
1928		"In a Sing Song Sycamore Tree" "She's a Great, Great Girl"
1929	Vagabond Lover	A Little Kiss Each Morning Heigh Ho, Everybody, Heigh Ho "What a Day!" "My Old Man"
1930	Roadhouse Nights A Lady's Morals	What a Little Moonlight Can Do "Here Comes the Sun" "Man from the South" "You Darlin'"
1931		"River Stay 'Way from My Door" "When the Moon Comes Over the Mountain" "Hang Out the Stars in Indiana" "It Looks Like Love" "Think a Little Kindly of Me"
1932		"Pink Elephants"

Year	Production Title	Popular Songs
1932		"We Just Couldn't Say Good-bye"
		"Just an Echo in the Valley"
		"A Little Street Where Old Friends Meet"
		"Try a Little Tenderness"
		"Lovable"
		"Little Locket of Long Ago"
		"All of a Sudden"
		"The Voice in the Old Village Choir"
		"We're a Couple of Soldiers, My Baby and Me"
		"The Clouds Will Soon Roll By"
1933		"Hustlin' and Bustlin' for Baby"
1934		"You Ought to See Sally on Sunday"
1935	Evergreen	Over My Shoulder
		Tinkle, Tinkle, Tinkle
		When You've Got a Little Springtime in Your Heart
	Jack Ahoy	My Hat's on the Side of My Head
		"I'll Never Say 'Never Again' Again" (HP-1)
		"As Long as the World Goes 'Round"
		"Dancing with My Shadow"
1936	It's Love Again	I Nearly Let Love Go Slipping Through My Fingers
1937		"So Many Memories" (HP)
1940		"I Hear Bluebirds"
1942		"Closer and Closer"

* * *

ALLIE WRUBEL

Composer Allie Wrubel was an accomplished instrumentalist

and played woodwinds in the Paul Whiteman Orchestra. He studied
medicine at Wesleyan University and music at Columbia. As a
member of his college band, he appeared at a Command Performance for the Prince of Wales in 1924. His first hit song, "Now
You're in My Arms," was published in 1931 when he was twenty-
six years old. The lyrics were supplied by singer Morton Downey.
Wrubel moved to the West Coast where he and lyricist Mort Dixon
became second only to Al Dubin and Harry Warren as the most
successful songwriters on the Warner Bros. lot during the Thirties.
Their popular film songs included "Pop Goes Your Heart," "Mr. and
Mrs. Is the Name," "Try to See It My Way" and "The Lady in
Red." In 1937, Wrubel began working with lyricist Herb Magidson
with whom he wrote such successes as "Music, Maestro, Please,"
"I Can't Love You Anymore (Anymore Than I Do)" and "I'll Buy
That Dream." The culmination of over a decade in Hollywood was
the Academy Award bestowed on him for "Zip-A-Dee-Doo-Dah"
(lyrics by Ray Gilbert) from the 1946 full-length cartoon "Song of
the South." Allie Wrubel was born in Middletown, Connecticut, in
1905, and was sixty-seven when he died in 1973.

Year	Production Title	Popular Songs
1931		"Now You're in My Arms"
1932		"As You Desire Me"
1933		"Farewell to Arms"
		"To Be or Not to Be"
		"Gypsy Fiddles"
		"I'll Be Faithful"
		"And So Goodbye"
		"Emperor Jones"
		"Please, Mr. President"
1934	Happiness Ahead	Pop Goes Your Heart
		Happiness Ahead
	Flirtation Walk	Mr. and Mrs. Is the Name
		Flirtation Walk
		I See Two Lovers
	Dames	Try to See It My Way
	The Key	
	Housewife	
1935	In Caliente	The Lady in Red (HP)
	Sweet Music	Fare-Thee-Well, Annabelle
	I Live for Love	Mine Alone
		I Live for Love
	We're in the Money	So Nice Seeing You Again
	Bright Lights	Toddlin' Along with You
	Broadway Hostess	
	Little Big Shot	
1937	The Toast of New York	The First Time I Saw You (HP)

Year	Production Title	Popular Songs
1937	Life of the Party	Let's Have Another Cigar-ette
	Music for Madame	
		"Gone with the Wind" (HP)
		"The You and Me That Used to Be" (HP)
1938	Radio City Revels	Good Night, Angel (HP)
		There's a New Moon Over the Old Mill
		"Music, Maestro, Please" (HP-1)
1939		"The Masquerade Is Over" (HP)
1940		"I Can't Love You Anymore (Anymore Than I Do)" (HP)
		"I'm Stepping Out with a Memory Tonight" (HP)
		"I'm Home Again"
		"Where Do I Go from You?"
1941		"There Goes That Song Again"
		"Why Don't We Do This More Often?"
		"Rancho Pillow"
		"Good-Bye Now"
		"My Own America"
1942	Private Buckaroo	Private Buckaroo
	Heart of the Rio Grande	
		"I Met Her on Monday"
		"A Boy in Khaki, a Girl in Lace"
1943	Swing Out the Blues	
		"May in Mexico"
1944	Hi, Beautiful	
1945	Sing Your Way Home	I'll Buy That Dream (AN) (HP-1)
1946	Song of the South	Zip-A-Dee-Doo-Dah (AA) (HP)
		Everybody Has a Laughing Place

ALLIE WRUBEL

Year	Production Title	Popular Songs
1946	Duel in the Sun	Gotta Get Me Somebody to Love
	Make Mine Music!	Johnny Fedora and Alice Blue Bonnet
	Swing Parade of 1946	"Why Does It Get So Late So Early?"
1947	I Walk Alone	Don't Call It Love
	The Fabulous Dorseys	"The Lady from Twenty-Nine Palms" (HP)
		"I Do, Do, Do Like You"
1948	Melody Time	Little Toot
	I Surrender Dear	
	The Strawberry Roan	"At the Flying 'W'"
		"I'm a-Comin' a-Courtin' Corabelle"
1949	Tulsa	
1952	Lady Possessed	
1959	Never Steal Anything Small	
1960	Midnight Lace	

* * *

JACK YELLEN

The parents of Polish-born Jack Yellen settled in Buffalo, New York, in 1897 when their son was five years old. The year he graduated from the University of Michigan, his lyrics were heard in the 1913 Broadway production "High Jinks." Yellen worked as a reporter for a Buffalo newspaper before moving to New York City. When he was released from the army after World War I, he continued with his Broadway career and placed songs in nine shows before answering the call to Hollywood. Among his successes during the 1920's were "Mamma Goes Where Papa Goes," "I Wonder What's Become of Sally?" and "Ain't She Sweet"--all with music by Milton Ager. Yellen and Ager's most famous number, "Happy Days Are Here Again," is included on ASCAP's list of 16 All-Time Favorites. In the mid-1930's, Yellen worked with composer Lew Pollack supplying songs for Alice Faye and Shirley Temple at Fox Studios. He went back to Broadway in 1939 to collaborate

on the scores for three revues with composer Sammy Fain, and in
1943 for "The Ziegfeld Follies" with music by Ray Henderson.

Year	Production Title	Popular Songs
1910		"I Used to Be Lonesome (Till I Found You)"
1913	HIGH JINKS	All Aboard for Dixieland
1915		"Are You from Dixie?" "Alabama Jubilee"
1916		"How's Ev'ry Little Thing in Dixie?"
1917		"Southern Gale" "Playmates"
1919		"Alexander's Band Is Back in Dixieland" "Johnny's in Town"
1920	WHAT'S IN A NAME FRIVOLITIES OF 1920	A Young Man's Fancy "Down by the O-Hi-O"
1921		"High Brown Blues"
1922	BOMBO THE BUNCH AND JUDY ZIG ZAG	Who Cares? Lovin' Sam, the Sheik of Alabam'
1923	TED LEWIS FROLIC	 "Mamma Goes Where Papa Goes" "Louisville Lou, the Vampin' Lady"
1924		"I Wonder What's Become of Sally?" "Bagdad" "Hardhearted Hannah" "Big Boy" "Big Bad Bill Is Sweet William Now"
1925		"Cheatin' on Me" "My Yiddishe Momme" "No One"
1926		"I Wish I Had My Old Gal Back Again"

Year	Production Title	Popular Songs
1926		"In Your Green Hat" "Lay Me Down to Sleep in Carolina"
1927		"Ain't She Sweet?" "Crazy Words, Crazy Tune" "I'm Waiting for Ships That Never Come In" "Forgive Me" (HP) "Could I? I Certainly Could" "Vo-Do-Do-De-O Blues" "Is She My Girl Friend?" "Ain't That a Grand and Glorious Feeling?" "Dream Kisses"
1928	RAIN OR SHINE WHOOPEE	Falling Star Forever and Ever Rain or Shine Hungry Women "If You Don't Love Me" "My Pet" "I Still Love You"
1929	MURRAY ANDERSON'S ALMANAC Honky Tonk This Is Heaven Glad Rag Doll Bulldog Drummond	Wait for the Happy Ending He's a Good Man to Have Around I'm the Last of the Red Hot Mamas This Is Heaven Glad Rag Doll
1930	Chasing Rainbows King of Jazz They Learned About Women Rain or Shine	Happy Days Are Here Again Lucky Me, Lovable You Happy Feet A Bench in the Park I Like to Do Things for You Song of the Dawn
1931	YOU SAID IT	Sweet and Hot You Said It "There's No Depression in Love"

Year	Production Title	Popular Songs
1934	George White's Scandals	(Oh, You) Nasty Man Hold My Hand My Dog Loves Your Dog
	Marie Galante	
1935	GEORGE WHITE'S SCANDALS	I'm the Fellow Who Loves You Life Begins at Sweet Sixteen
	George White's Scandals of 1935	It's an Old Southern Custom Hunkadola According to the Moonlight
	King of Burlesque This Is the Life Under Pressure	
1936	Sing, Baby, Sing Captain January	Sing, Baby, Sing (HP) The Right Somebody to Love
1938	Happy Landing Rebecca of Sunnybrook Farm	A Gypsy Told Me
1939	GEORGE WHITE'S SCANDALS	Are You Havin' Any Fun? (HP) Goodnight, My Beautiful Something I Dreamed Last Night
1940	BOYS AND GIRLS TOGETHER	I Want to Live
1941	SONS O' FUN	Happy in Love (HP)
1943	THE ZIEGFELD FOLLIES	Love Songs Are Made in the Night
1945	George White's Scandals	
1947		"The Wildest Gal in Town"
1949		"Church Bells on Sunday Morning"

* * *

VINCENT YOUMANS

Vincent Millie Youmans was born in New York City in 1898.

After serving in the Navy during the First World War, he began his professional career as a song plugger. He soon progressed to another occupation common to aspiring songwriters--playing the piano during rehearsals of new musicals. Youmans received his big break in 1921 when he was recommended to the producer of "Two Little Girls in Blue" and several of his melodies were used in the production. For his second musical, Youmans teamed with Herbert Stothart on the score for "Wildflower." The book and lyrics were the work of Otto Harbach and a young man named Oscar Hammerstein. Their collaboration resulted in one of the most phenomenal successes of the period. "Wildflower" ran for 17 months!

In 1924, an event occurred in Detroit, Michigan, that established Youmans as one of the greatest musical talents of the 1920's. The event was the opening of "No, No Nanette." The original score underwent several revisions before the show settled down to a year's run in Chicago. Its success prompted the producers to send out touring companies and to also open the show in London. By the time "No, No Nanette" had its Broadway premiere in 1925, audiences were already familiar with many of the songs. Among them was "Tea for Two" which became one of the most famous compositions ever written for the stage and is included among 16 numbers listed on ASCAP's All-Time Hit Parade. According to the tradepaper Variety, "Tea for Two" is one of the four most-recorded songs in popular music history.

The first song written by Vincent Youmans was "Hallelujah!" which he composed as a teenager in the Navy. The song was without a lyric until the composer decided to include it in his score for "Hit the Deck" (1927). The most popular ballad from the same show had a difficult time attaining success. Originally titled "Come On and Pet Me," it was dropped from the score of "Mary Jane Mc-Kane." The melody was then salvaged, equipped with a new set of words, and inserted in "A Night Out" which closed during its tryouts. As "Sometimes I'm Happy," the song finally became a standard.

During the first nine years of his career, the majority of Youmans' musicals were hits. While many of the melodies he composed during the last three years of his activity became popular, all but one of his later productions were financial failures. The exception was "Take a Chance" (1932) but Youmans long-awaited triumph had to be shared with Richard Whiting and Nacio Herb Brown who composed most of the show's music. "Take a Chance" was Youmans' farewell to the legitimate theatre. In 1933, he created the score for the film "Flying Down to Rio" and was nominated for an Academy Award for his music to "The Carioca." After the film was released, the composer's career came to a virtual standstill. He contracted tuberculosis and went into retirement at the age of thirty-five after only a dozen brief years of active composition. Vincent Youmans died in Denver, Colorado, in 1946 having spent his last 13 years as an invalid. Twenty-five years after his death,

"No, No Nanette" was revived on Broadway and played to capacity audiences for more than a year.

Year	Production Title	Popular Songs
1920		"The Country Cousin"
1921	TWO LITTLE GIRLS IN BLUE	Oh Me, Oh My, Oh You Dolly
1923	WILDFLOWER	Wildflower Bambalina
	MARY JANY MCKANE	Toodle-oo
1924	LOLLIPOP	Tie a String Around Your Finger
1925	NO, NO NANETTE	Tea for Two I Want to Be Happy Too Many Rings Around Rosie No, No Nanette You Can Dance with Any Girl at All I've Confessed to the Breeze
	A NIGHT OUT (closed in tryout)	
1926	OH, PLEASE!	I Know That You Know
1927	HIT THE DECK	Sometimes I'm Happy Hallelujah! Why, Oh, Why?
1928	RAINBOW	The One Girl I Want a Man Hay, Straw
1929	GREAT DAY!	More Than You Know Without a Song Great Day! Happy Because I'm in Love
	A NIGHT IN VENICE	
1930	SMILES	Time on My Hands I'm Glad I Waited
	9:15 REVUE What a Widow!	Love Is Like a Song You're the One
	Hit the Deck Song of the West	Keepin' Myself for You
1932	THROUGH THE YEARS	Drums in My Heart

Year	Production Title	Popular Songs
1932	THROUGH THE YEARS	Through the Years You're Everywhere Kinda Like You
	TAKE A CHANCE	Rise 'n' Shine So Do I Oh, How I Long to Belong to You Should I Be Sweet?
1933	Flying Down to Rio	The Carioca (AN) Orchids in the Moonlight Music Makes Me Flying Down to Rio

* * *

JOSEPH YOUNG

After attending public schools in his home town of New York City, Joe Young worked as a singer for a music publisher. The nation began singing his lyrics in 1911 when "When You're Away" was published. By 1916, Broadway star Al Jolson was introducing Young's songs to theatre audiences. During the first sixteen years of his career, he shared credit for no less than 49 hits including such standards as "Rock-a-Bye Your Baby with a Dixie Melody," "My Mammy," "Dinah," "Five Foot Two, Eyes of Blue" and "In a Little Spanish Town." Most of his biggest hits were written in collaboration with lyricist Sam Lewis, and he worked most frequently with composers Walter Donaldson and Fred Ahlert. Although his songs were heard in ten Broadway productions and nine motion pictures, the majority of his songs were published as independent numbers. Joe Young was fifty at the time of his death in 1939.

Year	Production Title	Popular Songs
1911		"When You're Away"
1912		"Down in Dear Old New Or- leans"
1913	THE PLEASURE SEEKERS	Don't Blame It All on Broad- way
1914		"When the Angelus Is Ring- ing" "Put It On, Take It Off (Wrap It Up, Take It Home)"

Year	Production Title	Popular Songs
1915		"Along the Rocky Road to Dublin"
1916	ROBINSON CRUSOE JR.	Where Did Robinson Crusoe Go with Friday on Saturday Night?
		Yaaka Hula Hickey Dula
	STEP THIS WAY	If I Knock the "L" Out of Kelly
	FOLLOW ME	When the Girls Grow Older They Grow a Little Bolder
		"Long Live the Ladies"
		"Arrah Go On (I'm Gonna Go Back to Oregon)"
		"Way Down in Iowa I'm Going to Hide Away"
		"Come on and Baby Me"
1917	THE PASSING SHOW	Meet Me at the Station, Dear
		"Huckleberry Finn"
		"In San Domingo"
		"I'm All Bound 'Round with the Mason Dixon Line"
1918	SINBAD	Hello, Central, Give Me No Man's Land
		Rock-a-Bye Your Baby with a Dixie Melody
		Why Do They All Take the Night Boat to Albany?
		How'd You Like to Be My Daddy?
		"Just a Baby's Prayer at Twilight"
		"Oh, How I Wish I Could Sleep Till My Daddy Comes Home"
1919		"Who Played Poker with Pocahontas When John Smith Went Away?"
		"I'll Be Happy When the Preacher Makes You Mine"
		"How Ya Gonna Keep'em Down on the Farm?"

Year	Production Title	Popular Songs
1919		"You're a Million Miles from Nowhere (When You're One Little Mile from Home)" "Daddy Long Legs" "Don't Cry, Frenchy, Don't Cry" "My Barney Lies Over the Ocean--Just the Way He Lied to Me" "Desert Gold" "Upstairs and Down"
1920		"Old Pal, Why Don't You Answer Me?" "I'd Love to Fall Asleep and Wake Up in My Mammy's Arms" "Singin' the Blues (Till My Daddy Comes Home)"
1921		"My Mammy" "Tuck Me to Sleep in My Old 'Tucky Home" "Cry Baby Blues"
1922		"Hello, Hello, Hello"
1923		"Lovey Came Back"
1924		"Dinah" "In Shadowland" "Put Away a Little Ray of Golden Sunshine for a Rainy Day" "In a Little Rendezvous" "Cover Me Up with the Sunshine of Virginia"
1925		"Five Foot Two, Eyes of Blue" (HP) "I'm Sitting on Top of the World"
1926	AMERICANA	"In a Little Spanish Town" "Take in the Sun, Hang Out the Moon"
1927	LADY DO	"There's a Cradle in Caroline"

Year	Production Title	Popular Songs
1927		"Keep Sweeping the Cobwebs Off the Moon" "High-High-High Up in the Hills"
1928		"Laugh, Clown, Laugh" "King for a Day" "Revenge" "Happy Go Lucky Lane" "In My Bouquet of Memories" "Just a Little Way Away from Home"
1929	Wolf Song Looping the Loop	Mi Amado "I Kiss Your Hand, Madame" "Then You've Never Been Blue" "Absence Makes the Heart Grow Fonder" "I Used to Love Her in the Moonlight"
1930	Spring Is Here Two Hearts in Waltz Time	Crying for the Carolines Have a Little Faith in Me Two Hearts in Three Quarter Time "Wasn't It Nice?" "Tellin' It to the Daisies" "I'm Alone Because I Love You"
1931	THE LAUGH PARADE	Ooh! That Kiss You're My Everything The Torch Song "Was That the Human Thing to Do?" "Starlight" "Don't Ask Me Why"
1932	High Pressure The Crooner Make Me a Star	I Can't Get Mississippi Off My Mind "Lullaby of the Leaves" "Sheltered by the Stars, Cradled by the Moon" "The Lady I Love"

Year	Production Title	Popular Songs
1932		"Snuggled on Your Shoulder" "The Night When Love Was Born"
1933	BLACKBIRDS	A Hundred Years from Today "In a Shanty in Old Shanty Town" "Annie Doesn't Live Here Anymore" "Two Tickets to Georgia" "You're Gonna Lose Your Gal" "Little You Know" "Shadows on the Swanee" "You're Beautiful Tonight, My Dear"
1934		"If I Didn't Care" "Dream Man, Make Me Dream Some More" "I Hate Myself (for Being So Mean to You)" "In a Little Red Barn (on a Farm Down in Indiana)"
1935	Woman in Red	"I'm Gonna Sit Right Down and Write Myself a Letter" "Sing an Old-Fashioned Song" "You're a Heavenly Thing" (HP) "Life Is a Song" (HP-1) "Because of Once Upon a Time" "I'm Growing Fonder of You"
1936		"Take My Heart" (HP-1) "You Dropped Me Like a Red Hot Penny" "There's Two Sides to Ev'ry Story"
1937	Danger Patrol	"Sweet Thing" "The Goona Goo" "I'm Happy, Darling, Dancing with You" "The Image of You"

Year	Production Title	Popular Songs
1937	Danger Patrol	"I've Got a New Lease on Love" "There's Frost on the Moon"
1939		"There's a New Day Coming"

Posthumous:

1950		"The Story of Annie Laurie"
1951		"Got Her Off My Hands (but Can't Get Her Off My Mind)"

* * *

VICTOR YOUNG

Victor Young composed over 300 film scores during his twenty year career in Hollywood. He was born in Chicago, and was educated in Warsaw, Poland. He became a concert violinist and toured in Europe and the United States. During the Twenties, he joined Ted Fiorito's orchestra and did many of the band's best arrangements. Young's first popular music success was "Sweet Sue-Just You" (lyrics by Will J. Harris) published in 1928. Throughout the 1930's, he was one of radio's leading arranger-conductors appearing regularly with such stars as Don Ameche and Al Jolson.

Victor Young began writing for motion pictures in 1936, and nine years later he received his first Academy Award nomination for his title song from "Love Letters." He interrupted his film and radio work twice to compose for Broadway: "Pardon Our French" (1950) and "Seventh Heaven" (1955). Neither production was successful. Young died in 1956 at the peak of his career. The fifty-six year old composer had completed the score for Mike Todd's film "Around the World in 80 Days" and the title song for "Written on the Wind." "Written on the Wind" received an "Oscar" nomination and Victor Young was awarded the statuette posthumously for the Best Score for a Dramatic or Comedy Film--"Around the World in 80 Days."

Year	Production Title	Popular Songs
1928		"Sweet Sue--Just You"
1929		"Can't You Understand?"
1930	BROWN BUDDIES	

Year	Production Title	Popular Songs
1930		"Was I to Blame for Falling in Love with You?"
1931		"Beautiful Love" "Too Late"
1932		"Lawd, You Made the Night Too Long" "The Old Man of the Mountain" "Street of Dreams" "Can't We Talk It Over?" "Waltzing in a Dream" "My Love" "Got the South in My Soul" "Love Me Tonight" "My Romance"
1933	MURDER AT THE VANITIES BLACKBIRDS	Sweet Madness A Hundred Years from Today "(I Don't Stand) A Ghost of a Chance" "I'd Be Telling a Lie" "Any Time, Any Day, Anywhere" "Shadows on the Window" "Love Is the Thing"
1934		"Give Me a Heart to Sing To" "Love Me"
1936	Accused Heart of the West Fatal Lady	
1937	Artists and Models Double or Nothing Hideaway Girl	
1938	Breaking the Ice	
1939	All Women Have Secrets Fisherman's Wharf Heritage of the Desert	
1940	A Night at Earl Carroll's	One Look at You

Year	Production Title	Popular Songs
1940	North West Mounted Police	
1941	I Wanted Wings Dancing on a Dime	
1942	Reap the Wild Wind	
1943	For Whom the Bells Tolls	A Love Like This
1944		"Stella by Starlight"
1945	Love Letters	Love Letters (AN) (HP)
1946	The Searching Wind	
1947	Golden Earrings	Golden Earrings
1949	My Foolish Heart Deadly Is the Female Song of Surrender Bitter Victory Chicago Deadline The Lucky Stiff	My Foolish Heart (AN) (HP-1) Mad About You Song of Surrender
1950	PARDON OUR FRENCH Our Very Own	Our Very Own "You're Not in My Arms Tonight"
1951	The Bullfighter and the Lady The Wild Blue Yonder	"Weaver of Dreams" "A Woman's Intuition"
1952	One Minute to Zero Something to Live For The Greatest Show on Earth Thunderbirds The Fabulous Senorita	When I Fall in Love
1953	Shane	The Call of the Far Away Hills
1954	Johnny Guitar Jubilee Trail	

Year	Production Title	Popular Songs
1955	SEVENTH HEAVEN Strategic Air Command	A Man with a Dream "Blue Star"
1956	Around the World in 80 Days Written on the Wind The Maverick Queen Drum Beat	Around the World (HP-1) Written on the Wind (AN)

Posthumous:

| 1957 | China Gate
Loves of Omar Khayyam | |

APPENDIX A: COMPARATIVE RANKINGS

When ranking the artists, it was necessary to take into account the considerably divergent periods in which they created. No valid comparison could be made between the successes of early writers, such as Stephen Foster, Paul Dresser, or Victor Herbert, and the successes of their later kin Cole Porter, Lew Brown, the Gershwins, etc. The primary consideration had to be the percent of the population that heard the songs and, therefore, purchased them in some form. To insure fairness in rating the subjects, they were placed in their respective eras: Before Tin Pan Alley, Tin Pan Alley, and After Tin Pan Alley.

Artists who were successful during Tin Pan Alley and continued to create after its demise are placed in the After Tin Pan Alley era; while many of the artists whose careers spanned these several decades failed to perpetuate their success, the increased opportunities of the era after Tin Pan Alley were still open to them. Within each era, the artists are listed in descending order according to the number of hit songs each artist produced as recognized in popular music histories.

The original list of composers and lyricists researched totalled 274. After each artist's popular songs were identified and the artists had been placed in their proper era, a standard was set for each era. The standard for "Before Tin Pan Alley" was set at six popular songs; the standard for "Tin Pan Alley" was 15; the standard for "After Tin Pan Alley" was 40. Any artist whose number of hit songs fell below the standard fixed for his era was eliminated.

Common sense makes it apparent that the resultant rankings are only indicative of available information. If previous historians failed to list any of an artist's popular songs, that artist has been ranked lower than he deserves. The rank achieved sometimes depends on only one song, and there are many ties. Some of the artists, such as George Gershwin, Lorenz Hart, Ralph Rainger, and Richard Whiting, died while relatively young and still highly productive. If they had lived a few decades longer, as did Irving Berlin, Richard Rodgers, and Jimmy McHugh, their records might well have surpassed the artists who appear to be their peers. In addition, artists such as Sammy Cahn, Burton Lane, Jule Styne, Hal David, etc., who are still active creators will undoubtedly improve their rankings in future years.

BEFORE TIN PAN ALLEY

Rank	Artist
1	Stephen Collins Foster
2	James A. Bland
3	William Shakespeare Hays
4	George Frederick Root
5	Septimus Winner
6	Henry Clay Work
7	Henry Russell
8	Daniel Decatur Emmett

TIN PAN ALLEY

Rank	Artist
1	Harry Von Tilzer
2	William Jerome
3	Victor Herbert
4	Andrew B. Sterling
5	Theodore F. Morse
6	Paul Dresser
7	George M. Cohan
8	Ernest R. Ball Egbert Van Alstyne
9	Will D. Cobb
10	David Braham & Edward Harrigan
11	Harry B. Smith
12	Edward Madden
13	Harry Williams

TIN PAN ALLEY

Rank	Artist
14	Monroe Rosenfeld P. G. Wodehouse
15	Charles K. Harris
16	Gene Buck Louis A. Hirsch
17	Henry Blossom
18	Chris Smith
19	Bob Cole
20	Jack Drislane Robert B. Smith
21	Arthur J. Lamb
22	Kerry Mills John Stromberg
23	Edgar Smith
24	James Thornton Rida Johnson Young

AFTER TIN PAN ALLEY

Rank	Artist
1	Irving Berlin
2	Gus Kahn
3	Harry Warren
4	Johnny Mercer
5	Jimmy McHugh Lew Brown
6	Jerome Kern
7	Mack Gordon Richard Rodgers

AFTER TIN PAN ALLEY

Rank	Artist
8	Oscar Hammerstein
9	Walter Donaldson
10	B. G. DeSylva
11	Al Dubin Leo Robin
12	Ira Gershwin
13	Sammy Cahn
14	James Van Heusen
15	Johnny Burke
16	Ray Henderson
17	George Gershwin Joseph Young
18	Charles Tobias
19	Cole Porter
20	Harold Arlen Frank Loesser
21	Al Hoffman
22	Samuel M. Lewis
23	Harold Adamson Alfred Bryan
24	Richard A. Whiting
25	Edgar Leslie Jule Styne
26	Benny Davis Harry Revel
27	E. Y. Harburg Lorenz Hart

AFTER TIN PAN ALLEY

Rank	Artist
28	Dorothy Fields Jean Schwartz
29	Cliff Friend
30	Milton Ager Hoagy Carmichael Ned Washington
31	Sam Coslow
32	Mitchell Parish Jack Yellen
33	J. Fred Coots James V. Monaco
34	Duke Ellington
35	Billy Rose
36	Paul Francis Webster
37	Hal David Sammy Fain Otto Harbach Arthur Schwartz
38	Albert Von Tilzer
39	George W. Meyer
40	Mack David Peter DeRose
41	Ted Koehler Irving Mills Sigmund Romberg
42	Fred Fisher
43	Ralph Rainger
44	Irving Caesar Joseph McCarthy Harry M. Woods
45	Burt Bacharach Carl Sigman

AFTER TIN PAN ALLEY

Rank	Artist
46	Bert Kalmar
47	Bob Hilliard
48	Andy Razaf
49	Gus Edwards
50	Joseph A. Burke Mort Dixon
51	Al Stillman
52	Burton Lane Abner Silver
53	Edward Heyman Jerry Livingston Allie Wrubel
54	Con Conrad Harry Ruby
55	Grant Clarke Arthur Freed Rudolf Friml Sam H. Stept
56	Howard Dietz Harry Tobias
57	Fred Ahlert Nacio Herb Brown
58	L. Wolfe Gilbert
59	Ray Evans & Jay Livingston
60	Louis Alter
61	Joseph Meyer Don Raye Bob Russell
62	Roy Turk
63	Herbert Magidson

AFTER TIN PAN ALLEY

<u>Rank</u>

64	Bob Merrill Sidney D. Mitchell Thomas (Fats) Waller
65	Ted Fiorito Vincent Youmans Victor Young
66	Harry Akst

The list of artists not covered in <u>Sweet and Lowdown</u> has been included to assure readers that the work of every songwriter of any stature whatever was thoroughly researched before making the final selection of the most successful songwriters.

Most of the composers and lyricists who were eliminated because the number of their popular songs did not meet the arbitrary standards set for their period created outstanding numbers. Notable examples are Ren Shields' "In the Good Old Summertime," W. C. Handy's "St. Louis Blues," Ralph Blane and Hugh Martin's "The Trolley Song," Carrie Jacobs Bond's "I Love You Truly" and "A Perfect Day," Shelton Brooks' "Darktown Strutter's Ball," Vernon Duke's "April in Paris," Johnny Green's "Body and Soul," Raymond Hubbell's "Poor Butterfly," Herman Hupfeld's "As Time Goes By," Mabel Wayne's "Ramona," and Meredith Willson's "Seventy-Six Trombones."

The memorable scores of such Broadway songwriters as Betty Comden and Adolph Green ("Bells Are Ringing"), Jerry Bock and Sheldon Harnick ("Fiddler on the Roof"), Fred Ebb and John Kander ("Cabaret"), Jerry Herman ("Hello, Dolly!"), and Alan Jay Lerner and Frederick Loewe ("My Fair Lady") have earned them a permanent place in the history of American popular music. However, the scores did not produce a sufficient number of songs that became popular with the general public to rank these artists with the composers and lyricists finally selected. <u>Sweet and Lowdown</u> could not truly set the record straight without acknowledging the contributions of:

Lee Adams	Ralph Blane
Stanley Adams	Jerry Bock
Richard Adler	Carrie Jacobs Bond
Robert Allen	J. Keirn Brennan
Leroy Anderson	Jack Brooks
Paul Anka	Shelton Brooks
Abel Baer	Walter Bullock
Dave Bartholomew	Anne Caldwell
Leonard Bernstein	Harry Carroll

Ivan Caryll
Saul Chaplin
Sidney Clare
Cy Coleman
Betty Comden
Will Marion Cook
Bobby Darin
Reginald DeKoven
Edgar De Lange
Gene DePaul
Fats Domino
Dorothy Donnelly
Dave Dreyer
Vernon Duke
Fred Ebb
Raymond B. Egan
Edward Eliscu
George Forrest
Dave Franklin
Ralph Freed
Percy Gaunt
Haven Gillespie
E. Ray Goetz
Al Goodhart
Jay Gorney
George Graff Jr.
Adolph Green
Johnny Green
Clifford Grey
Albert Hague
W. C. Handy
Benjamin H. Harney
Sheldon Harnick
Jerry Herman
Billy Hill
Frederick Hollander
Karl Hoschna
Joseph E. Howard
Raymond Hubbell
Herman Hupfeld
Howard Johnson
J. Rosamund Johnson
Arthur J. Johnston
Al Jolson
Isham Jones
Tom Jones
Irving Kahal
John Kander
Bronislau Kaper
Charles Kenny
Nick Kenny
Robert A. King
Raymond Klages

Alex Kramer
Dory Langdon
John Latouche
Vee Lawnhurst
Carolyn Leigh
Alan Jay Lerner
Sammy Lerner
Oscar Levant
Frederick Loewe
Gustav Luders
Ballard MacDonald
Glen MacDonough
Cecil Mack
Henry Mancini
Edward B. Marks
Hugh Martin
Josef Myrow
Alfred Newman
Jack Norworth
Ben Oakland
Chauncey Olcott
Al Piantadosi
Lee Pockriss
Lew Pollack
Andre Previn
Harold Rome
Ann Ronell
Jerry Ross
William J. Scanlan
Victor Schertzinger
Harvey Schmidt
Tot Seymour
Richard Sherman
Robert Sherman
Ren Shields
Maurice Sigler
A. Baldwin Sloane
Ted Snyder
Stephen Sondheim
Harold Spina
Dave Stamper
Joseph W. Stern
Herbert Stothart
Charles Strouse
Harry Tierney
Dimitri Tiomkin
Henry Tobias
Rudy Vallee
Mabel Wayne
Kurt Weill
Pete Wendling
Percy Wenrich
Joan Whitney

Bert Williams
Spencer Williams
Meredith Willson

Robert Wright
Hy Zaret

APPENDIX B: SOURCES OF DATA

The research for Sweet and Lowdown is based on the following fifteen volumes:

Burton, Jack. The Blue Book of Tin Pan Alley. Vol. 1-1776-
    1860-1910. Vol. 2-1910-1950. Watkins Glen, N.Y.: Cen-
    tury House, 1950

_____. The Blue Book of Broadway Musicals. Watkins
    Glen, N.Y.: Century House, 1952

_____. The Blue Book of Hollywood Musicals. Watkins
    Glen, N.Y.: Century House, 1953

Ewen, David. American Popular Songs from the Revolutionary War
    to the Present. New York: Random House, 1966

Kinkle, Roger D. The Complete Encyclopedia of Popular Music
    and Jazz. Vol. 1. New Rochelle, N.Y.: Arlington House,
    1974

Lynn Farnol Group, Inc. The ASCAP Biographical Dictionary of
    Composers, Authors and Publishers. New York: ASCAP,
    1966

Mattfeld, Julius. Variety Music Cavalcade. Englewood Cliffs,
    N.J.: Prentice-Hall, Inc., 1952, 1962, 1971

Shapiro, Nat, ed. Popular Music. Vol. 1-1950-1959 (1964, 1967).
    Vol. 2-1940-1949 (1965). Vol. 3-1940-1964 (1967). Vol. 4-
    1930-1939 (1968). Vol. 5-1920-1929 (1969). New York:
    Adrian Press

Spaeth, Sigmund. A History of Popular Music in America. New
    York: Random House, 1948

Williams, John. This Was Your Hit Parade. Camden, Me.: John
    R. Williams, 1973

The volumes consulted contained extensive lists of thousands
of song titles. Some included songs which were admittedly not popular but were listed for reasons such as: 1) they were important

to their creator's career, 2) they reflected a current event or personality, 3) they were introduced by a celebrated performer or one who later became famous, 4) they were memorable to theatre audiences, 5) they were representative of particular types of songs, etc. In other cases, authors listed every song from Broadway productions which were failures ("Ben Franklin in Paris," "Anyone Can Whistle," "Bajour," etc.). Songs such as the foregoing were not included in the research for Sweet and Lowdown nor, in general, were songs written after 1959 unless they were popularized on identified recordings. After 1959, it was almost impossible for a song to become popular without a hit record.

Titles of Broadway productions and their opening years are as reported in the annual Best Plays... publications. Motion picture titles and release years are as listed in Film Daily Year Book of Motion Pictures, Motion Picture Almanac, or other sources supplied by the Academy of Motion Picture Arts and Sciences Library.

Since no data were available in book form covering years after 1969, songs after that time were omitted. The exclusion of such songs would have little bearing on the ranking of the composers and lyricists since only 16 of the 144 artists included were still active creators during the Seventies.

APPENDIX C: ADDITIONAL BIBLIOGRAPHY

Arlen, Harold. Happy with the Blues. Garden City, N. Y.: Double-
    day & Co., Inc., 1961

Baral, Robert. Revue. New York: Fleet Press Corp., 1962

Cohan, George. Twenty Years on Broadway and the Years It Took
    to Get There. New York: Harper, 1925

Eells, George. The Life That Late He Led. New York: G. P.
    Putnam's Sons, 1967

Ellington, Duke. Music Is My Mistress. Garden City, N. Y.:
    Doubleday & Co., Inc., 1973

Ewen, David. The Life and Death of Tin Pan Alley. New York:
    Funk and Wagnalls, 1964

_____. Complete Book of the American Musical Theatre.
    New York: Holt, Rinehart & Winston, 1958

_____. Great Men of American Popular Song. Englewood
    Cliffs, N. J.: Prentice-Hall, 1972

Farnsworth, Marjorie. The Ziegfeld Follies. New York: Bonanza
    Books, 1956

Green, Stanley. The World of Musical Comedy. New York: Gros-
    set & Dunlap, 1960

Jay, Dave. The Irving Berlin Songography. New Rochelle, N. Y.:
    Arlington House, 1969

Kimball, Robert, ed. Cole. New York: Holt, Rinehart & Winston,
    1971

_____ and Alfred Simon. The Gershwins. New York:
    Atheneum, 1973

Klamkin, Marian. Old Sheet Music. New York: Hawthorn Books,
    1975

Lewine, Richard and Alfred Simon. Encyclopedia of Theatre Music.
    New York: Bonanza Books, 1961

_____ and _____ . Songs of the American Theatre. New York: Dodd, Mead & Co., 1973

Lynn Farnol Group. Richard Rodgers Fact Book. N.Y., 1968

Michael, Paul. The American Movies Reference Book: The Sound Era. Englewood Cliffs, N.J.: Prentice-Hall, Inc., 1969

Simon, Henry W., ed. The George and Ira Gershwin Song Book. New York: Simon & Schuster, 1960

Thomas, Tony. Harry Warren. Secaucus, N.J.: Citadel Press, 1975

INDEX OF SONG TITLES

My Funny Valentine   275, 277,
401
My Future Just Passed   480
My Future Star   481
My Gal Is Mine Once More   196,
420
My Gal Sal   42, 44
My Gee Gee from the Fiji Isles
130
My Guiding Star   422
My Guitar   230
My Handy Man Ain't Handy Any-
more   386
My Hat's on the Side of My Head
484
My Heart and I   395
My Heart Belongs to Daddy   375,
377
My Heart Cries for You   426
My Heart Goes Crazy   145, 454
My Heart Has Learned to Love
You   25
My Heart Is a Hobo   145, 454
My Heart Is an Open Book (David)
176
My Heart Is an Open Book (Hey-
man)   283
My Heart Is an Open Book (Revel)
258, 389
My Heart Is Singing   298
My Heart Is Taking Lessons   143,
367, 369
My Heart Reminds Me   435
My Heart Still Clings to the Old
First Love   43
My Heart Stood Still   276, 400
My Heart Tells Me   256, 260, 467
My Heart's Desire   480
My Home Town Is a One Horse
Town   427
My Honey Moon   24
My Honey's Lovin' Arms   359, 360
My Hopes Have Departed Forever
18
My Hula Lula Girl   54, 421
My Ideal   393, 480
My Impression of You   334, 470
My Inspiration Is You   319
My Irish Molly O   54, 421
My Irish Rosie   54, 422
My Isle of Golden Dreams   294
My Jealous Eyes (That Turned
from Blue to Green)   181

My Jersey Lily   82
My Josephine   69, 77
My Kind of Town   159, 456
My Kinda Love   106
My Kingdom for a Kiss   207,
466
My Lady Hottentot   54, 82
My Little Bimbo Down on the
Bamboo Isle   165, 200
My Little Coney Isle   75, 83
My Little Corner of the World
287
My Little Dream Girl   255
My Little Girl   321, 458
My Little Lady   38
My Little Lovin' Honey Man
337
My Little Red Book   114, 177
My Love   470, 499
My Love for You   284, 427,
430
My Love Loves Me   216
My Lucky Star   132, 192, 280
My Lula San   41
My Mad Moment   480
My Mama Says "No, No"   229
My Mammy   199, 200, 321,
322, 493, 495
My Man Is on the Make   276,
400
My Mississippi Belle   41
My Mom   202
My Moonlight Madonna   474
My Mother's Bible   21
My Mother's Eyes   139, 254
My Mother's Rosary   321, 357
My Musical Comedy Maid   39
My! My!   331, 344
My Ohio Home   201
My Old Aunt Sally   16
My Old Flame   172, 173
My Old Kentucky Home   17,
18
My Old Man   198, 483
My Old New Hampshire Home
74, 82
My One and Only   246, 250
My One and Only Heart   435
My One and Only Highland
Fling   252, 468
My Own   94, 343
My Own America   486
My Own Iona   254

INDEX OF PRODUCTIONS

Be Yourself 380, 411
Beautiful Blonde from Bashful
  Bend 261
Beautiful but Broke 204, 255
BEAUTY AND THE BATH 88,
  305
BEAUTY PRIZE 307
Because You're Mine 157, 476
Bedtime Story 380, 393
BEGGAR'S HOLIDAY 214
BEGUM 68, 69
Behind the Eight Ball 384
Bell for Adano 196, 417, 420
BELLE OF BOHEMIA 69
BELLE OF BOND STREET 138,
  231
BELLE OF BRIDGEPORT 41
Belle of New York 351, 468
Belle of the Nineties 173
Belle of the Yukon 144, 453
BELLE PAREE see LA BELLE
  PAREE
Belles on Their Toes 160
BELLS ARE RINGING 436, 437,
  440
Bells Are Ringing 440
Bells of St. Mary's 144, 453
Bernadine 352
Best of Everything 158
Best Things in Life Are Free
  279
Best Years of Our Lives 160
BETSY 123, 150, 276, 399
BETTY 56, 318, 423
BETTY BE GOOD 71
BETTY LEE 52, 53, 150, 167
BETTY LOU 269
BETWEEN THE DEVIL 195, 419
Beyond the Blue Horizon 332, 391,
  438
Big Beat 217
BIG BOY 130, 167, 189, 191,
  237, 279, 360
Big Boy 431
Big Broadcast 101, 320, 369,
  380, 392, 393, 450
Big Broadcast of 1936 173, 381,
  394, 481
Big Broadcast of 1937 381, 395
Big Broadcast of 1938 382, 395
Big Carnival 217
Big Circus 223
Big City Blues 380

Big Pond 220
Big Show 312, 431, 471
Big Sombrero 384
Big Street 391
Big Town 96, 199, 204
Big Town Girl 104
BILLIE 37, 40
BILLIONAIRE 70
BILLY ROSE'S AQUACADE
  339, 408, 409, 411, 452,
  453
BILLY ROSE'S CRAZY QUILT
  106, 196, 198, 251, 271,
  276, 400, 408, 411, 464
Bird of Paradise 189
Blondie Goes to College 155
Blondie of the Follies 229,
  234, 447
Blondie's Blessed Event 155
BLOOMER GIRL 108, 111,
  271, 273
BLOSSOM TIME 404, 406
Blossoms on Broadway 330,
  381, 395
Blowing Wild 476
BLUE EYES (Gershwin) 149,
  245
BLUE EYES (Kern) 308
Blue Gardenia 416
BLUE HOLIDAY 274
BLUE KITTEN 241, 269
BLUE MOON 210
BLUE PARADISE 68, 404,
  405
Blue Skies 117, 127
Blues in the Night 110, 350
BLUSHING BRIDE 406
BOMBO 98, 166, 190, 236,
  294, 406, 427, 482, 488
Bonanza 215, 218
Booloo 174
Border Legion 284
Born to Dance 377
BOTTOMLAND 66
Bottoms Up 93, 297, 314,
  480
Bourbon Street Beat 181, 325,
  328
Boy Friend 105
Boy of a Dolphin 477
BOYS AND BETTY 115, 118
BOYS AND GIRLS TOGETHER
  221, 490

-O-

INDEX OF NAMES